FINDING AMELIA

www.tighar.org

FINDING AMELIA

the true story of the earhart disappearance

ric gillespie

Naval Institute Press
291 Wood Road
Annapolis, MD 21402

ISBN-13: 978-1-59114-319-2

Library of Congress Cataloging-in-Publication Data

Gillespie, Ric, 1947–
  Finding Amelia : the true story of the Earhart disappearance / Ric
Gillespie.
    p. cm.
  Includes bibliographical references and index.
  ISBN 1-59114-319-5 (alk. paper)
  1. Earhart, Amelia, 1897–1937. 2. Women air pilots—United
States—Biography. 3. Search and rescue operations—Pacific Area. I.
Title.
  TL540.E3G55 2006
  629.13092—dc22

                                                    2006016663

Printed in the United States of America on acid-free paper ∞

12 11 10 09 08 07   8 7 6 5 4 3 2

Cartographer: Pat Thrasher
Book design and composition: David Alcorn, Alcorn Publication Design

CONTENTS

FOREWORD

I t is difficult to write about a legend. Write too richly, and you merely add to the fable; write too cynically, and you will be a mere debunker. It is even more difficult when the legend vanishes into oblivion. Yet, in these pages on the disappearance of Amelia Earhart, one of America's most famous aviators, Richard Gillespie has not only avoided these treacherous shoals but has also produced a narrative of epic scale, for he deals with the greatest elements of tragedy: human error and its awesome consequences.

Of Earhart herself, Gillespie writes with admirable professional detachment. "Earhart's piloting skills," he tells us, "were average at best, but good looks, genuine courage, a talent for writing, and [her husband] George Putnam's genius for promotion and media manipulation . . . made her one of America's most famous and admired women."

Yet Earhart is not really Gillespie's focus. Rather, it is the harrowing account, as far as anyone can trace it, of her last flight into the vast oblivion of the Pacific. In writing it, Gillespie has had to deal with three main challenges. First, that there is no incontrovertible physical evidence as to her fate, and what slender artifacts exist can at best provide the stuff of intelligent conjecture. Second, the most abundant evidence surrounding her disappearance is electronic—the records of radio telephone and telegraph—and those records have been so voluminous, at times so contradictory, and on occasion so self-serving by those who sent them, that the totality of their meaning and import have been not been clear until now. Third, much heat but little light has been generated by the unfounded assertions, the irrational theories, and the melodramatic perspectives of several generations of amateur Earhart sleuth/enthusiasts who have had extreme opinions but little fact to buttress them. Like curiosity seekers at a crime scene, they have merely raised the level of confusion.

Gillespie has brought to his task an array of formidable qualifications to research and write what will probably be the most detailed and factual account of Amelia Earhart's disappearance and the massive and failed attempt to find her that we shall ever have. An experienced general aviation pilot himself, a longtime risk-management specialist and aviation accident investigator, and a rigorous and determined researcher, he has tracked down numerous leads in government, business, industry, and aviation circles and has led a number of well-conceived and -organized search expeditions to the Equator and the possible terminus of Earhart's flight.

Over the decades, the author's search has involved him in investigations across a small range of artifacts—buttons, shoes, pieces of aluminum; in a painstaking study of radio logs and photographic and cartographic data; and in a growing familiarity with such esoterica as tidal research and geomorphology. Where the trail has led to a dead end he has had the courage and good sense to drop it and seek answers elsewhere. But of all Gillespie's tasks, none has been more important and more challenging than the collection, sorting out, and reintegration of the mass of radio communications surrounding the flight and the rescue effort into a comprehensible narrative, an effort that has combined careful and comparative analysis with the sensitivities of a skilled storyteller to weave a compelling narrative.

And what a narrative it is. Like viewers at a rerun of the old newsreel of the presidential motorcade entering Dallas on the morning of November 22, 1963, we read with growing dread of the Earhart departure from Lae, New Guinea, for her destination of Howland Island, a flyspeck on the map of the Pacific, knowing that she and her navigator, Fred Noonan, will never arrive. Thanks to Gillespie we also know how multiple were the miscalculations (a number by Earhart herself), the misapprehensions, the faulty equipment, and the faulty information that set her Lockheed Electra on its fatal trajectory and crippled all attempts to guide the pilot to a safe landing.

One reflects, too, on the fact that Earhart was six decades too early for access to a vital electronic system—global positioning—that could have identified for her and those seeking her where she was in the vastness of the ocean. Throughout the story, the hiss and crackle of empty airwaves that mark the futile efforts of Earhart and her would-be rescuers to communicate their locations to each other are a threnody of encroaching disaster. From this account it is also obvious, though not clearly stated, that the end of the crew of the Electra must have been quite terrible—death by drowning in the wreckage of a sinking aircraft or slow dehydration and death on the burning shores of a remote and uninhabited atoll hundreds of miles off their original course.

On other stages and at other times, Ric Gillespie has proposed a detailed and persuasive, if not conclusive, explanation of what happened to Amelia Earhart and Fred Noonan. I myself do not pretend to have strong views about her fate, nor would I argue that Gillespie has presented the final solution to the mystery of her disappearance. Indeed, in these pages, the author himself has not made this claim. He has, instead, attempted the most complete and fact-based history of the Earhart puzzle yet written. Brilliantly, he only hints at an explanation for the Earhart enigma here on the book's last page, a suggestion left hauntingly in the air for us to ponder.

As a historian, I think I know good history when I read it. By its display of technological expertise, by its careful weighing of complex evidence, by its objectivity, and by its humanity, this is certainly first-rate history.

Mark Peattie
Asia-Pacific Research Center
Stanford University
June 4, 2006

ACKNOWLEDGMENTS

The research that made this book possible has been an eighteen-year voyage of discovery. The International Group for Historic Aircraft Recovery has been the vessel and I, as TIGHAR's executive director, have been privileged to be the captain; but, like any skipper, I am only as good as the crew who work the ship. The facts presented in these pages testify to the dedication, intelligence, and generosity of the members of TIGHAR, without whom the boat would never have left the dock, let alone reached this point in our journey. Any errors in interpreting the facts are mine alone.

I am especially indebted to Dr. Randy Jacobson, without whose dogged pursuit of forgotten contemporary sources the true story of the Earhart disappearance could not have been told. Randy ferreted out the thousands of logs, letters, and official radio messages that detail the government's involvement in the tragedy; but finding the documents was only the first step. He then translated the archaic radio shorthand into Standard English and assembled the messages chronologically, converting innumerable, and often obsolete, time zones to Greenwich Time. Finally, he entered the assembled mountain of data into a computerized database. The enormous, yet easily searchable, files included on the DVD that accompanies this book are the product of his years of tedious, meticulous work.

Another special salute goes to Lt. Cdr. Robert L. Brandenburg, USN (Ret.). Bob's patient tutelage in the ways of the navy was of great help to a former army officer. More significant, his second career as a navy civilian scientist made it possible to quantify the credibility of the Earhart radio distress calls. Two of his research papers are included on the DVD.

The members of TIGHAR's board of directors—John Sawyer, Peter Luce, Richard Reynolds, Dr. Thomas King, Capt. Richard "Skeet" Gifford, Arthur Carty, and Russell Matthews—were unfailing in their support, both professional and financial, as were the thirty scholars, scientists, and expedition veterans of TIGHAR's Earhart Project Advisory Council. During the writing process dozens of TIGHARs provided critical commentary on draft chapters, and many more donated critical cash as participants in the TIGHAR Literary Guild. Their names are included on the DVD.

Any attempt to catalog all the TIGHAR researchers whose labors contributed to the book is doomed to failure, but I'll mention a few and beg the forgiveness of the many I am sure to omit. Forensic imaging specialist Jeff Glickman of Photek coaxed valuable information from historical photos. Oscar Boswell, Capt. Skeet Gifford, and Lockheed/Martin engineer Tom Roberts brought their awesome aviation expertise to bear on the question of the Electra's capabilities. Jerry Hamilton and Ron Dawson did unprecedented research on the life of Fred Noonan. Don Jordan brought two previously unknown Noonan letters to light. Russ Matthews reviewed the papers of Harry Manning. Bill Moffet did yeoman service squinting through weeks of microfilmed newspaper articles to find and catalog reports of radio distress calls from the Earhart plane. Ron Bright tracked down news coverage of the calls reported by Dana Randolph and Nina Paxton. Karen Hoy helped get accurate citations for newspaper references. Art Rypinski sorted out the history of the Bureau of Air Commerce. Historian Peter McQuarrie found the obscure British file that brought the castaway of Gardner Island from rumor to reality.

Several individuals with personal ties to the Earhart story came forward and generously shared documents that shed new light on the events of 1937. Capt. Jim Bible provided scans of the letters his mother, Helen Day, received from her friend Fred Noonan. David Bellarts generously shared the recorded recollections of his father, *Itasca*'s chief radioman, Leo G. Bellarts. And then there is Betty Klenck Brown, who may have been the last person to hear the voices of Amelia Earhart and Fred Noonan, and whose carefully preserved transcription of what she heard may reveal more about their fate than any existing document. Betty had the courage to come forward and subject herself to relentless cross-examination. She did so openly, cheerfully, and with sincere goodwill. My admiration and affection for her are immense.

Finally, I despair of finding words to express my gratitude for the unceasing encouragement, editorial guidance, and, all too often, thankless support of my wife and partner, Pat Thrasher.

INTRODUCTION

On July 2, 1937, Amelia Earhart vanished somewhere in the Central Pacific during an attempted flight around the world. Finding Amelia has been an American obsession ever since.

At the time of her disappearance, Earhart was the world's most famous female aviator and one of the most admired women in America. Accompanying her on the flight was Fred Noonan, a celebrity navigator in his own right. When the two flyers failed to arrive at their mid-Pacific refueling stop on Howland Island, the U.S. government launched what the press called "The greatest rescue expedition in flying history."

Expectations were high that the U.S. Navy and Coast Guard would rescue the missing flyers, and for more than two weeks, newspapers and newsreels led the public on a roller-coaster ride of promising leads and crushing disappointments. The ships and planes returned empty-handed, but the search for Amelia Earhart was not over. Indeed, it had just begun. Over the ensuing decades, researchers and enthusiasts have struggled to establish the validity of competing answers to the riddle of the flight's fate. Millions of dollars have been spent combing tropical islands and scouring the depths of the ocean. Hundreds of books, articles, and documentaries offer a dizzying array of solutions to the mystery, and Amelia remains America's favorite missing person.

What has been missing, among all the hype and the hoopla, has been the history. Not since George Washington chopped down the cherry tree has the story of an American hero been so shot through with myth and legend. In any investigation, establishing the known is essential to asking productive questions about the unknown. The information commonly accepted to comprise the facts of the Earhart case has traditionally been drawn chiefly from Earhart's own writings and from official government reports written after the search for her was abandoned. The stories those sources tell are necessarily colored by the motives and agendas of the people who wrote them.

Most of the arrangements for Earhart's two world flight attempts—the preparation of the aircraft, decisions regarding the route, the extent and nature of the U.S. government's involvement—were made via correspondence. Nearly all of those documents survive, as do the logs of the ships and the official records of the radio communications that directed the U.S. Navy and Coast Guard search. All told, these sources amount to more than five thousand individual items, each representing an undeniably genuine piece of the Earhart story. Some of the pieces are well known and have been used selectively in the past to support various theories, but the entire picture, scattered and dispersed among dozens of archival files and private collections, has been as indecipherable as a dropped box of jigsaw puzzle pieces. Once collected, compiled, and assembled, however, these items provide a day-by-day, and in some cases minute-by-minute, record of what really happened. With the historical record in hand, information replaces interpretation, documentation dispels speculation, and the mists of legend are swept away to reveal a far more accurate and informative picture of what happened than has ever before been available.

Finding Amelia means finding the real Amelia behind the public persona and understanding the events that led to an empty sky over Howland Island. Finding Amelia means sailing with the searchers, feeling their frustrations and following their failures. Ultimately, finding Amelia means realizing that there was always more mix-up than there was mystery.

Finding Amelia

CHAPTER ONE

An Airport in the Ocean
the american equatorial islands

tasca nodded gently in the tropical night, waiting, listening. The 2:00 AM deck log entry recorded a balmy 81° F, clear skies, a light breeze from the east, and a calm sea. In the Coast Guard cutter's cramped radio room, the smell of stale cigarettes, cold coffee, and shirtless men hung in the air amid the soft hum of the transmitters and receivers. Somewhere, far to the west, Amelia Earhart's Lockheed Electra droned through the darkness, drawing closer with each passing hour.

Nearby, invisible but for the faint moonlit line of surf breaking on its fringing reef, lay a narrow lozenge of coral sand and scattered scrub less than two miles in length. The captain of a Nantucket whaler had dubbed it Worth Island in honor of himself in 1822, but the name did not stick, perhaps because no one thought the barren outcropping was "worth" anything. Located in what was then the South Seas Whale Fishery, the island's small size and low profile made it a hazard to navigation, and in 1842 another American whaling captain bestowed a measure of immortality on the lookout who spotted it. All we know about that sharp-eyed sailor is that his name was Howland.

On a July night nearly a century later, Howland's island was inhabited by several thousand seabirds, a similar number of small gray Polynesian rats, and a half dozen Hawaiian and Chinese-American youths. The birds and rats were regular residents, but the young men were there on business. They were employed by the U.S. Department of Interior as "colonists" to establish American sovereignty over the birds, the rats, the coral, and what had to be the world's most improbable airport.

Stretching across the length and breadth of the island's surface were three intersecting runways. Each had been laboriously scraped out of the coral gravel, rolled smooth and firm, suitably marked, and equipped with windsocks. A handful of engineers and laborers, working under extreme conditions and using condemned and makeshift equipment, had accomplished the construction in strict secrecy and with great urgency. Built by the U.S. government with specific authorization from the president of the United States, the airfield was a civilian airport ostensibly intended to serve "the flying public" in a place nearly two thousand miles from the nearest flying and the nearest public.[1] The American taxpayers, in the throes of the Great Depression, had unwittingly built an entire airport for one-time use by a private individual engaged in a self-promotional publicity stunt.

The sequence of events that led to this bizarre situation had its beginning in 1932 when, among the telegrams received by Amelia Earhart upon the successful completion of her solo transatlantic flight from Newfoundland to Ireland, was one from the wife of New York governor and presidential candidate Franklin D. Roosevelt. Mrs. Roosevelt expressed her congratulations and those of her husband, and Amelia responded with a letter of thanks.[2] The two women met for the first time later that year shortly after FDR became the president-elect. Amelia was scheduled to give a talk at a high school in Poughkeepsie, New York, not far from the Roosevelt estate, and Eleanor took the opportunity to invite the famous flier and her husband, publisher and promoter George Palmer Putnam, to stop at Hyde Park for dinner on the way. Afterward, Mrs. Roosevelt introduced Amelia at the lecture. "I hope to know Miss Earhart more and more," she told the crowd, "but I never hope to admire her more than I do now. She has done so many things which I have always wanted to do."[3]

Earhart and Putnam were invited to the inauguration in March, and during an overnight visit to the White House in April, Amelia escorted the new first lady on her first night airplane ride to see the lights of Washington from the air. Airplanes were also on the president's mind. One of his first acts in office was to reorganize the federal agency charged with regulating civil aviation. Competition for the job of director of the Commerce Department's Aeronautics Branch was intense, and throughout the summer of 1933 Amelia lobbied President Roosevelt to appointment her dear friend Eugene Vidal. Her efforts were successful. In September, Vidal was made head of the agency that would soon be renamed the Bureau of Air Commerce.

Vidal faced many challenges in his new job. Dwindling budgets forced cuts in navigation services at the same time the public and the press were decrying a rash of domestic airline accidents. The nation's premier international airline, Pan American Airways, enjoyed a better safety record, but the "chosen instrument" for the projection of American aviation commerce was encountering obstacles to the expansion of its overseas routes.

International service required the development of terminal and refueling facilities in destination countries. To the frustration of Pan American and the U.S. State Department, the potentially lucrative routes across the North Atlantic to Europe were stymied by Britain's refusal to grant landing rights in Newfoundland and England despite the U.S. offer of reciprocal accommodations. The British did not yet have an aircraft that could profitably carry passengers and mail on such a long trip and had no desire to award a North Atlantic monopoly to the Americans.

With the Atlantic blocked for the moment, Pan American formed a Pacific Division and, in 1935, established routes across the North Pacific using American possessions as stepping-stones to Manila and Hong Kong. The southern routes to New Zealand and Australia, however, hit another British roadblock.

Transoceanic air commerce depended on aircraft that could safely carry large payloads over great distances. Large payloads meant large aircraft, and in the 1930s, the state of aircraft engine development dictated that large aircraft required very long takeoff runs to get airborne. Suitable runways were nonexistent. The answer was the flying boat, a compromise creature with the wings of an aircraft and the body of a boat. Neither fish nor fowl, flying boats were awkward on the water and slow in the air. They could, however, be built large enough to carry a profitable load of passengers and mail, and they could turn any stretch of water into an airport, so long as the water was relatively calm.

The refueling stops along Pan Am's North Pacific route—Hawaii, Midway, Wake, and Guam—featured harbors or lagoons that provided sheltered water for landings and takeoffs. On the projected route to New Zealand and Australia, however, most of the South Pacific atolls known to have usable lagoons already belonged to His Majesty King George V, or at least such was the opinion of His Majesty's government.

While the State Department squabbled with Whitehall over the ownership of long-neglected atolls, Vidal's Bureau of Air Commerce looked forward to a day when transoceanic air travel would be free from the need for long stretches of calm water. Aviation technology was advancing at a blinding pace. Vidal believed that large land planes with powerful, reliable engines would soon tuck up their wheels and span the oceans with greater speed and fewer refueling stops than the ponderous flying boats. The new airplanes would need runways, not lagoons, and Vidal saw a coming need for well-placed islands where American engineers could build airports.

In 1935, the Bureau of Air Commerce established an American presence on three small, desolate, lagoon-less Pacific islands near the equator. A young bureau employee by the name of William T. Miller was selected to head a project by which Jarvis, Baker, and Howland Islands were to be "colonized" as the American Equatorial Islands. The colonization was to be accomplished using furloughed U.S. Army personnel assisted by young native Hawaiian graduates of Honolulu's Kamehameha vocational school. Five men—"one NCO, one cook, one first aid man, and two Hawaiians who could look after such matters as fishing and boating, and other miscellaneous duties"—would live on each island for nine months at a time, resupplied with food and water at three-month intervals.[4]

The army lieutenant charged with selecting the colonists later recalled: "The requirements were that they must be grown up, that they be able to fish in the native manner, to swim excellently, and to handle a boat; that they be boys who were disciplined, boys who were friendly and unattached, and who had proven themselves of the type of disposition that could stand the rigors that might have to be undergone, who it was believed would be able to 'take it,' no matter what might come."[5] Their pay, at three dollars per day, would be better than the average factory worker's, and they would have no expenses. They were to keep logs of daily tide and weather observations, but their primary function was just to be there. The U.S. Coast Guard, at that time an arm of the Treasury Department, would provide transportation to and from the islands, but the boys would be well advised to remain healthy because they would be literally marooned on desert islands with no means of communication. The U.S. Navy supplied fuel for the Coast Guard ships and drums of drinking water for the colonists; the army provided engineers and materials for the construction of rudimentary accommodations. In March 1935, the first colonization expedition to the American Equatorial Islands set out from Honolulu aboard the Coast Guard cutter *Itasca*.

The project suffered some early setbacks. The soldiers squabbled among themselves and had to be removed, but it turned out that four Kamehameha youths on each island could handle the job just fine. The colonization program was a success, and William Miller supervised three replenishment missions by *Itasca* over the next year.

In February 1936, Secretary of State Cordell Hull sent a memorandum to President Roosevelt recommending that American ownership of the islands be cemented with an executive order placing the islands "under the administration of one of the Departments of the Government, possibly the Interior Department."[6] Legal authority for the claim was found in the American Guano Act of 1856, a relic of the days when accumulations of guano (bird dung) on Pacific islands were a valuable source of fertilizer. The law provided for the acquisition of uninhabited islands that were deemed vital to American commercial interests. The president was agreeable to the suggestion, but when the Bureau of Air Commerce learned that its project was about to be handed to the Interior Department, the bureau, out of either confusion or pique, took its ball and went home. In March, the bureau abruptly removed all of the colonists and supplies from the islands.

On May 13, 1936, the president signed the order annexing the three islands, and in June the Department of the Interior reinstalled the colonists. The department's Division of Territories and Island Possessions constructed better accommodations, provided communications equipment, and recruited young Chinese-American men in Hawaii who held amateur (ham) licenses to operate the radios. To replace the Bureau of Air Commerce's William Miller as the administrator of the American Equatorial Islands the Interior Department selected Richard B. Black. A tall, sturdily built

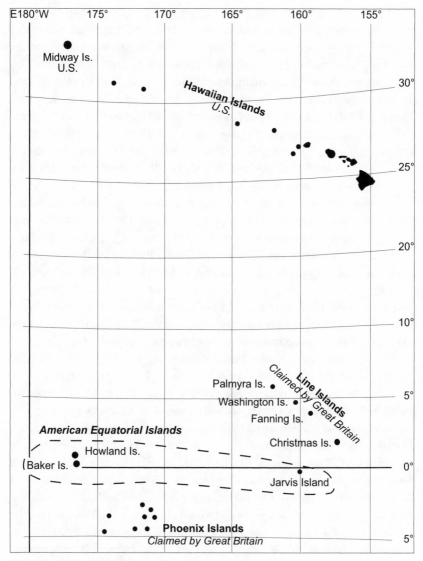

The American Equatorial Islands.

thirty-four-year-old civil engineer from North Dakota, Black was a seasoned explorer who had been a member of Admiral Byrd's 1933–35 Antarctic Expedition. The transition seems to have gone smoothly, with Miller and Black both making the first reprovisioning voyage to the islands following the reinstatement of the colonists. Miller then returned to the States while Black settled into his new job in Hawaii.

Surveys of the islands that Miller conducted early in the project identified Jarvis Island as the best candidate for the eventual construction of an airfield.

Commercial land planes capable of using a mid-ocean airport were still years away. It was therefore with considerable surprise that, on November 16, 1936, Black received a cable from his supervisor in Washington at the Interior Department's Division of Territories and Island Possessions asking him to look into the availability of tractor equipment in Hawaii for a January expedition to the Equatorial Islands. "Desire to have landing field prepared on Jarvis Island earliest date practicable."[7] Black replied the next day, asking where the money was going to come from, and was told there was no money. He would need to borrow a tractor from the army or the navy or somebody. His supervisor assured him: "Fully appreciate difficulties and urge your best efforts for their solution."[8]

The strange request was the unforeseen consequence of a conversation that had taken place at the White House six months earlier. Over the past four years Amelia Earhart and Eleanor Roosevelt had become fast friends, and during a May 14, 1936, overnight visit, Earhart and George Putnam told Mrs. Roosevelt about their still very confidential plans for Amelia to make a flight around the world. In June, George wrote to the first lady on his wife's behalf asking "to avail ourselves of the help you so kindly offered when we last saw you. Our wish is to be put in touch with the proper person in the State Department whose aid can be enlisted in connection with A.E.'s proposed world flight."[9]

True to her word, Eleanor had her secretary write a note to Richard Southgate, chief of the Division of Protocol, asking him to "take care of the things he [Putnam] wished done in the State Department." The note also cautioned Southgate that "Mrs. Roosevelt asked me to send you this special note to say that she had promised Mr. Putnam to keep this matter confidential. She is sure you understand and that you will be *very* nice to him" [emphasis in the original].[10] To take care of the things Mr. Putnam wished done, the State Department would need to be very nice indeed. Flying around the world meant corresponding with and obtaining permissions and clearances from every country whose territory Earhart would visit or fly over. Routes had to be set so as to avoid sensitive areas, and approvals were complicated by the fact that the airplane would not have a standard license but would be operating in the "restricted" category at very high weights. Arrangements concerning passports, visas, inoculations, and fumigations had to be addressed. Over the next months the State Department would send dozens of letters and telegrams clearing the way for Amelia's world flight. Putnam paid the postage and cable costs, but civil servants handled the hassle.

While the State Department worked on the diplomatic issues, Amelia grappled with the practical aspects of the trip. By later that fall she had another favor to ask of her friends on Pennsylvania Avenue. On November 10, 1936, she wrote a letter to the president asking him to support her unique approach to a major obstacle: the Pacific Ocean.

Some time ago I told you and Mrs. Roosevelt a little about my confidential plans for a world flight. . . . For some months Mr. Putnam and I have been preparing for a flight which I hope to attempt probably in March. The route . . . is east to west, and approximates the equator.

The chief problem is the jump westward from Honolulu. The distance thence to Tokio [the standard spelling in 1936] is 3900 miles. I want to reduce as much as possible the hazard of the takeoff at Honolulu with the excessive overload. With that in view, I am discussing with the Navy a possible *refueling in the air over Midway Island* [emphasis in the original].

A squadron of Consolidated PBY-1 (later to be dubbed "Catalina") flying boats was due to be ferried to Hawaii early in 1937. Amelia's plan was to practice aerial refueling from one of the "new seaplanes being completed at San Diego for the Navy. . . . That plane subsequently from Honolulu would be available for the Midway operation." She felt that

a project such as this (even involving a mere woman!) may appeal to Navy personnel. Its successful attainment might, I think, win for the Service, further popular friendship.

I should add the matter of international permissions, etc. is being handled very helpfully by the State Department.

Knowing your own enthusiasm for voyaging and your affectionate interest in Navy matters, I am asking you to help me secure Navy cooperation—that is if you think well of the project.[11]

The president did think well of the project. A week later, Chief of Naval Operations Adm. William Leahy received Amelia's letter and a memorandum saying that "the President hoped the Navy would do what they could to cooperate with Miss Amelia Earhart in her proposed flight."[12]

The job of assessing the practicality of the proposal landed on the desk of Rear Adm. Ernest J. King, the newly appointed Commander Aircraft, Base Force, and for the past three years the chief of the navy's Bureau of Aeronautics. The admiral was an experienced naval aviator, and he had some practical observations about Miss Earhart's plan. In a confidential memo to his superiors, King acknowledged that "the PBY-1 lends itself to the refueling uses discussed," but he pointed out that "the chief factor attending the feasibility of the proposed plan is that of airmanship." King felt confident the navy's pilots would be up to the task of holding the tanker aircraft steady, but he questioned whether Earhart had the skill required to approach and detach from the tanker without fouling the hose line in the propellers: "The ability of the pilot(s) of the receiving plane has not been demonstrated, and since this phase of flying is not ordinarily practiced by, or included in the training of, civilian or commercial aviators it is reasonable to assume that considerable special training will be required to assure the success of the undertaking."[13] Admiral King also pointed out that the extensive training stateside and the proposed operation at Midway were going to be expensive, and he did not think the navy should foot the bill. Meanwhile, in other government offices, a better and cheaper plan was already in the works.

On November 16, two weeks before Admiral King's memo raised concerns about the midair refueling idea, Richard Black in Hawaii had received his instructions from the Interior Department to build a runway on Jarvis Island as soon as possible. In Washington the next day, a Tuesday, Gene Vidal at the Bureau of Air Commerce sent a cable to William Miller telling him to contact Amelia Earhart at the Seymour Hotel in New York and arrange to meet her in South Bend, Indiana, on Saturday. Miller was to bring with him information about the three Pacific islands the bureau had colonized and that were now being administered by the Department of the Interior.[14]

Vidal's Bureau of Air Commerce had invested heavily in the proposition that the islands were of great value in the development of air routes to New Zealand and Australia. At least for the moment, however, transoceanic commercial aviation was the province of the flying boat, and Pan American Airways was preparing to send its first survey flight to New Zealand in March using the lagoon at Kingman Reef as a refueling stop. The three lagoon-less American Equatorial Islands were beginning to look like the American equatorial white elephants. To counter that impression, Vidal needed some good press for the islands. If one of them became a key element in a highly publicized crossing of the Pacific by a land plane, the islands' future utility would be demonstrated and the colonization program validated. When presented with the possibility, Earhart recognized that island-hopping southwestward across the Pacific to New Guinea would be safer and less expensive than a thirty-nine-hundred-mile nonstop hop from Hawaii to Japan that relied on midair refueling over Midway. The navy was notified that it was off the hook, and, on December 4, the chief of naval operations put out the word to his people that "arrangements for refueling [Earhart are] no longer required."[15]

In Hawaii, Richard Black still did not know why the Department of the Interior needed an airport in a hurry, but he was able to report that he had a line on an army "five-ton caterpillar and improvised scraper." He also mentioned that Robert Campbell, a Bureau of Air Commerce engineer who happened to be in Honolulu to do a survey of Hawaiian airports, thought some financial help might be obtainable through the Honolulu office of the Works Progress Administration. The local WPA administrator,

Mr. F. H. Lacey, had suggested the request should start in Washington. It was Black's opinion that if the necessary equipment, materials, personnel, transportation, and money could be rounded up, Jarvis could be "worked into fair emergency field" in three months.[16]

Although Black and Campbell may have been puzzled by the sudden urgency to build an airport in the middle of nowhere, it is not surprising that they looked on the WPA as a possible source of funding. Among its many "make work" projects during the Great Depression the WPA built more than a thousand airports around the United States. The agency was also reputed to be something of an easy mark; in fact, the term *boondoggle* entered the American political lexicon in 1935 to describe WPA projects that were considered trivial, wasteful, and motivated by political favoritism.

With Amelia's acceptance of Vidal's apparent assurance that he could build her a mid-Pacific airport came the realization that Howland Island's location made it far preferable to Jarvis as a refueling stop on her world flight. On December 7, 1936, without explanation, Black received notice from Washington that the plan had been changed. Acting Director Ruth Hampton advised him that the airfield was now to be built on Howland instead of Jarvis. Hampton also informed him that William Miller of the Bureau of Air Commerce was consulting with Aubrey Williams, the WPA's deputy director, and that he would "propose that Howland landing field be designated WPA project under Lacey. Suggest you keep in communication with Robert Campbell and Lacey as to developments."[17]

The next day, December 8, Vidal sent a cable to Robert Campbell in Hawaii informing him: "You will be temporarily retained in the Pacific and will be in charge of runway construction on Howland. More particulars will be mailed you. Release no information for publication concerning these activities."[18]

Campbell's reaction to the news that he was being sent to the middle of the ocean to build an airport on a desert island with a catch-as-catch-can assortment of equipment and labor is suggested by his announced decision to return to Hawaii with the Coast Guard cutter *Duane*, which had been tasked with dropping off the construction crew, and supervise the project from there. He had a change of heart, however, when he received the letter with the promised particulars: "For your information, be advised that Miss Amelia Earhart is contemplating a flight around the world, in a twin-motored land plane, and is including Howland Island, South Seas, as one of her refueling stops. Inasmuch as Miss Earhart is including Howland Island as one of her stops, it enables the Government to give immediate consideration to previous plans and to expedite the construction of a landing area on the Island which will be available to the flying public."[19]

On December 21, Campbell cabled Washington: "Air mail instructions received December 19th. Under circumstances withdraw my suggestion to start work and return with *Duane*. Appreciate opportunity and glad to remain Howland for purpose assuring completion. General Drum also feels necessary I remain account of equipment and personnel."[20] (Maj. Gen. Hugh A. Drum was the commanding officer of the U.S. Army's Hawaiian Department.) Lacey, the local WPA administrator, told Campbell the airport project would have to be formally approved by the sponsoring agency, in this case the Bureau of Air Commerce, before he could apply for funding. Accordingly, Campbell cabled a formal project proposal to headquarters "for the construction of three runways forming basic development in airport construction program on proposed route to antipodes."[21] On December 28, 1936, Campbell received confirmation that the bureau had approved the Howland Island airport project "for immediate prosecution."[22]

CHAPTER TWO

Kamakaiwi Field

preparations for the first world flight attempt

As the new year dawned, preparations for the airport construction expedition were coming together. General Drum had offered to send along a surveyor to lay out the runways and a couple of mechanics to help keep the equipment running. Army engineers from Oahu's Schofield Barracks were building a pontoon arrangement for getting the heavy equipment ashore over the reef, and arrangements had been made to assemble all of the equipment at the army's Hickam Airfield. From there it could be brought "through the fence" to an adjoining navy yard for loading aboard the Coast Guard ship "to prevent curious being admitted to dock."[1]

Most of the project's $9,981 budget was covered by in-kind contributions from the participating agencies, but nearly a third of the expenses required cash expenditures—$225 for gasoline, $65 for an acetylene welding unit, $60 to repair the blade on the grader, $9 for a set of socket wrenches, and $2500 in payroll—and that was a problem. Both the Bureau of Air Commerce and the Interior Department were adamant that they could provide no financial support for the project. The cash would have to come from the WPA, but that agency seemed to be living up to the popular joke that its acronym stood for "We Piddle Around." Lacey was sympathetic, but until he received clearance from Washington he could not release a nickel.

The Coast Guard cutter *Duane* was scheduled to embark the expedition on January 12, 1937, and on Tuesday the fifth, with one week left, Robert Campbell was getting nervous. "No release Howland project received today," he wrote to J. S. Wynne, chief of the Airports Section. "All materials, supplies, equipment should be ready to load Friday at latest. Normal purchase and delivery delays make imperative release by January 6 or sailing date *Duane* extended. Have three days work repairing county grader which must be paid for by WPA as no other funds purchase available. Repair work on WPA truck essential and truck cannot be released until project OK."[2]

January 6 came and went with still no word from the WPA. On the seventh Richard Black cabled his own frustration and concern: "Island welding company who will repair blade for condemned grader will require three days after authority to complete job. Sunday intervenes. Blade could be delivered Tuesday if authority from project cleared by 9 AM Honolulu

Time, January 8. Grader essential for project. Delay of grader repair would mean delayed sailing. Campbell and I cannot understand why Lacey has received no word of project status since he wired approval."[3]

Amelia planned to begin her world flight from California on March 15 and to land at Howland two days later. The construction of the runways had been predicted to take three months. Even if the expedition sailed from Hawaii on January 12, it might not be possible to get the airport finished, especially if equipment problems caused delays. Black and Campbell were concerned that any postponement of the sailing date meant an increased risk that the runways would not be ready in time. Back in the States, however, Amelia had just learned that the problem was much worse than that.

The WPA approval process was more complicated and went far higher than any of the planners had anticipated. Before the agency could release any money, the expenditure would have to be cleared by the Treasury Department's Bureau of Budget, and that required the specific approval of the president of the United States. As far as FDR knew, however, Amelia was planning on flying nonstop from Hawaii to Japan. The funding request that the WPA and the Bureau of Budget would lay before him was "for the construction of three runways forming basic development in airport construction program on proposed route to antipodes"—hardly an urgent matter.

Amelia had no choice but to bring the president back into the loop, and fast. On Thursday, January 7, the White House received a Western Union telegram from Amelia Earhart in Burbank, California, addressed to "Honorable Franklin D. Roosevelt." After briefly reminding him of his help in getting the navy's cooperation for her aerial refueling plan she informed him that

> since then the necessity for such difficult and costly maneuvers has been obviated and instead I hope to land on tiny Howland Island where the government is about to establish an emergency field. Commerce approves my plan, Interior very cooperative, Coast Guard ditto. All details arranged. Construction party with equipment due to sail from Honolulu next week. Am now informed apparently some question regarding WPA appropriation in amount $3000 which covers all costs other than those born [sic] by me for this mid-Pacific pioneer landing field which permanently useful and valuable aeronautically and nationally. Requisition now on desk of A. V. Keene, Bureau of Budget, Treasury Department. Understand its moving requires executive approval. Under circumstances could you expedite, as immediate action vital. . . . Please forgive troublesome female flyer for whom this Howland project is key to world flight attempt.[4]

The following Monday, January 11, the president approved the project.

The construction expedition was set to sail from Honolulu the next day, but trouble with *Duane*'s boiler delayed the departure until the thirteenth. The plan was to proceed immediately to Howland, but two days out, one of the crew became seriously ill and the captain decided to divert the ship to Fanning Island, the nearest hospital. It was January 22 when *Duane* finally arrived at Howland Island. Once there, the men found heavy surf on the reef. They managed to land one of the tractors and some supplies, but at the cost of wrecking the pontoon raft and "two men disabled but not seriously hurt."[5] It took them until midnight of the following day to rebuild the raft, and the landing of equipment and supplies could not resume until the twenty-fourth.[6] Finally, on January 28, Campbell could report that "*Duane* leaves today. Gear and personnel all landed and in working order. Actual grading operations start tomorrow." Black would return to Honolulu with *Duane*, which once again went by way of Fanning Island, this time to collect the body of the crewman, who had died despite the hospital's efforts to save him. On February 5 Campbell reported that work was under way and that, despite numerous difficulties, he thought he could have the runways finished by March 15 "exclusive of breakdown."[7]

The world flight appeared to be back on track. On February 12, at a packed press conference at Manhattan's Barclay Hotel, Amelia Earhart announced that she would fly around the world. Later that day Richard Black in Honolulu sent a cable to his boss in Washington: "Mainland press releases give Earhart itinerary. Mainland releases January 14 announced WPA airport project Howland. Many requests here for story and pictures of landing and airport construction. Please outline policy for me follow."[8] Black's boss told him to "refer all requests for news releases pictures etcetera to Bill Cogswell, Miss Earhart's representative Honolulu."[9]

The Howland airport was to have three 150-foot-wide runways. The coral would be graded and rolled to create a north–south strip 4000 feet long and a northeast–southwest strip 3000 feet long, but the prevailing easterly winds made the east–west strip the most likely to be used. Due to the shape and orientation of the island, this was necessarily also the shortest strip at 2400 feet. By March 4, Black was able to forward word from Campbell that the east–west strip was finished. The next day, however, brought news that the tractor had suffered a serious mechanical breakdown that "will not allow completion of northeast–southwest runway as originally planned."[10]

William Miller immediately replied, "Miss Earhart desires as long a runway as possible for takeoff. Advise if north and south runway will be ready, also length and possible wind direction and velocity in the evening."[11] Black was in Honolulu and Campbell was on Howland. Their only means of communication was through the island's amateur radio station. When there

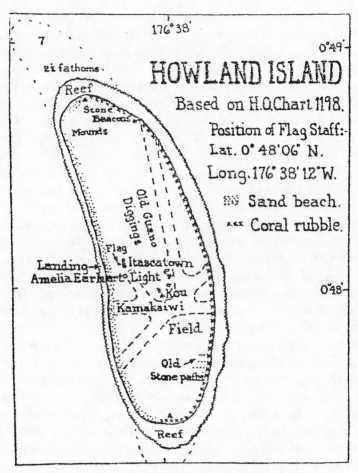

176° 38'

7

0°49'

HOWLAND ISLAND

Based on H.O.Chart 1198.

Position of Flag Staff:-
Lat. 0° 48'06" N.
Long. 176° 38'12"W.

≈≈ Sand beach.
⌐⌐ Coral rubble.

2¼ fathoms

Reef

Stone
Beacon

Mounds

Old Guano
Diggings

Flag
Itascatown
Light
Kou
Kamakaiwi

Field

Landing
Amelia Earhart

0°48'

Old
Stone path

Reef

Chart of Howland Island showing the runways of Kamakaiwi Field. "Landing" refers to the best place to cross the reef. Amelia Earhart Light was a small commemorative lighthouse erected in January 1938. *Source: National Archives*

was no response by the next day, Miller sent a more emphatic cable: "It is necessary and desirable to have suitable runway of sufficient length for take off of Miss Earhart's plane as her longest flight is from Howland to Lae, New Guinea. Your information on east and west runway received. Advise progress of construction of north and south runway which I understand will be longest runway. Also advise date of completion and latest information on length of all runways."[12] The same day he sent a cable to George Putnam advising him that "tractor broke down on Howland which was repaired and work progressing slowly."[13]

On Monday, March 8, with one week to go before the planned departure of the world flight, Miller still had not heard from Black about the situation on Howland. Miller sent his March 6 cable to Black a second time and followed it with another later that day: "Miss Earhart is ready to leave on schedule and it appears as if the completion of runways on Howland will delay her flight. It will be appreciated if you can expedite a reply from Campbell to my radios of March 6 and 8 requesting information on runway."[14]

Things were looking grim enough that Miller decided to ask the Coast Guard and navy to delay the sailing of the ships that would be supporting the flight "until further advised in order to allow for the completion of runway construction on Howland Island."[15] When Black saw the message, he quickly pointed out that the Coast Guard cutter going to Howland had to sail as scheduled because it was carrying the spare parts Campbell needed to fix the tractor.[16]

In a separate cable sent that same day, Black also explained to Miller why communication with Campbell on Howland was so slow. High-frequency radio signals travel best during the hours of darkness, and Black was able to communicate with Campbell only at night because "day light schedules with island impossible on present equipment." He had relayed Miller's message on the night of the sixth, and Campbell had replied on the night of the seventh, estimating that the work could be completed within twenty-four hours of the ship's arrival with the spare parts.[17] Meanwhile, the Coast Guard, acting on the earlier request, had already ordered the cutter to delay sailing, so Miller had to send another message to straighten that out.

On Monday, March 8, Putnam had informed Miller that the plane would be "probably ready after Friday, weather permitting." If the runway was not completed, the departure of the world flight would have to be delayed. Putnam was growing impatient: "Important know promptly as possible condition at Howland."[18] Miller still did not have the information Earhart wanted about the north–south runway. On Tuesday Miller's supervisor told Black to tell Campbell to "cable further information concerning Howland runways."[19] Black replied, explaining the delay: "Amateur short wave distance contest now in progress and poor atmospheric conditions causing delay handling messages to and from Campbell but hope contact him tonight and forward runway report to you."[20] Later that night he finally managed to get through to Howland. Black cabled Miller that "Campbell says tonight there is no need for delay." Assurances were fine, but what about the north–south runway?

Meanwhile, events in Washington had taken a turn that spelled trouble for the world flight. Amelia's close friend Gene Vidal had resigned as director of air commerce. Vidal's tenure as director had been contentious from the beginning, and the previous September he had nearly been fired. Amelia had saved him with a strong telegram to the first lady in which she threatened to withdraw her support for FDR's reelection unless Vidal was reinstated: "There is little use of my trying to interest others in the President's cause," she wrote, "when my heart is sick with the knowledge that an industry can be jeopardized and an individual's career blasted by what seems a personal feud."[21]

Vidal kept his job and so did Roosevelt. Without the help of both men later that fall Earhart would almost certainly have given up her plans for an around-the-world flight. Vidal's troubles continued, though, and by the end of February, fed up, he resigned. With her friend no longer running the Bureau of Air Commerce, Amelia's smooth ride through the bureaucracy came to a quick halt. Almost immediately she began facing regulatory issues.

On that busy Tuesday of March 9, with the world flight's scheduled departure just days away, William Miller received a cable from Robert R. Reining, chief of the bureau's Registration Section, suggesting that Miss Earhart renew her transport license, which was due to expire on April 15 during the proposed flight. Reining also wired Earhart directly, calling her attention to a letter sent to her husband back on October 20, 1936, in which Assistant Director J. Carroll Cone had pointed out that Amelia's transport license had expired on October 15. She would, of course, need to get her license renewed, and "in view of the long over water flights involved" in the proposed world flight, she would also need to obtain a nonscheduled instrument flying rating.[22]*

Amelia had renewed her six-month transport license but had done nothing about the instrument rating. Now Vidal was gone and the rating was an obstacle to her planned departure. Reining made it clear to Earhart and to Miller that the world flight would not proceed until the matter was settled.

The next day, Miller received word that the State Department had obtained all the necessary international permissions and clearances and had sent a letter to the Department of Commerce authorizing the world flight. He sent a cable to Reining asking him to forward the letter to Amelia at Oakland Airport via air mail special delivery.[23] Reining refused to budge: "Earhart letter authority withheld pending receipt inspector's report flight check approving instrument rating."[24]

The instrument rating examination tested three elements. The applicant had to pass a written examination, demonstrate ability to control the aircraft solely by reference to flight instruments, and show proficiency in the use of radio navigation aids. But the wording in Reining's cable to Miller offered a way out. Authority would be withheld pending Earhart's obtaining "a nonscheduled instrument rating or flight check ability to fly entirely by instruments."[25] In other words, she could skip the written exam and the radio navigation flight test. Seizing on the easier option, Amelia did not attempt to qualify for an instrument rating but chose rather to take a flight

---

*The examinations required for obtaining a nonscheduled instrument flying rating were less demanding than those for pilots who flew for scheduled air carriers.

check of her ability to fly entirely by instruments. On March 11 Reining received a telegram from the chief inspector in Oakland: "Flight check Earhart instrument flying satisfactory. Written and radio flying not given account her desire to expedite and save engines."[26] The next day, Reining sent the State Department authorization letter to Earhart via airmail, special delivery.

At the same time Earhart and company were sorting out Amelia's pilot certification issues and desperately trying to find out what was going on at Howland, they were also coming to the realization that she needed another navigator. The crossing of the Pacific Ocean to Hawaii, thence to Howland Island, and from there to New Guinea was obviously the most hazardous portion of the world flight, and Amelia had recruited Harry Manning to help her with radio and navigation on those legs. The two had met and struck up a friendship in 1928 when Manning was the captain of the ocean liner that brought Amelia home from her first aerial Atlantic crossing. As a mariner, Manning was well versed in ocean navigation. As an amateur radio enthusiast and private pilot, he was familiar with Morse code and radio direction-finding.

Manning seemed like a good choice to help Amelia cross the Pacific, but in the final days before the flight's departure, questions arose about his ability to adapt his nautical navigation skills to the very different aviation environment. Fortunately for Earhart, Capt. Frederick J. Noonan, arguably the world's finest aerial navigator, had recently left Pan American Airways and was available to help out. The very short notice did not allow Noonan to get the necessary visa to accompany the flight as far as New Guinea, but his skills in aeronautical-celestial and dead-reckoning navigation were most needed for the flight from Hawaii to tiny Howland Island. The new plan was for Earhart, her technical adviser Paul Mantz, and the two navigators to make the flight from Oakland to Honolulu. Mantz would stay in Hawaii while Earhart, Manning, and Noonan made the jump to Howland. Noonan would leave the flight there and return to Honolulu aboard the Coast Guard cutter *Shoshone*. Manning would continue on as far as Darwin, Australia, and Earhart would make the rest of the trip around the world solo.

At long last, on Saturday, March 13, 1937, a message arrived from Campbell on Howland with apologies that static interference had precluded communication for the past three days. Two runways had been completed: the 2400-foot east–west strip and the 3000-foot northeast–southwest strip. To accommodate Earhart's expressed desire for "as long a runway as possible for takeoff," the north–south strip would now be nearly a full mile long. Campbell promised that it would be finished by March 15.[27] Richard Black announced that the airport had been officially named Kamakaiwi

Field in honor of James Kamakaiwi, the Honolulu boy who had been the first Hawaiian to go ashore on Howland when the island was first colonized on March 30, 1935, and had been the leader of the colonists ever since.[28]

With this last hurdle cleared, Earhart hoped to depart as early as the next day, Sunday the fourteenth, but she would have to switch airports. Heavy rain had swept the San Francisco Bay area since Thursday, and the unpaved Oakland airfield was a mess. San Francisco airport had a 3000-foot paved strip, and Earhart decided that the world flight would depart from there at 5:00 PM on Sunday. But there was a problem. Mr. Doolin, the airport manager at San Francisco, was worried that the overloaded aircraft might not be able to clear obstructions just past the end of the runway and was reluctant to grant permission for the takeoff. Mr. Bedinger, the chief of the bureau's General Inspection Service and the same person who had given Earhart her instrument check ride, cabled Reining in Washington asking for instructions on how to handle the issue.[29]

The bureau's new director, Fred D. Fagg Jr., replied the next day. He noted that the flight was noncommercial and that the airplane had been given a "restrictive certificate" for the specified takeoff weight. Fagg was also under the mistaken impression that the pilot had been "certified for radio and instruments." Nonetheless, he said, "unless takeoff would interfere with interstate or foreign commerce, responsibility for place and manner of takeoff rests entirely with state and local authority and person making such takeoff."[30] This time the bureau would not bend the rules. The airport manager was the local authority, and Mr. Doolin apparently stood firm because the aircraft remained at Oakland.

On Monday, March 15, William Miller informed all government agencies cooperating with the flight that "Miss Earhart will not depart this date from Oakland airport on her round the world flight on account weather conditions. Will advise on March 16 further information relative to her departure from Oakland."[31]

The *Herald Tribune* newspapers carried a story that day by Carl Allen, a reporter who had covered Earhart for years. Oakland airport officials were scrambling to get the runway in shape for Earhart's takeoff, he wrote, but the flight had been delayed due to "head winds of unexpected strength on the 2410-mile course to Honolulu."[32] The weather was a legitimate concern—it had also delayed the departure of two Pan American flights to Honolulu—but there was another reason, mentioned by no one, that the world flight could not leave.

Fred Noonan, having had a chance to assess the plane's navigational equipment, had identified a major deficiency in the flight preparations. As described in a *Time* magazine article later that summer, Noonan was "dismayed that there was nothing with which to take celestial bearings except an ordinary ship sextant. He remedied that by borrowing a modern bubble octant designed especially for airplane navigation."[33] Modern bubble octants were expensive, and Noonan apparently did not own one himself. It is equally apparent that he was unwilling or unable to borrow one from his former employer, even though Pan American had a major terminal right there in Alameda. Harry Manning held a commission in the U.S. Naval Reserve, so he sent a telegram to the naval air station at San Diego urgently requesting that a bubble octant be sent via air express to Oakland for use on Earhart's transpacific flight. Manning would sign for the instrument.[34]

At 10:10 the next morning, Wednesday the sixteenth, the naval reserve air base at the Oakland airport received word that the octant would be on the United Air Lines flight scheduled to arrive at 2:50 PM. Three-quarters of an hour later, at 10:57 AM, Miller announced: "Weather conditions improving. Departure from Oakland on March 17 looks definite."[35] With Pioneer Bubble Octant No. 12-36 safely aboard, the world flight splashed through the puddles of the Oakland airport and lifted into the air at 4:37 PM on March 17.[36]

CHAPTER THREE

Hawaiian Debacle
the luke field accident

A melia Earhart's Lockheed Electra landed at the army's Wheeler Field early the next morning, having set a new record of fifteen hours and forty-seven minutes for the trip despite mechanical difficulties. On arrival, Mantz told Army Air Corps engineering officer Lt. Kenneth Rogers that for roughly the last half of the flight, the propeller on the right-hand engine had been stuck at a fixed angle of pitch. He also said that the generator had stopped showing a charge due to a failure in the electrical control box. After a brief photo session, Mantz, Earhart, Manning, and Noonan left the airfield. The army's investigation of subsequent events would determine that they left without leaving any instructions "whatsoever as to what was to be done to the plane in the way of service or check-over."[1] The previously announced plan had been for Earhart, Manning, and Noonan to take off from Wheeler on the flight to Howland Island at 10:00 PM that night, so Lieutenant Rogers and the local Pratt & Whitney service representative, Wilbur Thomas, "took it upon themselves to do what is usually done to put an airplane in suitable condition for the continuance of such a flight."[2] They changed the oil, cleaned and gapped the spark plugs, and performed a number of other routine checks. Nothing was wrong with the control box. The problem was that the current control had been set improperly, resulting in a blown fuse. In servicing the propellers they found that both hubs took a surprising amount of grease, although there was no sign of a leak.

At 2:45 PM, William Miller, back in Oakland, informed all government agencies supporting the flight that "Miss Earhart has postponed her departure from Honolulu to Howland Island 24 hours on account of weather."[3] In his later report to the chief of naval operations, however, the navy aerological officer (meteorologist) who prepared the forecast said that he had predicted "favorable flying conditions over the entire route, except for cloudiness and showers near Pearl Harbor. It is understood that her delay was occasioned by other reasons."[4]

About the time that Miller was sending notification of the postponed departure, and just as Lieutenant Rogers and Mr. Thomas were about to run up the Electra's engines to see if the grease had fixed the propeller problem, Paul Mantz returned to the airfield and was briefed on the work that had been done. Mantz performed the run-up himself and found that the right-hand prop still would not change pitch. The airplane was shut down and rolled into the hangar, where army mechanics partially disassembled the hub and found that the blades were "badly galled and frozen in place." The officer in charge judged the failure to be "due to improper or insufficient lubricant." It was the opinion of some of the technicians that "the hubs were nearly dry when the plane left the mainland."[5]

The engineering officer ordered that the propellers from both engines be taken across town to the Air Corps's Hawaiian Air Depot at Luke Field, Pearl Harbor, for overhaul. At 4:18 PM, the Coast Guard notified the support ships: "Earhart plane will probably take off late tomorrow afternoon, Friday, March 19th, according to latest information just received and authentic."[6]

At the depot, Lt. Donald Arnold consulted with Mantz, who said that the propeller malfunction had first occurred immediately following a brief encounter with icing conditions. On disassembling the hub Lieutenant Arnold found that a "soft putty-like compound" had been used as a lubricant. This material was much thicker than the grease used on army aircraft, and Arnold was of the opinion that the icing conditions encountered during the flight had rendered the lubricant useless, resulting in the seized blades.[7] Mantz left the depot but telephoned at 7:00 PM with the news that Earhart might want to depart as early as 8:00 or 9:00 the next morning. The work continued into the night, and at 2:00 AM the overhauled props arrived back at Wheeler Field, where Lieutenant Rogers had kept his men standing by to put them back on the airplane. "When the installation had been completed and the cowlings safetied and checked," the investigation report noted, "the crew retired for a much needed three hours sleep. The crew and the Engineering Officer were back on alert at seven in the morning but found they could have used the time for sleep to advantage when none of the Earhart party arrived until nearly eleven o'clock."[8]

The Earhart party that arrived did not include Earhart, Manning, or Noonan. It was Paul Mantz who showed up, with his fiancée and a local friend in tow. Mantz ran up the engines and found that both propellers appeared to be functioning properly. He informed the army personnel at Wheeler that he and his guests were going to take the plane up for a test flight and then land at Luke Field, a shared army-navy airstrip on Pearl Harbor's Ford Island, to see whether that airport's three-thousand-foot paved runway might be more suitable for Amelia's departure than Wheeler's sod field. The weather forecast for the route to Howland still looked good, but a possibility of local showers in the Honolulu area remained. Mantz undoubtedly wanted to avoid the type of delays the muddy field at Oakland had imposed, and this time there should be no bureaucratic obstacle to a last-minute airport change.

The army was indeed accommodating, but this was the first indication that Earhart might want to use Luke Field. The operations officer at Luke was notified, and "steps were immediately taken to recall all airplanes and clear the airdrome." Mantz landed the Electra there at noon and announced that the machine was "performing excellently." He said that Earhart would definitely be making her takeoff from Luke Field, but her time of departure would depend entirely on the weather. After making arrangements with Lieutenant Arnold to have the airplane serviced and fueled for the Howland flight, Mantz left with his guests at 1:30 PM.[9]

A little over an hour later Mantz got a phone call from Lieutenant Arnold. There was a problem with the fueling. The Standard Oil truck with Earhart's gasoline had arrived at 2:30, and fueling had begun using a chamois strainer to check for contamination. The strainer showed "considerable sediment" in the fuel that on closer inspection appeared to be flakes of rust. Arnold ordered the fueling halted and called Mantz. The latter's solution was to proceed with the fueling using the army's gas, and Arnold agreed. He then put Mantz on the phone with the Standard Oil representative to work out the details; "considerable arguing and wrangling" ensued. When Arnold took the phone again, Mantz said that he was coming to the airport and told him not to do anything until he got there. There was clearly going to be no late-afternoon departure for Howland. At 3:45 PM, *Shoshone*, standing by at Howland, received a message from Fleet Air Base, Pearl Harbor, that "Miss Earhart expects to depart [at] 2400 [midnight] today or daylight tomorrow, Saturday, depending on weather."[10]

The Standard Oil representative did not want to wait for Mantz to arrive and made a number of suggestions about how they might go ahead and fuel the airplane. Arnold resisted, informing him that "the Air Corps had no interest in the matter whatsoever and that [he] had neither official nor personal authority in connection with the flight, the crew, or the sponsors, and must wait for Mr. Mantz." Mantz arrived at 4:15, and some Standard Oil gas was put through the chamois strainer. Sediment was present. The army's report indicated that "the Standard Oil representative argued with Mr. Mantz that the dirt was already in the chamois and did not come from his tank. Mr. Mantz procured a new chamois and another test showed signs of sediment." The fueling of the Electra was completed using army gasoline, and the plane was locked in the hangar at 7:30 PM.[11]

That afternoon Amelia wrote a long article for the next day's Honolulu newspapers with a detailed explanation of how weather conditions had forced her to delay her departure. The plane's engines, she said, were "having a mechanical rub-down to keep them in perfect condition." She told her readers, "I went to Wheeler Field early yesterday morning to ride over the takeoff area. I changed the takeoff from Wheeler to Luke Field by permission.

Wheeler is being improved and worked, and is temporarily rough in spots. Luke Field has a 3000 foot hard surface runway which is adequate to my needs and would save the landing gear from the beating it would have on rough ground." She explained that, in consultation with her navigators, she had rejected a dawn takeoff because the trip was expected to take about twelve hours and the plane had to arrive at Howland in daylight.[12]

Nonetheless, at 9:30 that night the operations officer at Luke Field received word "that the takeoff was scheduled at dawn and that Miss Earhart and her party would arrive at Luke Field about 3:30 AM, March 20th."[13] It was closer to 4:30 when Earhart, Mantz, Manning, Noonan, and several reporters arrived. Mantz did the preflight inspection while Amelia and the navigators went to a back room in the hangar to review the charts and weather forecasts. After a brief discussion with Mantz she announced that she would wait for daylight before taking off. At 5:30 AM Earhart started the engines. "Captain Manning and Mr. Noonan took their places," the army's report noted, "and at 5:40 she taxied out."[14]

Later that day, Amelia Earhart watched the blue Pacific slide by below— not from the cockpit of her airplane but from the deck of the passenger liner *Malolo*, which was carrying her and her crew back to California. The Electra lay wrecked on a trailer in the same Luke Field hangar where it had been secured the night before. Before sailing Earhart had written another article for the Honolulu newspapers. In it she reported that "witnesses said a tire blew out. However, after studying the tracks carefully I believe that that may not have been the primary cause of the accident. The right shock absorber, as it lengthened, may have given way.... There was no indication that anything was off normal until something happened on the right side."[15]

The investigating board of army officers concluded that "after a run of approximately 1200 feet the airplane crashed on the landing mat due to the collapse of the landing gear as a result of an uncontrolled ground loop; the lack of factual evidence makes it impossible to establish the reason for the ground loop."[16] *Ground loop* is an aviation term used to describe a loss of directional control while the aircraft is on the ground, similar to an automobile "spinning out." Although the airplane had not burned and no one had been injured, the damage to the Electra was extensive.

Amelia was undaunted. "My present wish," she told her readers, "is to follow through as soon as the plane and engines are reconditioned. May I express my thanks to all who have been standing by so faithfully and warn them that I shall ask their cooperation again?"[17]

Amelia Earhart made good on her warning. A little more than three months later, another Coast Guard cutter stood by at Howland Island.

CHAPTER FOUR

Reversals
preparations for the second world flight attempt

tasca spent most of the July night drifting on the dark ocean just to the west of Howland, the island's surrounding reef being too steep to permit anchoring. At 2:39 AM, the deck log recorded "ahead one third speed on course 95°" as the ship moved closer to the island in anticipation of the coming dawn and the arrival of Amelia Earhart. In the narrow radio room high on the top deck, the ship's chief radioman listened for the first call from the approaching plane. Below, the crew members not on watch and the thirty-two guests aboard for this very special cruise slept—or tried to. Among them was one man who had more than the heat and humidity to blame for any sleeplessness he suffered.

As the head of the Interior Department's American Equatorial Islands project, Richard Black was the official leader of the reprovisioning expedition. His responsibilities were to service the islands' colonists and to act as "coordinator of governmental assistance to [the] Earhart flight as regards Howland Island."[1] He had waited here for Amelia before. In March he had led the mission to the islands aboard *Itasca*'s sister ship, USCG *Shoshone*, a trip that had been fraught with tension and frustration. The workmen had made heroic efforts to get the airfield finished in time for the Electra's expected arrival, only to have the date repeatedly postponed. When Amelia's flight from Hawaii finally began, it ended on the runway with a wrecked airplane. That same day, George Putnam, in California, had sent a message to Black aboard *Shoshone* at Howland: "Telephoning from Honolulu before boarding the *Malolo*, Miss Earhart asked me to send a message directly to Howland Island to tell you how sorry she is to break that engagement for tonight to which she had looked forward. She is sorrier for the trouble she has given you and the Coast Guard and Commerce officers and personnel with you. She is going to try again and next time hopes to be less of a nuisance."[2] Two days later, Black received a message from Bureau of Air Commerce liaison William Miller telling him that the airplane was being shipped to the Lockheed factory in California for repairs and that Earhart would begin her world flight again from Oakland in six to eight weeks.[3]

On March 20, the day of the accident, Putnam also sent a telegram to Secretary of Commerce Daniel C. Roper conveying Amelia's "deepest appreciation for the generous cooperation given her by the Department of Commerce." Earhart was "sorry for all the trouble" and wanted the secretary to know that she "intends to try again when repairs are completed and next time hopes to be less of a nuisance to all concerned." The telegram ended with a special plea: "Especially I want to add that Bill Miller has been of invaluable help and our greatest hope is that he may be on deck with us when we try it again."[4] Earhart and Putnam were sincere in their desire to retain Miller's services. As the bureau's point man in the colonization of the Equatorial Islands, Miller knew the ground and knew the people. Since his first wire to Earhart in November 1936, Miller had sent well over a hundred telegrams and cables coordinating every aspect of Earhart's projected flight across the Pacific with dozens of agencies and individuals in the United States and abroad.

Putnam sent several other telegrams that day to various government agencies; all of them passed along Amelia's thanks, announced her intention to try again, and expressed her hope to be less of a nuisance next time. There is no record of a telegram to Fred Fagg, William Miller's boss and Gene Vidal's successor as director of the Bureau of Air Commerce. Fagg's bureau had already demonstrated that the days of special treatment for Amelia were over. Putnam may have thought that he had a better chance of hanging on to Miller by going over Fagg's head and appealing directly to the secretary of commerce, but Roper's reply was not encouraging: "Please express to Miss Earhart my thanks for her cordial message to the Department of Commerce for its cooperation. Also my congratulations on her splendid feat and my most sincere regret that a disappointing mishap has delayed her effort. You may be sure that the Department of Commerce is proud to have had a part in this achievement."[5] For all its kind sentiments, the message made no mention of Miller and used the past tense in describing Department of Commerce support.

If Roper's letter implied a cooling of enthusiasm in Washington, there was nothing subtle about the sudden chill in Hawaii. Prior to the accident, the Air Corps's Hawaiian Air Depot had worked all night to rebuild the Electra's propeller hubs at no charge. After the accident, the work of preparing the wrecked plane for shipment was billed according to regulations. When Earhart requested that the Electra be shipped to California on an army transport ship, the answer was no.[6] Forced to buy space aboard a commercial vessel, she requested the use of a navy barge to move the plane from Pearl Harbor to Honolulu. Again, the answer was no.[7] The plane made the trip to the dock on a commercial barge and returned to California aboard the Matson liner SS *Lurline*. The price tag for the prep work and transportation came to more than $4000.

The press, too, was becoming less willing to give Amelia a free ride. Newspaper coverage of the mishap had been generally charitable, blaming the crash on a blown tire. *Newsweek* characterized the accident as "a tough bit of luck," but *Time* magazine took a critical view of the entire world flight endeavor:

> Between 1924 and 1933 the globe was girdled six times by aircraft. Last year, when Pan American Airways started carrying passengers across the Pacific, reporters Herbert Ekins and Leo Kieran circled the globe on commercial lines. Soon after, Pan American's President Juan Terry Trippe and a party of friends also flew around on commercial lines. Last week, Aviatrix Amelia Earhart Putnam took off from Oakland "to establish the feasibility of circling the globe by commercial air travel" and "to determine just how human beings react under strain and fatigue."

Time's description of the accident was no less sarcastic:

> Down the long concrete runway the ship shot at 60 m.p.h. Suddenly the left tire [*sic*] blew out. Lurching, the plane crumpled its landing gear, careened 1,000 ft. on its bottom in a spray of sparks while the propellers knotted like pretzels. With sirens screaming, ambulances dashed to the wreck just as Flyer Amelia stepped out white-faced. Said she: "Something must have gone wrong."[8]

The unkindest cut came from Maj. Alford Williams, a leading figure in aeronautical development. In 1923, as a young navy lieutenant, Williams had set two world speed records. He went on to become a highly respected innovator of air combat tactics and techniques. On resigning from the navy in 1930, he took a commission in the Marine Corps Reserve while continuing his aviation research and development work under the sponsorship of Gulf Oil.*

Like Amelia Earhart, Williams had a flair for the written word, and in 1937 the forty-six-year-old aviation expert wrote a weekly column on aeronautical matters that was syndicated in newspapers all across the United States. His March 31 offering excoriated "individually sponsored trans-oceanic flying" as "the worst racket" in aviation. Williams charged that "the personal profit angle in dollars and cents, and the struggle for personal fame, have been carefully camouflaged and presented under the banner of 'scientific progress.'" The major was not bashful about naming names: "Amelia Earhart's 'Flying Laboratory' is the latest and most distressing racket that has been given to a trusting and enthusiastic public. There's nothing in that 'Flying

---

*Army aviator James H. "Jimmy" Doolittle had a similar arrangement with Shell Oil.

Laboratory' beyond duplicates of the controls and apparatus to be found on board every major airline transport. And no one ever sat at the controls of her 'Flying Laboratory' who knew enough about the technical side of aviation to obtain a job on a first-class airline." Williams did not buy the blown tire story either. "She lost control of the airplane during a takeoff on the concrete runway of a standard Army airdrome and wrecked the 'Flying Laboratory.'... That ship got away from her—that's the low down." Most ominous for Earhart, Williams called for government action to stop her. "It's time the Bureau of Air Commerce took a hand in this business and it's my guess that the bureau will not grant Mrs. Amelia Earhart permission to make another attempt."[9]

The army was more circumspect in its assessment of the accident. A sixty-two-page confidential report, "Proceedings of a Board of Officers Appointed to Investigate the Crash of Miss Amelia Earhart at Luke Field, March 20, 1937," found no support for Amelia's contention that a mechanical failure caused her to lose control of the aircraft, but neither did it place the blame on pilot error.[10] The report concluded that the army had accorded Earhart "every reasonable assistance and facility . . . to facilitate her flight" and that the airplane crashed "due to the collapse of the landing gear as the result of an uncontrolled ground loop," but the "lack of factual evidence makes it impossible to establish the reason for the ground loop."[11] The army's report, however, was not released to the press.

The Electra arrived back in California on April 2 and was trucked to Burbank, where Lockheed engineers assessed the damage. The crash had wiped out the main landing gear, both propellers, the entire right wing outboard of the engine, and most of the underside of the fuselage. Repair would involve a major rebuild at an estimated cost of $12,500.

More serious for Earhart and Putnam than the financial consequences of the accident was the loss of their Bureau of Air Commerce liaison. Despite Putnam's request, William Miller had been reassigned to more conventional duties and would no longer be available to coordinate support for the hazardous transpacific legs of the world flight. If Amelia needed further evidence of a wind shift at Commerce, it came on April 19, 1937, in a letter from the General Inspection Service. She had failed to submit a Report of Accident Form on the Luke Field crash, a violation of regulations subject to a fine of $500. The inspector in Honolulu had recommended that no action be taken, but the matter was "being made of record."[12]

As the end of April approached, a second world flight attempt was still mostly brave talk. Lockheed was proceeding with repairs to the Electra, and Earhart was in New York with her husband trying to raise the money needed to put the flight back on track. The sponsors who had put up the funding for the first trip had not pledged the dollars needed for another try, but money was not the only problem. The team had lost some key players. Harry Manning, the only member of the crew who was familiar with radio navigation and adept at Morse code, was no longer part of the team. The reason released to the press was that his leave of absence from his duties as a sea captain would expire before the plane could be repaired. Manning later said he quit because he had lost faith in Earhart's skill as a pilot and was fed up with her "bullheadedness."[13]

Most damaging of all was the loss of friends in high places. Without Vidal's influence and Miller's services in cajoling and coordinating government support, Alford Williams's prediction of a federal ban on a second attempt was a real possibility. To make sure the problems she was having with the Commerce Department did not spread to other agencies, Amelia took matters in hand to ensure continued support from the Coast Guard, the U.S. Navy, and the Department of the Interior.

On April 27, Earhart sent a telegram to Rear Adm. Russell R. Waesche, commandant of the Coast Guard, asking to see him the next day, preferably in the morning. Waesche replied that he would be "delighted" to see Earhart at any time convenient for her.[14] She also visited the chief of naval operations. Apparently the visit was a success. Later that day, the CNO advised the U.S. naval station in Samoa that "Amelia Earhart second flight starting within two or three weeks. Please have *Ontario* ready to render same service as on previous attempt. Will advise time plane departure Oakland."[15]*

Earhart also paid a call on Richard Black's superiors at the Interior Department's Division of Territories and Island Possessions. After the meeting, Black was notified that Earhart had said she would be departing for Hawaii at the end of May and would proceed to Howland after a short layover. Although the letter to Black mentioned how charming Amelia had been, it also instructed him to work with other agencies to arrange for the island to receive a precautionary visit by a military aircraft before the date of Earhart's anticipated arrival.[16]

The directive did not surprise Black. He was being ordered to implement his own idea. A week earlier, Black had advised Washington that he had, on his own initiative, written a memorandum to the local navy intelligence officer offering the use of "Howland Island emergency landing fields in projected fleet operations." Black cabled his bosses that "best interest of government served if service plane were first to use fields. This recommendation made as result of recent happenings."[17]

The division's acting director, Ruth Hampton, replied to Black's cable and authorized him, after the fact, to "inform Army and Navy that all

---

*The oceangoing tug USS *Ontario* had been positioned halfway between Howland and New Guinea in March.

facilities JHB [Jarvis, Howland, Baker] islands available to them for flight operations or otherwise as may be required." She also asked Black what he meant by "recent happenings."[18] Black explained that the term referred to "Army, Navy and Commerce unofficial attitude toward Earhart accident Luke Field. Campbell [the Commerce Department engineer who had built the Howland runways] and I feel that in view of such uncertainty better for service plane to make first use Howland fields."[19]

Hampton responded with a short encrypted message.[20] Messages originally sent in cipher are not at all unusual among the archived official government communications relating to the Earhart flights. All have been decoded, however, except one: Hampton's message is the only un-decoded message among the thousands in the Earhart archives. The cipher Hampton used is no longer available, so the telegram's content remains a mystery. Black replied with an unencrypted telegram saying that he was sending a letter with "full explanation . . . on Clipper flying Tuesday."[21] It seems clear that the acting director wanted more information about the "unofficial attitude" toward Earhart's accident and the "uncertainty" it caused.

Although subsequent correspondence confirms that Black's "full explanation" letter arrived in Washington, it has not been found. In fact, it is the only example of a known piece of correspondence missing from an Earhart-related archived file. Neither Hampton's encrypted query nor Black's missing letter was designated classified, so any information they contained was not officially secret. The context of the discussion in which the two communications occur, however, and the documented disparity between Earhart's popular image and her performance in Hawaii leave little doubt about the nature of Black's concerns.

As head of the Equatorial Islands project, Black's primary interest was in the islands' continued development, and Earhart's landing on Howland seemed likely to promote that. A Pan American Airways flying boat had just completed the first survey flight from Hawaii to New Zealand, landing and refueling in the lagoon at Kingman Reef. Newspapers had covered the prospect of commercial air service to the South Pacific extensively, but Howland was not part of the equation.[22] If Earhart successfully crossed the Pacific Ocean in a land plane, the usefulness of Howland's airport—and the value of the American Equatorial Islands—would be dramatically demonstrated. But the portents were not promising.

Despite setting a speed record from California, Earhart had arrived in Hawaii in an airplane crippled by shoddy maintenance. Regardless of whether the accident that ended her first attempt to fly to Howland Island was the result of a mechanical failure, as she claimed, or simply poor piloting, it did nothing to inspire confidence that another try would have a happier result. If Earhart's second world flight attempt ended in failure, perhaps this time with a crash at Howland Island, it would be very difficult for the Division of Territories and Island Possessions to argue for further development of the islands. Some politically embarrassing questions asked about how the airport came to be built might arise as well.

Black felt that the best protection against such eventualities was to validate the utility of the island airfield before Earhart had a chance to try again— hence his attempt to interest the navy in making some use of the island during upcoming fleet maneuvers. All that was needed was a plane from an aircraft carrier to land and take off as a demonstration that the island could be used as an emergency landing facility. In the end, the navy was not interested and the projected fleet operations took place without using Howland.

For the rest of April and the entire month of May, Black heard not another word about Earhart's plans. Finally, on June 1, he sent a cable to Acting Director Ruth Hampton asking if she had any information about a number of confusing developments and rumors. Reports in the press were saying that Earhart had reversed her course around the world, but Black had also heard that the Bureau of Air Commerce might ban Earhart's world flight as unnecessary.[23] Hampton replied the next day, saying only that "Earhart completed first lap east/west [sic] flight arriving San Juan but we have no further information than contained in press. No requests have been received from Miss Earhart or Mr. Putnam. Suggest you contact Navy, Coast Guard and Putnam's representative Honolulu and endeavor secure information."[24] The navy and Coast Guard personnel in Hawaii knew no more than Black, and Putnam had no representative in Honolulu. Earhart was off on her second attempt to fly around the world, and coordination of support for the most dangerous part of the trip had been exactly zero.

Earhart's decision to reverse the direction of her flight surprised almost everyone. The surviving correspondence indicates that Amelia did not mention it during her fence-mending visits to the Coast Guard, navy, and Interior Department in late April. The plan was first revealed in a May 5 letter from George Putnam to Richard Southgate, his State Department contact:

> For your information it now appears that Miss Earhart will be able to renew her world flight attempt the latter part of May.
>
> The original plan contemplated proceeding from Venezuela to Los Angeles via Central America and Mexico. Confidentially, because of increasing rains in that region it is now likely that she will attempt to fly from California, via a point in Texas, to Miami, and thence to Venezuela and on to Natal, via Porto Rico. That is, going West–East. . . . Because of changed weather conditions it is now possible that the route in Africa may also be changed.[25]

Putnam asked Southgate whether the revised routes would require further permissions from the countries involved.

Three days later, on May 8, Putnam revealed the new plan to the chief of naval operations.

This note is to lay before you the exact situation. It is for the moment very confidential. Aside from Miss Earhart and myself only two people know the revised plan.

The delay from the chosen mid-March date has resulted in changed weather conditions on several stretches of the proposed route. In a couple of instances these are drastic. Specifically, the weather probabilities in the stretch from Natal north are increasingly bad as June advances. The same is true of the Dakar–Aden–Karachi route. Obviously it is therefore desirable to get to Natal and across the South Atlantic and Africa as promptly as possible.

So Miss Earhart has decided to reverse the route and to proceed *from west to east* [emphasis in the original].[26]

Putnam went on to explain that there would be "no announcement." The takeoff from Oakland would "be simply the commencement of another 'trial flight.' . . . As matters stand, this 'sneak' takeoff from Oakland will occur probably between May 18th and May 24th."

Putnam said that his best estimation was that his wife would reach Howland Island "somewhere between twenty-five and thirty days from the date of takeoff" and expected to be able to provide the navy with more specific information "about a fortnight in advance" of the Lae–Howland flight. It appears that neither the Coast Guard nor the Interior Department was notified of the change.

Southgate replied to Putnam that same day. Not only would new clearances be needed from the various countries to be visited, but Southgate, on his own initiative, had discussed the matter "informally with an officer of the Department of Commerce, who stated in view of the changed circumstances it would be necessary to issue a new letter of authority for the flight. He suggested that you be advised to communicate directly with the Department of Commerce, furnishing the latest information concerning Miss Earhart's plane."[27]

The news that Commerce was going to require a new letter of authority for the flight was not welcome, but neither was it unexpected. Since Eugene Vidal's departure, the Bureau of Air Commerce had been more hindrance than help to Earhart, and at least one prominent aviation figure had suggested that the government ban a second attempt. The decision to reverse the direction of the world flight may have been influenced as much by the need to mollify the Bureau of Air Commerce as by weather considerations.

Earhart and Putnam had been able to secure the loans and sponsorships needed to make a second attempt possible. Much of the money had been donated, but George and Amelia had gone heavily into personal debt to complete the budget. In mid-April, the promise of another try at a trip around the world was enough to land a contract with publisher Harcourt Brace for a chronicle of her trip to be called *World Flight*.* The book was an ingenious way to further capitalize on the press coverage that had always been the journey's primary purpose.

In her initial letter to FDR soliciting navy support for her planned world flight, Earhart had assured the president that "the flight . . . has no commercial implications. The operation of my 'flying laboratory' is under the auspices of Purdue University. Like previous flights I am undertaking this one solely because I want to, and because I feel that women now and then have to do things to show what women can do."[28]

The sentiment was noble, and was without question sincerely felt, but Earhart was being less than accurate. As Al Williams had so acidly pointed out, the airplane was not a flying laboratory, and for Earhart to say that she was operating under the auspices of Purdue was a stretch, to say the least. The university had given Amelia the money with which to buy the Electra, but the title was in her name and decisions about how the airplane was used were hers alone. The purpose of the world flight, like that of her previous record-setting flights, was to generate publicity for Amelia Earhart and her sponsors.

Earhart's piloting skills were average at best, but good looks, good luck, genuine courage, a talent for writing, and George Putnam's genius for promotion and media manipulation had made her one of America's most famous and admired women. Amelia's self-deprecating public persona belied a ferocious determination, but her drive was not aimed merely at self-aggrandizement. Earhart used her celebrity to advocate both public acceptance of commercial air travel and her other great passion, equal opportunities for women. A flight around the world, the first ever by a woman, and done simply "because I want to," would advance both causes while enhancing her own fame.

The central feature of the trip was a plan to use state-of-the-art telecommunications to bring the experience of international air travel to the public with unprecedented immediacy. By 1937, telegraph—and in many cases long-distance telephone—service was available from nearly all of the planned stops on Earhart's world flight. Putnam had negotiated an arrangement with the *Herald Tribune* newspaper syndicate for Amelia to phone, or when necessary wire, the syndicate's New York office from each

---

*Subsequent events resulted in the title being changed to *Last Flight*.

destination with a travelogue about her flight and the exotic people and places she saw along the way. Earhart's bylined story would be carried in the next morning's paper. For the syndicate this was an opportunity to give *Herald Tribune* readers a first-person, serialized, near-real-time account of what it was like to travel the world by air. For Earhart and Putnam it was a publicist's dream come true: coverage of Amelia's adventures, as told by Amelia, featured in major papers around the country virtually every day for a month or more.

The book contract with Harcourt Brace expanded the original concept. After some introductory chapters, the stories she would file with the *Herald Tribune* during the trip would be combined and edited to make up the rest of the book. She began writing immediately, relating the story of the preparations for the first attempt and the disaster that ended it. She acknowledged that "the stress and strains of an airplane accident and its aftermaths are just as severe financially as they are mechanically. On the prosaic dollar-and-cent side friends helped generously, but even so, to keep going I more-or-less mortgaged the future. Without regret, however, for what are futures for?"[29]

In fact, she had little choice. Neither Earhart nor her husband was independently wealthy, and their income depended on Amelia's market value as a celebrity. If she was to salvage her fame, she had to make good on her promise to fly around the world—and she had to do it soon because the newsworthiness of such a flight was steadily diminishing. At the same time Earhart was mortgaging the future, Eastern Airlines pilots Dick Merrill and Jack Lambie were making headlines with another specially modified Lockheed Electra almost exactly like hers. On May 9, they carried photos of the *Hindenburg* disaster nonstop from New York to England, and a few days later they brought photos of the coronation of King George VI back to the United States, again nonstop. Their achievement was heralded as the first commercial round-trip transatlantic flight and was yet another indication that transoceanic international air travel was becoming routine.

Earhart and Putnam were counting on sales of *World Flight* to put their finances back in order, but time was running out. The book had to be ready for the Christmas market, so the trip would have to begin as soon as the plane left the repair shop later in May. Setting off across the Pacific in a newly repaired airplane, however, would be blatantly foolhardy. Even if Earhart had been willing to try it, the chances of the Bureau of Air Commerce issuing the necessary letter of authority for such an endeavor, especially in light of Earhart's recent track record, were slim. It was also obvious that the enterprise could not survive another false start. The request for renewed permission to make the flight, dated May 10, went to J. Monroe Johnson, assistant secretary of commerce.

In her book, Earhart wrote: "It is only fair to record that the Bureau of Air Commerce probably would have preferred that I abandon the effort. Its policy was to discourage all such extracurricular undertakings of the kind, the common or garden term for which sometimes is 'stunt flights.' But having granted me permission once, the ship, personnel and flight plan being the same, it would have been difficult to withdraw it."[30]

Of course, neither the ship nor the personnel nor the flight plan was the same. The ship had been rebuilt, the personnel reduced, and the flight plan reversed. Given the dismal outcome of the first attempt, the Commerce Department might easily have justified banning a second attempt, if only to save Amelia from herself. In the end, the revised itinerary was approved, and on May 14 a new letter of authority was issued and the State Department was asked to "go forward with the matter of notifying the various foreign Governments involved."[31]

The plan conceived by Earhart and Putnam did have some disadvantages. She would have to mislead the press and the public about the true nature of the flight from California to Florida, and then, if all went well, admit she had misled them. But Amelia had often been coy about upcoming flights. The publicity surrounding the Oakland takeoff of the first world flight attempt had been something of an anomaly. Both of her previous transoceanic flights, Newfoundland to Ireland in 1932 and Hawaii to California in 1935, had grabbed headlines with surprise departures.

For the second world flight attempt Earhart and Putnam went to extraordinary lengths to make sure the press did not discover the plan. To minimize the danger of leaks, only a few key people were told that the flight to Miami was the provisional beginning of a second attempt. Not even Earhart's technical adviser, Paul Mantz, out of town for an air show, was in on the secret. The tight security meant that detailed coordination of support for the Pacific legs of the trip would have to wait until after the world flight had publicly begun. On the other hand, reversing the direction meant crossing the Pacific at the end of the trip rather than the beginning, leaving plenty of time to make the necessary arrangements.

On Wednesday, May 19, the Bureau of Air Commerce inspector in Burbank certified the rebuilt Electra as fit to fly.[32] The second world flight attempt officially, but secretly, began the very next day. For the trip to Miami, Amelia was accompanied not only by Fred Noonan but also by George Putnam and her mechanic, Ruckins D. "Bo" McKneely.

The shakedown flight across the country shook down several problems—some with the airplane, some with the pilot. Earhart's attempt to restart the left engine after refueling in Tucson, Arizona, caused an engine fire that nearly got out of hand. An unplanned overnight stay was necessary to repair the damage. As the trip continued, Earhart discovered that the automatic pilot needed adjustment and the radio transmitter had a very short range. Her arrival in Miami on the afternoon of May 23 was downright embarrassing. Amelia landed at the wrong airport, took off again, and on landing at the correct field, Miami Municipal, misjudged her height and dropped the airplane onto the runway in what she reportedly said was the hardest landing she had ever made in the Electra. An inspection by Pan American mechanics turned up no damage, and they worked on the autopilot and radio problems over the course of the following week with varying degrees of success.

On May 30, the cat was officially let out of the bag. The front page of the *New York Herald Tribune* carried the headline "Miss Earhart Set to Fly Eastward around the World." The article, written by Amelia, explained that "there are several reasons for the change in direction. Or, perhaps, one basic one on which all others hang. The weather." She also justified the subterfuge about the beginning of the world flight with an appeal for sympathy:

So much was written before and after the March 17 take-off at Oakland, and following the Honolulu accident that I thought it would be a pleasant change to just slip away. . . . Incidentally, the career of one who indulges in any kind of flying off the beaten path is often complicated. For instance, if one gives out plans beforehand, one is likely to be charged with publicity seeking by those who do not know how difficult it is to escape the competent gentlemen of the press. On the other hand, if one slips away, as I have generally tried to do, the slipper-away invites catcalls from those who earn their living writing and taking photographs. So I am hoping the pros and cons of the whole undertaking can wait until it is finally over.

The changes in the weather, she said, had also "brought an increase in personnel. Originally I planned to be alone except for a navigator on the Pacific, where objectives were small islands on a vast ocean. Now I am taking Captain Noonan the whole distance to save time on occasion."[33]

The radios and autopilot continued to give trouble, and it was June 1 before the world flight resumed, publicly this time, with the flight from Miami to San Juan, Puerto Rico.

CHAPTER FIVE

Not for Publication

crossing the south atlantic

As Fred Noonan tracked the Electra's progress southward, Amelia let "Sperry" (the Sperry automatic pilot) do much of the flying while she made notes for her book about the "opalescent sea" and islands where "small streams look like green snakes." Earhart and Noonan worked alone together for the first time on the seven-and-a-half-hour trip to San Juan, and her jotted comments about the navigator speak rather dismissively of "Freddie." "Freddie looking for lighthouse." "Freddie points out a partly submerged wreck off shore." But there is a growing admiration in notations such as, "6:35. We sight a reef. Freddie said we'd pass one at 6:40. Pretty good." And, "Freddie says San Juan at 1:10 EST from white hankies of foam?" (an allusion to Noonan's ability to judge surface wind speed and direction from the appearance of the sea). Familiarity, in this case, seems to have bred respect, and Earhart's notes written later in the world flight refer to Noonan as "Fred" or "F.N.," never "Freddie."[1]

If it took some time for Amelia to get to know her navigator, that was because Frederick J. Noonan, for all his affable nature and well-publicized accomplishments as Pan American's star navigator, was a very private individual. Amelia lived and thrived in the spotlight, writing and speaking freely about her feelings and opinions. Fred Noonan's personal life, however, was not for publication, and his public writings were confined to professional treatises on navigation.[2] The letters and telegrams Earhart and Putnam sent to various government agencies survive as part of the public record, and much of Earhart's private correspondence was later donated to libraries and archives. By contrast, nearly all of Noonan's surviving letters and telegrams are in private collections. Some have been released to researchers. Others, regrettably, have not.

In the years since his death, Noonan's preflight inaccessibility has made him a one-dimensional figure in the Earhart legend: the expert navigator with a drinking problem. Newly available contemporary sources, however, reveal a more complete—and very different—picture of the man who flew with Amelia, permitting a better understanding of how the two aviators worked, and ultimately died, together.

Noonan's addition to the Electra's crew just days before the departure of the first world flight attempt appears to have been occasioned by the discovery that the flight's designated navigator, Harry Manning, needed help. Manning was an experienced sea captain and a licensed pilot, but he was accustomed to applying his celestial navigation skills from the deck of a slow-moving ship at sea level. Shooting the sun and stars through the windows of a high-flying, often turbulence-tossed airplane traveling at 150 miles per hour was a very different proposition.

Noonan too held maritime ratings and a pilot's license, but he was also a celebrated aerial navigator. Born in Chicago in 1893, he went to sea at an early age, serving in a succession of merchant ships and steadily advancing in his ratings and certifications. During the Great War, Noonan lived in New York and served aboard several American and British ships in the merchant marine, but he was never in the U.S. Navy. In 1926, the U.S. Shipping Board awarded Noonan his license as "master of steamers of any gross tonnage." His career was moving ahead, and the next year, at age thirty-four, he married Josephine Sullivan in Jackson, Mississippi. The couple settled in New Orleans, where Fred worked for the Mississippi Shipping Company as chief mate on SS *Carplaka*.[3]

If Fred Noonan hoped that his master's papers would bring him a ship of his own, the next few years brought disappointment. Employment was steady despite the onset of the Great Depression, but Noonan sailed always as a mate, never as captain. In 1930, perhaps hoping for better advancement in a newer, and in some ways similar, field, he obtained a limited commercial airplane pilot's license and landed a job with Pan American Airways' Caribbean Division in Miami. Later that year, the Noonans moved to Port au Prince, Haiti, where Fred had been made field manager of the company's new Haitian operation. Adapting his maritime navigational expertise to aviation, Fred was instrumental in developing techniques for the company's nascent Pacific Division.

In March 1935, he and Josie moved to Oakland, California, and for the rest of that year Noonan served as navigating officer on the survey flights that pioneered commercial air service across the Pacific. From Pan Am's Alameda base, the planes hopscotched first to Honolulu and Midway, then to Wake Island, and finally all the way to Guam and Manila. On November 22, 1935, a new Pan American Airways Martin M-130 dubbed the "China Clipper" lifted from the waters of San Francisco Bay and headed westward over the ocean, its course set by the company's star navigator, Capt. Fred Noonan. Two weeks later, the giant flying boat returned safely, having completed the first scheduled transpacific airmail flight.[4]

Fred Noonan made at least twenty-one flights for Pan American in 1936, including numerous, often lengthy, test hops and five round-trip Pacific crossings to Manila. His last flight with the airline—a sixteen-day marathon as navigator of the "Philippine Clipper"—concluded on December 7, 1936. Sometime later that month he left the company. The reason for his departure is not documented; no letter of resignation or notification of termination is known to exist. The most contemporaneous explanation is found in a 1939 book written by Pan Am pilot William Grooch, who reported something of a rebellion among the airline's flight crews following the November–December Manila trip.

> On the outbound voyage the crew had reacted normally; then, as they wearied of the long grind, tempers became frayed, movements sluggish. It was an effort to remain awake on duty. . . . [P]ilots were averaging a hundred and twenty-five hours a month in the air. This was far in excess of the limit established by the Department of Commerce regulations. Ed [Pacific Division Chief Pilot Capt. Edwin Musick] felt they had a just grievance. He championed their cause with company officials, pointing out that his own promised raise in salary had not materialized. They shrugged and passed the buck to the New York office. There the matter was pigeonholed. Ed strove to convince the pilots that the delay was due to the press of more urgent business. . . .
> Fred Noonan said, "We've lived on promises for a year. I'm through." He resigned immediately. The others grumbled but carried on.[5]

Fred Noonan's professional record, both nautical and aeronautical, is spotless. References in his own correspondence make it clear that Noonan enjoyed an occasional drink, and it is possible—and even probable—that he sometimes overindulged, but stories about excesses arose only after his death. There is nothing in the historical record to support later allegations that he was fired by Pan American for drinking.

The first months of 1937 were an unsettled time for Fred Noonan. He was forty-three years old and his six-year career with Pan American had come to an end—as had his ten-year, childless marriage to Josephine. The extent to which the stress and the long separations of the past two years were factors in the breakup is not known but, on March 3, 1937, Noonan's attorney filed divorce papers in Juarez, Mexico.[6] Around this time Fred was also involved in a serious automobile accident.[7] A more positive development was the new love in his life. Mary Beatrice "Bee" Martinelli, herself a divorcée with no children, ran a beauty salon in Oakland. The couple planned to marry as soon as Noonan's divorce became final.

Ten days after Noonan filed for divorce, and just two days before Amelia Earhart's scheduled March 15 departure for Hawaii, Noonan's name appeared for the first time in the press as a member of the Electra's crew.[8] No record of any agreement Noonan may have had with Earhart and Putnam regarding compensation for his services has come to light, but other documents provide clues to the arrangement.

When Earhart took off from Oakland on her first attempt to fly around the world, her plan called for navigators Fred Noonan and Harry Manning to guide the Electra to Honolulu and from there to Howland Island. Noonan would leave the crew at Howland, and Manning would continue on with Earhart as far as Australia. Amelia would span the remaining two-thirds of the globe alone. That plan, however, appears to have been altered after the plane reached Hawaii.

On March 19, the night before the takeoff for Howland, Noonan sent a telegram to Bee: "Leaving 1:30 AM your time. Amelia has asked me to continue with her at least as far as Darwin, Australia and possibly around the world. Will keep you advised. Trip around world will be completed before I can return from Australia. I love you, Fred."[9] In his message to his bride-to-be, Noonan did not appear to be concerned about the cost of a steamer ticket if he left the flight in Darwin; nor did he mention anything about increased compensation for his services if he were to continue on as Earhart's navigator. His sole concern seemed to be the length of time it would take him to get home. He assured Bee that flying around the world with Amelia would be faster than sailing back across the Pacific from Australia. The content of Noonan's telegram is consistent with an agreement by which Earhart and Putnam covered his expenses but left it up to him to turn fame into fortune.

The wreck at Luke Field the next morning ended the first world flight attempt and did not enhance anyone's fame or fortune, but Fred did get back to his sweetheart sooner than expected. Noonan, Earhart, and Manning sailed for California that same day, and one week later, on March 27, 1937, Fred and Bee were married in Yuma, Arizona. According to newspaper accounts, the couple planned to settle in Oakland but would "spend a brief honeymoon in Hollywood as Noonan is now engaged with Miss Earhart in preparing plans for the re-start of the world flight."[10]

Eight days later, Fred Noonan found himself in yet another wreck. April 4, 1937, was his forty-fourth birthday, and that night, as he and his bride drove through Fresno on their way back to Oakland along the Golden State Highway, they hit another car head-on. Fred escaped with minor bruises, but Bee was hospitalized with "an extensive laceration on the knee and other injuries." The other driver was not injured, but the man's wife and infant daughter were treated for bruises at Fresno Emergency Hospital and released. Noonan was cited for driving in the wrong lane.[11]

Little is known about Noonan's activities during the following six weeks. He maintained a post office box address in Hollywood, and a business directory published later that year lists a residence address in Los Angeles. During that time, Earhart and Putnam traveled back and forth between the two coasts, fund-raising and fence-mending on the East Coast and

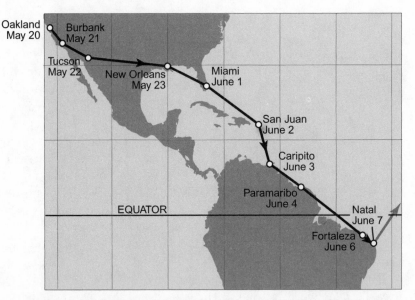

The progress of Earhart's second world flight from Oakland, California, to Natal, Brazil. Dates shown are for the departure from each location.

monitoring the progress of repairs to the airplane in Burbank. Noonan did not attend the meetings in Washington, however, and he does not appear in the photos and newsreels of Amelia inspecting the Electra in the repair shop in California.

A Bureau of Air Commerce inspector examined and certified the Electra on May 19, 1937, and Fred was on hand in Burbank the next day for the "sneak takeoff" of the second world flight attempt. Three days later, Amelia, Fred, George Putnam, and mechanic Bo McKneely arrived in Florida, having completed the Electra's cross-country test flight.

Fred was on familiar turf in Miami, and he took the opportunity to renew his acquaintance with Helen Day, a young woman he had met when he worked for Pan American's Caribbean Division. He wrote to Day at least four times during the world flight, and his letters, recently released by her family, provide a rare glimpse of Noonan's personality and his perspective on the trip around the world.

Fred's first letter to Helen Day was written from Fortaleza, Brazil, five days into the trip. In it he described crossing "hundreds of miles of unexplored dense virgin jungle. . . . It was interesting because of the lack of recogniz-able landmarks—a jungle is equally as devoid of distinguishable landmarks as an ocean. In consequence, at several times we had to rely upon celestial navigation to ascertain our position."[12]

From Fortaleza, Earhart and Noonan made the short hop to Natal on the easternmost tip of Brazil. At 3:15 AM on June 7, 1937, they set off across the South Atlantic for Africa. The predawn takeoff was intended to allow the flight to reach its destination—Dakar, French Senegal—before dark, but thirteen hours and twenty-two minutes later, at 7:35 PM local time, three minutes before sunset, the Electra touched down unannounced at St. Louis, 163 miles beyond Dakar.

That same evening, June eighth, Amelia sent a press release to the *Herald Tribune* explaining what had happened.

> Here at St. Louis are the headquarters of Air France for the trans-Atlantic service and I am grateful for the field's excellent facilities, which have generously been placed at my disposal. But it is only fair to say that I had really intended to land at Dakar 163 miles south of St. Louis. The fault is entirely mine.
>
> When we first sighted the African coast, thick haze prevailed. My navigator, Captain Fred Noonan, indicated that we should turn south. Had we done so, a few minutes would have brought us to Dakar. But a left turn seemed to me more attractive and fifty miles of flying along the coast brought us here.
>
> Once arrived over the airport and having definitely located ourselves, it seemed better to sit down rather than retrace our track along a strange coast with darkness imminent.[13]

It was a good story, but it was not true. The chart Noonan used to track the flight's progress was sent home later in the trip and is now in the Amelia Earhart Collection at Purdue University.[14] Noonan's hand-drawn course lines and notations, and two notes he passed to Amelia during the flight, document what really happened.

In a letter to a friend written from Dakar, Noonan described the weather conditions that prevailed during the trip: "The flight from Natal, Brazil to Africa produced the worst weather we have experienced—heavy rain and dense cloud formations necessitated blind flying for ten of the thirteen hours we were in flight."[15] For most of that long day over the South Atlantic, the Electra hung suspended in a world of gray murk as rain beat a staccato tattoo on the windshield. Earhart let the automatic pilot do the flying while she made notes for her book. "Have tried to get something on radio. No go. Rain, Static. Have never seen such rain. Props a blur in it. See nothing but rain now through wispy cloud. Fred dozes."[16]

The navigator, slumped in the copilot's seat, might as well catch some sleep. Unable to monitor their progress by landmarks or celestial observations, Noonan could do no more than give Earhart his best guess at a compass heading that would keep them more or less on track. Popular legend has Noonan confined to the navigator's station in the rear cabin and able to communicate with Earhart only in notes passed forward over the fuel tanks by means of a bamboo pole. In fact, he spent much of his time in the cockpit with Amelia, clambering over the fuel tanks into the rear cabin only when he needed room to spread out a chart or use the lavatory.

Earhart and Noonan did, however, communicate primarily in writing. Even when sitting side by side, the din of the engines prohibited anything but shouted verbal exchanges. The Lockheed Model 10 had been designed with the comfort of the passengers, not the pilot, in mind. The propellers, the source of most of the noise in a propeller-driven aircraft, were placed well forward, directly opposite the cockpit. The standard airline version of the airplane featured extensive soundproofing, but in the long-range Model 10E Special, the insulation had been sacrificed to save weight. Consequently, the decibel level in the cockpit was truly punishing. Dick Merrill and Jack Lambie had been rendered temporarily deaf by their round-trip flight to England in the other 10E Special in May.

After six and a half hours the weather began to improve. Earhart noted, "Clouds seem to be changing. Formation seems thinner. Rather bright in spots. Can hardly believe sun is north of us but so it is."[17] An hour later, Noonan was able to get a shot of the sun through the cockpit windows. He then climbed over the fuel tanks into the rear cabin and took another celestial observation through the glass panel in the cabin door. A few minutes later he passed a note forward to Earhart. "By a second observation crossed with the first taken in the cockpit, find we are north of course—have averaged 147 mph. Now we have a tail wind—alter course to 76° M[agnetic]."[18]

Noonan hoped that the new course would take them directly to Dakar, but as it turned out, he had overcorrected for the wind. His next observation showed the Electra to be well south of its course, so he had Amelia reduce the amount of correction. An hour later, another observation established the airplane's position about 50 miles from the African coast and almost 150 miles south of Dakar. Noonan passed Earhart another note ordering a turn to the left: "3:36 change to 36°. Estimate 79 miles to Dakar from . . ." and here the note was later altered by someone (the handwriting is entirely different) to read "3:36 PM."[19] Matching the note to Noonan's map, the note probably originally read, "Estimate 79 miles to Dakar from landfall."

Across the bottom of the note Earhart scribbled "What put us north?" referring to the earlier need for a mid-course correction. The note, which was reproduced in *Last Flight*, was probably changed by the book's editor because it did not agree with Earhart's allegation that the flight arrived on the African coast 50 miles north of Dakar. Altering the note made it appear as though Earhart was asking Noonan why they had struck the coast north of Dakar.

When the flight came within sight of the coast, Earhart and Noonan encountered another problem. As Fred wrote in his June 9 letter, "To add to our woes the African coast was enveloped in thick haze, rendering objects invisible at distances over a half mile, when we made the landfall. And our radio was out of order—it would be, in such a jam. However, with our usual good luck, if not good guidance, we barged through okay."[20]

Dakar sits on a peninsula extending out into the Atlantic. The Electra had made landfall south and east of the city. In hazy conditions such as Noonan described, forward visibility while flying toward a setting sun is virtually zero. Turning back toward the ocean to try to find Dakar with no radio, limited fuel, and failing daylight was not an attractive proposition. Finding St. Louis was a simple matter of following the coastline northeast-ward to where the Senegal River meets the sea.

No one knows why Earhart was so quick to put out a different story, but at least one good reason is apparent. The decision to bypass Dakar under the prevailing circumstances was operationally correct but bureaucratically risky. The world flight's path across Africa lay over French colonial posses-sions, and there had been a great deal of State Department correspondence with Paris discussing specific routes and the various restrictions that would apply to each. Once the French authorities had been told which of the approved routes Earhart would follow, they expected her to go where she had said she would go. All of the approved routes across Africa began in Dakar. Failing to land there, if seen as willful disregard of the approved itinerary, might result in the airplane and crew being impounded and fined. If missing Dakar was represented as a navigational mistake, however, especially one for which the female pilot took the blame for not listening to her male navigator, the French authorities might be less likely to hold it against her. Whatever Earhart's motivation, the American public and the French authorities accepted her version of events, and the next day the flight repositioned to Dakar without incident.*

The letter Fred Noonan wrote from Dakar on June 9, 1937, was addressed to "Eugene Pallette, Hollywood Roosevelt Hotel, Hollywood, California, Etats-Unis." Pallette was a popular and prolific film actor, best remembered today for his role as the rotund and raspy-voiced Friar Tuck in the 1938 Warner Brothers film *The Adventures of Robin Hood*. It is clear from the letter that Noonan had promised to keep Pallette informed about the prog-ress of the world flight via telegram. Fred was having difficulty meeting that

---

*Earhart's bogus account, cleverly expedient as it was, has become a staple of the Earhart legend and has been used to justify endless speculation about Amelia's relationship with Noonan and whether and how she might have disregarded his instructions during the Lae–Howland flight.

obligation, and his letter, sent back across the South Atlantic via airmail, was apologetic.

Dear Gene,

Having trouble sending messages such as I promised you—but I am doing the best that I can. Facilities are not always available, and therefore I am sending one message when possible, naming stop made since the previous message. Tried to get one off last night but some trouble developed at the cable station. As I had sent the cablegram to the cable office by messenger I have not yet ascertained the cause of the delay in transmission—but will do so later to-day.

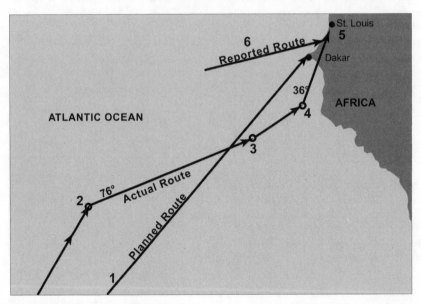

What really happened on the coast of Africa.
1. The Electra's planned route from Natal, Brazil.
2. Emerging from bad weather, Noonan was able to take a celestial observation and determine that the flight was north of course. He instructed Earhart to alter her heading to 76°.
3. Two hours and forty-five minutes later, Noonan took another observation. He realized he had over-corrected and instructed Earhart to take a slightly more northerly heading.
4. An hour later, the flight was close enough to the African coast for Noonan to get a better fix on their position. He instructed Earhart to turn to 36° and estimated that they were 79 miles from Dakar.
5. With evening approaching, the visibility in the Dakar area was down to one half mile in haze. Earhart and Noonan prudently decided to continue up the coast to St. Louis.
6. Not wanting to admit that she had intentionally bypassed her approved destination, Earhart claimed that she had hit the coast north of Dakar and turned the wrong way.

After describing the flight so far and the expected itinerary for the next few days, Noonan closed: "With kindest personal regards, and looking forward to a highball together in the not too distant future—I am, Sincerely, Fred Noonan."[21]*

Noonan's letter to Pallette differs markedly in tone from the newsy missives that Fred wrote to his wife and to Helen Day during the world flight; nor does it appear to be intended for publication. Earhart's press releases, such as the one she wrote after landing in St. Louis, were sent to the *Herald Tribune* under the deal negotiated by Putnam for exclusive newspaper coverage of her trip around the world. No stories attributed to Noonan appeared in the press, and it can be safely assumed that Putnam would not have permitted such competition.

Just what Noonan and Pallette were up to is a matter for speculation, but Noonan's promise to feed Pallette information is not—Fred's letter from Dakar is unequivocal—and the promised updates must have had a purpose that justified the considerable cost of sending international telegrams and airmail letters. Whatever the arrangement, it probably reflected Noonan's plans to capitalize on the expected success of the world flight.

---

*Noonan's letter to Pallette ended up in the possession of Fred's widow and eventually in a private collection of his correspondence. If there are other letters or telegrams from Noonan to Pallette, they have not been released.

CHAPTER SIX

Stand to Sea

preparations for the flight to howland island

As Earhart and Noonan pursued their own agendas on the coast of Africa, Capt. Stanley V. Parker, commander of the Coast Guard's San Francisco Division, discovered that, like Richard Black in Hawaii, he had been blindsided by Earhart's surprise departure. On June 7, 1937, a message arrived from the commandant in Washington asking, "Have arrangements been made to have vessel at Howland Island end of June cooperation Earhart flight?" Captain Parker replied, "Earhart negative. No official information of itinerary and schedule received but private information promised two weeks advance notice of time of expected arrival Howland Island."[1]

If that time was going to be late June, there was a problem. Parker explained to the commandant that all of the ships currently assigned to the Hawaiian Section were either laid up for maintenance or committed to other duties until the end of June. He added: "Please advise closest estimate expected arrival time Howland."[2] Admiral Waesche's response dumped the problem squarely back in Parker's lap. "Best estimate Earhart flight is depart from New Guinea June 20 for Howland. Advise action contemplated by you."[3]

The commandant had ordered him to pay Paul, so Captain Parker had no choice but to rob Peter. The cutter *Itasca* was in port near Los Angeles, having recently been assigned to the Coast Guard's Southern Section for duty on the West Coast. He would have to send it back to the Hawaiian Section. Parker alerted the cutter's captain to "be prepared on short notice to proceed Howland Island via Honolulu."[4]

Meanwhile, the Department of the Interior was also trying to cope with the schedule change. On June 8, 1937, the day Earhart and Noonan arrived in St. Louis, Acting Director Ruth Hampton received a letter from George Putnam saying that Earhart would probably be at Howland in the latter part of June or early July. Hampton immediately responded, cautioning him that Interior could not support a late June arrival because "the next regular quarterly expedition to Equatorial Islands cannot leave Honolulu before July 1st due to the nonavailability of appropriations before that date."[5] Hampton then cabled Black in Hawaii to bring him up-to-date on the situation and to suggest that he proceed with arrangements for the island reprovisioning and Earhart flight support expedition to leave Honolulu early on the morning of July 1.[6]

In San Francisco, Captain Parker, having been told to send a cutter to Howland in late June and unaware that Interior was out of money until July 1, sent a message to the commander of the Hawaiian Section: "In view *Itasca*'s early departure for Honolulu and Howland Island, suggest possibility her performance routine line island cruise."[7] The Coast Guard commander in Honolulu ran the idea past Richard Black, who told him about the appropriations problem. Later that day, Black cabled Hampton with the news that the Coast Guard was sending *Itasca* to Honolulu and offering a suggestion: "Since Putnam has been advised sailing date July 1st, please advise me whether combine cruise to aid flight and regular cruise visiting JBH [Jarvis, Baker, Howland], or special cruise immediately and regular cruise mid July. Commander Hawaiian Section leaves decision to us but respectfully suggests conference Coast Guard Washington would obviate necessity such early departure of *Itasca* from coast if cruises combined."[8]

Howland Island was nearly two thousand miles from Hawaii. Black and the Coast Guard commander could hardly believe that their superiors in Washington were contemplating two separate trips. The sensible course of action was to wait and do the island resupply and flight support as a combined cruise after July 1, but the decision rested with the Interior Department's Division of Territories and Island Possessions and its acting director, Ruth Hampton.

Faced with the prospect of Amelia cooling her heels somewhere on the far side of the world until it was convenient for the Department of the Interior to resupply the Equatorial Islands' colonists, Putnam quickly wrote back to Hampton.

> I hasten to reply to your letter of June 8th. . . . I have today received a letter from Admiral Waesche of the Coast Guard. He informs me that a cutter is at Honolulu and will depart for Howland when required. . . . From my understanding, as above set forth, it would appear that the departure for the Island of Mr. Black, even before July 1st, would not necessarily necessitate the expenditure of Department funds as transportation, and I assume sustenance, are supplied by the Coast Guard. . . . I have taken the liberty of assuming that Mr. Black would, so far as Howland Island is concerned, be in charge of the entire matter. I have had very pleasant and helpful exchanges of letters with him and am deeply grateful for his intelligent and efficient cooperation and his evident intention to follow the matter through thoroughly.[9]

Putnam's representations in the letter were disingenuous at best. The letter from Admiral Waesche did not say that "a cutter is at Honolulu and will depart for Howland when required." Waesche's letter said only, "I have notified our San Francisco representative to be prepared to have a vessel at Howland Island the latter part of June."[10] *Itasca*, at that moment, was still tied to a California pier. Putnam's assumption that the Coast Guard was covering the cost of "sustenance" for the colonists was also in error. The Interior Department was responsible for provisioning the islands and, as Hampton had told him in her letter, could not resupply the colonists until appropriations became available on July 1. Putnam's claim to have exchanged pleasant and helpful letters with Black is not supported by the historical record. All of the correspondence with Black to coordinate support for the first world flight attempt had been handled by the Bureau of Air Commerce liaison, William Miller. The only communication Black had ever received from Putnam was the telegram Putnam sent to him aboard *Shoshone* on the day of the Luke Field wreck, and that message merely relayed Amelia's apologies for breaking their "engagement for tonight."[11]

Putnam was right about one thing. With regard to government support of Earhart's second attempt to fly to Howland Island, Black was, indeed, in charge of the entire matter. Putnam was also correct in saying that it was Black's intention to follow the matter through thoroughly. But at that moment Richard Black was growing apprehensive at the lack of communication from George Putnam.

Nonetheless, Putnam's letter had the desired effect, and Hampton sent Black a cable authorizing two expeditions to Howland Island:

> Letter from Putnam just received indicates possible arrival Earhart at Howland before July 1st . . . Putnam states all arrangements with Coast Guard and Navy have been made and cutter will leave Honolulu sufficiently in advance to permit several days at Howland to recondition runways and disperse bird population, also to establish radio contact with Earhart plane. . . . You are authorized to proceed with coordination all arrangements and if departure necessary before July 1st to make special trip to Howland, regular expedition to follow at such time as you may decide after 1938 appropriation becomes available. Please cooperate and assist in every way possible and keep this division closely informed as to developments.[12]

Black would do as he was told, but he needed information about the flight he was supposed to support. He replied, "Will proceed with coordination of arrangements as directed. . . . Please give me direct radio address Putnam or other direct contact flight."[13]

The Coast Guard's San Francisco Division also needed information. Captain Parker was upset that Putnam had failed to provide the promised two weeks' advance notice of Earhart's anticipated arrival at Howland. On June 10, 1937, he asked the commandant that "Putnam be required to keep this Division advised daily of progress of Earhart flight." The reply from Washington was not encouraging: "Headquarters unable contact Putnam."[14]

Itasca was at sea, steaming for Honolulu. Its captain, Cdr. Warner K. Thompson, also needed instructions. On June 11, he queried Parker, "Please advise any radio schedules to be observed with Earhart plane and frequency guarded." Parker replied with what little information he had: "No plane schedules have been arranged with this Division. On previous trip plane was equipped with 50 watt transmitter for operation on 500, 3105 and 6210 kilocycles with receiver covering all frequencies and direction finder covering 200 to 1500 kilocycles. All transmissions were by key although the transmitter may be used for voice. Will advise all details possible to obtain when received from headquarters."[15]

The next day Parker also passed along to *Itasca* a comment forwarded by the Coast Guard air station in Miami: "When Amelia Earhart took off from Miami she stated she would not try to communicate with any radio station but would broadcast her position every 15 and 45 minutes past each hour on 6210 kcs. She also transmits on 3105 kcs. She stated that her receiver will be used most of the time taking radio bearings."[16] This was outdated information and hearsay, but Earhart's flight to Howland might be as little as eight days away and Putnam had still sent no word about what support she wanted and how the Coast Guard and navy ships were supposed to communicate with her.

As division commander, Parker also faced the prospect of ships from his Hawaiian Section making back-to-back trips to Howland. On June 12, he sent a strongly worded appeal to Admiral Waesche: "Failure to combine Earhart mission and routine Equator Island cruise so awkward and embarrassing in variety of aspect[s] it would seem higher authority could compel action on basis of emergency funds." Parker pointed out that if *Itasca* did not resupply the islands on this trip, that job would have to be done in July by the cutter *Roger B. Taney*, which would thus not be available for law enforcement duties for the entire month of July. In addition, Parker added, "some adverse comment may flow from special detail of *Itasca* to flight cooperation alone."[17]

Admiral Waesche saw Parker's point. Rather than risk adverse comment, the Coast Guard would pay for the supplies. He notified Parker: "*Itasca* authorized to obtain and issue to Department Interior necessary stores for islands. Invoice Coast Guard supplies to Interior after June 30."

Waesche then telephoned Interior, and the good news was wired to Black in Hawaii the same day. The flight support and the island resupply missions would be combined in a single voyage that would sail according to Earhart's schedule.[18]

But what was Earhart's schedule? And what radio protocols would she be using? On June 14, 1937, Black wired Hampton with a message for Putnam which she included in a letter sent to his New York address. "The following radiogram for you from Mr. Richard B. Black: 'Request latest estimate arrival date Howland Island and frequent supplementary information via Coast Guard radio to reach me here or aboard *Itasca*. Please give me full instructions on radio contact with plane as verification of information Earhart gave at Miami regarding frequencies and times of transmission. We have two radios dated March 13 covering plan on first flight.'"[19]

The "radios" Black referred to were messages sent to the Coast Guard a few days before the first world flight attempt was scheduled to leave California. The navigator/radio operator for that flight, Harry Manning, and the Bureau of Air Commerce liaison, William Miller, had designed the plan based on the capabilities of the aircraft and crew at that time. The information was now dangerously obsolete. In his appeal to Putnam for information, Black also explained what arrangements had and had not been made to provide Earhart with weather predictions: "Lieutenant True, Aerologist, Fleet Air Base, will give forecast from Howland to Honolulu and suggest you arrange forecast New Guinea to Howland through weather facilities at Lae."[20]

Itasca arrived from California on the morning of June 15, 1937, mooring to Honolulu's Pier 27 at 11:55 AM. Commander Thompson immediately went ashore to report for duty. At the Hawaiian Section offices Thompson met the section's deputy commander, Lt. Cdr. Frank T. Kenner, and the Interior Department's representative, Richard Black. Kenner had skippered *Itasca* on earlier trips to the islands, had been in charge of landing construction equipment from USCG *Duane* to build the Howland runways, and had helped to coordinate support in Honolulu for Earhart's March attempt. Because the mission to Howland was to be Thompson's first cruise to the equatorial Pacific, Kenner was going along in an advisory capacity. His presence on this trip would provide a measure of continuity.

Itasca's mission would be "to act as Earhart plane guard at Howland and furnish weather." On completion of its work in connection with the Earhart flight, the ship was to "continue on regular Line Island cruise." Black was the designated "leader of the expedition and coordinator of government assistance to Earhart flight as regards Howland Island."[21] It was his job to match Earhart's needs to the services offered by the various agencies, and he could already see that competent, reliable radio communication was going to be critical to the success of the mission.

The transmitters the colonists on Howland and Baker operated were low-powered ones that could send only code. It was the cutter's radio operators who would handle the preflight coordination, provide weather information, and send the signals on which Earhart would take bearings to guide her to Howland. *Itasca*, however, arrived in Hawaii with only one experienced chief radioman. He was assisted by three young men rated radioman third class, the lowest rating for operators. As leader of the expedition, Black felt justified in arranging to have the men replaced with experienced U.S. Navy personnel. Commander Thompson would have none of it. He later explained: "This arrangement was not acceptable to the Commanding Officer of the *Itasca* for the reason that the Coast Guard has sufficient radiomen to perform its work."[22]

Thwarted in his attempt to improve the level of radio expertise aboard the ship, Black did what he could to give the island better radio capability. During the preparations for the first world flight in March, Manning and Miller had suggested that a radio direction finder be set up on Howland Island "if practicable."[23] A direction-finding radio receiver can determine the direction, or "bearing," from which an incoming signal is being transmitted. If Earhart was having trouble using the plane's direction finder to home in on signals sent from the ship, the receiver on the island could take bearings on the transmissions from the plane, and the operator could then radio her with instructions about what course to follow. Direction finders work best on relatively low radio frequencies, and the plan designed in March was for the plane to transmit signals on 500 kilocycles. Setting up a direction finder on Howland had been a good idea, but the request had not been made until the supply ship was already at sea. Richard Black revived the idea for the second world flight attempt, but the very limited information available about Earhart's intentions made no mention of the lower frequency and spoke only of Earhart transmitting on her two higher frequencies.

High-frequency direction finding was problematic, but Black conspired with Army Air Corps lieutenant Daniel A. Cooper, who would be in charge of servicing the Electra at Howland, to borrow an experimental unit from the navy. Commander Thompson was not supportive of this idea either: "Mr. Black and Lieutenant Cooper of the Army had the Navy send a high frequency direction finder on board. The Coast Guard did not request the equipment and did not receipt for it." Thompson later explained his skepticism: "It was the impression of Coast Guard officers that limits of accuracy reasonably to be expected from this equipment in the circumstances which would obtain on Howland Island were decidedly not sufficiently close to warrant its use as a dependable navigational device to bring the plane safely on the island. It was considered desirable however to set the equipment up at Howland as a necessary precaution."[24]

Itasca had a direction finder, but it was not able to take bearings on high-frequency signals, and there was no expectation that it would be used. The plan, as Thompson understood it and as Earhart had implied when she left Miami, was for the Coast Guard to be the passive partner in the direction-finding procedure. *Itasca*, standing just off Howland Island, would send signals, and Earhart would use the direction finder aboard her Electra to home in on the ship.

If Black and Cooper insisted on setting up the navy high-frequency direction finder on Howland, someone would have to operate it. Thompson had already made it clear that navy radio operators were not welcome aboard *Itasca*, but Black thought he might be able to find a top-notch Coast Guard radioman for the job. The cutter *Roger B. Taney* was in dry dock, and its crew was temporarily unemployed. The first operator selected was found to be "medically unfit," and the job ultimately fell to Radioman 2nd Class Frank Cipriani, who reported aboard *Itasca* the next day.[25]

June 16, 1937, was also the day that George Putnam broke his silence. In telegrams sent to the chief of naval operations, the commandant of the Coast Guard, and Ruth Hampton at Interior, he advised that Amelia had wired from Karachi, India, saying that she expected to arrive in Lae, New Guinea, one week hence. Putnam estimated that she would fly to Howland on June 24 or possibly June 25.[26] The telegrams said nothing about radio arrangements.

Two days later, on June 18, as *Itasca* was about to put to sea, Black was handed a cable from Ruth Hampton in Washington. The message relayed long-awaited radio information she had just received in a letter from Putnam.

> Earhart will broadcast radio phone quarter after and quarter to hour. Her frequencies 6210 and 3105, former used daylight. Also has 500 but dubious usability. Advise what frequencies *Itasca* will use, ditto naval vessels, so she can listen. Suggest Coast Guard and Navy coordinate so that helpful weather data be broadcasted to her after Lae takeoff on the hour and half.
>
> Will confirm arrangement with her by wire at Lae.
>
> Can *Itasca* forward Howland weather forecast to Lae possibly via the *Ontario* prior takeoff?[27]

Responding to Black's request of June 14, Putnam was verifying what Amelia had reportedly said before her departure from Miami. There was still nothing about her radio direction finder or how she planned to use it to find Howland Island, but Putnam's message did include new information. Putnam said that Earhart would broadcast using radiotelephone and that her 500 kilocycle frequency was of "dubious usability." In fact, the usability of the 500 kilocycle frequency was not dubious, it was virtually nonexistent. Low frequencies require long antennas. On the first world flight attempt, the Electra had been equipped with a "trailing wire" that could be run out and reeled in electrically from a short mast under the cabin. That mechanism was destroyed in the Luke Field crash, and Earhart chose not to have it reinstalled when the airplane was rebuilt at Lockheed Burbank.

Her decision was symptomatic of a larger problem. With Harry Manning's departure, there was no longer anyone on the crew who was technically proficient in radio matters or was even adept at sending and receiving Morse code. The low frequency could be used only to send code. In omitting the trailing wire, Earhart was eliminating the weight of a system she could not use anyway.*

In the absence of updated instructions, Black and the Coast Guard had been studying the old radio protocols set up by Manning and Miller. Those procedures specified the use of telegraphy for most communications with the plane. Putnam now indicated that Earhart would broadcast using radiophone, but he did not make it clear that the plane could no longer communicate using Morse code.

Putnam's letter reveals another problem as well. In his June 14 message to Putnam, Black had told him, "Lieutenant True, Aerologist, Fleet Air Base, will give forecast from Howland to Honolulu and suggest you arrange forecast New Guinea to Howland through weather facilities at Lae." Now Putnam was asking Black, "Can *Itasca* forward Howland weather forecast to Lae possibly via the *Ontario* prior takeoff?" And to Hampton he wrote, "As you will readily understand a matter of vital importance is for Miss Earhart to get the best possible weather data concerning the Howland region and that along the route to Howland from Lae prior to her takeoff."[28]

Black replied by wire to Hampton. He would arrange for U.S. stations in the Central Pacific (Howland, Baker, Jarvis, Fanning, Christmas Island, and the navy ships USS *Swan* and *Ontario*) to send their weather observations to the main U.S. Navy radio stations in Hawaii and Samoa. The navy would be asked to forward the data to the weather bureau at Lae, New Guinea.[29] Black made it clear that Putnam would have to cover the cost of forwarding the weather data to Lae via commercial services.

Over the next several days, the various stations made their weather reports to the navy. Radio Tutuila in American Samoa had difficulty transmitting the information onward, but some of the compiled weather observations

---

*Legend has it that the trailing wire was removed in Miami, but photos of the plane taken in Burbank on May 20, 1937—the day after it came out of the Lockheed repair shop—clearly show that the system was not present at that time.

did reach Lae. Ultimately, it did not matter. There was no weather bureau in Lae to make use of the raw data.

The same day that George Putnam wrote his letter to Hampton he sent a plea for help to J. M. Johnson, the assistant secretary of commerce: "I am venturing this note to inquire the present whereabouts of W. T. Miller. I have the impression that he is due shortly back from his trans-Pacific trip." Putnam reminded Johnson how helpful Miller had been prior to Amelia's previous attempt to fly to Howland Island. Amelia was expected to be ready to try again on June 24, he told Johnson, and Putnam would soon be flying from New York to Oakland to help coordinate with the Coast Guard for the difficult Pacific legs. "Perhaps [Miller] could put in a few days there with me. He is, of course, intimately familiar with the entire Pacific situation, knows the personnel involved, etc. . . . I will be grateful for word as to Miller's whereabouts and doubly grateful if it is possible for him to lend me a hand should he be returning in time." Johnson replied that Miller was due back in a few days, but "several very important matters are being held in abeyance awaiting his return here. I would be glad to have him consult with you there but he would not be able to spend any time out at Oakland."[30]

Meanwhile, in Hawaii, as *Itasca* was preparing to put to sea, Black and the Coast Guard at last had some current information about Earhart's radios, but questions were now being raised about the cutter's own equipment. San Francisco Division sent a message to the Hawaiian Section saying that *Itasca's* transmitter was faulty and ordering the section to send someone to check it out. Warrant Officer Henry Anthony, the Hawaiian Section's radio technician, went down to the dock and performed some tests but could not find anything wrong. "Transmitter checked and operation excellent," he reported; "no defects noted."[31]

At four o'clock on the afternoon of June 18, 1937, the 250-foot Lake class cutter cast off from Pier 12. *Itasca* normally carried a complement of ninety-seven officers and men, but for this cruise it carried eleven additional sailors borrowed from the cutters *Taney* and *Reliance*. There was also an extra officer aboard—the ship's previous captain, Lt. Cdr. Frank Kenner, who would act as adviser to Commander Thompson.

Richard Black had loaded the ship with forty drums of water and several tons of supplies for the islands, and nine Hawaiians were coming along to relieve the colonists. The army sent Lt. Daniel Cooper and two enlisted men to service the Electra, an engineer captain and an enlisted assistant to examine the runways, and a photographer. The navy contributed two airplane mechanics and its own photographer. Also aboard was a doctor from the U.S. Public Health Service. The press was represented by two wire service reporters: Howard Hanzlick from the United Press and James Carey from the Associated Press. Rounding out the ship's company were three civilian "guests of the wardroom," Mr. P. Fricks and Mr. E. W. Walsh, the latter accompanied by his eleven-year-old son, Geoffrey. In all, there were about 133 souls aboard as *Itasca* "stood to sea shaping course for Howland Island."[32]

The ship had barely cleared the harbor when there was more trouble about the radios. The San Francisco Division communications officer had monitored the previous day's radio traffic and insisted that *Itasca's* transmitter was not working properly. Worse, one of the ship's radio operators had refused to cooperate when directed to make adjustments. The division commander demanded "name of radioman responsible for disregarding orders." The cutter's captain replied, providing the name of the offender but also disagreeing with headquarters and begging their indulgence. "Transmitter not, repeat not, faulty based on repeated checks. *Itasca* has difficult communication problem with inexperienced personnel and desires Division's cooperation."[33]

The next day, as *Itasca* steamed southward, Black sent a message to Ruth Hampton in Washington answering Putnam's question about what frequency the Coast Guard would use to send weather reports: "*Itasca* can give her almost any frequency desired." If Earhart was going to find Howland Island by homing in on signals sent by *Itasca*, however, Black needed more information—and he needed it from Amelia, not from Putnam. He asked Putnam to have Earhart contact him with "what frequency best suited her homing device. Also, have her designate time and type of our signal."[34]

Amelia had no way of communicating directly with Black. She was in Southeast Asia and he was on a boat in the middle of the Pacific. Black suggested that Putnam have her send a commercial wire to the governor of American Samoa. The governor's office would then pass the message to the local U.S. Navy radio station at Tutuila, which would in turn relay it to *Itasca*.[35] It was an awkward, time-consuming arrangement, but as far as Black knew, it was the only one available. Putnam responded that it was difficult for him to get in touch with Amelia but promised that she would contact Black via Samoa when she reached Australia, and that she would confirm all arrangements before leaving Lae for Howland.[36]

In fact, Amelia had been in daily telephone communication with the *Herald Tribune's* New York office for more than a week, providing a series of exclusive first-person narratives of her travels. As she made her way down through South America and across the South Atlantic, she sent her daily travelogues as telegrams and they appeared in the paper under a byline that read "By Amelia Earhart—via wireless." She filed no stories during her three-day trip across Africa, so the *Tribune* published Associate Press coverage of that part of the flight. Once she reached Khartoum in Anglo-Egyptian Sudan, she resumed sending her daily contributions, but now the byline appearing above her articles in the newspaper read, "By Amelia Earhart—via telephone."[37] Over the next nine days she phoned in stories from Massawa, Eritrea; Karachi, India; Calcutta, India; Akyab, Burma; Rangoon, Burma; Singapore; and Bandoeng, Java, in the Netherlands East Indies.

Late on the night of June 20, 1937, the same day he had sent a telegram to Ruth Hampton telling her "Difficult contact Earhart satisfactorily before arrival Darwin," George Putnam talked to his wife again by telephone. She had just landed at Bandoeng after an easy 630-mile hop from Singapore. For Amelia it was midmorning on June 21. As Amelia reported in the story she phoned in to the *Herald Tribune* later that day, "The conversation mostly concerned arrangements being made for the two flights from Lae, New Guinea to Howland Island and thence to Honolulu. The United States Navy and Coast Guard are kindly co-operating to help make these rather longish jumps a bit easier. There were details to settle about radio frequencies, weather reports, and the like."[38] If any details were, in fact, settled during the phone call, Putnam did not pass them along to the navy or the Coast Guard—or to Richard Black.

The Electra arrived in Bandoeng needing what Noonan called "some minor instrument adjustments."[39] Royal Netherlands East Indies Airlines operated American-made aircraft, and the shop at Bandoeng was well equipped to address the problem. Weather delays in Burma had put the world flight a day behind schedule, and Earhart hoped that the repairs could be completed in time for a morning departure the next day. That afternoon, while the technicians worked on the airplane, she and Noonan visited an active volcano. "Tonight we go to the home of one of the K.L.M. pilots, for international 'ground flying' is one of the few social events our recent lives have permitted," she informed her *Herald Tribune* readers. "We are staying tonight at a very good hotel. My room is filled with flowers and everything is as neat and clean as Dutch reputation prescribes. I wish we could stay longer, but we must push on as soon as the plane is in condition."[40]

Whether or not she really wanted it, Amelia got her wish. On checking with the airfield later that night, Earhart learned that the needed repairs were taking longer than anticipated and that it would be another day before the Electra was ready. There was time for more sightseeing. Noonan had friends living in Batavia (today's Jakarta), about eighty miles away. He telephoned them that night and they invited him and Amelia to spend the following day, June 22, with them. Fred wrote to Helen Day the next night that "the local Nash automobile representative placed a car and driver at our disposal—so we drove down this forenoon—had a fabulous lunch at the famous 'Des Indies' hotel with a charming group—toured the town by car—and flew back on the local airways."[41]

While she was in Batavia that afternoon, Amelia had phoned her husband to say that she expected to be able to leave Bandoeng in the morning and would be in Lae by June 24. The next day, Wednesday the twenty-third, brought further frustration. Her story for the *Tribune*, written that afternoon, explained the situation: "My plans for leaving Bandoeng today cannot be carried out, as K.L.M. engineers and mechanics pleaded for two hours more to complete their work on my plane, so we now plan to hop off some time after midnight, trying to reach Darwin, Australia, by nightfall." She described the previous day's visit to Batavia and concluded with: "Bandoeng is a charming place. If I must delay I am glad of such surroundings."[42]

Her June 23 press release, however, did not reach the newspaper; nor did her husband receive a phone call from her that day. Transpacific telegrams and phone calls went by radio, and it may be that atmospheric conditions were bad that day. For whatever reason, there was no word from Amelia. Wednesday's *Herald Tribune*, for the first time since her departure from Miami, carried no news about Amelia Earhart's trip around the world.

That same day, Putnam confessed his puzzlement in a letter answering Ruth Hampton's request for updated information about when Amelia might make the flight to Howland. He wrote that he had spoken with his wife at 2:00 AM on June 22, and at that time Amelia had hoped to leave Bandoeng "tomorrow." "However, we have no word from her whatsoever this morning so I just don't know. All I can report is that when I talked to her yesterday she expected to be in Lae by the 24th, ready to take off for Howland. . . . I expect to leave tonight for the coast."[43]

CHAPTER SEVEN

The Long Road to Lae

delays on the way to new guinea

Amelia had not checked in, and for once Putnam did not know where she was. Neither did Richard Black. As *Itasca* neared the end of its five-day voyage from Honolulu to Howland, Black apparently reasoned that because he had not yet received the promised communication from Darwin, she was probably still in Bandoeng, Java. To be safe, he sent telegrams to both Darwin and Bandoeng, giving her the radio capabilities of the three ships that would help guide her flight and asking her to "please confirm and designate signals desired from *Ontario*, *Itasca* and *Swan* within these ranges best suited to your homing device." The oceangoing tug USS *Ontario* was positioned halfway between Lae and Howland; USCG *Itasca* was approaching the island; and the seaplane tender USS *Swan* (with no seaplane aboard) was on station halfway between Howland and Hawaii. He also cautioned her that any messages she might send from Lae via Samoa would take four hours to reach *Itasca*.[1]

A few hours after Black sent his telegrams, Commander Thompson sent two as well, one addressed to Earhart in Port Darwin (now Darwin), Australia, and the other to Lae, New Guinea: "Request you advise this vessel 12 hours prior to your departure from New Guinea full information regarding your desires in matter of radio frequencies and communication schedule. We will conform to any frequencies desired. Important anticipate your departure as communication via Port Darwin very slow."[2] Amelia did not see Thompson's message until she reached Australia five days later.

Yet another message reached *Itasca* from San Francisco Division insisting that the ship had a faulty transmitter. Heeding Commander Thompson's earlier plea for patience with the cutter's inexperienced radio operators, headquarters provided a detailed diagnosis of the problem (a faulty relay). By later that day the problem had finally been fixed.[3]

Midday, June 23, at Howland Island was evening in New York as George Putnam boarded a United Airlines Douglas DC-3 for the all-night trip to Oakland, California. If all was going according to plan, Amelia should be on her way from Darwin to Lae about now.

In Java it was the morning of June 24, and Amelia was not on her way to Lae. She was not even on her way to Darwin. Earhart was still stuck in Bandoeng. The maintenance problems were taking longer to fix than expected. The Electra spent the whole day of June 23 in the hangar, and mechanical difficulties once again frustrated an early-morning departure on the twenty-fourth. By the time the work was completed that afternoon there was not enough daylight left to fly any farther than Surabaya, a major city just 355 miles away.

At 1:15 PM (1:45 AM in New York) on Thursday, June 24, 1937, Amelia succeeded in placing a phone call to the *Herald Tribune*'s office in New York. She gave the paper the previous day's press release and reported that she was still in Bandoeng but was ready to depart for Surabaya. She also needed to talk to her husband. It was important that he know about this most recent delay before he made press commitments for her arrival in Oakland. But Putnam, she learned, was at that moment on an airplane en route to California. He was scheduled to arrive in Oakland at 9:00 AM Pacific Time, ready to start the business day. She needed to catch him before he got there.

The United flight was scheduled to land in Cheyenne, Wyoming, for a brief refueling stop at 2:33 AM Mountain Time, about three hours from the time Amelia called New York. The flight to Surabaya should take only about two and a half hours, but if there were delays or unexpected headwinds she could easily miss him. If she played it safe and waited to make the call from Bandoeng, it would then be too late to fly to Surabaya before dark. Playing it safe was not Amelia's style. When the United DC-3 arrived at the terminal in Cheyenne, passenger Putnam was told that there was an international phone call waiting for him from Surabaya, Java. Earhart told him of the delay but assured him that she would be able to continue on to Australia in the morning. The three-minute call cost $24.[4]

While Earhart and Noonan were flying to Surabaya and Putnam was flying to Oakland, the Coast Guard cutter *Itasca* was completing its five-day voyage from Honolulu. At 8:56 PM on June 23, 1937, the ship "raised Howland Island, bearing 90 degrees true, distance 7 miles. Stopped, drifted to the westward of the island awaiting daybreak."[5] The first thing the next morning, Richard Black led a delegation ashore to check the airfield. He found the runways to be in good condition, time and some rain having served to settle and compact the coral surface. Lieutenant Cooper erected windsocks and marked the boundaries with red bunting. The island's birds, however, presented a problem.

Black thought their numbers had increased since March. Cooper considered them to be a "significant hazard" and estimated the population at "10,000 Frigates, 8,000 Booby and 14,000 Terns. The Frigates and Boobies are the size of large buzzards while the Terns are the size of young pigeons."[6] Sailors used blocks of TNT and riot guns in an attempt frighten the birds away, but succeeded only in shifting them from place to place around the island.

The best they could hope to do was clear the birds away from the approach end of the runway Earhart was most likely to use.

The expedition was ready at Howland, but where was Amelia? In his first report sent from *Itasca*, Associated Press correspondent Jim Carey described the preparations being made for the flight's arrival and ended with a query: "Earhart whereabouts? *Itasca* not informed." United Press reporter Howard Hanzlick also filed his first story, painting a picture of "minute preparations for every emergency" with "all personnel on toes."[7]

Late in the afternoon on Thursday, June 24, *Itasca*'s radio operators picked up press reports that Earhart was still in Java and was expected to remain there for three days. If Earhart was not going to fly to Australia until Sunday, there was plenty of time to attend to other business. Black sent a message to Washington saying that *Itasca* would proceed to Baker Island and resupply the colonists there on Friday. "Please tell Putnam we would appreciate direct notification of all progress," he added.[8]

Earhart, in fact, was not making progress. During early-morning preflight checks before leaving Surabaya for the flight to Darwin, she discovered that the Cambridge Exhaust Gas Analyzer—vital for obtaining maximum fuel efficiency—which she thought had been repaired was again malfunctioning. Earhart and Noonan had no choice but to return to Bandoeng. In a press release filed from Bandoeng later that day, by wireless this time, Earhart expressed her frustration: "Today for the second time in a week I had to do what is unquestionably the most difficult thing I have ever done in aviation. It was necessary to return to Bandoeng this morning from Sourabaya [*sic*] for readjustment of certain long-distance flying instruments. . . . I do not know how long we shall have to be here, but it is probable that the trouble will be located today.[9]*

Word of the reversal traveled fast. Within a few hours, *Itasca*, unloading supplies at Baker Island, received a message from San Francisco Division: the Associated Press was reporting that Earhart had attempted to resume her trip yesterday but had gotten only as far as Surabaya, Java, before experiencing instrument problems. She was returning to Bandoeng, Java, and it was not certain when she would continue.[10]

Later, another message from San Francisco Division brought word that Putnam, now in Oakland, had confirmed that Earhart was indeed back in Bandoeng, "departure indefinite." Putnam promised that once she got to Darwin, Amelia would cable the communication details for the Lae–Howland flight directly to the Coast Guard in San Francisco, which would then convey

---

*Earhart's comment that she had been forced to reverse course "for the second time in a week" is a reference to a flight on June 19 when heavy rain forced her to turn back less than half an hour after departing Akyab, Burma, for Bangkok, Siam.

them to *Itasca*. Putnam also tried to provide some of the radio information the Coast Guard had been clamoring for. "Communication from plane will be on 500, 3105 or 6210 kilocycles by voice."* He also repeated the previously given information that Earhart would broadcast her position at fifteen and forty-five minutes past the hour. *Itasca*, he said, should adjust its transmitter "for possible use 3105 kilocycles for voice."[11]

This was the first time the Coast Guard radio operators learned what frequency Earhart might want them to use when transmitting to her. It was an unusual request because, by federal regulation, only aircraft were allowed to transmit on 3105 kilocycles. Ground stations replied on a different frequency. In closing, Putnam added, "direction finder on plane covers range of about 200 to 1400 kilocycles."[12] That evening, *Itasca*, having completed its resupply of the Baker Island colonists, steamed the forty miles back to Howland.

In Bandoeng, it was the morning of June 26 and the Electra was once again in the Royal Netherlands East Indies Airlines hangar. On her unscheduled return to Bandoeng Earhart received a telegram that had arrived there after she left for Surabaya. The message was the one from Richard Black aboard the Coast Guard cutter *Itasca* informing her of the ship's radio capabilities and asking that she "designate signals desired from *Ontario*, *Itasca* and *Swan* within . . . ranges best suited to your homing device."[13]

While technicians worked on her airplane, Amelia drafted a response to Black's request and gave it to the local telegraph office. By midday the instrument problem seemed finally to be fixed, but once again there was time for just a few hours of flying before nightfall. Earhart and Noonan flew back to Surabaya while Amelia's telegram began its journey to Black.

That afternoon the Electra landed in Surabaya for the second time in as many days. Amelia did not file a *Tribune* story from Surabaya, and *Last Flight*, the book later compiled from her narratives, does not mention the second stop at that city. Apparently Earhart made another phone call to her husband later that night, because the next morning—at 8:00 AM aboard *Itasca* and 11:30 AM in California—the Coast Guard's San Francisco Division sent a priority message to the cutter: "Repairs made and Earhart now at Surabaya. Expects leave dawn this date for Port Darwin and next day for Lae. Following information from Earhart this date; homing device covers from 200 to 1500 and 2400 to 4800 kilocycles. Any frequencies not repeat not near ends of bands suitable."[14] The admonition to avoid frequencies near the ends of the bands was to permit tuning the receiver slightly above and below the frequency, thus allowing for possible calibration discrepancies.

---

*The plane had never had voice capability on 500 kilocycles. With the elimination of the trailing wire antenna during repairs at Lockheed, the frequency became essentially useless.

Just the day before, Putnam had said her homing device covered 200 to 1400 kilocycles. Earhart was now saying that it had much broader frequency limits, and she seemed to be asking the Coast Guard to designate what frequencies she should use for direction finding. San Francisco Division's commanding officer, Capt. Stanley Parker, was happy to oblige. In his message to *Itasca* he said: "We suggest using suitable frequencies having in mind uncertain characteristics of high frequencies. Use 333 kilocycles or frequency in that vicinity and try 545 kilocycles after tests with stations your locality to determine which is best." After several more suggestions and admonitions he added: "Am advising Earhart that *Itasca* will voice radio her on 3105 on hour and half hour as she approaches Howland."[15]

San Francisco's suggestions were not welcome aboard *Itasca*. From the beginning, Black and Thompson had assumed that they were there to accommodate Earhart. It was up to her to tell them what she wanted. Black's June 23 telegram had asked Earhart to "designate signals desired from *Ontario*, *Itasca* and *Swan* within these ranges best suited to your homing device," and Thompson had asked her for "full information regarding your desires in matter of radio frequencies and communication schedule. We will conform to any frequencies desired."[16] Now, not only was Parker pressing Commander Thompson to assume more responsibility for Earhart's flight by telling him to suggest what frequencies she should use, he was also taking it on himself to tell Earhart what Thompson would do.

Not long after Parker's message reached *Itasca*, the U.S. Navy's main radio station in Hawaii, Radio Wailupe near Honolulu, contacted the cutter with a wire for Black from Earhart. Amelia's telegram from Bandoeng had taken more than sixteen hours to wend its way through the system. Her instructions were very specific. For the flight from Lae to Howland she wanted *Ontario*, the navy ship positioned halfway along the route, to be ready to transmit on 400 kilocycles. When she got close, she would call the ship and it should then send the Morse code letter *N* (dash-dot) repeatedly for five minutes. At the end of each minute the ship should also send its call letters, NIDX, twice. By hearing the letter *N* and identifying the call letters Amelia could be sure that she was listening to *Ontario*. She would then, presumably, use her direction finder to home in on the ship and make sure she was on course for Howland. Her instructions for *Itasca* were somewhat different. Rather than wait for her to call, the cutter was to transmit the Morse code letter *A* (dot-dash), the ship's position, and its own call letters, NRUI, every hour on the half hour on a frequency of 7500 kilocycles. "Position ships and our leaving will determine broadcast times specifically. If frequencies mentioned unsuitable night work inform me Lae."[17]

The receipt of Earhart's detailed plan reinforced Commander Thompson's view that his job was to deliver the services the flyer requested, not design a flight plan for her. The ship had now received a direct communication from Earhart via the navy. The information being relayed though San Francisco Division was contradictory, and its commanding officer seemed to be trying to micromanage *Itasca*'s mission. Warner Thompson had had enough. A few hours after receiving Earhart's telegram, he fired off a strongly worded message to Parker: "Consider present relationship Division–*Itasca* communications unsatisfactory and potentially dangerous to Earhart contacts and other vital schedules. Urgently request *Itasca* be given complete communication independence. *Itasca* has reliable communications with Navy and routine traffic can be routed via that system. Recommend discontinuance all San Francisco Radio–*Itasca* schedules until Earhart flight reaches Hawaii."[18]

Parker acceded to Thompson's request; further messages from San Francisco were confined to Putnam's queries about press arrangements. Still, sorting out just what procedures Earhart desired was a bit of a challenge.

The day before, Putnam, via San Francisco, had informed *Itasca* that Earhart might want the ship to send voice on 3105 kilocycles. Amelia's telegrammed instructions contained no such request, but Parker had advised Earhart that *Itasca* would send voice on that frequency on the hour and half hour. Accordingly, Commander Thompson ordered the cutter's transmitter adjusted to enable voice transmissions on 3105 kilocycles.

Earhart's stated plan with regard to *Ontario* could have been more specific, but it was at least reasonable. She did not say what frequency she would use to call the ship, but presumably it would be either her daytime frequency of 6210 kilocycles or her nighttime 3105, depending on when she arrived in the area. Her request for signals on 400 kilocycles was within the stated limits of her direction finder.

Her announced plan for finding Howland Island, however, was at odds with information received via San Francisco. She was asking *Itasca* to send signals on 7500 kilocycles—signals useless to her direction finder, which, according to Putnam's message covered a "range of about 200 to 1400 kilocycles," and according to San Francisco's latest message covered "from 200 to 1500 and 2400 to 4800 kilocycles."[19] Neither Richard Black nor Commander Thompson questioned Earhart's choice of frequencies, even though Thompson, at least, was well aware of the discrepancy. As he later wrote in his official report:

> The above message [referring to Earhart's instructions] is the first contact that the *Itasca* has had with Earhart previous to the anticipated flight. The *Itasca* bases this message as the key message of the flight. It will be noted that the frequencies requested were high frequencies with the exception of *Ontario*. This is contradictory to the last message received from Commander San Francisco Division suggesting 333 and

545 kilocycles. It will also be noted that the requested 7.5 megacycles
is beyond the frequency range, that at least to our knowing [sic], of
the plane direction finder.[20]

Thompson's implication that Earhart had rejected San Francisco
Division's suggestion that she use lower frequencies is misleading. The suggestion was made to Thompson, not Earhart. He and Black had declined
to pass the recommendation along to Amelia. Thompson's misrepresenta-
tion would later create the impression among senior Treasury Department
officials that Earhart had disregarded instructions given to her by the
Coast Guard.

Just what range of frequencies the Electra's homing device could cover
is an important question but not a difficult one to answer. A hoop-shaped
"loop" antenna mounted above the Electra's cockpit received the signals for
direction finding. Numerous photos taken from the time of its installation
just prior to Earhart's first world flight attempt in March until the final takeoff from Lae, New Guinea, in July leave no doubt that the loop antenna on
Earhart's Electra was one of a new line of Bendix direction finders pictured
and described in the August 1937 issue of *Aero Digest* magazine: "Bendix
D-Fs are designed to operate in conjunction with Bendix Type RA-1 receiver,
but will also give accurate and dependable bearings when used with any
standard radio receiver covering the desired frequency range." The article
also notes that these receivers can be used "as navigational direction finding instruments within frequency range of 200–1500 kilocycles."[21] Those
parameters generally agree with the limits described by Manning and Miller
prior to the first world flight attempt ("Plane has direction finder covering
200 to 1430 kcs").[22] They also agree with Putnam's message of June 25, 1937,
saying that the plane's direction finder "covers range of about 200 to 1400
kilocycles."[23] Where Earhart got the idea that her direction finder could cover
"from 200 to 1500 and 2400 to 4800 kilocycles" is not clear, but the signals
she requested on 7500 kilocycles were far beyond even those limits.[24]

The morning of Sunday, June 27, 1937, in Surabaya found the world flight
ready to leave Java at last. The plan was to make the thirteen-hundred-mile
flight to Darwin that day, but although the Electra was now cooperating, the
winds were not. Earhart and Noonan spent the night in the town of Koepang
on the island of Timor. As Fred explained in a letter to Helen Day:

We arrived here about noon from Surabaya, Java, with intention of
going on to Port Darwin, Australia, but upon arrival received a weather
report indicating head winds of about forty miles per hour lay ahead
of us. As Port Darwin time is two hours ahead of local time—that is—

the sun sets there two hours earlier than it does here—we decided not to risk landing at a strange airport after darkness had fallen.

So here we be—in a town without hotel accommodations—for the night.

However, it is not as bad as it would appear at first sight. Throughout India, Burma, Siam, and Dutch East Indies the various governments have established what they call "Rest Houses"—comfortable habitations erected to take care of the infrequent travelers who drop in unexpectedly.[25]

Earhart wired a story to the *Tribune* with her impressions of the town "perched as it is on cliffs with winding paved roads" and the airport "surrounded by a stone fence a few feet high to keep out roaming wild pigs."[26]

Sunday night in Koepang was Sunday morning aboard *Itasca*. The ship expected no further word from Earhart until she reached Lae, so Black, the Hawaiian colonists, and the army contingent used the time to build a small extension on the west end of the island's east–west runway. With a length of only twenty-four hundred feet it was the shortest of the three airstrips, but the prevailing easterly winds made it the most likely to be used. "We found that with only a thin hand-placed layer of coral, it was better not to roll, as the rolling seemed to push the coral into the sand," Black reported.[27] The new area was to be marked unsafe for landing but could be used to extend the takeoff.

Earhart and Noonan arrived in Darwin on the afternoon of June 28, 1937. Asked why she had not answered the airport's radio calls, Amelia explained that her receiver was inoperative. A local technician inspected the set, replaced a blown fuse, and conducted a successful ground test of the radio.[28] Earhart did not mention the incident in her Darwin press release, sent by wire to the *Tribune*; nor does it appear in *Last Flight*. The book, however, does include the passage: "At Darwin, by the way, we left the parachutes we had carried that far, to be shipped home. A parachute would not help over the Pacific."[29]

The correspondent for the Sydney, Australia, newspaper who was present for the Electra's arrival in Darwin told a different story: "The first thing she did after being officially welcomed was to inquire if parachutes, part of the emergency equipment for the Pacific crossing in front of her, had arrived from America. They reached here more than a week ago. . . . Fully tested and ready for immediate use, the parachutes were waiting in Mr. Collins's office."[30] (Alan Collins was the civil aviation officer for Darwin.) Earhart made no mention of the parachutes in her press release, but a photograph taken that day shows her and Noonan in front of the Electra's cabin door with what appears to be a pile of items about to be loaded aboard the airplane. Two parachutes are clearly visible.

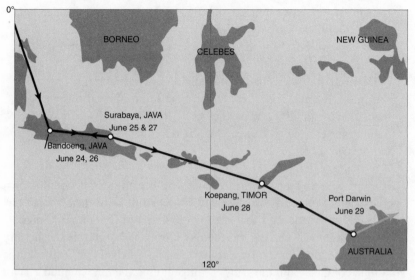

Earhart's route from Bandoeng, Java, to Darwin, Australia.

In Darwin that evening, Earhart sent information to Guinea Airways in Lae intending to arrange radio communications for her flight to New Guinea the next day. To make sure the message got through, she sent two cables via separate commercial services. Both telegrams expressed the desired radio frequency as wavelength in meters in accordance with the British system. One telegram said that she would be sending and receiving on a wavelength of 36 meters.[31] The second telegram had it that she would be "receiving and transmitting 36.6 meters D-F loop."[32] The message is ambiguous in that the "D-F loop" (the hoop-shaped radio direction finder antenna mounted on the cockpit roof) was a receiving antenna and could not be used for transmitting. Its mention in the telegram implies that Earhart intended to use her direction finder to home in on signals sent by Lae on 36.6 meters.

Early the next morning, Tuesday, June 29, Earhart and Noonan left for New Guinea.

CHAPTER EIGHT

"Denmark's a Prison"

confusion and frustration in lae

Earhart and Noonan made the twelve-hundred-mile flight from Darwin to Lae without incident except that, once more, there was radio trouble. After takeoff she was able to talk to Darwin for the first part of the journey, but as she approached New Guinea she was unable to establish contact with the airfield at Lae. This time the problem was procedural rather than mechanical. The airline manager at Lae later reported: "On arrival Miss Earhart pointed out that whereas these radios [the two telegrams she had sent from Darwin the night before] advised us of a wave length of 36 metres, in reality her wave length was 49 metres which explained why we failed to pick up any messages from her."[1]*

Lae had not heard Earhart's transmissions because the Lae radio operator had been told to listen on the wrong frequency. But Amelia would not have been able to hear Lae even if the conversion from kilocycles to meters had been correctly computed. In her telegrams she had intended to advise Lae that she would be both transmitting and receiving on her daytime frequency of 6210 kilocycles. For her to receive on that frequency, Lae would, of course, have to be transmitting on that frequency. The radio station at Lae transmitted on 6522 kilocycles, though, and, like most stations at that time, had neither the capability nor the legal latitude to alter its broadcast frequency. Because she did not receive any of Lae's transmissions, Earhart could not try to use her radio direction finder to navigate. Consequently, she did not discover that her direction finder was unable to home in on high-frequency transmissions.

When Earhart landed at Lae, Black's reply to the message she had sent to him from Java was waiting for her. In outlining the radio procedures to be used on the flight to Howland, Earhart had asked Black to tell her if any of the frequencies she had requested were "unsuitable for night work."[2] The problem, of course, was not the time of day, but rather that her request for signals on 7500 kilocycles was at odds with her own description of the capabilities

---

*The conversion formula is very simple. Divide 300,000 by kilocycles to get meters. Divide 300,000 by meters to get kilocycles; 36 meters is 8333 kilocycles; 36.6 meters is 8197 kilocycles; 49 meters is 6122 kilocycles; 3105 kilocycles is 96.6 meters; 6210 kilocycles is 48.3 meters.

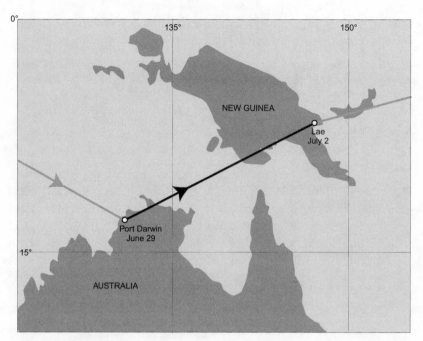

Earhart's route from Darwin to Lae.

of her direction finder. Black's telegram did not point out the discrepancy, but simply assured her that *Itasca*'s transmitters were calibrated and ready to send her signals on 7500, 6210, 3105, 500, and 425 kilocycles.[3]

In the same message, Black advised Earhart that *Itasca*'s own direction finder had a frequency range of 270 to 550 kilocycles. Since the Electra could transmit only on 3105 and 6210 kilocycles, the cutter would be unable to take bearings on her signals. Black made no mention of the high-frequency direction finder that had been set up on Howland Island. He did, however, "request we be advised as to time of departure and zone time to be used on radio schedules."[4] The "zone time" was important. Amelia's twenty-five-hundred-mile flight from Lae to Howland would be crossing several time zones. For the radio schedules to work, the ship and the plane would need to be in agreement about what time it was. Black's telegram did clear up one issue. Earhart's earlier request that *Itasca* transmit the ship's position along with its call letters revealed that she was not sure exactly where the cutter would be. Black specified, "*Itasca* at Howland Island during flight."[5]

Early the next morning, Wednesday, June 30, 1937, in Lae, Earhart sent off a reply to Black via Samoa, addressing her cable to "Commander USS *Itasca*": "Plan midday takeoff here. Please have meteorologist send forecast Lae Howland soon as possible. If reaches me in time will try leave today.

Otherwise July 1st. Report in English, not code, especially while flying. Will broadcast hourly quarter past hour GCT. Further information later; Earhart."[6]

She had, as best she could, answered Black's query about when she would depart. She had also answered his question about what zone time to use for her radio schedules. The flight would use GCT (Greenwich Civil Time; now Greenwich Mean Time, or Universal Time), and she would transmit at quarter past each hour, not at quarter past *and* quarter to the hour as specified in earlier messages. She also asked that messages sent to her, "especially while flying," be sent in "English, not code." Neither Earhart nor Noonan was adept at sending or reading Morse code. Both could "recognize an individual letter [only] if sent several times."[7]

Earhart next cabled her husband in Oakland: "Radio misunderstanding and personnel unfitness probably will hold one day. Have asked Black for forecast for tomorrow. You check meteorologist on job as FN must have star sights. Arrange credit if *Tribune* wishes more story."[8] The message reveals a number of problems and misconceptions that were to plague preparations for the flight to Howland Island.

A few minutes earlier, she had sent a message to *Itasca* saying she would depart at midday if the weather forecast reached her in time. Now she seemed resigned to delaying her departure until the next day, Thursday, July 1, due to "radio misunderstanding and personnel unfitness." What Earhart meant by "radio misunderstanding" is obvious. During the previous day's flight from Australia, confusion about frequencies had prevented her from establishing radio contact with Lae. The misunderstandings would have to be sorted out and the radios tested before she could undertake the long and difficult flight to Howland.

Her reference to "personnel unfitness" seems equally clear. Amelia's wire to her husband was sent at 6:30 AM local time in Lae. The previous day's eight-hour flight from Australia had capped a week of early mornings and frustrating delays. It is hardly surprising that Earhart and Noonan did not feel up to immediately setting off on a journey that was expected to take a minimum of eighteen hours.*

In her wire to her husband that morning, Earhart asked him to "check meteorologist on job as FN must have star sights." But there was no meteorologist on the job. Two weeks earlier, on June 14, Richard Black had advised Putnam that once Earhart reached Howland Island, Lt. Arnold E. True, the

---

*Tired and stressed they undoubtedly were, but none of the contemporary accounts of their stay in New Guinea indicates that either was in less than good health. Allegations that Earhart was ill and that Noonan was drinking heavily are based on stories told years later and are not supported by the historical record.

navy meteorologist at Fleet Air Base, Pearl Harbor, would provide a forecast for the flight to Honolulu. Black suggested that Putnam arrange for a
Lae–Howland route forecast through the weather facilities at Lae. Putnam's
response, "Can *Itasca* forward Howland weather forecast to Lae?" suggests
he was confused on several points.[9]

When Earhart was ready to leave Lae she would need more than a prediction of what the weather was likely to be when she got to Howland. She
needed a forecast for the entire twenty-five-hundred-mile route. To provide
such a forecast, a meteorologist needed observations and measurements
from many points on and near the route over a period of several days.
Lieutenant True could provide a forecast for Earhart's Howland–Honolulu
flight because he had good weather data for that part of the northern
Pacific. He did not, however, routinely receive weather observations from
the southwestern Pacific because U.S. Navy operations in that region were
very limited in 1937.

Except in the immediate vicinity of Howland Island, Earhart's route from
Lae lay exclusively over the waters, territories, and colonial possessions of
Great Britain. Black reasoned that the British/Australian administration
in New Guinea would be better equipped to provide the weather services
Earhart required, hence his suggestion that Putnam make arrangements
with Lae. Doing what he could to assist the presumed meteorologist at Lae,
Black set up a system intended to provide the weather bureau there with
data from U.S. ships and islands in the Central Pacific. Neither Putnam nor
Black seems to have inquired whether there was, in fact, a weather bureau
or forecasting facility at Lae. There was not. In the end, Earhart arrived in
New Guinea with no way to obtain a weather forecast for the longest and
most dangerous leg of her world flight.

The "FN" who must have star sights was Fred Noonan, of course, who
would be using celestial navigation and dead reckoning to bring the flight
close enough for Earhart to use radio direction finding to fine-tune the
approach to Howland Island. Although his job was critical to the flight's
success, he performed it autonomously aboard the airplane and required
no particular coordination with external support services. Consequently,
none of the messages sent to Black, the Coast Guard, or the navy during
the planning for the second world flight attempt and the preparations for
the Lae–Howland trip included a reference to Noonan. Earhart mentioned
Noonan regularly in her stories to the *Tribune*, but the men at sea did not
see newspapers. The unintended effect was that no one aboard the ships
that would be supporting the flight knew for certain that Noonan would
be on the airplane.

Earhart's June 30 cable to her husband reveals yet another apparent information gap. Referring to the message she had addressed to "Commander USS

Itasca," Amelia told Putnam that she had "asked Black for forecast for tomorrow."[10] It appears that Earhart was under the impression that Richard Black was the captain of *Itasca.* She and the Department of the Interior representative had never met. Earhart's first direct contact with Black was the telegram she had received from him while she was in Java. It was sent from "USCG *Itasca*" and signed simply "Black."[11]

The last line of Earhart's telegram to Putnam, "Arrange credit if *Tribune* wishes more story," refers to her precarious finances. The delays in Java and the consequent flurry of international phone calls were expensive, and she was apparently running low on cash.

For Earhart and Noonan, Wednesday, June 30, was a day of recuperation and preparation. Fred Noonan helped the Guinea Airways maintenance staff service the Electra and address a number of minor problems. The mechanics were familiar with the aircraft type because the airline operated a Lockheed Electra of its own. Meanwhile, Eric Chater, the Guinea Airways general manager, did what he could to get weather information for Earhart. He sent a telegram to the chief wireless inspector in Rabaul, New Britain, saying: "Amelia Earhart would be grateful if you could obtain weather reports by about ten AM first July from Nauru or Ocean Island, Tarawa and Rabaul. Also, for your information, her plane KHAQQ will transmit on 6210 kcs quarter past each hour on her flight across to Howland Island."[12]

Rabaul passed along the request, but the only response was from the radio operator on Nauru, an island about halfway along and just north of the route to Howland. The wind there was from the southeast at three knots, and the weather was "fine but cloudy."[13]

Sometime that day, Amelia phoned in a story to the *Tribune* describing the flight from Darwin and the airfield at Lae: "Everyone has been as helpful and cooperative as possible—food, hot baths, mechanical service, radio and weather reports, advice from veteran pilots here—all combine to make us wish we could stay. However, tomorrow about noon we hope to be rolling down the runway, bound for points east."[14]

Across the International Date Line in California, it was Tuesday afternoon, June 29, and George Putnam was trying to generate media interest in the imminent completion of Amelia Earhart's world flight. The only firm commitment he had was a guest spot on a popular radio program that aired on Monday nights, and he needed to know whether she would be back in time do the show on July 5. The last information he had about his wife's whereabouts was an Associated Press report that she had left Darwin for Lae the previous afternoon, his time.[15] He had not yet received the telegram Earhart sent from Lae saying that she would "hold one day," nor was he aware of her phone call to the *Tribune.*[16] As far as Putnam knew, Earhart could already be on her way to Howland. A wire sent to Lae might miss her. The Coast Guard's San Francisco Division, on the other hand, was in direct radio communication with *Itasca*. To be sure his message reached Amelia, Putnam had the Coast Guard send it to the cutter: "Following for Miss Earhart upon arrival Howland Island: Flight contingencies permitting, is Saturday arrival likely? Sunday latest? Either perfect. Confidential: Want you to know very important radio commitment Monday night. Nothing else whatever. Signed Putnam."[17] *Itasca* was not asked, and made no attempt, to forward the message to New Guinea. Earhart never saw it.

At noon in Lae, Amelia watched the airfield's radio operator, Harry Balfour, as he checked the aircraft's ability to receive "long-wave" (low-frequency) signals of the sort most useful for radio direction finding. The test went well and Balfour was able to receive signals sent by a nearby station on 500 kilocycles.

Although the radio receiver aboard the airplane seemed to be functioning well, other radio-related problems were threatening to delay the flight's departure. The accuracy of Fred Noonan's celestial navigation on the trip to Howland depended on the accuracy of his chronometer. Radio stations at selected locations around the world broadcast special signals at specified times each day to enable navigators to set their timepieces correctly. Lae, New Guinea, could usually receive the broadcasts from stations in Australia and French Indochina, but on this day local interference frustrated Balfour's attempts to get time signals for Noonan. The flight to Howland could not begin without a successful time check.

That afternoon—Wednesday, June 30, in Lae—Earhart sent another message to Black via Samoa announcing her latest departure plans and asking him to try to establish direct radio contact between *Itasca* and Lae: "Account local conditions plan start July 1st, 23:30 GCT, if weather okay. Will *Itasca* try contact Lae direct on 25 metres—Lae on 46 metres—so can get forecast in time? Particularly interested probable type percentage clouds near Howland. Now understand *Itasca* voicing 3105 on hour and half hour with long continuous signal on approach. Confirm and appoint time for operator here to stand watch for direct contact; Earhart."[18]

She wanted *Itasca* to call Lae on a frequency of 12,000 kilocycles and listen for a reply on Lae's transmitting frequency of 6522 kilocycles. If the two could establish a direct radio link, the uncertainty, confusion, and hours of delay involved in routing messages through Samoa would be eliminated. Still unaware there was no meteorologist aboard *Itasca*, Amelia hoped to have a forecast in hand in time for her planned departure at 9:30 AM local time the next morning, July 1.

That evening, nearly twelve hours after it was sent, Earhart's early-morning message asking for the meteorologist's forecast finally reached *Itasca*. Commander Thompson immediately had a radio transmission sent to Fleet

Air Base, Pearl Harbor, asking that Lieutenant True be contacted at his home. "Earhart appears to think *Itasca* has Navy aerologist aboard. Black requests you give at least an opinion."[19] While Thompson and Black waited for True to respond, they sent a reply to Earhart via Samoa: "Reference your message. Have no aerologist aboard. Have requested forecast from Fleet Air Base, Pearl Harbor, for Howland to Lae though doubtful if obtainable. Will forward Honolulu Howland forecast as indicated."[20] This message does not appear to have reached Lae at all.

Late that night, Lieutenant True sent a message to Earhart, via Samoa, with his best attempt at a forecast for the Lae–Howland route. As weather forecasts go, it was largely meaningless. True's only sources of weather data for the area in question were USS *Ontario*, the navy ship on station roughly halfway along her route, and *Itasca* at Howland. *Ontario* was getting some rain squalls. The weather was good at Howland. Other than that, True's forecast was based on his knowledge of what was "generally average" for the region.[21] Even this minimal information does not appear to have reached Earhart.

Around 9:00 PM that night, *Itasca* received Earhart's message requesting that the ship make direct radio contact with Lae. She had, however, neglected to provide Lae's call letters, so at 10:00 PM another telegram was sent to her via Samoa: "Request *Itasca* be advised call letters of station to be contacted." In the same message, *Itasca* confirmed its understanding of the radio procedures to be used during the upcoming flight: "Will transmit letter *A* with call letters repeated twice end every minute on half hour and hour on 7.5 megacycles. Will broadcast voice on 3105 kcs on request or start when within range."[22] Once again, the cumbersome system of relaying communications through Samoa appears to have failed. *Itasca* received no reply to its request for the station's call letters but seems to have made some attempt at direct communication anyway. The effort was not successful.[23]

The next morning was Thursday, July 1, in Lae. Earhart and Noonan were rested. The plane had been serviced and the radio receiver tested. A weather forecast from the meteorologist assumed to be aboard *Itasca* was expected shortly. Noonan still needed to set his chronometer, but everyone hoped that the necessary time signals would arrive in time for a midmorning departure. Rising terrain off the northwest end of Lae's three-thousand-foot turf runway dictated that Amelia would have to make the heavily overloaded takeoff to the southeast out over the Huon Gulf. The early-morning offshore breeze was blowing the wrong way, but the wind direction typically reversed as the day progressed. At 6:00 AM Earhart sent a message to *Itasca*: "Plan leave by ten this morning New Guinea time."[24]

Before having the plane fueled for the flight to Howland, Amelia made a short test flight to confirm that everything was working. She was, at last, able to establish two-way voice communication with the ground, transmitting to Lae on her daytime frequency of 6210 kilocycles and receiving Balfour's reply on Lae's frequency of 6522 kilocycles. Balfour's assessment of the aircraft's transmitter was that the "carrier wave on 6210 kc was very rough and I advised Miss Earhart to pitch her voice higher to overcome distortion caused by rough carrier wave, otherwise transmitter seemed to be working satisfactorily."[25] Earhart then asked him to send a "long dash" while she attempted to take a bearing on the station, but this attempt to use her homing device was unsuccessful as well.

The airplane's radio direction finder was based on the principle that a circular antenna is most efficient when oriented edgewise to the incoming signal. When the loop antenna over the cockpit was rotated, the sound got louder or softer depending on the orientation of the antenna to the incoming signal. It was easier to tell when the signal was quietest, so the pilot turned the loop until a minimum signal was heard and from that could determine the direction from which the signal was coming.

During the test flight, Earhart found she could receive Lae's signal, but the intensity of the sound did not change when she rotated the loop. In the terminology of the time, she could not "get a minimum," and so could not get a bearing on the sending station. The problem was that although the radio receiver could pick up the signal and she could hear the tone in her headphones, the direction-finding aspect of the system could not respond to such a high frequency. Amelia, however, decided that the test had failed because the airplane was too close to the station and the signal was too strong.

It is not clear whether Balfour's previous ground test of the receiver included taking a bearing using the direction finder, but it is known that he carried out his test on a signal of 500 kilocycles, a frequency well within the loop antenna's 200 to 1500 kilocycle capability. In the flight test, Earhart tried to take a bearing on Lae's 6522 kilocycle signal but could not get a minimum. Balfour accepted Earhart's diagnosis of the problem, and so passed another opportunity to discover the flaw in her plan for finding Howland Island.

In Balfour's defense, it must be said that the Bendix direction finder was new, and a wireless operator working in the wilds of New Guinea was unlikely to be familiar with it. Nor had Balfour been privy to earlier messages to the Coast Guard concerning the frequency limitations of Earhart's homing device.

Earhart concluded her test flight shortly after 7:00 AM, and the Guinea Airways ground crew began fueling the airplane for the long flight to Howland. There were still two unresolved problems: Earhart had not received a weather forecast for the route, and Noonan still needed to get a time check on his chronometer. The trip was expected to take at least eighteen hours. The arrival had to be in daylight, but Noonan's best celestial navigation required the stars. The approach to Howland, therefore, was best made in the hours immediately after sunup, and that meant a morning takeoff from Lae the previous day.

The departure window came and went with still no forecast and no time signals. Around 11:00 AM Earhart reluctantly postponed the flight. At noon, she sent a message to Richard Black aboard *Itasca*: "Due local conditions takeoff delayed until 21:30 GCT, July 2nd. Any forecast Lae/Howland before then appreciated. Notify *Ontario* change."[26] Earhart was saying that she now planned to depart from Lae at 7:30 AM the next morning.

Back in California, George Putnam, having learned that his wife had not left Lae on June 30 but not yet aware that the July 1 departure had also been canceled, was still trying to find out whether she would be home in time for the radio engagement Monday night. Knowing that *Itasca* was trying to establish direct contact with Lae, and hoping to catch Amelia before the scheduled takeoff, he had the Coast Guard's San Francisco Division send an urgent message to the ship: "Please forward Earhart, Lae. Rush. Is there likelihood Oakland by Monday morning? Reply via *Itasca*. Important."[27] *Itasca* never established direct radio contact with Lae, and the message was not forwarded to Lae as a telegram.*

Throughout the remainder of the day—Thursday, July 1—in Lae, Balfour continued his effort to receive time signals. Earhart and Noonan, as they had done during earlier enforced delays, used the time to do some local sightseeing. At some time during the day, a weather forecast for the Lae–Howland route came in from Lieutenant True at Fleet Air Base, Pearl Harbor. Guinea Airways manager Eric Chater, in a letter written three weeks later, recalled that the forecast had come in via Samoa at 7:30 that morning.[28] U.S. Navy records, however, show that True's forecast was not transmitted from Hawaii until more than an hour after that time, and that messages relayed through Samoa were taking a minimum of three and a half hours to reach Lae, if they got there at all. Whenever the forecast actually reached New Guinea, the picture it painted of the weather to be expected along the route was typical for the region:

Earhart, Lae. Forecast Thursday.
    Lae to *Ontario*—Partly clouded. Rain squalls 250 miles east Lae. Wind, east south east, 12 to 15.

---

*Over the years there have been accusations that George Putnam pressured his wife to make the flight to Howland before she was ready. While there is no doubt that the messages he sent to her via *Itasca* conveyed a sense of urgency, Earhart never saw them.

Ontario to longitude 175—Partly cloudy, cumulus clouds about ten thousand feet. [Visibility] mostly unlimited. Wind, east north east, 18.

Thence to Howland—partly cloudy. Scattered heavy showers. Wind, east north east, 15.

Avoid towering cumulus and squalls by detours as centers frequently dangerous.

Fleet Air Base, Pearl Harbor.[29]

When no storm systems are present, virtually every day in the Central Pacific is partly cloudy with big, puffy cumulus clouds often building to around ten thousand feet. Some get big enough to develop into localized squalls with heavy showers. Any pilot knows that it is a good idea to stay out of such clouds. The forecast surface winds would be moderate quartering headwinds, as they would be almost any day in that part of the world. Winds at altitude might be quite different, but that information was not available.

The forecast was for "Thursday," but whose Thursday? True had sent the forecast at 12:20 Hawaiian time on Wednesday, June 30. Across the International Date Line in Lae, New Guinea, at that moment, it was 8:50 AM on Thursday, July 1. Was this a forecast for Earhart's today or for True's tomorrow? Unclear as the intended day may have been, the prognostication was so typical of the region that it did not much matter.

That evening, Amelia wrote another press release for the *Tribune*. She had received no reply to her suggestion that a charge account be arranged, so she sent her story as a telegram, collect. Echoing Hamlet to express her frustration, she wrote: " 'Denmark's a prison' and Lae, attractive and unusual as it appears to two fliers, just as confining. Lockheed stands ready for longest hop weighted with gasoline and oil to capacity, however clouds and wind blowing wrong way conspired keep her on ground today. In addition FN has been unable, account radio difficulties, to set his chronometers. Lack knowledge their fastness or slowness. We shall try to get off tomorrow, though now we cannot be home by Fourth of July as hoped. Earhart."[30]

Finally, at 9:00 PM, the anxious listeners heard a marginal signal from Sydney, Australia, and at 10:30 the Adelaide time signal came through clearly. The time check indicated that Noonan's chronometer was three seconds slow. For a flight requiring the degree of precision needed to bring the plane as close as possible to such a small island, however, Noonan wanted more than one time check.

The next morning—July 2, 1937—the planned takeoff time of 7:30 AM came and went. Finally, at 8:00 AM, another clear time signal came in, this time from Saigon, and the chronometer checked out the same as the night before. Chater later reported that "both Captain Noonan and Miss Earhart expressed their complete satisfaction and decided to leave at ten o-clock."[31] That hour happened to also be 00:00 Greenwich Civil Time. For a flight departing at that time, the GCT time throughout the trip would be the same as the flight's time aloft.*

The Electra had been fueled for the trip following Earhart's test flight the previous morning. Although Amelia's press release described the aircraft as being "weighted with gasoline and oil to capacity," the plane was actually about 50 gallons shy of its maximum fuel load. The reason was simple and sensible. The Lockheed's engines performed best for takeoff on 100 octane aviation fuel, but the new high-test gasoline was not yet widely available. All but one of the Electra's twelve fuel tanks carried the standard 87 octane gas. An 81-gallon tank in one wing had been filled with the 100 octane fuel at the last stop where it could be had, probably Bandoeng. Now that tank was about half empty, leaving an adequate 40 gallons or so for the heavily overloaded takeoff; it could not be topped off with Lae's lower-grade fuel without diluting its contents.

Earhart's aircraft had a well-documented total fuel capacity of 1151 U.S. gallons.[32] Accounts written shortly afterward by Eric Chater, Guinea Airway's manager, and James Collopy, the district superintendent for civil aviation, indicate that after fueling at Lae for the trip to Howland Island, the airplane had about 1100 U.S. gallons of gasoline aboard.[33] Because the tanks were filled in the morning hours of the previous day, the loaded airplane necessarily sat through the heat of an entire New Guinea day, and it is reasonable to expect that some fuel was lost due to expansion and leakage through the fuel tank air vents. Such losses are common, fairly negligible, and quite apparent from the dribbling vents and wet patches on the ground. Although neither Chater nor Collopy mentioned it specifically, it is also reasonable to expect that, for such a fuel-critical flight, any such loss would have been replaced during the final inspection on the morning of the takeoff.

Given the controversy surrounding subsequent events, there has been a great deal of discussion and speculation about how long and how far the Electra could fly on 1100 gallons of gas. The answer is, it depends. In the spring of 1936, when she was selecting an aircraft for her anticipated globe-circling flight, range was Earhart's primary consideration. Her original plan called for a nonstop flight of nearly 3000 miles to Japan

---

*Some historians have alleged that Earhart's takeoff time was selected specifically for that reason, but her earlier plans to depart at 9:30 and 7:30 local time argue against that assertion. The juxtaposition of the takeoff time with 00:00 GCT appears to have been nothing more than a convenient coincidence.

after midair refueling over Midway Island. Lockheed got the order with a promise that their Model 10E Electra could be modified to carry enough fuel to fly for 4500 miles. On June 4, 1936, while Earhart's Model 10E Special was under construction, the company published a study explaining how that phenomenal range could be accomplished.

The thirty-seven-page document, entitled "Lockheed Report No. 487— Range Study of Lockheed Electra Bimotor Airplane," was authored by engineers C. L. Johnson* and W. C. Nelson and includes seventeen graphs and nine pages of tables and computations. The study concludes that "it is possible to fly a Lockheed Electra Model 10E non-stop for a distance of between 4100 and 4500 miles starting out with 1200 gallons of gasoline and the proper amount of oil."[34] There were caveats, of course. The range projections were for "zero wind" conditions and required the meticulous management of numerous variables such as airspeed, throttle settings, and propeller RPM. Of critical importance was the adjustment of the fuel-air mixture to ensure that the engines were functioning at peak efficiency.

According to the Lockheed study, an Electra carrying a fuel load of 1100 gallons should be able to cover 3680 miles in zero wind in twenty-four to twenty-seven hours, depending on a fairly narrow range of airspeed choices. Put another way, 1100 gallons would give the Electra between twenty-four and twenty-seven hours of endurance at airspeeds between 135 and 150 miles per hour. Headwinds or tailwinds would determine the actual distance covered. A flight equivalent to the distance from Lae, New Guinea, to Howland Island in zero wind could be expected to take between seventeen and nineteen hours depending on the airspeed selected. If Earhart used the higher airspeed profile specified in the study, she could fly against an average headwind of 15 miles per hour for the entire flight, arrive in the vicinity of Howland nineteen hours after takeoff, and still have at least a five-hour—26 percent—reserve.

The long-range capabilities of the Model 10E Special were not merely theoretical. During the preparations for the world flight, Johnson had flown with Earhart in her Electra to gather further data and make sure Amelia understood how to implement the fuel management techniques and procedures he and Nelson had worked out. In March, Earhart had departed Oakland, California, with 947 gallons of fuel aboard and landed in Honolulu, Hawaii, nearly sixteen hours and 2400 miles later. According to Amelia, the tanks still held more than four hours' worth of fuel, a comfortable 25 percent reserve.[35]

---

*Clarence L. "Kelly" Johnson helped design the Model 10. He went on to become one of the world's most famous aeronautical engineers, leading the design teams on such aircraft as the P-38 Lightning, the F-104 Starfighter, the U-2, and the SR-71 Blackbird.

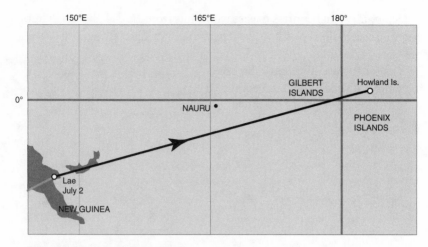

Earhart's route from Lae to Howland Island.

In May 1937, while Earhart's Electra was still under repair following the Luke Field wreck, the performance predicted in "Lockheed Report 487" was again dramatically validated when Dick Merrill and Jack Lambie made back-to-back nonstop Atlantic crossings in the other Model 10E Special, the "Daily Express."

As Earhart contemplated her impending 10:00 AM departure from Lae on July 2, 1937, the only weather forecast to reach her had indicated more or less average conditions along her entire route. She could expect moderate headwinds, and she might have to divert around occasional squalls, but if she could get the Electra airborne with the heaviest fuel load she had ever carried, she had every reason to expect that she could fly all that day, all night, and arrive in the Howland area around 7:00 AM the next morning. If the island did not appear on schedule, she would have about five hours—until at least noon—to locate it or find somewhere else to land.

In the closing line of her press release to the *Tribune*, Amelia had written: "Not much more than a month ago I was on the other shore of the Pacific, looking westward. This evening, I looked eastward over the Pacific. In those fast-moving days which have intervened, the whole width of the world has passed behind us—except this broad ocean. I shall be glad when we have the hazards of its navigation behind us."[36]

The hazards of its navigation were greater than she supposed. Her declared intention to take bearings on high-frequency signals sent by *Itasca* was doomed to failure, as were any efforts by the cutter to take bearings on the high-frequency signals she could send. Unless Noonan's navigation was uncannily accurate, the only glimmer of hope was the borrowed high-frequency direction finder set up on Howland, and Earhart did not know it was there.

She had begun her press release with a line from *Hamlet*, but it is a quote from *Macbeth* that speaks to her departure from Lae:

I'm for th' air; this night I'll spend
Unto a dismal and a fatal end:
Great business must be wrought ere noon.[37]

CHAPTER NINE

Lost

communications failure on the flight to howland island

Across the International Date Line, it was July 1 and the Howland Island airport was ready for its first customer. Just offshore, the men aboard the Coast Guard cutter *Itasca* were preparing to provide weather and navigational assistance to the plane and trying to find out if Amelia Earhart was finally on her way.

The cutter's communications capabilities were considerable, but they were not unlimited. Of *Itasca*'s four transmitters, two could send the high-frequency signals Earhart had requested, but only one could provide the Morse code letter *A*s on 7500 kilocycles that Amelia hoped to home in on. That radio, however, was also needed for communication with the outside world. The other high-frequency transmitter, if tuned somewhat beyond its normal limits, could handle Earhart's request that *Itasca* talk to her on 3105 kilocycles. *Itasca* had only one high-frequency transmitting antenna, so the two transmitters could be not be used simultaneously. A switch mounted on the ceiling of the radio room selected which of the two units was connected to the antenna.

Situated on the top deck just behind the funnel, the radio room measured sixteen feet from side to side with a door at each end, and a scant nine feet front to back. Large metal cabinets that housed the ship's transmitters and receivers stood on the floor and hung from the walls, leaving just enough room for the desks of two operators. Each man had a telegraph key for sending Morse code and a typewriter that he used to keep a running log of incoming and outgoing transmissions. Normally, the operators listened over headphones, but incoming signals could also be broadcast over a loudspeaker mounted on the wall.

The principal players on this narrow stage were the cutter's radiomen. *Itasca*'s communications officer was Ens. W. L. Sutter, but apart from certifying the retyped, clean copies of the logs, he is virtually invisible in the official record. As in most small military detachments, the person running the show was the senior noncommissioned officer. In *Itasca*'s communications section, that person was Chief Radioman Leo G. Bellarts. The thirty-year-old Bellarts had joined the Coast Guard to follow his passion for radio.

Under Bellarts's supervision aboard *Itasca* were three young men who had not yet progressed beyond the Coast Guard's lowest rating for radio technicians. Many years later, Leo Bellarts remembered Radioman 3rd Class William Galten as his most trusted operator. "I could give Galten a job and Galten would go ahead and carry it through. He would do what I told him to and I was perfectly . . . at ease because I knew Galten was a reliable man. He was a good man."[1]

Bellarts was less complimentary about Radioman 3rd Class George Thompson (no relation to the cutter's captain). "Thompson was a very peculiar individual. He was an ex-army man—ex-army operator—and you'd tell him to do something and he'd do it as long as it fit with his idea." It was George Thompson who had disregarded orders from San Francisco Division during the dispute about *Itasca*'s transmitter. "Thompson was a good operator. Maybe better than Galten as [far as being an] operator is concerned. But as far as reliability, I'd put Galten ahead of Thompson."[2]

Radioman 3rd Class Thomas O'Hare was, in Bellarts's opinion, a "fast operator" in more ways than one. Everyone aboard *Itasca* knew that the Earhart flight was of great interest to the press and to the public. O'Hare seems to have been ready to take full advantage of the situation. Bellarts recalled:

> I started missing little papers that was around the shack—radio shack. . . . [S]omebody was picking souvenirs up. . . . I knew there was somebody in the radio shack that was doing it. Snitching that stuff. . . . O'Hare, I think was one of 'em because I never got a copy of his log. And I got a little bit disgusted so I passed the word—absolutely those things, when they get off a watch, they are to deliver [the logs] to me by hand only. Lieutenant Commander Baker, he was the exec and I told him about it and he said, take care of the logs. Keep all that stuff, he says. Don't let it out of your hands.[3]

Radioman 2nd Class Frank Cipriani, the fourth operator under Bellarts's supervision, was an outsider aboard *Itasca*. Normally assigned to the cutter *Roger B. Taney*, Cipriani had been brought aboard at the request of Richard Black specifically to operate the high-frequency direction finder to be set up on Howland Island. "Temporary. He was a temporary man," Bellarts remembered. "And so he went over on the beach and it was just as good. . . . We didn't want him."[4]

George Thompson had the watch just after midnight on July 1 when a radiogram arrived for Black from U.S. Navy Radio in Tutuila, American Samoa. Earhart had sent the message from New Guinea the previous afternoon: "Due local conditions, take-off delayed until 21:30 GCT, July 2nd. Any forecast Lae/Howland before then appreciated."[5]

Earhart was saying that she intended to take off from Lae at 7:30 AM on Friday, July 2. That would be 10:00 AM on Thursday, July 1, aboard *Itasca*. Richard Black had less than ten hours to get a new forecast to her. The only means of communication with her was by telegram via Samoa. That was taking a minimum of three and a half hours, and often much longer. The forecast had to come from Lieutenant True, but it was now the middle of the night in Hawaii and True was probably at home and asleep. *Itasca* immediately sent a message to Fleet Air Base, Pearl Harbor: "Request forecast Lae to Howland Island for Earhart. Anticipate early departure this date."[6]

Seven and a half hours passed before Fleet Air Base transmitted a forecast to be forwarded to Earhart via Samoa. Once again, True cautioned that he did not have much information: "Accurate forecast difficult account lack of reports your vicinity. Conditions appear generally average over route. No major storm. Apparently partly cloudy with dangerous local rain squalls about 300 miles east of Lae and scattered heavy showers remainder of route. Winds east southeast about 25 knots to *Ontario* then east to east northeast about 20 knots to Howland; Fleet Base Pearl Harbor."[7] *Itasca* received the forecast, but Earhart did not. The general manager of Guinea Airways would later report that the telegram arrived in Lae "as the machine was leaving the ground."[8]

Aboard *Itasca*, the morning, noon, and afternoon passed with no word as to whether Earhart had left Lae. At 4:45 PM, Thomas O'Hare, who was on duty in the radio room, asked U.S. Navy Radio in Tutuila to "give me flash if you find out. . . . We don't think she took off or we would know by now."[9] An hour later, just to be safe, O'Hare made his first attempt to pick up the plane: "Tuning for KHAQQ [Earhart's radio call sign] on 3105 kcs—Results negative."[10]

At 6:10 PM, San Francisco Division sent word that United Press was reporting that Earhart had taken off at noon Lae time.[11] If that were true, she had been in the air for several hours. Commander Thompson considered the news reliable enough to order a special radio watch specifically to listen for the inbound aircraft. He also sent Frank Cipriani, the radioman borrowed from *Taney*, ashore to man the high-frequency direction finder that had been set up on the island.[12]

The Associated Press correspondent aboard *Itasca*, James Carey, filed a report that described the situation as it was understood aboard the cutter at that time: "Earhart arrival expected 10:30 morning. Estimate 20 hour plus flight. Easterly winds forecast Howland. Headwinds en route."[13]

In setting up the special radio watch to communicate with the Electra, *Itasca*'s chief radioman had to sort out Amelia's desired frequencies, schedules, and procedures from the fragmentary instructions received in the past weeks. The protocols Bellarts and his operators later used in trying to communicate with Earhart indicate that he was missing a key piece of the puzzle.

Bellarts does not seem to have been aware of instructions contained in a cable Earhart sent the morning after she arrived in Lae. Addressed to "Commander USS *Itasca*," it said, "Plan midday takeoff here. Please have meteorologist send forecast Lae Howland soon as possible." The realization that Earhart was counting on the cutter to provide a weather forecast for the upcoming flight had prompted the frantic effort to contact Lieutenant True at home in Honolulu and get him to come up with some kind of prognostication. The information in the second half of Earhart's message was vital but required no immediate action: "Report in English, not code, especially while flying. Will broadcast hourly quarter past hour GCT."[14]

In 1937, virtually all marine and aviation long-distance communication was conducted in Morse code. Most ships did not use radiotelephone at all, and aircraft used voice radio only for short-range calls. Earhart's request that *Itasca* use exclusively English was thus highly unusual. The idea that an aviation professional, especially a famous long-distance flyer, would not be fluent in Morse code was almost inconceivable. That was why Earhart had gone to some pains to explain to her hosts in New Guinea that both she and Noonan "entirely depended on radiotelephone reception as neither of them were able to read Morse at any speed but could recognize a single letter sent several times."[15] And it was also why she had warned *Itasca* to "report in English, not code." Bellarts, however, either never got the word or disregarded it. The vast majority of the cutter's transmissions to the plane were sent in Morse code.

Equally important, and equally missed, was Earhart's stipulation that she intended to transmit only once each hour, at quarter past the hour, and that she would keep her radio schedule according to Greenwich Civil Time (GCT). In this respect, Earhart was very much up-to-date. Recognizing the need for standardized time coordination with aircraft that were crossing several time zones during a single flight, Pan American Airways used Greenwich time for all communications schedules. Coast Guard captains—and for that matter the U.S. Navy—had no such need, and often operated according to a system of half-hour time zones while at sea. Throughout the time Earhart was in flight, *Itasca*'s radio operators used local time calculated as Greenwich time minus eleven and one-half hours. In practice, being eleven hours out of synch was of little consequence, but the half-hour discrepancy was a problem. "On the hour" for Earhart was "on the half hour" for *Itasca*. When Earhart's watch read quarter past the hour, the clocks aboard *Itasca* were at quarter to the hour. As a result, the men aboard the cutter had the impression that Amelia was contradicting herself, when in fact she was doing exactly what she had said she would do.

How it came about that *Itasca*'s chief radioman seems to have not seen this crucial message is not known. One obvious explanation is that the radio room's copy of the message was one of those "little papers" that went missing as a souvenir and so was not available to Bellarts when he tried to piece together Earhart's instructions.

Bellarts took the first special watch himself and began listening for signals. He soon heard "very weak signals on 3105. Unreadable and seemed [to] shift about." Later that hour he typed, "No sigs on [3105] during period 7:45–48."[16]

Earhart was transmitting at about that time. Bellarts did not hear her because she was sixteen hundred miles away and sending on her other frequency. However, Harry Balfour, the wireless operator in Lae, New Guinea, did hear the transmission. "Position 4.33 South, 159.7 East. Height 8,000 feet over cumulus clouds. Wind 23 knots."[17] This report, the third that Balfour heard, put the plane in the vicinity of the Nukumanu Islands, not yet halfway, but on course and on schedule for Howland Island. The Electra had covered the roughly nine hundred miles from Lae in about six hours, for an average speed of somewhere in the neighborhood of 150 miles per hour. Estimates of the Electra's speed, position, and progress during the flight from Lae are of necessity rough approximations. The accuracy of Earhart's few reported positions cannot be verified; nor is it possible to know how old the information was at the time Earhart made the report.

At eight thousand feet, the airplane was where it should have been for maximum efficiency. And with the approach of nightfall, the report that it was above the tops of the cumulus clouds was good news. As the day cooled off, the clouds should not build any higher. Earhart's "Wind 23 knots," however, was meaningless without mention of the wind's direction.*

Finally, just before 8:00 PM aboard *Itasca*, official notification of Earhart's departure arrived from Lae, via Samoa: "Urgent, Black, *Itasca* . . . Amelia Earhart left Lae at 10 AM local time July 2nd. Due Howland Island 18 hours time."[18] This information presented a new picture. The plane had left Lae two hours earlier than previously reported, and the eighteen-hour time-en-route estimate indicated that Earhart anticipated lighter headwinds than predicted in the most recent forecast. *Itasca* should now expect the plane to arrive at around 6:30 AM.

At about the same time the message arrived from Lae, Leo Bellarts handed off the special Earhart radio watch to George Thompson. Following Bellarts's

*Recent speculation that the aircraft ran out of fuel far sooner than Lockheed fuel consumption tests suggest it should have is based on speculative interpretation of Earhart's reported statements. "Wind 23 knots" is assumed to refer to a headwind, and "speed 140 knots," in an earlier report, is taken to be airspeed rather than ground speed. In this scenario, strong headwinds were present and Earhart compensated by running her engines at higher power settings, thus increasing her airspeed and burning fuel at a far higher rate. There is no evidence to suggest that strong headwinds were present, however, or that Earhart increased her fuel consumption.

instructions, Thompson listened for signals from Earhart on 3105 kilocycles, especially at quarter to and quarter past the hour. On three occasions during his six-hour watch he heard unreadable voice transmissions, but nothing he could identify as coming from the airplane. Thompson also followed Bellarts's instructions regarding the signals *Itasca* was to transmit. A few minutes before each hour and half hour he sent the local weather in Morse code, followed on the hour and half hour by the Morse code letter *A* repeated for three minutes, all on 7500 kilocycles.

As night settled over the island, Frank Cipriani set up the borrowed high-frequency direction finder and began listening for Earhart. He started listening at 9:00 PM on July 1, although his radio log indicates that he began his watch at 10:00 PM on July 2.[19] The log is one day and one hour ahead of the actual local time. Apparently, when Cipriani went ashore at Howland on the evening of July 1 he was confused about what day it was (not at all unusual aboard a ship on a long voyage) and believed the date to be July 2. Consequently, events recorded in the Howland radio log as happening on July 3 actually occurred on the second. July 4 is really July 3. By July 5 Cipriani had figured out his error, and the log is correct from then on.

The date discrepancy was an error, but the time difference was intentional. Cipriani, like the radio operators aboard the cutter, kept his radio log in local time. *Itasca* used actual local time as computed according to U.S. Navy conventions. On the island, however, the colonists used Honolulu time for the sake of convenience in coordinating radio schedules with Hawaii. In 1937, Hawaii was using Greenwich minus ten and a half hours. Local time in the Howland area, as used by *Itasca*, was Greenwich minus eleven and a half hours. (For the sake of clarity, events on Howland will be described in *Itasca* local time.) The net result was that local time on Howland was an hour later than local time aboard the ship standing just offshore. The obvious errors and apparent contradictions in the various radio logs have prompted charges of negligence where there was in fact only a lack of information, and allegations of conspiracy where there was merely confusion.

Aboard the cutter, as George Thompson stood the special Earhart radio watch, William Galten performed the ship's regular radio duties. When he was not handling routine administrative traffic, Galten, too, listened for Earhart at quarter to and quarter past each hour, noting in his log what he did and did not hear. Like Thompson, he heard nothing he could be sure was the plane, but a few minutes before 10:00 PM he heard a very weak Morse code transmission, "KHAQQ [the Electra's call sign] this is VK [Galten could not get the rest of the sender's call sign]. What is your position now?"[20] The station Galten heard was the island of Nauru, call letters VKT. Earhart's planned route passed roughly one hundred miles south of the British colony, and the operator there later reported that he had heard voice transmissions from the plane shortly before Galten heard his transmission.[21] At the time, however, all Galten knew was that someone, somewhere was trying to call Earhart.

At two o'clock in the morning, Thomas O'Hare relieved Galten on the administrative watch and Bellarts once more took the Earhart watch. Half an hour later, he spoke into the microphone for the first time, "*Itasca* to Earhart."[22] At this point the plane had been in the air for fourteen hours and should have been within radio range, but the only sound in Bellarts's headphones was the familiar crackle of static.

No word of Earhart's progress had come in since the initial report of her departure from New Guinea. If Lae or anyone else had heard from Earhart since then, they had not told *Itasca*. The sleeping ship drifted on the dark ocean to the west of Howland. On the bridge, the officer of the deck ordered the engine ahead one-third to ease the ship to within five miles of the island. In the radio room, Bellarts continued to send weather reports and *A*s.

At quarter to three he listened for her scheduled broadcast and heard a voice. It was barely discernible against the background noise, but Bellarts was sure he was hearing Earhart. The transmission lasted three minutes, and he could not make out a word of what she was saying. He typed: "Heard Earhart plane but unreadable thru static" and notified the bridge that first contact had been made.[23]

Commander Thompson, in his official report, later claimed that at this time "Bellarts caught Earhart's voice and it came in through loud speaker, very low monotone 'cloudy, overcast.' Mr. Carey, Associated Press representative, was present. Also Mr. Hanzlik [*sic*] of United Press, both gentlemen recognized voice from previous flights to and from Hawaii. There was no question as to hearing Earhart."[24] Overcast conditions would have prevented Fred Noonan from using star sightings to track the flight's progress. But the ship's radio logs do not support Thompson's allegation. Asked about the discrepancy many years later, Bellarts vehemently denied that he had heard Earhart say "cloudy, overcast" and explained that, at that time, the loudspeaker was not in use: "That static was something terrific, you know, just crashing in on your ears. And I'll guarantee you that Hanzlick and that other joker never heard that. Oh, I would definitely be on the phones. Absolutely. Not on a loudspeaker."[25]

Exactly an hour after the first reception, Bellarts heard her again. Although Bellarts did not know it, Earhart was transmitting precisely when she had said she would—once an hour at quarter past the hour Greenwich Civil Time. The signal was a bit stronger this time, and he could make out that she "will listen on hour and half on 3105."[26] To Bellarts, it appeared that Earhart was changing the agreed-upon procedure. Following the instructions Earhart sent from Java, he had been sending her Morse code letter *A*s and the ship's call letters, NRUI, on the hour and half hour on 7500 kilocycles.[27] He was apparently not aware that on the same day Earhart had sent her instructions, San Francisco Division had advised her (presumably via Putnam) that "*Itasca* will voice radio on 3105 [to] her on hour and half hour as she approaches Howland."[28] Earhart confirmed that change in a telegram she sent to Black from Lae on June 30—"Now understand *Itasca* voicing 3105 on hour and half hour"—and, she added, "with long continuous signal on approach."[29] It appears that another little paper had gone missing from the radio room.

Her request for a long, continuous transmission when she got close clearly implies that she intended to find the island by homing in on the signal using her radio direction finder. On June 26, she had said that her direction finder "covers from 200 to 1500 and 2400 to 4800 kilocycles."[30] A signal sent on 3105 kilocycles would fall within that range. It seems to have been a workable plan if she was right about the capabilities of her direction finder. But Bellarts either disregarded the request or never saw it.

In the predawn hours of July 2, as Earhart passed her fifteenth hour aloft en route from Lae, she was probably wondering why she had heard nothing from *Itasca*. Her transmission, "Will listen on hour and half on 3105," was a reminder, not a change.[31]

Commander Thompson's version of the 3:45 AM reception, as related in his official report, is quite different from the entry that appears in Bellarts's original log. The raw logs were often strewn with errors and revisions, and it was standard practice to "smooth"—that is, retype—the rough logs before filing them as part of the official record. Most of *Itasca*'s surviving radio logs are "smoothed" versions. Fortunately, Chief Bellarts saved the raw log of the special Earhart radio watch. According to Commander Thompson, Earhart's 3:45 transmission was: "*Itasca* from Earhart . . . *Itasca* from Earhart . . . overcast . . . will listen on hour and half hour on 3105 . . . will listen on hour and half hour on 3105."[32] Again, a cloudy sky could have serious consequences for the flight's navigation. There is no "overcast" in the original radio logs, however; nor does the word appear in the transcript filed by Army Air Corps lieutenant Daniel Cooper, who joined the group in the radio room at 3:40 AM.[33] Cooper's version of the 3:45 reception matches Bellarts's log entry, "Will listen on hour and half hour on 3105—(very faint, S-1)."[34]

"S-1" means strength 1. The strength of received radio signals was rated on a subjective scale of 1 to 5. According to accepted international standards in 1937, strength 1 was "hardly perceptible, unreadable"; strength 2 was "weak, readable now and then"; strength 3 was "fairly good, readable but with difficulty"; strength 4 was "good, readable"; and strength 5 was "very good, perfectly readable."[35] In fact, Cooper should have rated the 3:45

reception as S-2. Some researchers have tried to determine how far away the Electra must have been at a given time based on the signal strength estimations included in the various logs and reports, but strength numbers represent general impressions, not precise measurements.

Just before 4:00 AM *Itasca* time, San Francisco Division sent a message asking *Itasca*, "Have you established contact with plane yet?" Radioman O'Hare replied, "Heard her but don't know if she hears us yet."[36]

On the hour, in accordance with Earhart's request, Bellarts sent the current weather using voice ("fone" in Coast Guard parlance) on 3105 kilocycles. Two minutes later, he sent the weather again on the same frequency, this time using Morse code. At quarter past the hour he listened on 3105 for a transmission from Earhart but heard nothing. On the half hour, he broadcast the weather again by voice and in code.

During this time, O'Hare, at the other radio position, was switching back and forth between keeping schedules with other stations and listening for Earhart on 3105. Radio Wailupe, the main U.S. Navy radio facility in Hawaii, asked, "Do you hear Earhart on 3105?" O'Hare replied, "Yes, but can't make her out."[37]

There should have been a transmission from Earhart at 4:45 AM (16:15 aboard the Electra), but there was none. O'Hare listened for five minutes and logged: "Tuned to Earhart. No hear."[38] Bellarts was presumably listening as well, but his log contains no entry for that time.

What happened next can only be pieced together from the two radio logs. Although the logs were intended to provide a minute-by-minute record of what the operators heard and the messages they sent, the logs kept by the two operators do not always agree. Operators in the same room often recorded the same event in their respective logs as occurring at times that vary by as much as three minutes. When things got hectic, discipline often lapsed. Phrases were sometimes inserted and logged times changed after the fact to maintain an appearance of chronological integrity. Consequently, although the surviving *Itasca* radio logs are an invaluable nearly real-time record of events, the times shown must be considered to have a margin of error of two or three minutes. Just as the forecast winds and interpretations of Earhart's ambiguous comments about wind and speed cannot be used to determine the Electra's rate of fuel consumption, so the *Itasca* radio logs do not place the airplane in time and space except within relatively broad limits. It appears that a few minutes before the top of the hour, Bellarts, knowing what he was going to do at five o'clock, typed: "Sent weather/code/fone/3105 kcs." But before he got to the end of that line on the log sheet and entered the time as 0500, Earhart's voice was suddenly in his headphones. On the same line he typed "(heard Earhart (part cldy)" and instead entered the actual time: 4:53.[39]

At the other position, O'Hare was also caught off guard. He was sending a message to Radio Wailupe when "Earhart broke in on fone 3105 / now ???? unreadable."[40] He logged the time of this event as 4:55. Despite subsequent official claims to the contrary, this ambiguous incident is the only report in either of the cutter's two radio logs of Earhart commenting about the weather.

Bellarts and O'Hare continued to listen but heard only static. By six o'clock more than an hour had passed since the last transmission from the plane. So far, they had heard Earhart's voice three times. Bellarts had logged portions of two receptions as intelligible phrases. O'Hare had not been able to understand anything she said.

The long night was coming to an end. All hands were up and breakfasted, and the ship was now standing just offshore of Howland Island. The eastern sky blushed with the promise of dawn as the cutter's boats headed shoreward carrying the various teams designated to support the aircraft's landing, greet the famous flyer, and service the airplane.[41] Somewhere over the dark western horizon, the Electra drew closer with each passing minute.

Then, at quarter past the hour, Earhart was back on the air. "Wants bearing on 3105 // on hour // will whistle in mic." She then announced that she was approximately two hundred miles out and started whistling.[42] Earhart's request for a bearing came as a surprise. It was never the plan for the ship to take bearings on signals from the plane. While she was in Lae, Black had informed Amelia that *Itasca*'s direction finder was limited to frequencies from 270 to 550 kilocycles.[43] Now she was asking *Itasca* to take a bearing while she whistled into the microphone on 3105 kilocycles.

Bellarts later said that she did not actually whistle. "I put down 'whistle' because she said she was whistling. Actually it was an audible sound. . . . It was higher than a hum. A shrill note." In Bellarts's opinion, Earhart was trying to mimic the steady, high-pitched tone of a telegraph key being held down. He felt that if *Itasca*'s direction finder had been able to respond to such a high frequency, "We could have handled it. But, notice, notice when she did that. One minute after she asked 'on the hour.' "[44]

Although it is apparent that Earhart did not understand the frequency limitations of radio direction finding, she was not behaving as erratically as Bellarts believed. Amelia was using Greenwich time, as she had said she would. For her, the time was not 6:15, it was 17:45. She was transmitting right on schedule and asking *Itasca* to send the bearing at the ship's next transmission time at the top of the hour. Bellarts, however, saw an irrational woman who refused to answer his calls, changed her plans from one minute to the next, and was now asking him for help he could not provide. "And I was sitting there sweating blood because I couldn't do a darn thing about it."[45]

The only person who might be able to do something about it was Frank Cipriani, the radioman Commander Thompson sent ashore the previous evening to set up the high-frequency direction finder Black had borrowed from the navy. As Earhart "whistled," O'Hare called Cipriani and told him take bearings on the signal.[46] Cipriani could hear Earhart at strength 3 ("fairly good") using a long antenna rigged to the receiver, but when he switched to the smaller loop antenna on the direction finder, reception dropped to almost nothing. Then she stopped transmitting. "Bearing nil."[47]

While the radio operators struggled to accommodate Earhart's request for a bearing, the sun arrived and Commander Thompson gave the order for the ship to begin making smoke so as to be more visible.[48] In his official report, Thompson implied that *Itasca* continued to lay down smoke for some two hours.[49] There is, however, a problem with that claim. *Itasca* was a steamship powered by two oil-fired boilers.[50] Water was pumped through tubes in the boiler fireboxes to generate the steam. The only technique available to *Itasca* for making smoke was to reduce the amount of air in the fuel-air mix being pumped into one of the fireboxes. The procedure produced thick clouds of heavy black smoke but also deposited soot on the steam tubes. More than about fifteen minutes of such abuse could result in uneven soot buildup, hot spots, tube rupture, and catastrophic failure of the boiler. Although *Itasca*'s deck log notes that the ship began making smoke at 6:14 AM, there is no corresponding entry for when smoke making ceased.[51] It is possible, and perhaps probable, that no smoke was being generated after about 6:30 AM, or that smoke making was intermittent after that time.

In the radio room, the two operators kept trying to establish communication with the plane. At about this time O'Hare abandoned any attempt to maintain communication with San Francisco and Hawaii. For the rest of the morning, both radio positions were occupied exclusively with trying to reach out to Earhart while Coast Guard headquarters, the navy, George Putnam, and the press waited anxiously for news of the plane's arrival.

At 6:45 AM, Earhart was back on, stronger now. Bellarts logged her words as: "Please take bearing on us and report in half hour." On the next line he typed: "I will make noise in mic" and added "—about 100 miles out."[52] O'Hare's log records the event somewhat differently. He typed: "Earhart on now. Reception fairly clear now." "Want bearing and want report in ½ hour."[53]

Reviewing the log more than thirty-five years later, Leo Bellarts was still baffled by Earhart's request, "Take bearing on us and report in a half an hour. Well, why do that? [I]f you take a radio bearing you get the bearing back like that. You don't wait no thirty minutes to get it back to them."[54] Once again, the time discrepancy between ship and plane created a false impression that Earhart was acting irrationally. For Amelia, the time was quarter past the hour and she was undoubtedly asking for the bearing to be sent at *Itasca*'s next scheduled broadcast time "*on* half hour," not "*in* half hour."

On Howland Island, Cipriani heard the transmission as well, although he was "using the direction finder and receiver sparingly due to heavy drainage on batteries."[55] The signal Cipriani heard was strong. He rated it strength 4 ("good, readable"), but it was too short and obscured by too much static for him to get a bearing.

Coming as it did only half an hour after both Bellarts and O'Hare heard her say she was two hundred miles out, Earhart's assertion that she was now one hundred miles away caused further concern. If true, it meant either that the aircraft was traveling at the unlikely speed of two hundred miles per hour or that her earlier distance estimate was significantly in error. There is, however, reason to doubt that she ever said she was one hundred miles out.

Three operators—Bellarts, O'Hare, and Cipriani—heard and separately logged the transmission. All three logs agree that Earhart asked for a bearing, and both Bellarts and O'Hare noted that she wanted the bearing sent to her "in [*sic*] half hour." O'Hare and Cipriani both mentioned that the signal was strong. Only the chief radioman's log, however, includes a comment about the plane being one hundred miles out. A platen misalignment in Bellarts's original log reveals that the phrase was inserted after the carriage return for the next line.

It may be that the notation "—about 100 miles out" was Bellarts's estimate based on the strength of the signal and was misinterpreted as a quote from Earhart by those reading the log. Whether she said it or not, the estimate was attributed to Earhart and contributed to the growing impression among the ship's company that they were dealing with someone who did not know what she was doing.

For the next half hour the two operators shared the single high-frequency antenna as O'Hare sent *A*s on 7500 and Bellarts tried to reach Earhart on 3105. If she made another report at quarter past the hour, it was blocked by a transmission that Bellarts was sending at that moment.[56]

At 7:18 AM Bellarts sent her a voice message on 3105: "Cannot take bearing on 3105 very good. Please send on 500 or do you wish to take a bearing on us? Go ahead please." There was no reply. On the chance that Earhart would comply with his request that she send a signal on 500 kilocycles, Bellarts handed the special Earhart radio watch off to William Galten and went forward to the bridge to operate the ship's own direction finder.[57]

The flight was now approaching its nineteenth hour aloft, and the growing strength of the plane's radio transmissions through the early morning hours meant that it was drawing steadily closer to *Itasca* and the island airfield. James Kamakaiwi, the leader of Howland Island's colonists and the man for whom the airport was named, described the morning and the mood in the island's daily log: "The sky was partly cloudy, mostly with high scattered cumulus drifting slowly past. The *Itasca* kept in close to the lee of the island, sending out huge clouds of smoke to aid Miss Earhart in finding the island. Rescue party were stationed on the runways and out in boats, while the official greeters waited anxiously at the reception spot. All eyes gazed fondly, proudly, and eagerly over the horizons."[58] But for the radio operators, there was more frustration than fondness. As the sun and the temperature rose, so did their sense of foreboding.

On the bridge, Bellarts had the ship's direction finder working but heard nothing on 500 kilocycles. He told George Thompson to keep trying while he returned to the radio room to see if there had been any further word from Earhart. All five of the Coast Guard radiomen were now engaged in trying to establish contact with the plane. On the island, Frank Cipriani listened on 3105, hoping to be able to get a bearing with the high-frequency direction finder if and when Earhart transmitted again. On *Itasca*'s bridge, George Thompson manned the ship's direction finder and monitored 500 kilocycles in case she sent a signal on that frequency. In the radio room, William Galten sent both voice and code on 3105 when Thomas O'Hare was not sending *A*s on 7500 kilocycles. The receiver set to listen on 3105 was plugged into the loudspeaker so that everyone in the room could listen. All the while, Chief Radioman Bellarts stood by, directing the effort.

At 7:30, Galten asked Earhart, "Please reply to our signals on key, please," and listened in vain for a reply.[59]

From 7:35 to 7:40, O'Hare sent *A*s on 7500. Then the antenna was switched to Galten, who sent more *A*s on 3105. At about this time a third transmitter, this one with low-frequency capability and its own antenna, was fired up so that O'Hare could send code on 500 kilocycles at the same time Galten was transmitting on 3105. As Bellarts recalled, "We have everything blasting on her. And it appeared to us that she just didn't—wasn't even trying to hear us."[60]

And then, suddenly, Earhart was back on again, very strong now. None of the radio logs assigns a strength value to the transmission, but later reports have it at strength 5 ("very good, perfectly readable"). Bellarts described his reaction many years later: "I actually did go outside and stand right outside the radio shack and started listening like that—you know, thinking, well, I must hear a motor any second. Actually we had people out on deck. We thought she was going to be flying right down into our rigging the way—oh, man—she came in like a ton of bricks. I mean that."[61]

Galten's log records Earhart's message as "KHAQQ calling *Itasca*. We must be on you but cannot see you. But gas is running low. Been unable to reach you by radio. We are flying at 1000 feet."[62] The entry was logged at 7:42.

O'Hare logged: "Earhart on now. Says running out of gas. Only ½ hour left. Can't hear us at all." He then commented, "We hear her and are sending on 3105 and 500 same time constantly and listening for her frequently."[63] He had the time as 7:40.

This was real trouble. Earhart had apparently reached the place where she expected her destination to be but could see neither the island nor the ship. To the men of *Itasca*, it was equally apparent that no airplane was visible or audible in the sky above and around them. There was no escaping the fact that the plane could no longer be considered to be en route to Howland. Amelia Earhart was lost.

CHAPTER TEN

Probably Down
the last in-flight radio messages

T he radiomen now realized that Earhart had not heard their transmissions. She had not heard the weather sent in code, she had not heard the *A*s they were sending, and she had not heard any of the information they had given her by voice. As Bellarts later said: "And it appeared to us that she . . . wasn't even trying to hear us. . . . 'Gas is running low. Been unable to reach you by radio. We are flying at one thousand feet,' and bingo—she turns the thing off. Not saying nothing at all or go ahead, or this or that or the other thing. That's what made us, as operators, disgusted with her."[1]

She was down low, flying below the base of the clouds at one thousand feet. To Leo Bellarts, who had never flown, it did not make sense: "They were puffy clouds, you know. Just billow . . . and there was plenty of blue in between them. Plenty of blue."[2] Lieutenant Cooper could have explained to Bellarts that even widely scattered clouds, when seen from above, quickly merge to mask from view anything that is not directly below the airplane, but the Air Corps lieutenant was ashore preparing to meet the arriving flight.

Worst of all, Earhart was low on fuel—but how low? Galten heard her say that her gas was running low. O'Hare thought he heard her say she had only half an hour of gas left. Which version was correct?

Lieutenant Cooper later wrote in his official report that the Electra's fuel supply was "estimated to last 24 hours with a possibility of lasting 30 hours." He also noted that "a 20% gas reserve is usually required."[3] The pilot of an airplane with a total endurance of twenty-four hours should therefore consider the last five hours of fuel to be reserve. Earhart's radio call was made just over nineteen hours into the flight. She was in the middle of the ocean, she did not know where she was, and she was now burning into her fuel reserve. She might reasonably be expected to describe her situation as "gas is running low." If O'Hare's interpretation was correct, however, the situation was far more critical than that.

Years later, Bellarts's opinion of the discrepancy was unequivocal:

Well, don't go on O'Hare's log, because I say—I wasn't even aware that O'Hare was putting that stuff down. . . . No, I mean that. . . .

O'Hare shouldn't have been putting that down because it was not his responsibility. It was actually mine and Galten, you know. [Laughs] . . . That stinkin' O'Hare. . . . It's in error . . . it should never have been in O'Hare's log. He's just adding confusion to it and that's not correct. Possibly O'Hare might have had something in his little punkin' head that he might have, you know, thought he was going to make a bundle of jack on that or something.[4]

At the time, however, *Itasca*'s commanding officer knew only that he had two different, but not necessarily contradictory, reports of Earhart's fuel situation. He had little choice but to accept the more pessimistic version. Commander Thompson was not present in the radio room and did not personally hear the call. In his official report, he quoted both versions accurately, but after O'Hare's "running out of gas, only ½ hour left," he added the parenthetical comment "(unverified as heard by other witnesses)." Sometime later, the "un" in "unverified" was crossed out by hand.[5]

Galten immediately replied to Earhart's call: "KHAQQ from *Itasca*. Your message okay. Please reply with voice." Onshore, Cipriani heard Galten's transmissions, but his batteries were now so weak that he had not been able to hear Earhart's call, let alone take a bearing on her.[6]

At 7:58 Earhart was back, still at strength 5 and so loud that it was almost too much for the loudspeaker. Galten recorded her words as "KHAQQ calling *Itasca*. We are drifting but cannot hear you. Go ahead on 7500 with a long count either now or on the scheduled time on half hour."[7] O'Hare did not log that message; nor did Cipriani. To the men in the radio room, Earhart was once again not making any sense. What could she mean by "we are drifting"? And *Itasca* could not give her a long count on 7500 kilocycles. A long count was a voice transmission, slowly counting from one to ten and back down to one, but *Itasca* could not send voice on 7500. Earhart's original instructions were for the ship to send Morse code *A*s on 7500, and that is what they had been doing faithfully for the past twelve hours. And why would she ask for the signal "either now or on the scheduled time on half hour"? According to O'Hare's version of her previous message, she would be out of fuel before then.

Aboard the Electra, the time was 19:28 GCT. Earhart was asking *Itasca* to transmit on 7500 either now or two minutes from now. She had not heard the cutter's earlier transmissions on 7500 because her receiver was tuned to 3105 while she tried in vain to communicate with the ship and get the radiomen to take a bearing on her. And she almost certainly said, "We are listening but cannot hear you," not, "We are drifting but cannot hear you."

Galten himself was uncomfortable with "drifting." After thinking about it, and possibly discussing it with the others in the room, he decided that she must have said she was "circling." He went back and erased "drifting" and typed "circling" over the erasure. The remnants of the word "drifting" are still apparent on the original log, and the overtyped word "circling" is misaligned with the rest of the line. All future versions of the transmission—in the ship's deck log, in the "smoothed" version of Bellarts's radio log, and in the many official reports—accepted that Earhart said she was circling.

Although he could not send the long count Earhart requested, Galten immediately responded with a series of *A*s on 7500 kilocycles and, at 8:00 AM, was rewarded with a direct response from Earhart on 3105: "KHAQQ calling *Itasca*. We received your signals but unable to get a minimum. Please take bearing on us and answer 3105 with voice."[8] This was both good news and bad news. For the first time Earhart had heard *Itasca*'s signals, but she had not been able to take a bearing using her own direction finder. And which signals had she been receiving—the *A*s on 7500 or the calls on 3105?

Years later, Bellarts recalled his frustration. "She didn't . . . she didn't actually say 7500. . . . 'We received your signals.' But she didn't say where. . . . Well we was just nuts that she didn't tell us to go ahead on this or go ahead on that—we would have did what she wanted. Because she's the king."[9]

Earhart sent long dashes on 3105 kilocycles while Galten tried to call Cipriani to alert him to the transmission. But it was no good. Cipriani was trying to conserve his weak batteries and heard only the tail end of Earhart's transmission.[10]

Bellarts instructed O'Hare to do nothing but concentrate on sending *A*s on 7500 whenever Galten was not using the antenna to call her on 3105. Meanwhile, Galten tried again to explain the problem to Amelia: "KHAQQ from *Itasca*. Your signals received okay. We are unable to hear you to take a bearing. It impractical to take a bearing on 3105 your voice. How do you get that? Go ahead."[11] The loudspeaker crackled with static, but there was no reply from Earhart. The antenna was switched over and O'Hare banged out a steady stream of *A*s on 7500.

At 8:11, Galten tried again: "KHAQQ from *Itasca*. Did you get that on 7.5 megacycles? Go ahead on 500 kilocycles so that we may be able to take a bearing on you. Impossible to take a bearing on 3105. Please acknowledge this transmission with voice on 3105. Go ahead."[12] Nothing. Four minutes later, Galten again blocked any quarter-past-the-hour call from Earhart on 3105 with his own transmission on the same frequency: "KHAQQ from *Itasca*. Do you hear my signals on 7500 kilocycles or 3105 kilocycles? Please acknowledge with receipt on 3105 with voice. Go ahead."[13] There was no reply.

The temperature in the radio room climbed with the tropical sun, the heat generated by the constant use of the massive transmitters, and the tension of each passing minute. As Bellarts remembered, "Believe me, we was trying everything we knew. . . . We tried stuff that actually is not in the log. . . . Really, I mean it. We was frantic."[14]

The men on shore knew the plane was overdue. As Richard Black wrote in his report, "After eight o'clock uneasiness was felt by the party ashore, but all stood by searching the sky in all directions."[15]

Aboard *Itasca*, the clock approached and then passed O'Hare's "½ hour left" deadline. The cutter's commanding officer decided the game was up. On the island, Black and the others received "a blinker message . . . from the ship stating that the plane was probably down at sea and recalling all hands to the ship as soon as possible. The parties were summoned from their stations and all ran at top speed for the beach where ferrying to the ship started at once."[16]

The word reached Frank Cipriani at 8:26 AM. "Received information that *Itasca* believe Earhart down. Landing party recalled back to vessel."[17] Cipriani remained ashore with the colonists to keep operating the high-frequency direction finder.*

The senior colonist, James Kamakaiwi, described the moment in a press release he wrote later that day:

> We were waiting near the west end of the east west runway about half mile from the government house. 8:30 and the minutes dragged. Then word wigwagged from *Itasca*, Amelia's signals on direction finder showed she was northwest of the island. Had she overshot? To the northwest was a big bank of clouds. What a grand background that would make. Why doesn't she come? The wigwag man was flashing to us. From the government house the receiver shouted to us "Amelia believed down. All shore parties return to ship." My heart stopped beating. It didn't seem real. Men were running to the house.
>
> Boats put off from *Itasca*. No one was laughing. Orders were passed sharply and, before we realized it, the loaded boats were back at the *Itasca*. Eight of us colonists were left behind. We were alone again on the island. The noise of the birds seemed louder.[18]

In the ship's radio room, Galten continued his efforts to reach Amelia. At 8:27 he sent another voice message, this time calling her by name: "*Itasca* to Earhart. We [are] transmitting constantly on 7.5 megacycles. Do you hear us? Kindly confirm receipt on 3105. We are standing by."[19]

---

*The report Black wrote and the cruise report Commander Thompson filed both have the shore party being recalled to the ship after the receipt of a subsequent transmission from Earhart at 8:43 AM. Cipriani's log entry, however, leaves no doubt that the recall order was issued earlier.

No answer.

For the next fifteen minutes both operators repeatedly tried to contact the plane, but each time, the only reply was the empty hiss and pop of static on the loudspeaker. At 8:44, Galten entered in his log that he was listening on 3105 but heard "nil." He also noted that the chief radioman was tuning up for a transmission to San Francisco Division. It was time to let headquarters know about the crisis. Galten tried to raise Division, but there was no answer.[20]

At some point during this period Earhart's voice suddenly burst from the speaker, as Bellarts recalled, "so loud she couldn't hardly get any louder."[21] Galten typed her words as: "KHAQQ to *Itasca*. We are on the line 157 337. We will repeat message. We will repeat this on 6210 kilocycles. Wait."[22] He added the notation that the transmission had been heard on 3105 kilocycles in voice at strength 5.

Galten logged the time the message was received as 8:43. However, the actual time Galten typed the "We are on the line . . ." entry had to have been later than 8:43 because he had already made entries for 8:44 and 8:45. To keep the log sequential, Galten went back and crossed out the 8:44 time notation, changing it to 8:42. He also crossed out 8:45 and made it 8:43. This break in the log's chronology raises the question of who actually heard the transmission and when it was really received.

It seems clear that Galten himself missed the message, because it was logged out of sequence. His original 8:44 entry says that he listened for Earhart on 3105 but heard "nil," so the message evidently came in after that time. The log also indicates that at 8:45 Galten was trying unsuccessfully to contact San Francisco. To do that, he had to put on his earphones and concentrate on listening for a reply through the static. Earhart probably transmitted right on schedule at 8:45 (quarter past the hour for her). Galten missed it, but Bellarts and anyone else in the radio room not wearing earphones heard it loud and clear over the speaker. It is easy to imagine an exchange that might have gone something like this:

Bellarts: Bill, did you get that?
Galten [removing his earphones]: Get what?
Bellarts: Earhart! She was just on again!
Galten: When?
Bellarts: Couple of minutes ago. I thought you heard it.
Galten: I was trying to raise Division. What'd she say?
Bellarts: Something about running on the line north and south.

Neither O'Hare's nor Cipriani's log records the transmission.

After Galten entered Earhart's message and typed the time as "43," he probably began tuning a receiver to 6210 kilocycles and listening for the repeated message. Again, this would involve using the earphones. But then Earhart's voice again came over the loudspeaker, still on 3105, with additional information. Galten seems to have missed her again and gotten the quote from someone who heard it over the speaker.

The log is a mess, but it appears that Earhart made a transmission at her regularly scheduled time. Those who heard the message understood her to say, "KHAQQ to *Itasca*. We are on the line 157 337. We will repeat message. We will repeat this on 6210 kilocycles. Wait." A minute or so later she added, "We are running on line north and south."

Later, the men who heard the transmission discussed the quality of Earhart's voice. Commander Thompson heard this call himself and, in his official report, described her message as "hurried, frantic, and apparently not complete." Lt. Cdr. Frank Kenner was also present. In a letter he wrote to his wife a few weeks later he said, "I heard her last broadcasts myself. She realized too late that she was in trouble, then she went to pieces, her voice clearly indicated that fact, by the desperate note in her transmissions."[23]

The anxiety in Earhart's voice was still fresh in Leo Bellarts's memory many years later: "I'm telling you, it sounded as if she would have broken out in a scream, it would have sounded normal. She was just about ready to break into tears and go into hysterics. That's exactly the way I'd describe her voice, now. I'll never forget it."[24]

The sun was well up, and Earhart had said she was switching to her daylight frequency of 6210 kilocycles. Galten listened but heard nothing. The *A*s broadcast on 7500 kilocycles were the only signals from *Itasca* that Earhart seemed to have heard, so he tried repeatedly to contact her in code on that frequency: "Heard you OK on 3105 kilocycles. Please stay on 3105 kilocycles. Do not hear you on 6210. Maintain sending on 3105. Your signals OK on 3105. Go ahead with position on 3105 or 500 kilocycles.[25]

Nothing.

By 9:15 AM, the shore party was back aboard and the boats hoisted.[26] *Itasca* was ready to begin searching for the lost plane, but the situation had changed. Earhart's most recent radio call meant that the airplane was not out of gas, even though her supposed fuel deadline had expired. She was transmitting on schedule, and she was talking about navigating, not landing in the water. Amelia was clearly worried and upset, but she was just as obviously still in the air and trying to find the island.

Her statement that she was "on the line 157 337" was presumed to be a reference to a line of position—a navigational line heading south-southeast (157 degrees) in one direction and north-northwest (337 degrees) in the other—but the line was meaningless without a reference point. She probably meant she was on a line of position that passed through Howland. "Running on line north and south" would make sense as a means of locating the island given the failure of radio direction finding.

Commander Thompson decided to sit tight. The plane was supposed to have at least twenty-four hours of endurance—enough gas to stay aloft until noon. *Itasca* would maintain its vigil at Howland until then. The Electra might appear overhead any minute. The radio room might at last be able to establish communication with the plane, and there was still a chance that Cipriani might be able to get a bearing with the high-frequency direction finder. If the plane had to land at sea, they would at least know in what direction to start searching.

With the shore party back aboard ship, the clouds of birds reclaimed their island. On the cutter's deck, every eye scanned the horizon for any speck or glint that might not be a booby or a frigate bird. Every ear strained through the squawking din to hear the rumble of distant engines. In the sweltering radio room, shirtless operators pounded out pleas in Morse code and listened in vain for a reply.

At 9:35, O'Hare called Cipriani on Howland and told him to "get the direction finder going at all cost." But it was no good. Half an hour earlier, Cipriani had logged: "All batteries on the island are discharged. Commenced to charge them." He did not hear O'Hare's directive and could not have done anything about it if he did.[27]

Earhart's scheduled broadcast time of fifteen minutes before the hour came and went, marking a full hour since her last anguished transmission. Ten o'clock, and another futile call to Cipriani on Howland to "get the D/F going at any cost."[28]

Three and a half hours had passed since *Itasca* cut off communication with the outside world to concentrate on Earhart. It was time to advise headquarters of the situation. At 10:15 AM, the word went out: "Earhart contact 07:42 reported one half hour fuel and no landfall, position doubtful. Contact 06:46 reported approximately one hundred miles from *Itasca* but no relative bearing. 08:43 reported line of position 157–337 but no reference point; presume Howland. Estimate 12:00 for maximum time aloft and if non-arrival by that time will commence search northwest quadrant from Howland as most probable area. Sea smooth, visibility nine, ceiling unlimited. Understand she will float for limited time."[29]

Anticipating the worst, Commander Thompson also sent a request to the Hawaiian Section that they contact the navy for a "seaplane search," noting that there was plenty of aviation fuel and oil available on Howland.[30] Then, having just advised his superiors that *Itasca* would remain at Howland until noon, Warner Thompson changed his mind and decided to leave. *Itasca* would abandon its plane guard station and initiate a search before the aircraft's estimated maximum time aloft had expired. At 10:40 AM, having "definitely assumed that the plane was down,"[31] Commander Thompson gave the order for *Itasca* to get under way "at full speed" to begin searching "the area which at that time seemed most logical."[32]

It is difficult to fault Commander Thompson's decision. In dealing with the question of whether Earhart said "gas is running low" or "only one-half hour left," he had prudently acted on the more pessimistic possibility, recalling the shore party and beginning preparations for a search as soon as the half-hour deadline expired. When a subsequent transmission from Earhart had made it apparent that the plane was still in the air, the captain had amended his plan and kept the ship on station at Howland.

Two anxious hours had passed with no further word from the plane. *Itasca*'s presence was not required for the Electra to make a safe landing on the island should the flight make a belated arrival over Howland. On the other hand, if Earhart was already down, she was in urgent need of assistance, and minutes could mean the difference between life and death. Under the circumstances, Thompson's order to begin the search seems justified.

As the ship got under way, the officers and men tried to make sense of the confusing and frustrating events of the morning. Frank Kenner later described the consensus that prevailed:

We all admired her nerve and pluck to attempt such a flight, but we cannot admire her good sense and judgment in her conduct of it. She was too sure of herself and too casual. She devoted no effort to the details at all. When it was too late and she was going down, she hollered for our aid but that was too late. We did all we could. She never gave us any of her positions as we repeatedly requested her to do, she never answered or acknowledged any of our messages. She gave us no information as to her plans, what plans she had for communication she changed in the middle of the flight. All in all, it was a mess.[33]

It was, indeed, a mess, but rather a different mess from the one Kenner and his shipmates perceived. Their frustration with Earhart's fragmented preflight coordination with the Coast Guard was understandable, but it is also apparent that *Itasca* failed to keep track of all the fragments. During the flight, the airplane and the ship were following different communication protocols. Although Earhart was adhering to her announced plan, those on *Itasca* had the impression that she was changing her mind.

In his official report, Commander Thompson complained that "Earhart asked *Itasca* to take bearings on her. This was never planned."[34] The statement is true, but it is also true that Earhart was never informed that a high-frequency direction finder had been installed on Howland.

Thompson also noted that "the signals that Earhart acknowledged were transmitted on 7500 [kilocycles]. Her direction finder loop could not handle this frequency."[35] The criticism is legitimate, but the conflict between the described frequency limitations of Earhart's direction finder and her obvious intention to try to find Howland by homing in on high-frequency signals was apparent from her earliest telegrams. In none of the many preflight coordination exchanges with Earhart did either Richard Black or Commander Thompson question her obviously unworkable plan.

The perception aboard *Itasca* that Earhart was acting irrationally colored the way events were interpreted. Amelia's failure to reply to radio calls was attributed to arrogance. Only later did Commander Thompson acknowledge that "Earhart probably had receiver trouble."[36] The impression that Amelia was thoroughly incompetent also made it easier to assume she had grossly mismanaged her fuel. With more information about the aircraft, the radios, and the events leading up to the flight's failure to arrive at Howland, the actual causes of the tragedy are apparent. As in most aviation accidents, the loss was not due to a single catastrophic event, but rather to the snowballing of a number of mishaps and errors.

The problems began with Earhart's poor preflight preparation and *Itasca*'s failure to alert her to obvious flaws in her plan for finding the island. Even so, these difficulties could have been sorted out had there been good in-flight communication between the plane and the cutter. Fred Noonan had brought the flight to within radio range of its goal, but Earhart and *Itasca* never established two-way communication. Contrary to Commander Thompson's perception, it was not receiver trouble. It was antenna trouble.

The Electra had three radio antennas. A wire running in a V from a mast mounted just behind the cockpit to each of the airplane's two vertical tail fins was dedicated to transmitting. The primary antenna used for receiving voice communications was a wire that ran along the belly of the aircraft, supported by short masts, from the nose to just forward of the cabin door. There was also a second receiving antenna, a circular "loop" over the cockpit that could be manually rotated for direction finding. A switch in the cockpit selected which receiving antenna was in use.

In motion picture film taken during Earhart's departure from Lae, the belly wire antenna is visible as the aircraft taxies out for takeoff. The film also shows that the airplane's heavy load placed the end of the antenna's aftmost supporting mast perilously close to the turf runway. Later, as the Electra comes back past the camera on its takeoff run, both motion picture and still photography show that the belly antenna is now missing.[37] Apparently, at some point while taxiing on the airport's uneven surface, the antenna mast struck the ground, breaking the shaft which was then dragged along the ground by the antenna wire. A puff of dust that erupts

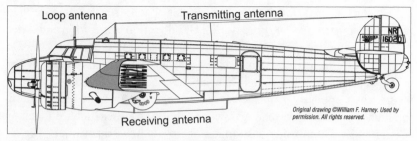

Loop antenna   Transmitting antenna

NR 16020

Receiving antenna

The receiving antenna on the underside of Earhart's Electra was lost during the takeoff from Lae, New Guinea.

under the aircraft during the takeoff may have been the dragged mast catching in the dirt and tearing loose the rest of the antenna. The lightness of the antenna structures in comparison to the great mass of the overloaded airplane meant that Earhart and Noonan, in the cockpit, did not feel the mishap. Stories told years later mentioned a length of antenna wire found on the runway at Lae sometime after Earhart's takeoff.

The loss of the belly antenna explains Earhart's inability to receive radio transmissions during the flight. The one time she was successful in hearing *Itasca* was when she decided to try to use her own direction finder. Asking *Itasca* to transmit on 7500 kilocycles, she dialed in that frequency on her receiver and switched to the loop antenna. She heard the Morse code *A*s, but the frequency was far higher than the loop's 1500 kilocycle upper limit. Unable to take a bearing on the signal, she switched back to the (missing) belly antenna, dialed the receiver back to 3105, and again tried to communicate with the cutter using voice—and again heard only static.[38]

The solution to Earhart's crisis was literally at her fingertips. Although her direction finder could not take a bearing on the high-frequency signal, the loop was clearly working as a receiving antenna because she was able to hear *Itasca*'s *A*s in her earphones. To hear *Itasca*'s voice transmissions on 3105, all she had to do was leave the antenna switch in the loop position. With the ability to have a conversation with the cutter, it should have been possible to sort out the direction-finding confusion so that either the plane or the ship could take a bearing and bring the flight to a happy landing at Howland.

Despite the loss of the belly antenna, the aircraft had sufficient fuel, communication, and navigational capability to safely reach its destination. Its failure to do so was the direct result of the crew's inability to diagnose and work around a relatively simple in-flight communications problem.

No one aboard *Itasca* had enough information to understand the problem; nor could they have done anything about it if they did. All that mattered was that Earhart was overdue and probably down. Ashore on Howland, James

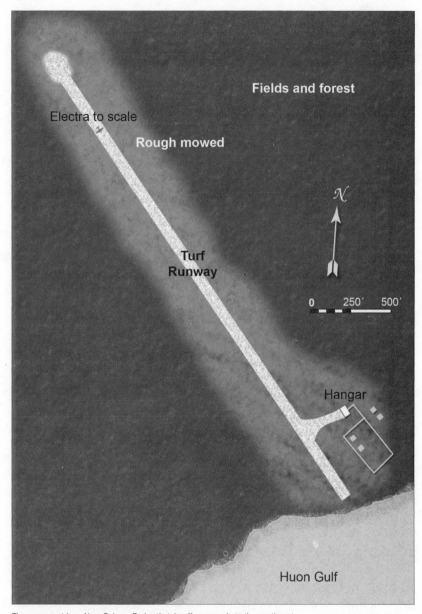

The runway at Lae, New Guinea. Earhart's takeoff was made to the southeast.

Kamakaiwi was distraught. "I couldn't make myself believe Amelia had missed us. We kept watching the sky. [T]he *Itasca* started out to sea towards the northwest. Soon she was disappearing over the horizon. I hope with all my heart they find her."[39]

CHAPTER ELEVEN

The Search Begins
the first day

A shudder ran through *Itasca* as the engine came to maximum revolutions, and within minutes the blue Pacific was hissing along the ship's sides. As the cutter steamed away from Howland, each passing minute of silence from the radio room seemed to validate the decision to begin a search. Exactly where Commander Thompson intended to look was still evolving. His initial message to headquarters indicated that he considered "the northwest quadrant" of a circle centered on Howland to be the most logical search area, but he offered no explanation of his reasoning at that time.

In the United States, the news that Earhart had not arrived at Howland and might be down at sea arrived like a thunderclap. It was 1:45 PM in San Francisco when Division received *Itasca*'s message and immediately forwarded the word to all commands and agencies involved in supporting Earhart's flight. Major media outlets began to scramble for access, and the Coast Guard was quick to recognize the public relations benefits of a high-profile rescue. Within an hour and a half of receiving *Itasca*'s message, the commandant's office in Washington was advising San Francisco Division that "if plane is located, headquarters has no objection to commanding officer *Itasca* broadcasting for National Broadcasting Company or other broadcasting company if requested after official report is made by radio to headquarters. Don Thompson of National Broadcasting Company will contact you."[1]

San Francisco Division and the Hawaiian Section were more concerned about whether there was going to be a rescue than about which broadcasting network was going to cover it. Two hours after *Itasca*'s first alert, they had still not received an update on the situation. No news was bad news. If the plane had not arrived by now, it was almost certainly out of gas. Another three-quarters of an hour passed, and still nothing more from the cutter. The Hawaiian Section finally sent *Itasca* a direct order: "Advise by dispatch full details concerning Earhart plane such as position reports, bearings, and all information Earhart flight that will be of value to naval search if plane dispatched from here. Recommend you broadcast data to all ships to be on lookout."[2]

In Oakland, George Putnam assumed the plane was down and sent a telegram to Adm. William Leahy, the chief of naval operations, in Washington:

"Technicians familiar with Miss Earhart's plane believe, with its large tanks, can float almost indefinitely. With retractable gear and smooth sea, safe landing should have been practicable. Respectfully request such assistance as is practicable from naval air craft and surface craft stationed Honolulu. Apparently plane's position not far from Howland."[3] Putnam need not have bothered. Leahy had already sent a wire to Hawaii addressed to the commandant of the Fourteenth Naval District, Rear Adm. Orin G. Murfin: "Use available naval facilities to conduct such search for Miss Earhart as, in your opinion, is practicable."[4]

An hour and quarter after the expiration of the noon fuel deadline, and three hours after Commander Thompson first reported Earhart's "non-arrival" at Howland, the Coast Guard's San Francisco Division received a terse message from *Itasca*: "Earhart unreported Howland at 12:00. Believe down shortly after 09:15 AM. Searching probable area and will continue."[5]

Amelia Earhart was officially missing and presumed down. Thompson now believed the plane had been in the water for four hours, but, again, he did not explain his reasoning. He seems to have taken the "½ hour gas left" version of the 7:42 message and applied it to the 8:43 "We are on the line . . ." message to arrive at his estimate that the plane had landed in the ocean shortly after 9:15.

A few minutes later, Thompson followed the recommendation from headquarters and broadcast an alert to "all ships, all stations": "Amelia Earhart plane en route Howland Island from Lae, New Guinea unreported since 20:45 GCT July 2 and apparently down at sea, position unknown. *Itasca* searching probable northwest sector off Howland Island. Request ships and stations listen on 500 kcs for any signals from plane. Commanding officer, U.S. Coast Guard cutter *Itasca*."[6]

From the very beginning of the search, Thompson recognized that the plane might send distress calls after it was down, but his "all ships" alert mentioned only one of the three wavelengths Earhart might use. Five hundred kilocycles was the international nautical distress frequency monitored by all ships at sea. All of Earhart's in-flight calls heard by *Itasca* had been on 3105 kilocycles, however, and when last heard from, she had said she was switching to 6210 kilocycles. *Itasca*'s "all ships" alert mentioned neither frequency.*

As *Itasca* steamed into the northwest quadrant, scouring the ocean for any sign of the downed plane, Commander Thompson and the other officers

*The "all ships" broadcast unwittingly set a trap for anyone who might send a hoax distress call. Earhart's decision not to reinstall the Electra's long trailing wire antenna after the accident in Hawaii meant the plane had virtually no capability to transmit on 500 kilocycles. Any alleged signal from Earhart on 500 kilocycles would be, by definition, bogus. Although virtually every ship on the ocean had the ability to send and receive on 500 kilocycles, throughout the entire search, no one claimed to hear Earhart on that frequency.

were still trying to figure out what had happened. Headquarters wanted "full details," but that was the problem: they did not have any details.[7] What they did know was that the world's most famous woman aviator had gone missing on *Itasca*'s watch. In their view, they had done everything they were supposed to do, and more, but her refusal to cooperate had defeated their best efforts. Now she was down at sea and, if not already drowned, might soon be. *Itasca* was the only means of rescue within hundreds of miles. The focus now had to be on figuring out where the plane had come down and getting there as quickly as possible.

At 2:00 PM, Thompson tried to explain in a message to San Francisco: "We have had no positions, speed, or courses from Earhart's plane except so called line of position at 0843 which had no reference point. She gave us none of her bearings. Believe she passed to north and west of island about 0800 and missed it in the glare of rising sun though we were smoking heavily at that time. Judge she came down between 337° and 90° from Howland and within 100 miles. Have broadcast as indicated."[8]

Thompson's catalog of Earhart's shortcomings was somewhat disingenuous. The "so called line of position" was so called by *Itasca*, not Earhart; and Thompson's statement that "she gave us none of her bearings" implied that she had bearings to give, when, in fact, Amelia had made it quite clear that she was unable to use her homing device.

Commander Thompson now believed that Earhart "passed to the north and west" of Howland at about 8:00 and continued to fly for another hour and a quarter before running out of fuel shortly after 9:15 "between 337° and 90° from Howland." He offered no rationale for his opinion that the plane had come down within one hundred miles of Howland. Just before two o'clock in the afternoon, having run northwestward from Howland for three hours, the captain ordered a cut back to the east.[9]

It was midafternoon in Honolulu when the Pan American Airways office received word that Earhart was down. At 3:30 PM, the company's radio direction-finding station at nearby Mokapu Point began a constant radio watch on 3105 kilocycles and 6210 kilocycles.[10] The airline's capabilities were formidable. Pan Am had been offering scheduled passenger service across the northern Pacific for nearly a year using radio direction-finding facilities erected at Mokapu, Midway, and Wake Island to guide its flying boats across vast reaches of open ocean. Until recently, Fred Noonan had been one of their own. The Pan Am radio operators listened intently for any possible signal from the lost plane, but, like their counterparts aboard *Itasca*, they heard nothing but static.

Shortly after Pan Am began listening, another "all ships" alert went out, this time from the U.S. Navy Hydrographic Office radio station in San Francisco: "All ships, all stations. US Coast Guard ship *Itasca* believes

Miss Amelia Earhart down between 337 and 90 degrees from Howland Island and within one hundred miles of island. Possibility plane may use radio on either 3105, 6210, or 500 kcs voice. Request any vessel that vicinity listen for calls and contact *Itasca*. Call NRUI [*Itasca*'s call sign] on 500 kcs."[11] This was the first request for all stations to listen on 3105 and 6210 kilocycles.

Later that afternoon, Commander Thompson received a message from San Francisco Division: "Possibility plane may attempt use of radio on water as radio supply was battery and antenna could be used on top of wing. Putnam and Lockheed state possibility of floating considerable time excellent and that emergency rubber boat and plenty of emergency rations carried on plane."[12] The message appeared to provide important new information. In fact, it was nothing more than wishful thinking. Technicians familiar with Earhart's Electra would later confirm that the plane could not send radio transmissions if it was afloat on the ocean. The news about a rubber boat and rations was speculation. No one in the United States, including Putnam, could possibly have known what emergency gear was aboard the aircraft on the Lae–Howland flight.

About an hour after San Francisco advised that the plane "may attempt use of radio on water," *Itasca* came back with: "Request frequencies Earhart emergency transmitter." Nobody had said anything about an emergency transmitter, but San Francisco replied: "Same as main transmitter. Possibility plane may be able receive *Itasca* 3105 voice." The message compounded *Itasca*'s misimpressions by seeming to confirm the presence of an emergency radio.[13]

The anxious afternoon wore on. *Itasca*'s deck rose and fell as the cutter rode the peaks and troughs of a heavy swell from the east, while every available pair of eyes scanned the ocean for some sign of a floating airplane or life raft. Visibility was unlimited; overhead, a few scattered clouds drifted on a light easterly breeze.[14] In the radio room, the operators kept a constant watch on 3105 but heard only the steady crash of static.

In Hawaii, Admiral Murfin was marshaling what few search resources he had. In 1937, Pearl Harbor was not yet the home of the Pacific Fleet. At Fleet Air Base, however, Patrol Squadron Six (VP-6) was equipped with the new long-range PBY-1. In theory, one of these aircraft could make the sixteen-hundred-mile flight from Honolulu to Howland by flying all night and, on arrival in the morning, still have enough fuel to conduct aerial search operations all day. In the evening, the plane could land and refuel using the gasoline originally intended for Earhart. But such a flight would involve significant risks.

First, the navy air crew would need to find Howland Island at the end of a very long overwater flight. In other words, they would have to do what Earhart and Noonan had just failed to do. If they did succeed in locating the island, they could not use the airfield. The PBY-1 was a flying boat; it would have to land offshore and refuel alongside *Itasca*. But flying boats were designed to land and take off in the protected waters of harbors and lagoons. Open-ocean operations in less than ideal sea conditions were extremely hazardous.

The aircraft commander, VP-6 squadron leader Lt. Warren Harvey, later described the situation in a letter to his mother:

> The flight never had much chance of success because of the distance involved, the total lack of facilities in that area, and total lack of information as to where to look. My prospects of cracking up were about 10 to 1 after searching for a little over 10 hours. I would have had to land down there by sundown in the open sea which had heavy swells with numerous white caps showing. There is no anchorage available either for a plane or a ship so the *Itasca* would have tried to take me in tow for several days until our small tender [USS *Swan*] could arrive to hoist me on board. Even the tender would have broken the plane's hull because the plane was bigger than the available space.[15]

Admiral Murfin ordered the mission to proceed, but he was careful to hedge his bet. As Lieutenant Harvey later told his mother: "[M]y orders on leaving here were not to hesitate to return if any adverse conditions were encountered."[16]

Sending the PBY was a gallant gesture, but what Murfin really needed was some way to put reliable aerial search capability on the scene for an extended period. What he needed was, at that moment, moored to Pier 2 in Honolulu. Just a day before, the battleship USS *Colorado* (BB-45) had put in to port. On its decks were three catapult-launched Vought O3U-3 "Corsair" floatplanes used for reconnaissance and spotting for the ship's eight 16-inch guns. Murfin sent a wire to the chief of naval operations in Washington: "*Colorado* at present in Honolulu [on] ROTC cruise. If she can be made available for dispatch to Howland Island, her planes would be of great value."[17]

The battleship was at the midpoint of a month-long training cruise for the Naval Reserve Officers Training Corps (NROTC) and was host to 185 college students and four "distinguished guests of the navy"—two university presidents, a dean, and a professor.[18] As later described by one of the students: "The West Coast NROTC summer cruises in the mid-1930s were gala events. Freshmen and sophomores from the Universities of California and Washington would board a battleship on a four-week excursion to the Hawaiian Islands, including a week of liberty in Hilo and Honolulu."[19]

Colorado was scheduled to remain in port for five days over the Fourth of July holiday. On the afternoon of July 2, as Murfin was asking Washington for permission to hijack their ship, the students, "dressed in [their] best white trousers and blue coats," were attending a tea dance in their honor at the Roof Garden of the Alexander Young Hotel. One of these young men later recalled the event:

> This affair exceeded our wildest expectations. All of Oahu's best-looking young women were there, each wearing two leis—one for herself and one for some lucky (or skillful) NROTC student. Each of us met someone lovely, danced all afternoon, and drank and dined into the evening. All of us made important plans for the following days: We each dreamed of being entertained by a lovely lady who was friendly and charming, had unlimited permission to charge her father's account at the Outrigger Canoe Club bar, and had a Buick convertible.[20]

The mood at Fleet Air Base was less festive as Patrol Plane 6-P-3 with four officers, four enlisted men, and a full fuel load taxied out onto the dark waters of Pearl Harbor. Shortly after 7:00 PM, Lieutenant Harvey pushed the throttles forward. The prop blast from the flying boat's engines sent back a cloud of spray as the PBY began its takeoff run. At first there was more noise than progress, but soon the waves were rattling against the hull as the aircraft raced across the water and lifted ponderously into the air to begin a slow climb to the southwest.

A few minutes later at Fourteenth District headquarters, Admiral Murfin received a short message from Washington: "*Colorado* is made available." Available, but hardly ready. The battleship was in need of refueling, and its three airplanes were in pieces on the hangar floor at Fleet Air Base. One of the pilots, Lt. (j.g.) William Short, described the situation in a letter to his father: "On the way in to Honolulu they sent us off and we went in to the air base at Pearl Harbor while the ship docked at Honolulu. That was last Thursday, the 1st [of July]. Friday morning, we 'turned to' on the planes as the primary object of sending us in to Pearl Harbor was to get some overhaul work done. We managed to get things pretty well torn apart Friday morning and the carburetors and such up to the shops—figuring on getting them back in shape for flying Monday."[21]

Short was the only member of the ship's aviation section present at the air base that evening when word arrived that *Colorado* might be designated to search for the missing Electra. "That kind of put me on the spot as you can well imagine—with the planes all out of commission and everybody scattered all over the place on liberty."[22]

As Short scrambled to round up *Colorado*'s aviation section and reassemble its airplanes, the battleship's commanding officer, Capt. Wilhelm

L. Friedell, tried to come to grips with his new mission. Admiral Murfin had ordered *Colorado* to get under way "as soon as possible with planes to conduct search for Amelia Earhart," but the all-important question of where to search was left to the captain's discretion. To help evaluate the scant information available, Friedell "conferred with the Commanding Officer, Fleet Air Base, Captain Kenneth Whiting, U.S. Navy, and other officers of the District and Air Base relative to the probable path and location of the Earhart Plane in the event of a forced landing."[23]

It is not surprising that Friedell sought the advice of the Fleet Air Base commander. Kenneth Whiting, Naval Aviator no. 16, had been taught to fly by Orville Wright in 1914. In 1918, he commanded the 1st Naval Air Unit in France, and after the war he became a major figure in the development of naval aviation. Ken Whiting was also acquainted with the subject of Friedell's search. Amelia Earhart had been Whiting's house guest for several days in 1930 after her Lockheed Vega flipped over on landing at the naval air station in Norfolk, Virginia. As the air station's commanding officer, Whiting had offered the hospitality of his home while Amelia recovered from a scalp laceration. Their paths crossed again in March 1937. Whiting by that time was commanding Fleet Air Base, Pearl Harbor. He was at Luke Field when Earhart's Electra crashed on takeoff.

In considering where *Colorado* should conduct its search, the officers had very little to go on. According to the information received thus far from *Itasca*, Earhart had said she was on a 157–337 degree line of position that presumably passed through Howland Island. If she was, in fact, on such a line, she was obviously either too far to the northwest or too far to the southeast to see the island. *Itasca*'s Commander Thompson had said that he believed the plane was "down between 337 and 90 degrees from Howland Island and within one hundred miles."[24]

Friedell, Whiting, and the other officers (almost certainly including meteorologist Lt. Arnold True) reached a different conclusion. They decided that the available information "seemed to indicate that the most probable reason for missing Howland Island would be that of stronger winds than normally expected in the region, and that the plane had probably been carried southeast of Howland, a greater distance than that from which Howland could be sighted."[25] Captain Friedell decided that *Colorado* would search for Earhart to the southeast of her intended destination.

By later that evening the three floatplanes had been reassembled and were "more or less ready," but the battleship still had to be moved from Honolulu to Pearl Harbor for fueling.[26] The NROTC students returning to the ship were in for a shock: "Once we arrived on the quarterdeck, we received the news that Amelia Earhart had managed to get herself lost somewhere in the vast Pacific while making a publicity-seeking round-the-world flight

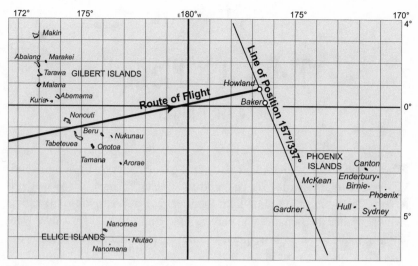

Earhart's planned route to Howland Island and the 157–337 degree line of position.

and that the *Colorado* was going to search for her. All Honolulu liberty was cancelled, and we were to get under way early in the morning. As more and more distraught NROTC students arrived back in the casemates and began to realize the enormity of this turn of events, silent thoughts turned to mutiny."[27]

CHAPTER TWELVE

"Think It Is Plane?"
the first night

F ar to the south, evening had also come to the men on Howland Island, the crew of the cutter *Itasca*—and to Amelia Earhart, if she was still alive. Although the fading light hampered visual searching, the radiomen knew that their chances of picking up signals from the lost flyer were better at night when high-frequency radio waves were not inhibited by the sun's effect on the upper atmosphere.

In *Itasca*'s radio room, Leo Bellarts was manning the special Earhart watch and listening intently, but there had been nothing but the everpresent static since Earhart's "We are on the line . . ." transmission that morning. At 5:30 PM, Bellarts, tired and hungry, turned the position over to George Thompson and went to get some dinner. Thompson settled into the routine, tuning constantly on Earhart's frequency but hearing only the usual scratch and hiss. Just on the hour of six o'clock, behind the static, there was a voice.[1] The signal was very weak and he could not make out any of the words.

Thompson immediately sent a voice transmission: "KHAQQ, KHAQQ from *Itasca*. You are very weak. Repeat on 3105. Please go ahead." He repeated the message in code followed by a string of *A*s. Immediately afterward, William Galten, at the other radio position, set his transmitter to 7500 kilocycles and tapped out "KHAQQ this is NRUI. Go ahead on 3105 again please if you are on."[2]

Neither operator heard anything in reply, but this was still a very exciting development. Fresh ears quickly manned the radio positions as Chief Bellarts took over from Thompson and Thomas O'Hare replaced Galten. At seven minutes past the hour, Bellarts sent a Morse code message asking Earhart to send "again please on 3105."[3] No reply. Five minutes later, he sent a voice message and tried something new: "KHAQQ, KHAQQ from *Itasca*. Please give long dashes if you hear us. Go ahead."[4] Still no answer.

Just as the sun sank below the horizon, the voice was back. Bellarts missed the call because at that moment he was sending a general broadcast asking all ships to contact *Itasca* if they had any information, but O'Hare heard and logged it: "We hear her on 3105 kcs now. Very weak and unreadable voice."[5]

The operators on Howland heard nothing because they were off the air, still recharging batteries, but at the same moment O'Hare heard what he believed was a call from Earhart, the Pan American Airways station in Hawaii heard "steady carrier on 3105—no modulation, very weak."[6]

Pan Am Mokapu had been listening steadily for signals from the missing plane since midafternoon but, like *Itasca*, had heard nothing until evening brought improved reception conditions. When O'Hare was hearing an unintelligible voice transmission, Mokapu heard a minimal signal with only the basic "carrier" getting through. If the two stations were hearing the same signal, the sender was located closer to *Itasca* than to Hawaii. Although some ships and shore stations could communicate by Morse code on 3105 kilocycles, only U.S.-registered civilian aircraft—and by special arrangement *Itasca*—were authorized to send voice transmissions on that frequency. If *Itasca* was hearing an aircraft in Hawaii, Mokapu should have heard it loud and clear.

A ship or a shore station somewhere in the Central Pacific could have been transmitting voice illegally on 3105 either in a sincere effort to contact Earhart or in an attempt to perpetrate a hoax. The other possibility is that the signal was coming from the Electra. If so, the plane was on land in one of the island groups of the Central Pacific region.

At 6:30, Bellarts tried again to get Earhart to send dashes. O'Hare logged the request as: "Phone very bad. If you hear us please give us a series of long dashes. Go ahead please."[7]

A thousand miles to the southeast of Howland Island, the Royal New Zealand Navy cruiser HMS *Achilles* was steaming en route from Samoa to Hawaii. Having heard the "all ships" request to listen for possible calls from Earhart, the warship was monitoring 3105. At the same moment Bellarts asked Earhart to send dashes, the radio operator aboard the cruiser heard an unidentified voice say: "Please give us a few dashes if you get us."[8]

Immediately after sending his request to Earhart, Bellarts heard on-again-off-again signals he described in his log as "something like generator start and then stop on 3105." Two minutes later, the same sound was repeated. At one point he heard the word "Earhart."[9] *Achilles* heard the signals too, and interpreted the intermittent transmissions as dashes: "A second transmitter was then heard to make dashes."[10]

In reply, *Itasca* tried again to call Earhart, this time using Morse code. *Achilles* heard only the first part of the call. "First transmitter was then heard to make KHAQQ twice before fading out." The radio operator aboard *Achilles* did not know whom he had heard, but in reporting the reception to the U.S. Navy, the ship's commanding officer said, "The evidence exists that either transmitter was the airplane itself."[11] The radio operators aboard *Itasca*, unaware of what *Achilles* had heard, did not know what to make of the incident either. O'Hare's 6:37 PM radio log entry expressed cautious hope. "Signals on and off. Think it is plane?? Signals are unreadable [but] heard the word Earhart."[12]

Both ships had heard someone respond to *Itasca*'s request for Earhart to send dashes. The sound Bellarts described is particularly significant. Normally a radio operator transmits dashes by alternately holding down and releasing a sending key. The transmitter stays on and the key simply breaks the signal to create dots or dashes. The signals Bellarts heard were made by repeatedly turning the power supply to the transmitter on and off.

Earhart had no sending key aboard the Electra. She could send dashes by alternately holding down and releasing the push-to-talk button on her microphone. Every time she depressed the button, the plane's transmitting system powered up, and each time she released the button the whole system shut down again. Dashes sent in this manner might sound, as Bellarts said, "something like [a] generator start and then stop." O'Hare's statement that the word "Earhart" was heard during these transmissions is a further indication that the signals were sent using a microphone. This time, the Pan American Airways station in Hawaii did not even hear the basic carrier signal. *Achilles* heard dashes but not the voice, suggesting that the sender was somewhat closer to *Itasca*.

Who might have sent the signals heard by *Itasca* and *Achilles*? An operator on a ship or at a shore station in the region might have overheard and misunderstood Bellarts's request "for a few dashes if you get us," but such an operator would almost certainly respond using a sending key, not a microphone. The signals could have been a hoax, but the hoaxer would have to be located somewhere in the Central Pacific, have the ability to transmit voice signals on 3105 kilocycles, and would have to know that Earhart could not send dashes in the customary manner. Not even *Itasca* had that information.

Itasca again called the plane in both voice and code. This time, a man's voice answered, "still distorted and unreadable." Disappointed, O'Hare logged, "Guess it isn't her now."[13]

For the next twenty minutes, Bellarts and O'Hare tried to figure out what was going on, but their efforts were complicated by interference on the frequency. Someone was sending code, trying unsuccessfully to raise other stations. During breaks in the interference, *Itasca*'s operators called the plane twice again and each time got an immediate response from the unintelligible man. For the past hour, the radiomen had been receiving unexplained intermittent voice transmissions on the plane's frequency in direct response to their calls to Earhart. The one word they had been able to understand was "Earhart," but when they decided that the voice was male, they discounted the possibility that the signals were coming from the missing plane. None of the messages sent to *Itasca* prior to Earhart's flight had mentioned Noonan, and all of the transmissions the *Itasca* operators had heard during the flight had been made by Amelia. Just before 7:00 PM, they concluded, "Phone signals definitely not Earhart."[14]

Itasca kept calling, but the garbled voice responses stopped. Half an hour later, Commander Thompson sent a status report to headquarters: "*Itasca* Earhart search up to this time negative results. Broadcasting to steamers but few in this area."[15] Thompson also provided his first detailed estimate of what had happened. Faced with a seemingly inexplicable series of events, he constructed a reasonable explanation by changing the events. "Earhart apparently handicapped through night by cloudy weather as portions of received messages indicated overcast and cloudy weather. Earhart direction finder apparently not functioning as well, as she could not get cut on *Itasca* on agreed frequencies. Earhart had barely sufficient fuel under the conditions to make Howland. Thought close to Howland at 07:58 when circling trying to pick up land and attempts [by] *Itasca* to give Earhart radio bearings failed after thorough tests both ways."[16] Speculation that overcast conditions may have hampered her navigation had evolved into certainty that she had actually described such conditions; and it was now an accepted fact aboard *Itasca* that Earhart was carrying just enough fuel to make it to Howland Island.

Thompson continued his report, for the first time describing his reasons for searching to the north: "Belief, based on signal strength only, that at 07:58 Earhart passed close to and to northward of Howland as believed that she would have seen Baker Island if passing to southward." In closing, Thompson said: "Have heard no signals from Earhart since 08:55 this morning when she gave *Itasca* a line of position believed to mean radio bearing and stated she was running north and south. *Itasca* using every resource to locate plane."[17] Thompson misstated the time of the last in-flight reception from the Electra and chose not to mention the strange dashes and unexplained voice transmissions his radiomen had recently heard on Earhart's frequency.

Up to this point, decisions about what had probably happened to Earhart and where *Itasca* should search for her had been the exclusive province of the cutter's commanding officer; but that was about to change. Ten minutes after Thompson sent his report to Coast Guard headquarters, Admiral Murfin ordered *Itasca* to "be at Howland Island at daylight tomorrow" to meet the PBY that was now en route. Once the flying boat was within five hundred miles of Howland, Thompson was to "keep the plane advised of your position, be prepared to provide radio bearings, and make smoke as requested."[18] The cutter was back on plane guard duty, this time for the navy. By this time *Itasca* was nearly one hundred miles northeast of Howland.

The ship would have to put about and steam back toward the island to be there by dawn. But not just yet; there was time for another couple of hours of searching.

In the radio room, Leo Bellarts was listening "on 3105 continuously but no signals heard."[19] Seven minutes later, the U.S. Army radio facility at Fort Shafter near Pearl Harbor heard dashes on that frequency.[20] No one else seems to have heard them. *Itasca*'s radio log does not say whether Bellarts was still listening at that time.

At eight o'clock, *Itasca* received a message sent out by the U.S. Navy radio station in Tutuila, Samoa, to all the stations involved in the search. HMS *Achilles* had just informed Tutuila: "Unknown station heard to make 'please give us a few dashes if you get us.' Heard good strength both on 3105 kcs. First station then made KHAQQ twice [then] disappeared. Nothing more heard of either at 06:20 GMT."[21] This secondhand account mentioned nothing about the dashes the cruiser had heard and misstated the time of the incident. Not surprisingly, no one aboard *Itasca* saw the connection to events earlier in the evening, and as far as anyone else knew, the cutter had "heard no signals from Earhart since 08:55 this morning."[22]

For the next thirty minutes everything was quiet, but then, exactly on the half hour, government radio operators in Hawaii heard dashes and a weak voice signal, this time on Earhart's other frequency, 6210 kilocycles.[23] It is not clear whether Coast Guard operators at the Hawaiian Station or army operators at Fort Shafter—or both—heard these signals. Dashes and voice heard together suggest that, once again, the transmissions were being sent using a microphone rather than a sending key. *Itasca* did not hear the signals; the ship's radio operators were not listening on that frequency. Howland Island did not hear anything either; Cipriani was still recharging his batteries. There is, however, a report that someone else heard a voice at that moment.

In Amarillo, Texas, thirty-one-year-old homemaker Mabel Larremore finally had some time to herself. Her husband and two sons had gone to bed, and Mabel, as she often did, stayed up to listen to overseas radio programs on the family's "very good shortwave set." At 2:00 AM, she was astonished to hear Amelia Earhart calling for help. The signal came in "very clear," and Mabel recognized Amelia's voice, having heard her interviewed on the radio and in newsreels. Earhart was sending the same message over and over. "She would complete one and start right in again," Larremore later reported.[24]

"Her message stated the plane was down on an uncharted island. Small, uninhabited. The plane was partially on land, part in water. She gave the latitude and longitude of her location," but she never said the name of the island. Earhart also "gave two frequencies."[25] "She stated that her navigator Fred Noonan was seriously injured. Needed help immediately. She also had some injuries but not as serious as Mr. Noonan."[26] Mabel's story continued: "I listened to her for thirty to forty-five minutes after waking my family to also listen. . . . And I called our local paper to let them listen to her message also. . . . I'm sorry I can no longer remember the latitude and longitude of the island. With that, we had no trouble locating [the island] on a map the next day. I had it all written down but over the years, a lot of moves, a second marriage, it has been lost. I have tried to think of some way I could remember that important information [but] have not come up with the answer. Sorry."[27]

Mabel did not come forward with her story until 1990, when she was eighty-four years old. She died the next year. The *Amarillo Globe News* did not run a story at the time, and, with no supporting documentation, her account can be judged only by how well it tracks with known events. Some of Mabel's recollections are not consistent with the historical record. For example, Mabel wrote: "I heard her SOS loud and clear, not on the frequency but on the one President Roosevelt said she might use. . . . [O]ne member of the family reminded me that our President had asked that no one give out any information if they heard anything, as it might endanger her life. . . . My family and I decided not to discuss this with anyone. The government of the U.S.A was supposed to take care of everything, so [we] did not listen for any later messages from her."[28] There is no record of Roosevelt making any kind of public statement about Earhart's disappearance during the search.

Elements of Mabel's story may have been colored by subsequent events. Indeed, Mabel came forward with her recollections in response to press accounts about researchers who were investigating precisely the scenario she said she heard Earhart describe. On the other hand, several stations in the Pacific heard voice transmissions at the very time Mabel claimed to have heard the calls from Earhart. In 1990, that information had not yet been compiled, let alone published.

Is it really possible that Mabel Larremore in Texas heard a loud and clear voice message from Earhart on her home shortwave set when radio operators thousands of miles closer to where the plane disappeared were getting a signal that was too weak to understand? The calculated probability of anyone on the U.S. mainland hearing intelligible voice signals from Earhart's low-powered transmitter on either of her primary frequencies is so small as to be virtually zero. If Mabel heard signals from the plane, the most likely explanation is that, in tuning her shortwave set looking for a foreign broadcast, she stumbled upon a harmonic of Earhart's frequencies.

When Earhart's transmitter sent out a signal on one of her primary frequencies, it also broadcast a weaker signal on higher multiples of that frequency called harmonics. These higher frequencies, although less powerful than the primary signal, are also less susceptible to degradation and can travel great distances. Under unusual and unpredictable propagation conditions, unexpectedly good reception can occur in places where nothing would ordinarily be heard. Earhart's "daytime" frequency of 6210 kilocycles happened to be the second harmonic (double the frequency) of her "night-time" frequency of 3105. Transmissions on 3105 might also be heard on the third, the fourth, or even the fifth harmonic (15,525 kilocycles). The higher the harmonic, the lower the power—but the greater the signal's ability to travel. Shortwave listeners often tuned for broadcasts in those frequency ranges. The reception Mabel described would be a rare event, but it was far from impossible.[29]

Half an hour after the Coast Guard's Hawaiian Section reported "dashes and voice, weak" on 6210 kilocycles and Mabel Larremore allegedly started hearing Amelia, Radioman George Thompson aboard *Itasca* noted in his log: "There is a weak signal on 3105 kilocycles, but cannot read it." After listening for two minutes, Thompson sent, "*Itasca* to Earhart plane: repeat message please again. Go ahead."[30]

While Thompson was calling Earhart, the radio operator aboard the PBY was informing Fleet Air Base that the flying boat had reached a point five hundred miles to the northeast of Howland. The patrol plane had received U.S. Navy Radio Tutuila's broadcast about what the British cruiser heard and was "setting watch on voice frequency 3105 kilocycles." The operator added that he would "attempt to establish communication."[31]

Aboard *Itasca*, George Thompson listened for two minutes and typed: "There are still weak voice signals on 3105 kilocycles."[32] He listened for another three minutes, but he still could not make out the words. Earhart's signal was not strong enough to carry understandable voice, but it should be good enough for code, if only he could get her to send code. For the first time, it occurred to Thompson that Earhart might not have a sending key: "KHAQQ from *Itasca*. Cannot read your phone. Please go ahead on key. If no got key, make and break your antenna connection where it connects to transmitter and send us your position in code."[33]

George Thompson had correctly diagnosed the situation aboard the Electra and had told Earhart how to solve the problem. Reasoning that she might be having as much trouble understanding his words as he was having reading hers, he sent his instructions in a more reliable format: he sent them in Morse code. But Amelia Earhart and Fred Noonan could not understand Morse code. If they received Thompson's transmission, they heard only an incomprehensible series of dots and dashes. Three minutes after asking Earhart to send her position in code, Thompson logged, "Still weak voice signals on 3105 kilocycles, but cannot read them."[34]

At about this time, according to the much later recollection of one of the pilots, the radio aboard the PBY picked up dashes.[35] There is no corroboration for his claim in the official record.

Sometime during the evening, the steamer SS *New Zealand* also heard dashes on 3105 kilocycles. The report, relayed to *Itasca* by San Francisco Division, did not specify the exact time or the ship's location other than "1200 miles from Howland."[36]

While the radio operator aboard *Itasca* was struggling to understand the garbled voice transmissions on 3105, a thousand miles to the west on the British island of Nauru, another operator was having the same problem with signals he was hearing on the second harmonic of that frequency—Earhart's "daytime" frequency of 6210 kilocycles. Like the radiomen aboard the Coast Guard cutter, the Nauru operator was familiar with Earhart's voice, having heard her position reports the previous night as the Electra passed south of the island.

On three occasions, at twelve-minute intervals, during the period when *Itasca* was receiving unintelligible voice and Mabel Larremore later claimed to have heard Amelia repeatedly sending a distress message, the Nauru operator heard "fairly strong signals. Speech not interpreted owing bad modulation or speaker shouting into microphone. No hum of plane in background but voice similar to that emitted from plane in flight last night."[37]

Six minutes after the last transmission heard at Nauru, George Thompson aboard *Itasca* logged: "Still weak voice signals on 3105 kilocycles again." Two minutes later he tried once more: "KHAQQ, Earhart plane, from *Itasca*. Please go ahead again with position."[38]

This time there was no response. The voice signals had stopped.

Aboard the cutter the time was 9:32 PM. An hour later, the ship took up a course for Howland to keep its dawn rendezvous with the PBY. *Itasca*'s operators continued to listen for signals and periodically called the plane, but they heard nothing more that night.

For Commander Thompson it had been an anxious and frustrating day. He was convinced that Earhart had come down at sea, and he had devoted all of his ship's resources to looking for her. Now, under orders from the navy, the cutter was on its way back to the one place he was sure she was not.

Itasca's visual search had turned up nothing. The results of the electronic search were more ambiguous. San Francisco Division had said that radio calls from the floating plane were possible. Thompson believed that Earhart might even be able to send distress calls from a rubber boat using an emergency transmitter. Starting just before sunset and continuing intermittently for three and a half hours, *Itasca*'s operators had heard radiotelephone transmissions on 3105. The signals were weak and the voice was garbled, but on one occasion the word "Earhart" had been understood. Was it her?

Whoever had been transmitting on that first night of the search seemed to be responding directly to *Itasca*'s voice calls to Earhart. The sender also seemed to be located somewhere in the Central Pacific. Other professional

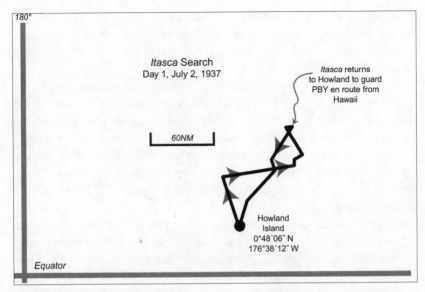

Itasca's movements on day 1 of the search.

operators farther from the search area had heard some of the signals, but not as consistently or as clearly as *Itasca*. However, to the men aboard the cutter, unaware of Noonan's presence on the flight, there was, one disqualifying observation. In at least some cases, the voice had been male.

Incomplete information and misconceptions about the flight and its capabilities had crippled *Itasca*'s attempts to guide the flight to a safe landing. Now those misconceptions, compounded by assumptions and bad information, were making it impossible to accurately assess the clues the search had turned up so far.

The situation was about to get worse.

CHAPTER THIRTEEN

Hoaxes and Hopes
the second day

At about the time *Itasca* turned for Howland, San Francisco Division received word that the radio operator at Nauru had heard a voice "similar to that emitted from plane in flight last night but with no hum of plane in background."[1] Wondering if Nauru might have overheard *Itasca* trying to call the plane, Division sent a message to the cutter asking, "Was *Itasca* on air from 0843 to 0854 GMT on 3105 kilocycles using voice?" Commander Thompson replied that the ship had not been transmitting but had heard weak voice signals during that time.[2] San Francisco passed along the Nauru report and relayed other news that had just come in: "Los Angeles men report hearing position report from KHAQQ [at] eleven thirty but as '1.6 179.' "[3]

There was much more to the story than Division told *Itasca*. The Los Angeles men, it seems, had heard quite a number of radio transmissions from the missing plane. Their spokesman was an amateur radio enthusiast and Amelia Earhart fan by the name of Walter McMenamy. McMenamy first told the Associated Press that "he picked up weak signals on 6210 kilocycles at 6 PM and heard the letters 'L-A-T,' which he took to mean latitude. The letters were followed by undecipherable figures. The signals continued for some time."[4]

Six o'clock in the evening in Los Angeles was two-thirty in the afternoon aboard *Itasca*. The cutter was monitoring 3105, not 6210. However, Pan American Airways in Hawaii started a listening watch on both frequencies at the same time McMenamy said he began hearing signals that continued for some time. Pan Am heard nothing. McMenamy's friend Karl Pierson, the chief engineer for the Patterson Radio Corporation, alleged that, at 8:00 PM, he "picked up similarly weak signals on 3105 kilocycles." Pierson added that "they were erratic and undecipherable."[5]

Both *Itasca* and Pan American were listening on 3105 at that time, but neither heard the signals. At the times reported by McMenamy and Pierson, nearly the entire radio propagation path between the U.S. mainland and the Central Pacific was in daylight. The probability of anyone in California being able to receive a transmission from the Earhart plane on either of the aircraft's primary frequencies is less than one in one hundred million.

According to the AP story, "Both Mr. McMenamy and Mr. Pierson said the signals came from a hand-cranked generator. Miss Earhart carried one in her plane."[6] There is no evidence that there was ever a portable generator or emergency transmitter aboard the Electra, but an exchange of messages between San Francisco Division and *Itasca* earlier in the day had mistakenly created that impression. Most Coast Guard radio traffic was sent in the clear and could be easily monitored by anyone with a good shortwave set.

By shortly after 11:00 PM that Friday night, McMenamy and Pierson had gotten together at the same location. McMenamy later mentioned that another radio amateur, Robert Rypinski, was also present. According to the *New York Times*, the three men reported that "a weak signal was received on 6210kc, not understood. On another radio receiver set tuned to 3105kc in the same room, they heard two distinctly separate signals they say were from the *Itasca* and from the plane; apparently not hearing each other."[7] During that period, stations in the Pacific were hearing no signals on either frequency and *Itasca* was not attempting to contact Earhart.

By the time McMenamy was interviewed by the *Oakland Tribune* on Saturday morning, the fish was bigger.

> He recognized the voice he heard during the night distinctly as that of Miss Earhart. "SOS, SOS, SOS, KHAQQ, SOS, SOS. It was Miss Earhart all right," he said. "I know her voice very well. She just kept repeating that over and over again. Once she said something else but I couldn't make it out. She can't use code herself so I assume Noonan was asleep or busy or something. How did her voice sound? Pretty good. Not scared at all—she never sounds that way. It is weak but very clear. The calls are coming every 15 minutes. About every third time they are signed by the call letters KHAQQ. No position is given. Regularly by my watch we hear an SOS every 15 minutes. It's just a single SOS each time—they are apparently conserving their batteries."
> The powerful Los Angeles amateur station had been hearing code SOS signals all night. This morning what appeared to be a radioed position of the plane was picked up. "It was 179 and what sounded like 1 point 6," said McMenamy.[8]

McMenamy's claim that he was familiar with Earhart's voice and capabilities was true. He was one of several amateurs who communicated with Earhart during her flight from Honolulu to Oakland in 1935. But in 1937, while McMenamy was hearing calls from Earhart every fifteen minutes, no one in the Pacific was hearing anything.

The same *Oakland Tribune* article mentioned another Los Angeles area operator who claimed to have heard a call from the missing plane:

"Kenneth Bartell of nearby Huntington Park said he got the signals from KHAQQ, the call letters of the famous woman flier's plane. The signals came in a man's voice, Bartell said, leading him to believe that it was the voice of Capt. Fred Noonan, navigator for Miss Earhart. At the same time Walter McMenamy, amateur radio operator in Los Angeles, reported picking up signals from the missing plane. . . . McMenamy, like Bartell, also said it was Noonan's voice he heard."[9]

That night, San Francisco advised *Itasca*: "Four separate radiomen at Los Angeles reported receiving Earhart voice this morning and verify '179 with 1.6 in doubt.' Position given as 'southwest Howland Island.' Above heard on 3105 kilocycles and call of plane distinctly heard and verified according to amateurs."[10] The four radiomen were never identified by name in Coast Guard radio traffic, but the message created the impression that four operators at separate locations had independently received the same transmission. That does not seem to have been the case. By McMenamy's own description, he, Pierson, and Rypinski were together at his house when they allegedly heard the calls. Bartell may have been with them. The four men were all members of the same amateur radio club.

A few days later, McMenamy's account of what he heard that night changed again. After Paul Mantz affirmed that Earhart carried no emergency power supply, the hand-cranked generator disappeared from McMenamy's story. Now, "There was a background of airplane motors. I can distinguish between motors and static of any kind. I feel sure of my contact with her."[11]

Coast Guard inquiries made more than a week after McMenamy's initial report still found him credible. On July 11, San Francisco Division informed the Hawaiian Section that "further investigation this date of radio reports by amateurs at Los Angeles on night of July 3 [*sic*] confirmed by four separate stations and indicate credibility of receipt of distress call from Earhart plane about 0920 GCT [1:20 PST] giving position as 179 and 1 point 6. At 1330 GCT [5:30 PST] woman's voice heard making distress call giving position as southwest Howland and motors were heard in background. This transmission repeated six or seven times."[12]

In 1959, Walter McMenamy made an audio tape in which he confessed to the hoax, claiming that Naval Intelligence forced him and Pierson to cooperate in a conspiracy. Earhart, it seems, landed safely but secretly at Howland Island after spying on the Japanese. Whatever their motivations, on Saturday morning, July 3, the interceptions alleged by McMenamy and Pierson seemed credible. San Francisco Division knew that ships and shore stations in the Pacific had heard signals that might be from the plane. These new reports appeared to support a growing suspicion that Earhart and Noonan were alive and calling for help.

By midmorning another amateur had surfaced. Oakland ham Charles McGill telephoned the Coast Guard with a report that he had heard SOS calls at 6:55 AM on a frequency of 3480 kilocycles. "Twenty-five NNW Howland. Ask Putnam to fly kite."[13] The reported frequency, time, and location reveal the report to be a crude hoax. Over the following days, McGill would claim further receptions, but a Coast Guard investigation on July 6 "definitely determined report false. Verify [sic] and reputation of man making report extremely dubious after investigation."[14]

Across the country, in Ashland, Kentucky, Nina Paxton also heard Amelia Earhart calling for help—or so she told the local newspaper almost a week later. According to Paxton, at two o'clock on the afternoon of Saturday, July 3: "The message came in on my short wave set very plain, and Miss Earhart talked for some time. I turned the radio down at one time to talk to my little child and then turned it back up to catch the last part of the message. I didn't understand everything Miss Earhart said because there was some noise."[15]

The newspaper article described the message as Mrs. Paxton understood it: " 'Down in ocean' either 'on' or 'near' 'little island at a point near . . .' and then something about 'directly northeast' although Mrs. Paxton was not sure about this part. 'Our plane about out of gas. Water all around. Very dark.' Then she said something about a storm and that the wind was blowing. 'Will have to get out of here,' she said. 'We can't stay here long.' " This message was preceded by Miss Earhart's call letters, "KHAQQ calling, KHAQQ calling."[16]

Two o'clock in the afternoon in Ashland, Kentucky, was 7:30 AM aboard *Itasca*. At that time the cutter was busy trying to communicate with the PBY, but multiple other stations around the Pacific were monitoring both of Earhart's primary frequencies and hearing nothing. The entire radio propagation path between Paxton's location and the search area was in daylight, and the probability that it was physically possible for her to have heard a transmission from the Earhart Electra is less than one in ten million.

Improbable is not the same as impossible, of course, and extraordinary events can and do occur. There is, however, nothing in Nina Paxton's claims that argues for her credibility. All the elements of Earhart's situation, as Paxton first described it, can be found in press accounts published in the days before Paxton contacted the newspaper. In 1943, her memory improved. When the RKO film *Flight for Freedom* prompted rumors that Earhart had been on a secret government mission to spy on Japanese installations in the Marshall Islands, Paxton wrote letters to the Office of Naval Intelligence and to columnist Walter Winchell. She now remembered that Amelia had made specific references to geographical features in the southern Marshalls.

Nina Paxton surfaced again in the 1960s amidst speculation that Earhart had come down at Mili Atoll in the Marshall Islands. She now remembered that "the first SOS message was heard on July 3, 1937, in which Miss Earhart stated. 'We lost our course yesterday and came up here. Directly Northeast of a part of the Marshall Islands near Mili Atoll.' "[17] She also revealed that she had heard messages from Earhart on several later occasions.

Nina Paxton, it seems, had received other unusual transmissions on her shortwave set. Prior to hearing Amelia she had "picked up Hitler giving commands that I doubt he had expected the world to hear." She also intercepted a message, apparently in English, which she quoted as: "We have just shot Mussolini, Madame, and eight co-patriots."[18] Nina Paxton's many and varied allegations elicited wide debate among later researchers, but her initial report never went further than the local Ashland paper.

Although Paxton's claims had no influence on the conduct of the 1937 search, the reports that did reach the authorities were the only bright spots in an otherwise bleak picture. On that Saturday morning of July 3, Earhart and Noonan had been missing for a full day, and the search for them was at a standstill.

Itasca was still the only ship on the scene. Its rescue efforts of the previous day had been fruitless, and now the cutter was back at Howland, waiting for another plane that would never arrive. The PBY had run into severe weather three hundred miles to the north of Howland. After trying for some time to find a way through, the pilot turned around and began the long trip back to Hawaii.

USS *Swan*, the Navy seaplane tender that had been positioned halfway between Howland and Hawaii, was headed south but was days away.

In Hawaii, *Colorado* had rounded up its crew and was taking on fuel at Pearl Harbor for the coming voyage. The battleship's three airplanes were still being reassembled ashore.

At Fourteenth Naval District headquarters, Admiral Murfin responded to pressure from Washington to do more to find Earhart by raising the stakes: "If more extensive search operations are contemplated, dispatch of aircraft carrier most practicable, efficient method."[19]

At the Navy Department it was late on Saturday afternoon, the day before the Fourth of July, and the chief of naval operations had a decision to make. On Friday he had told Admiral Murfin to "use available naval facilities to conduct such search for Miss Earhart as, in your opinion, is practicable."[20] It was now apparent that the only naval facilities available that could be practicably employed in the search were a small seaplane tender with no seaplane and a commandeered battleship with three spotter planes.

If Washington wanted more of a search than that, Murfin needed an aircraft carrier. In 1937 the U.S. Navy had three aircraft carriers: USS *Lexington*

(CV-2), USS *Saratoga* (CV-3), and USS *Ranger* (CV-4). None was anywhere near the Central Pacific. Just getting a carrier to the search area would take at least a week. By that time there was a good chance that Earhart and Noonan would be either rescued or dead—if they were not dead already. Whether or not to send an aircraft carrier was essentially a public relations decision. To buy some time before making a final decision, the CNO sent a message to the commander in chief of the U.S. Fleet: "Request aircraft carrier be fueled and prepared for search Amelia Earhart, if so directed by Navy Department."[21]

Like everyone else, Earhart's husband had been encouraged by the news that a British cruiser had heard the plane's call letters. At his request, the Coast Guard's San Francisco Division sent a message to the Hawaiian Section: "Putnam asks that effort be made to confirm that HMS *Achilles* got call letters KHAQQ clearly and certainly."[22]

George Putnam also wanted to be sure the navy had the latest information about radio receptions by amateurs. Shortly after noon, the navy commander in California informed Admiral Murfin in Hawaii: "Putnam reports amateur operators vicinity of Los Angeles have intercepted position reports. Earhart plane one degree 36 minutes south latitude, 179 degrees east longitude. He believes possibility plane on land and sending intermittent signals."[23]

Earhart's husband was trying to reconcile the amateur reports with what he was hearing from Paul Mantz. As reported by the Associated Press in a story datelined Oakland, July 3:

> A theory that Amelia Earhart might have brought her plane down safely on a small coral atoll south of Howland Island was advanced today by her technical adviser, Paul Mantz, in a telephone conversation with George Palmer Putnam. Putnam, husband of the Aviatrix, said he conferred with Mantz at Burbank.
>
> "Several of the Phoenix Islands are large enough to allow a plane to land," Mantz was quoted by Putnam. "The undercarriage may have been damaged, but the flyers could have walked away from the plane uninjured."[24]

Paul Mantz knew that if signals were being sent from the plane, it had to be on land. Putnam trusted Mantz's knowledge of the Electra, but the islands of the Phoenix Group were hundreds of miles southeast of where *Itasca* was searching. Putnam interpreted McMenamy's vague "179 with 1.6 in doubt" to be 1°36'S, 179°E, a position roughly three hundred miles southwest of Howland. Perhaps there was land there.[25]

Noon in California was morning in the Central Pacific. At 8:00 AM, *Itasca* arrived back at its plane guard station. For the past two hours it had been apparent that there would be no plane to guard, but the navy had not released the cutter from its assigned duty. Commander Thompson complained to the Coast Guard's Hawaiian Section: "Drifting off Howland [in] compliance [with] commander 14th Naval District dispatch. . . . Plane apparently returning to base. Imperative continue search today. Time element vital." An hour later, Hawaiian Section replied: "Navy plane reports returning Pearl Harbor due bad weather. *Itasca* resume search all possible speed. Advise if you concur."[26]

Commander Thompson concurred, and by nine-thirty his ship was again headed northward toward the area where he believed the plane had come down. He hoped the Electra was still floating or that Amelia had managed to deploy the rubber boat she supposedly had with her, but he had little confidence that any of the radio signals received the night before were from the lost flier. Shortly after leaving Howland, he debunked the idea that *Achilles* had heard Earhart. The Hawaiian Section relayed the disappointing news to San Francisco: "*Itasca* advises that call received by HMS *Achilles* was sent by *Itasca*."[27]

Thompson was basing his judgment on the communication he received the night before from the U.S. Navy radio station in Tutuila, Samoa, but the information in that message was both inaccurate and incomplete. In relaying *Achilles*'s report, the navy operator got the time of the incident wrong and failed to mention that the cruiser had heard dashes. As it turns out, Thompson was correct. The Earhart call letters *Achilles* heard *were* sent by *Itasca*. But it is also true that radio operators on both ships heard a response to *Itasca*'s request for dashes. If the Earhart aircraft was on the ground somewhere in the Phoenix Group, the probability that it could receive and understand a voice transmission sent by *Itasca* on 3105 kilocycles is 99 percent. The probability that *Achilles* could hear and understand *Itasca*'s call is 69 percent. The chance that both ships could hear dashes sent from the Electra is 99 percent.

While *Itasca* steamed northward from Howland on a bright Pacific morning, Henry Morgenthau was working late on a Saturday evening in Washington. As secretary of the treasury, Morgenthau was ultimately responsible for the actions of the Coast Guard, and on this Fourth of July weekend, one of his cutters was center stage in a drama that was playing out on the front pages of every newspaper in the country. Just before 6:00 PM he had the Coast Guard commandant send a message to *Itasca*: "Secretary of Treasury Morgenthau requests latest information search of plane Amelia Earhart. Request information be sent Coast Guard headquarters immediately upon receipt of this message."[28]

Despite the request for an immediate response, an hour and an half passed before Commander Thompson sent a reply:

Itasca searched three thousand square miles [since] daylight yesterday. Guarded Navy plane during night and arrived Howland daybreak this morning under orders Commandant Fourteenth Naval District. Depart[ed] Howland 0900 today, plane having returned to base owing bad weather.

Search being pressed with all possible energy and weather conditions favorable thereto. Area searched north of Howland on assumption most logical as no definite position from Earhart plane received at any time.[29]

The secretary was not satisfied with Warner Thompson's brief summary. The cutter's commanding officer had not addressed the question that was on everyone's mind. Was Earhart really out there calling for help? Before Morgenthau left for the night, he had another message sent to *Itasca*: "Secretary Morgenthau desires that you furnish the latest information available on Earhart plane at time of preparation of a dispatch which will reach headquarters not later than 0630 [Washington time] 4 July 1937. Advise if signals have been heard at any time and if so when they started and when they ceased."[30]

It was just after 2:00 PM aboard *Itasca* when Morgenthau's demand for a more complete report arrived. The deadline for sending the dispatch was midnight for *Itasca*, which left ample time to compose the message. During the afternoon, both of the wire service reporters aboard the cutter took the opportunity to file stories describing the situation as they saw it. Howard Hanzlick's report to the United Press was long on drama and short on accuracy:

Men at stations tensely alert. Long wait capped by anxiety. Search felt deeply. Men working with grim efficiency. Great concern over why Amelia short of fuel in air only approximately twenty and half hours. Should have had several hours more fuel.

Why Amelia never gave position? Her radio evidently not working properly. *Itasca* requested [in] each broadcast [that Amelia] give position. Never given. At 8:42 Amelia radioed "half hour fuel left. No landfall. Position doubtful." Last message 9:43 "Line of position 157–337. Am circling. Please give radio bearing." Her voice sounded very tired, anxious, almost breaking.

Lack [of] information from Amelia making search difficult. Last night at 6:50 PM sailing east, investigated seeming light flash [on] horizon port beam. No result. Eleven thirty PM started back toward Howland.

Several times excitement aroused. Stars low on horizon, seeming flares. Daybreak morning seeming smoke [on] horizon. Investigated. Futile.

Searching full speed today area 150 miles northwest Howland, 100 miles north. Weather same [as] yesterday.[31]

Hanzlick's account illustrates the extent to which folklore had already replaced fact aboard *Itasca*. The men of the cutter were now wondering why, not whether, Earhart had run out of fuel far too soon.

James Carey's story to the Associated Press described how the search was being conducted.

Combing search area [where] Earhart probably down. Aboard ship, crows nest [and] bridge both [have] four lookouts continuously [searching with] glasses. Night, use two searchlights skyward. Friday PM crew [and] rest [of] party tense on deck [ready to] aid [in] track[ing] down any flare [or] clue. Flashes reported. Followed. Result be stars rising out horizon [and] lifting cloud banks.

Early this AM chased down what turn[ed] out [to] be waterspout. Off 10:37AM from Howland [to] comb area again. Water aboard rationed to two hour use daily. Previously five.[32]

Neither journalist mentioned the radio calls heard the night before.

Just before nightfall, Commander Thompson sent his dispatch to Secretary Morgenthau: "No information Earhart plane since 0843 2 July. Heard faint signals between 1825 and 1858 2 July which developed, as nearly as could be ascertained, into call Q85. Signals unreadable and, from call letters, definitely not Earhart. Unable contact Q85 after 1858."[33]

Once again, Commander Thompson's description of the incident was at odds with the ship's radio logs. According to those records, the radiomen heard faint calls from an unknown station intermittently between 6:00 and 6:43 PM. The signals included unintelligible voice transmissions and on-and-off signals sent in apparent direct response to *Itasca*'s request for Earhart to send dashes. At one point the word "Earhart" was heard. Beginning at 6:43 and continuing until 6:58, further transmissions from the unknown station were partially blocked by Morse code transmissions from station QZ5 (not Q85) trying to raise stations KACA and KCWR. *Itasca* was never successful in establishing contact with QZ5.*

---

*Extensive research has failed to determine the identities of stations QZ5, KACA, and KCWR.

In his message to the treasury secretary, Thompson neglected to mention that weak voice signals, assumed by *Itasca*'s radio operators to be transmissions from the missing plane, began again at 9:00 PM and continued for half an hour. During this second period of unexplained transmissions, the operator on Nauru heard "fairly strong signals. Speech not interpreted owing bad modulation or speaker shouting into microphone. No hum of plane in background but voice similar to that emitted from plane in flight last night."[34] *Itasca*'s captain either did not see or chose to disregard the coincidence. Because he said nothing about *Itasca*'s receptions during this period, no one else had a chance to connect the dots.

With an inaccurate impression of what had transpired in his ship's own radio room, Commander Thompson had an explanation for the reports of calls from the missing flier: "We are calling Earhart frequently and consistently on 3105 kilocycles and, undoubtedly, amateur and other stations mistake us for Earhart plane. We are pushing search at top speed day and night in logical areas north of Howland and have thoroughly search 2000 square miles daylight today with negative results."[35]

There was, however, one amateur report that could be interpreted to fit Thompson's own belief about where the plane might be. He had been told that "Los Angeles men" had heard Earhart give her position as "1.6 179."[36] If the numbers meant latitude 1.6°N, longitude 179°W, it put the plane within the area Thompson believed was most logical. He was willing to check it out: "Amateur stations report unverified position from Earhart plane west of Howland which area we will search during daylight tomorrow. If party afloat on plane or raft they are drifting north and west at estimated maximum two miles per hour. Visibility and general search conditions excellent. Sea conditions to present time now favorable if plane or raft is afloat. Have auxiliary radio listening stations Howland and Baker Island and all reported commercial craft over large area familiar with situation and on the alert, both visual and radio."[37]

As sunset in the Central Pacific marked the close of the second day of the Earhart search, *Itasca* was seventy-five miles north of Howland and steaming westward toward Thompson's interpretation of the position reported by the Los Angeles men.

USS *Colorado*, fully fueled and with its airplanes aboard, was five hours out of Pearl Harbor on the four-day, sixteen-hundred-mile voyage to the search area.

In California, the aircraft carrier USS *Lexington* and four destroyers were being readied in case the Navy Department decided to commit them to the effort to save the missing fliers.

Skeptical as *Itasca*'s captain may have been that legitimate distress calls had been heard, in Honolulu and San Francisco, nightfall and the improved

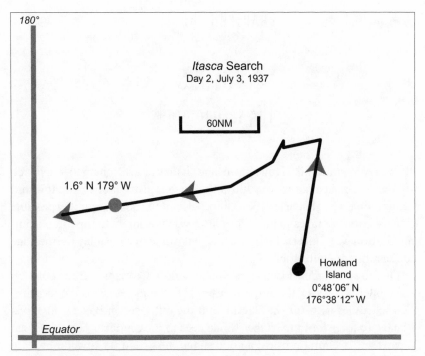

Itasca's movements on day 2 of the search.

radio reception it brought was greeted with great anticipation. *Itasca* had been advised by headquarters to "not, repeat not, use 3105 or 6210 kilocycles next two nights to permit absolute check on authenticity of calls and to permit monitoring of above frequencies by use of directional antennae."[38]

As evening fell on Oahu, the Coast Guard's Hawaiian Section picked up on a suggestion Earhart's husband had made the night before: "Radio station KGU Honolulu offers to broadcast whatever desired on theory Earhart plane may be able to receive. Suggest use this means for aiding in search and sending encouragement to occupants of plane. Please contact Mr. Coll of KGU. Signed Putnam."[39]

Arrangements for a special broadcast to Earhart were made with NBC affiliate KGU and with Honolulu's other major commercial station, KGMB. Earhart was known to be familiar with both stations from her previous flights, and it was not unreasonable to suppose that she might be listening for news of efforts to come to her aid. Coast Guard and navy stations would listen for any reply while Pan American Airways' direction-finding receivers in Hawaii, Midway, and Wake Island, as well as the Coast Guard's own direction-finding radio facility in San Francisco, would try to determine where the signals were coming from.

They were all in for a busy night.

CHAPTER FOURTEEN

Voices

the second night

The radio station on Howland Island, its batteries recharged, was back on the air. At sundown on July 3, *Itasca* sent instructions "for Howland and Baker [to] listen [on] 3105 kilocycles continuously" for any possible signals from Earhart's plane.[1] The cutter was not maintaining direct communication with Baker Island, so Howland would need to relay the message to the radio operator there.

On Howland, Coast Guard radioman Frank Cipriani and the colony's radio operator, Yau Fai Lum, were using the island colony's radio to maintain schedules with *Itasca*, Hawaii, and the outposts on Baker and Jarvis islands. To listen for Earhart they would need to use Cipriani's portable Coast Guard set. If Cipriani heard a good signal, he would try to get a bearing with the high-frequency direction finder Richard Black had borrowed from the navy. The problem was that the portable Coast Guard receiver was not very sensitive. Yau Lum replied to *Itasca*'s directive saying that Howland would be "unable" to comply with the orders to keep a continuous watch due to the portable's inability to receive weak signals.[2] He did, however, pass the instruction along to Baker Island's radio operator, Paul Yat Lum.

Aboard *Itasca*, Chief Radioman Leo Bellarts took the watch himself. Because he did not know that Earhart's transmitter was crystal-controlled and therefore not susceptible to drifting off its designated frequency of 3105, Bellarts widened his search for signals that might be from the plane. At 7:15 PM, on a frequency of 3110 kilocycles, he picked up something that sounded like a weak voice signal but he could not make out the words. He kept listening, and eight minutes later he heard the same sounds.[3]

While Bellarts was struggling with the off-frequency signal, Paul Yat Lum on Baker Island, listening on 3105 kilocycles, signaled that he "heard Earhart plane, S4, R7."[4] According to the 1937 edition of the *Radio Amateur's Handbook*, an S4 signal (strength 4 on a scale of 1 to 5) was "good, readable." An R7 reception (readability 7 on a scale of 1 to 9) was a "good strong signal, such as copiable through interference."[5]

The signal received at Baker Island was markedly different from anything that had been heard so far. On the previous night, stations in and around the search area had reported dashes and faint, unintelligible voice signals in apparent response to *Itasca*'s calls to Earhart. Now a government radio operator in the search area had heard a clear and strong transmission he unequivocally identified as being from the missing plane.

Who did Paul Lum hear? *Itasca*, under orders from headquarters, was no longer transmitting on Earhart's frequencies, so he did not overhear and misunderstand a call from the cutter. If Lum heard a strong signal at Baker, others in the region should have heard it too—if they were listening; but mostly they were not. Aboard *Itasca*, Bellarts was off frequency at the time. Howland Island was not listening at all. In Hawaii, the Pan American Airways station would not begin its radio watch on Earhart's frequency for another ten minutes. The only other station known to have been monitoring 3105 at that moment was the Coast Guard's Hawaiian Section. Operators there were hearing a weak carrier wave but no distinguishable voice.[6]

If Baker Island and the Hawaiian Section were hearing the same transmission, whether sent from the plane or by a hoaxer, the origin point was almost certainly much closer to Baker than to Hawaii. A hoaxer could have been aboard a ship, and a ship could be anywhere, but if the transmission heard at Baker and Honolulu was genuine, the Electra had to be on land, and the land had to be otherwise uninhabited. Most of the island groups in the Central Pacific were densely populated. Only the Phoenix Group remained largely unsettled. The uninhabited southwestern islands of the archipelago are 350 miles south of Baker Island and more than 2000 miles from Hawaii. If Earhart's Electra was on one of those islands, the probability of a voice transmission from the aircraft being received at Baker Island as a good, strong signal is 99 percent. The chance of the Coast Guard's Hawaiian Section hearing an understandable voice message sent from the Phoenix Group is only a little better than 2 percent. If the Hawaii operators heard anything at all, it would probably be only the underlying carrier wave, just as they reported.

Itasca, meanwhile, was not aware that anyone else was hearing anything. Unable to resolve the voice signals on 3110, Bellarts handed off the radio watch to George Thompson at 7:45 PM. Thompson resumed listening for Earhart on 3105 but heard nothing.

An hour later, as the cutter settled into another night of searching and listening, wire service reporter Howard Hanzlick summarized the situation aboard *Itasca* in an update to the United Press: "Unresulting search covered over two thousand square miles north and northeast [of] Howland area [during] daytime today. Weather cloudy [with] afternoon rain squalls. Tonite heading southwest towards line of flight from Lae. Assumption Amelia fell short on course. Hope still expressed. Seas slightly choppy. Two searchlights constantly."[7]

Amelia fell short? On Friday morning, when the flight failed to arrive, Commander Thompson decided that the sector northwest of Howland was the most logical area to search. By midafternoon he had come to believe that "she passed to north and west of island about 0800 and missed it in the glare of rising sun. . . . Judge she came down between 337° and 90° from Howland and within 100 miles." That evening, when he made his report to Secretary Morgenthau, Commander Thompson's expressed belief was that the plane had flown past Howland to the north.[8]

Thompson's new theory that the plane had never gotten as far as Howland was based on the position west of Howland the four amateurs in Los Angeles had reported. He reasoned that Earhart might be sending distress calls from the floating plane or from a life raft using a portable generator. Maybe the flight had come down at sea short of the island. Maybe not, but no trace of the plane had been found so far, and the position reported by the amateurs was the only lead he had.

Hanzlick's press release continued with some human interest. "Personnel [have] waited, thought, [and] talked [about] Amelia so long now, [that it is] like searching for close friend, though most have never seen her. Some heard her voice. Those who did have great admiration for [her] courage when she called in slow measured words 'half hour fuel left, no landfall.' Not until last message did [her] voice show emotion." He closed his report with: "Unverified here [that] Noonan [is] with Amelia. *Itasca* proceeding [to] investigate an amateur position rumor to westward."[9]

At 10:00 PM in Honolulu (9:00 PM aboard *Itasca*), the NBC Radio affiliate KGU made a special broadcast on its regular frequency asking Earhart to reply if she heard the request. Immediately afterward, the Pan American Airways station at Mokapu heard "a faint carrier on 3105. Too weak to distinguish any words."[10] The Coast Guard Hawaiian Section also heard a weak carrier. *Itasca* was busy with other traffic and heard nothing. Howland was not listening, and if Lum on Baker heard anything he did not say so. Neither the Coast Guard cutter nor the island radio operators had been told that commercial stations would be making broadcasts asking Earhart to respond.

When Itasca resumed monitoring 3105 twenty minutes later, Radioman George Thompson picked up the weak carrier. There was a voice, but he could not make out the words.[11] He continued to hear the signal sporadically for more than half an hour. Just after 10:00 PM he logged an exchange with the operator on Howland:

Itasca: K6GNW [Lum's call sign] this is NRUI [*Itasca's* call letters].
Howland: Go ahead.
Itasca: We have heard a weak carrier on 3105 kilocycles for the last

40 minutes. Do you hear it?
Howland: No. The static is bad.
Itasca: Roger. Try to get him and take a bearing. See you in half an hour.
Howland: Roger. See you in half an hour.[12]

Thompson continued to hear the weak signal, although at times it almost faded away completely. At 10:30 PM, another powerful commercial station in Honolulu, KGMB, made a call on its broadcast frequency asking Earhart to respond on 3105. Pan American listened for a reply, but the static was especially heavy and the operators heard no signals.[13]

Itasca was still hearing the faint carrier, and it was time to check back with the operator on Howland.

Itasca: K6GNW this is NRUI.
Howland: Go ahead.
Itasca: Do you hear the carrier now?
Howland: Yes, maybe the second harmonic from a broadcasting station.
Itasca: No, it is impossible for a second harmonic to go 1000 miles. [Only the higher harmonics are capable of spanning great distances.] Did you get a bearing?
Howland: No, will get one now.
Itasca: Roger, see you in half hour.
Howland: Roger.[14]

For the next thirty minutes *Itasca* continued to hear the weak carrier on Earhart's frequency. KGMB made another broadcast at midnight (11:00 PM for *Itasca*) asking Earhart for signals. This time, three stations in the Honolulu area heard a reply. Pan American Airways at Mokapu heard a carrier but no voice on 3105; the static was too bad to try for a directional bearing. The Coast Guard's Hawaiian Section radio operator heard the signal a little bit better and was able to discern a weak voice, but could not understand what was being said. The U.S. Navy radio station at Wailupe also heard the voice and was able to pick out the number "thirty-one."[15] (The radio frequency 3105 is usually spoken as "thirty-one-oh-five.")

The Hawaiian Section now decided that *Itasca* should know about the KGMB broadcast and the response that had been heard. At 11:05 PM, the cutter received a message: "Radio Oahu, PAA, [and] this office heard voice carrier [at] end [of] KGMB broadcast 3105. Continuing broadcast. Concentrating [on] 3105 for reply. Several dashes also heard."[16] Someone out there was sending voice on 3105, and everyone—*Itasca*, Howland Island, the Coast Guard's Hawaiian Section, the navy, and Pan American—was hearing it.

Only U.S.-registered civilian aircraft were permitted to talk on that frequency. An aircraft operating in the Territory of Hawaii was not a likely source. In 1937, the lack of lighted airfields in the islands limited civilian night flying. In any event, Hawaiian stations should have heard a local aircraft loud and clear. A call from an aircraft on the U.S. West Coast might be heard weakly in the distant Pacific under the right conditions, but the Coast Guard's monitoring station in California was listening on 3105 and heard nothing.

What direction were the signals coming from? *Itasca* immediately queried Yau Lum and Cipriani on Howland:

Itasca: K6GNW this is NRUI.
Howland: Go ahead.
Itasca: Did you get a bearing?
Howland: No, the signals were very weak and when I shifted to the direction finding antenna the signal faded out completely.
Itasca: Roger, well how about a schedule in one hour?
Howland: How about some sleep?
Itasca: Roger, will see you at 8 AM Honolulu standard time, that is 7 AM here.
Howland: Roger, see you at 8 AM, signing off.[17]

Howland was done for the night, but *Itasca* continued to hear an inter-mittent carrier on 3105.

An hour and a half later, the Coast Guard monitoring station in California informed *Itasca* that its operators had been hearing a "strong carrier on 6210 kcs being on about fifteen minutes. We have three receivers picking it up. . . . Signal is stronger from westerly direction."[18]

In Honolulu, the time was 1:30 AM and the Hawaiian Section again heard a transmission on 3105, "One minute duration, speech identified as man's voice." A few minutes later, the Pan American station on Wake Island heard an intermittent voice signal with "rather wobbly characteristics . . . male voice although unreadable through static."[19] Another person claimed to have heard a man's voice during that time. Later that night, the U.S. Navy radio station at Wailupe described the incident in a message to *Itasca*, *Colorado*, and others.

A man named Donaldson, who lived in the town of Wahiawa, about twenty miles from Honolulu, had heard a man's voice make "three or four calls." Donaldson had been able to make out the figures "31.05 and "31.07," the word "help," and the call letters "KHAQQ."[20] The half-hour period during which Donaldson heard the calls coincided with the time the Hawaiian Section and Pam Am Wake had heard an unintelligible man's voice on 3105 kilocycles.

The frequency or frequencies Donaldson was listening on are not known. His account references readings on the dial of his Zenith radio without specifying what model Zenith he had. The details of his story may also have suffered in translation. Wishing to report what he had heard, Donaldson phoned his local Mutual Wireless telegram office. Mutual sent a wire to the U.S. Navy radio station at Wailupe, which in turn forwarded the message "for what it may be worth" to the various search authorities. The navy message seems to be the only surviving account of Donaldson's report.

The Donaldson incident is similar to the Baker Island reception earlier that same night. In each case, a listener heard an identifiable call from the missing plane at a time when other stations were hearing a much weaker signal. Baker Island was listening on Earhart's primary nighttime frequency. The strength of the signal received there was probably a function of Baker's geographical proximity to the sender. Donaldson, on the other hand, might have heard more than the Coast Guard station in Honolulu twenty miles away because he was listening on a harmonic. Both incidents are consistent with the sender being somewhere south of Howland.

Of course, like Walter McMenamy, Donaldson could have been fabricating the whole thing. Unlike McMenamy's, though, Donaldson's claim was synchronous with other reported receptions. At the time he made his call to the local telegram office, Donaldson could not have known that the Coast Guard's Hawaiian Section and the Pan Am station on Wake Island had both heard a man's voice during the time he said he heard a man calling from KHAQQ.

After four hours of intermittent receptions on Earhart's frequencies by multiple stations, the Pacific went quiet. *Itasca* heard its last "unreadable signals" on 3105 at 1:20 AM. Half an hour later, Leo Bellarts logged: "On 3105 constantly but nothing heard."[21]

In Los Angeles, McMenamy and Pierson were having better luck. According to an Associated Press report datelined Los Angeles, July 4:

Walter McMenamy, amateur radio operator, said he picked up Amelia Earhart's call letters "KHAQQ" at 5 AM Pacific time [1:30 AM aboard *Itasca*] today. He said the call was in voice, but was "too faint to tell definitely if actually from Miss Earhart."

R. D. "Bo" McKneely, Miss Earhart's mechanic at Burbank, California, also heard the call on McMenamy's powerful set. He called Paul Mantz, Miss Earhart's technical adviser, reporting that the radio call was fast, "too fast to distinguish clearly." He said after the call letters something else was sent, "probably a position."

"We heard nothing decipherable during the night," Pierson said, "and at 5:30 the carrier wave faded out. Just before that we heard a voice, definitely that of a woman and sounding like the voice I had heard more clearly yesterday." McMenamy has said he was familiar with Miss Earhart's radio voice, having heard it many times, and that the words of distress, spoken so calmly Saturday morning, were those of the aviatrix, now down in the South Pacific.[22]

At the time McMenamy and Pierson claimed to hear Amelia's voice transmitting her call sign on 3105, none of the stations in the Pacific heard anything on that frequency. The probability of a voice message from the Electra on 3105 kilocycles being heard in Los Angeles is less than one in ten million.

The press asked Paul Mantz what he thought of McMenamy's claims.

Mantz, who serviced Amelia's plane, said she could send radio messages only if her plane were on land.

"She has no hand-crank aboard to generate power," Mantz said. The right engine, turning over at 900 R.P.M. creates about 50 amperes. This burns almost six gallons of gas hourly.

"To the best of my knowledge, Miss Earhart did not have much fuel when she was forced down. Yet, the signals appear to be sent regularly."[23]

Mantz was skeptical of McMenamy's claims because of the number of transmissions he was claiming to hear. The Electra's radios were powered by the plane's batteries, which were charged by a generator on the right-hand engine. In theory, the transmitter could be used without running the engine, but the batteries would be quickly drained, leaving no way to start the engine to recharge them. As a practical matter, if signals were being sent from the plane for a protracted period, the engine had to be running and turning with enough power to keep the batteries charged. For every hour that signals from the plane were being received, the engine had to be burning at least six gallons of gas. Mantz was having a hard time believing the plane could have enough fuel to support McMenamy's claims, but he remained hopeful. "If I heard the voice, I could tell instantly if Amelia were sending. She speaks right into the microphone with her lips almost on the instrument. The resultant sound is calm, drawling, and sort of whispery."[24]

Itasca's radio operators were familiar with Earhart's speaking style too, but the voice that was being reported by the Hawaiian stations was male, and as Hanzlick had told the United Press earlier that night, no one on *Itasca* was certain Noonan was with Amelia.[25] And the men aboard the cutter were still operating under the assumption that the plane had an emergency generator and could transmit distress calls if afloat on the ocean.

As the cutter steamed southwestward, the airwaves on 3105 remained quiet. At 2:00 AM, searching slightly off frequency as he had done before, Bellarts found a familiar sound and typed, "Signal on about 3110. Sounded like QZ5." An hour later, Pan American's facilities at both Midway and Wake heard a "wobbly" signal on 3105 that "sounded like a phone but was too weak to identify." No one else heard it.[26] A few minutes later, Midway heard "a very faint broad signal, apparently a phone," but was unable to take a bearing. Wake heard nothing, but according to the operator at Midway, the Pan American station at Mokapu in Hawaii "reported taking a bearing on it which might be 175 approximately."[27]

A bearing of 175 degrees goes into a part of the Pacific far beyond where the plane could possibly be and where no known sources for a signal existed. The directional estimate was so uncertain that the operator at Mokapu did not even mention it in his report. He did, however, confirm that three minutes later he began hearing "rough, weak signals" that continued for the next quarter of an hour. During that time he was able to get a "doubtful bearing of 213 . . . may be plus or minus ten degrees." The information was passed along to *Itasca* with the caution that it was "offered only as [a] possibility."[28]

In trying to take bearings on signals that, if they were legitimate calls from the Electra, had to be coming from the search area, Pan American was pushing the limits of its direction-finding system. The stations at Mokapu, Midway, and Wake were designed to guide the Pan Am Clippers as they island-hopped across the North Pacific. The refueling stops were roughly twelve hundred miles apart, so the island stations were never required to take bearings on a plane that was more than about six hundred miles away. The Earhart Electra had vanished somewhere in an area that was three times that distance from each of the three Pan Am stations.

The "plus or minus ten degrees" margin of error for Mokapu's "doubtful bearing of 213" takes in Howland, Baker, and the Phoenix Group as potential locations for the source of the signal. Neither Howland nor Baker nor *Itasca* was transmitting on 3105 at that time. The islands of the Phoenix Group were uninhabited except for a small coconut plantation on Hull Island. The overseer there had a transmitter, but it had been out of service since June. In short, there is no known source for the signal heard by Mokapu, but the bearing passes closest to the uninhabited islands in the southwestern part of the Phoenix Group—McKean and Gardner.

Aboard *Itasca*, the airwaves had been quiet for the past several hours. While the Pan Am station in Hawaii was taking a doubtful bearing on rough, weak signals, the cutter's radio operator was hearing nothing but heavy static. But five thousand miles away, yet another amateur was hearing a call from the missing plane. A more unlikely witness in a more unlikely place is difficult to imagine.

Rock Springs is a precarious patch of green in the Red Desert of south-western Wyoming. In 1937, New Deal programs had somewhat softened the impact of the Great Depression on the coal-mining town, and perhaps for that reason Cyrus Randolph was able to support his son Dana's hobby. Dana was sixteen years old, and for the past eight years he had been fascinated with radio. Under the tutelage of his uncle John Randolph he had "studied and worked on the mechanics of radio" and "built his own sets." At 8:00 AM on the morning of the Fourth of July, Dana was listening on a commercial set with a shortwave receiver using "a new antenna he had designed and just had erected." His father was in the kitchen when he heard Dana yell, "Hey, Paw! I got Miss Earhart!"[29]

As the local *Rock Springs Rocket* later reported, Dana had heard a woman say, "This is Amelia Earhart. Ship is on a reef south of the equator. Station KH9QQ [*sic*]." Then the signal died away.

The elder Randolph came running and he and his son listened closely. Again the woman's voice came from the loud speaker, repeating her name, the call letters of her station, and fading away again as she began to give her location. The procedure was followed for 25 minutes.

Dana's Uncle Victor Randolph, who lives next door, came in and was told about the reception of the call for help.

"Everybody wants to know about that," he told his nephew. "Get down town and report that."

Cyrus and Victor Randolph immediately went to the police station to learn where the report should be made. They were directed to a local Department of Commerce radio operator. He notified Washington of their report, saying that the plea for help had come in at 16,000 kilocycles, and then the three of them dashed to the Randolph home to listen again.

But despite constant vigilance at the radio almost day and night, no other clear message came through. Sounds that seemed almost to be the voice of the flier were heard but they were not clear enough to be understood.[30]

It was almost noon in the Central Pacific before word of the incident reached *Itasca*. A message from San Francisco Division read: "Unconfirmed reports from Rock Springs, Wyoming, state Earhart plane heard 16,000 kilocycles. Position on a reef southeast of Howland Island. This information may be authentic as signals from mid-Pacific and Orient often heard inland when not audible on coast. Verification follows."[31]

Verification did follow three hours later. "Following received from Rock Springs in response to inquiry. 'Investigation reveals signals heard near sixteen megacycles [are] thought to be from KHAQQ, signed KDN.' "[32] Station KDN was the Department of Commerce aeronautical radio facility in Rock Springs. The operator there believed that Dana Randolph had heard Amelia Earhart because he knew from personal experience that receptions like the one the boy reported were possible. He undoubtedly realized that the frequency Dana read from the dial of his commercial set was very close to 15,525 kilocycles—the fifth harmonic of 3105.

In assessing the credibility of the story, the government investigator may have also been influenced by another consideration. The Randolph family was African American. In the Rock Springs of 1937, for these men to spread false information about a famous white woman would be, to say the least, unwise.

The probability of a fully intelligible voice message from the Earhart aircraft, assuming it was on Gardner Island in the Phoenix Group, being heard in Rock Springs on the fifth harmonic of 3105 at the specific time in question, using the type of receiving antenna typical of home shortwave sets, is just shy of 1 percent.[33] Dana, however, was not using a typical antenna. He was a knowledgeable amateur using "a new antenna he had designed and just had erected."[34] Without knowing the particulars it is impossible to say for sure, but Dana's new antenna may have considerably improved his odds of receiving at least a partially understandable signal.

The Randolph family's claim appears to have no bandwagon aspect. The local paper was published only every other day, and the news of distress calls from the lost fliers had not yet reached Rock Springs. When Dana's story appeared in the July 6–7 edition of the *Rock Springs Rocket*, the headline read "First Radio Contact with Miss Earhart Made by Springs Boy."[35]

The content of the call the Randolphs heard is a departure from the transmissions other amateurs reported. According to the Rock Springs newspaper, Dana heard the woman say, "This is Amelia Earhart."[36] It was the first time someone claimed to hear Amelia giving her name rather than her call letters. The call sign mentioned in the newspaper article, KH9QQ, is incorrect, but the Department of Commerce radio operator who investigated the report made no mention of the discrepancy. It seems likely that the newspaper reporter simply got it wrong.

The description of the plane's position and situation reported by the Randolph family was at odds with the prevailing assumption that Earhart was afloat on the ocean. On the morning of July 4, neither the public nor the searchers had yet received the news that the plane had to be on land to transmit. According to the *Rocket*, Dana heard Earhart say, "Ship is on a reef south of the equator." The position information given to the Coast Guard by the Department of Commerce investigator was more specific. According to his report, the reef was "southeast of Howland."[37]

There are reefs southeast of Howland. One of them encircles Gardner Island, the atoll that lies closest to the bearing Pan American took during the time Dana Randolph was hearing the woman who claimed to be Amelia Earhart.

Manager and client, publicist and celebrity, husband and wife. George Putnam and Amelia Earhart; with executives of the Sperry Corporation circa 1936. *TIGHAR Collection, courtesy of Honeywell Commercial Avionics Division*

The Stars and Stripes go up over Howland Island. The man standing in front of the flagpole appears to be James Kamakaiwi, leader of the U.S. Department of Interior colonists and the man for whom the airport on Howland was named. *TIGHAR Collection, courtesy of Frank Stewart*

For the Oakland to Honolulu leg of Earhart's first World Flight attempt in March 1937, the Electra carried a four-person crew; (l. to r.) technical adviser Paul Mantz; Amelia Earhart; and navigators Harry Manning and Fred Noonan. *TIGHAR Collection*

Earhart's Electra arrived in Hawaii on March 18, 1937, with serious mechanical problems. In the hangar at Wheeler Army Airfield mechanics can be seen working on the starboard propeller. *TIGHAR Collection*

A few minutes before dawn, March 20, 1937. Luke Field, Pearl Harbor. This is the earliest known photo of the Electra after the takeoff accident that ended the first World Flight attempt. Earhart looks on as Manning reaches into the cockpit. The person behind Manning appears to be Paul Mantz. *TIGHAR Collection*

The Coast Guard cutter USCG *Itasca* was detailed to "act as plane guard and furnish weather" for Earhart's flight in June 1937. *TIGHAR Collection, courtesy of Frank Stewart*

Itasca's commanding officer, Cdr. Warner K. Thompson. The lei around his neck suggests that this newspaper photo was taken upon *Itasca's* arrival in Hawaii from California on June 15, 1937. *TIGHAR Collection*

Bandoeng, Java, June 1937. Earhart and Noonan confer with Royal Netherlands East Indies Airlines mechanics. Instrument problems delayed the flight for several days. *TIGHAR Collection, courtesy of Mrs. Wiersma*

NR16020 en route from Bandoeng to Surabaya, Java, on either June 24 or 26, 1937. The Electra made the short trip twice. *TIGHAR Collection, courtesy of Francis Furman*

Port Darwin, Australia, June 28, 1937. Earhart and Noonan prepare for the flight to Lae. Identifiable items include two cans of tomato juice on the cabin floor, a can of "Mobilubricant" carried by AE, a metal canister (probably nitrogen for servicing landing gear struts), two parachutes, a spare tail wheel, a control wheel, and another can of lubricant on the ground behind Noonan. *TIGHAR Collection*

Lae, Territory of New Guinea, 10:00 AM, July 2, 1937. This is the only known still photograph of the Earhart Electra taken during its final takeoff run. The loop antenna and dorsal transmitting antenna are visible but the receiving antenna on the underside of the aircraft is missing. *TIGHAR Collection, courtesy of Alan Board*

In this publicity photo, Earhart demonstrates how she tunes the Electra's Western Electric radio receiver using the remote controls on the instrument panel. The actual receiver was installed under the copilot's seat. *TIGHAR Collection*

Itasca's Chief Radioman, Leo G. Bellarts, saved the original radio log of the cutter's attempts to communicate with Earhart. *TIGHAR Collection, courtesy of David Bellarts*

The radio room of the Coast Guard cutter USCG *Tahoe* was virtually identical to that of its sister ship *Itasca*. *National Archives*

Adm. Orin G. Murfin, Commandant of the Fourteenth Naval District, directed the search for Earhart from his headquarters at Pearl Harbor. *National Archives*

Visiting Honolulu on its annual Navy ROTC training cruise, the battleship USS *Colorado* (BB-45) was commandeered to search for Earhart. *National Archives*

Radio distress calls reported by Karl Pierson and Walter McMenamy received national press attention and significantly influenced the Coast Guard's search for Earhart. McMenamy later admitted that the messages were bogus. *National Archives*

"Hey Paw! I got Miss Earhart!" Sixteen year-old radio amateur Dana Randolph said he heard Earhart say, "Ship is on a reef south of the equator." A government investigation found his report to be credible. *TIGHAR Collection, courtesy of the Rock Springs Rocket*

Betty Klenck in St. Petersburg, Florida, heard anguished distress calls on her family's shortwave radio. The notes she took appear to contain information that could only have come from Amelia Earhart. *TIGHAR Collection, courtesy of Betty Klenck Brown*

The west end of Gardner Island as it appeared in the late 1930s before the island was inhabited. The wreck of SS *Norwich City* is clearly visible, aground on the edge of the reef at right. The tide is high and the reef flat is awash. Inland from the sand beach, the island is covered by dense vegetation. The main passage into the central lagoon is at center top in the photo. *TIGHAR Collection, courtesy of Royal New Zealand Air Force*

The reef flat at Gardner Island at low tide on a calm day in 2001. The boundary between ocean and reef flat is visible as a thin line of surf at left. The beach and island are roughly 150 yards out of frame to the right. *TIGHAR Collection, courtesy of Ric Gillespie*

USS *Colorado* carried three Vought O3U-3 "Corsair" floatplanes for scouting and spotting for the ship's guns. During the Earhart search, the planes were used for aerial inspections of the reefs and islands of the Phoenix Group. This aircraft, Plane No. 4-0-6, was flown by Lt. (jg) Leonard Fox. *U.S. Navy photo*

USS *Colorado's* Senior Aviator, Lt. John O. Lambrecht, saw "signs of recent habitation" on Gardner Island one week after the Earhart plane disappeared. The island had been uninhabited since 1892. *TIGHAR Collection*

The northern shoreline of Gardner Island photographed from one of USS *Colorado's* aircraft on July 9, 1937. The tide is high and seaward portion of the reef is obscured by surf. The hand-drawn north arrow points due West. *New Zealand National Archives*

The aircraft carrier USS *Lexington* devoted its entire search to areas of open ocean west and north of Howland Island. *National Archives*

CHAPTER FIFTEEN

Negative Results
the third day

It was Sunday, the Fourth of July, and just as George Putnam and his wife had hoped, Amelia Earhart's name was on the front page of every newspaper in the country. The headlines, however, were not what they had planned:

Storm Turns Back Plane Sent to Find Miss Earhart; Several Radio Calls Heard[1]
Storms Balk Navy Plane on Earhart Hunt; U.S. Battleship and Aircraft Carrier Sent to Join Search as Radio Signals Die Out[2]

On Independence Day morning, the American public awoke to the news that Amelia was out there somewhere calling for help but her signals were dying out. The navy plane had been forced to turn back, but now a battleship and an aircraft carrier were rushing to her rescue. It was not drama. It was melodrama.

Truth be told, the press had jumped the gun. The navy had not yet committed to sending the aircraft carrier and its escort of destroyers. Reporters had found out that USS *Lexington* had been ordered to "prepare for a south seas cruise that might last four weeks." Word had also leaked that the naval air station at North Island in San Diego was preparing to put "six squadrons of aircraft" aboard the carrier. There could be no doubt about the ship's projected mission.[3]

At noon in Washington, Admiral Leahy did the only thing he could do. He issued the order to the commander in chief of the U.S. Fleet: "When *Lexington* Group is in all respects ready, proceed to assist in search for Earhart plane. Cooperate with Commandant Fourteenth Naval District, *Colorado*, and *Itasca*."[4]

The Navy Department now had a new reason for finding Earhart and Noonan as soon as possible. Critics of the Roosevelt administration were sure to protest the cost of sending an armada of warships thousands of miles to search for one lost private airplane. If the missing fliers could be rescued quickly, the ships could stand down. But finding Earhart and Noonan meant looking in the right place.

On Friday, naval aviation officers in Hawaii had reasoned that strong winds had probably carried the plane "southeast of Howland."[5] On Saturday night, Pan American had taken a directional bearing on a radio signal that seemed to be coming from somewhere in the Phoenix Group southeast of Howland. On Sunday morning, an amateur report that was judged to be authentic put the plane on a reef southeast of Howland. Now the newspapers were quoting Paul Mantz as saying that the plane had to be on land to transmit. Mantz believed that "Miss Earhart landed on one of the Phoenix Islands, a group southeast of Howland Island."[6]

What the navy needed was for someone to search the Phoenix Islands as soon as possible. *Itasca* was the only ship actively searching, and it was concentrating on the ocean north and west of Howland. *Colorado* was still days away. What about that British warship that had heard possible signals from the plane? It was down there somewhere, on its way from Samoa to Hawaii, and British cruisers carried a catapult-launched seaplane. An hour after the chief of naval operations activated the *Lexington* Group, the U.S. Navy radio station at Tutuila, American Samoa, sent a message to HMS *Achilles*: "What is your present position? The Navy Department requests this information in connection with Earhart search now in progress."[7] The cruiser replied with a position that put it some thirteen hundred miles east of the search area—almost exactly as far away as *Colorado* was to the north. There was no point in getting the British involved if they could not get there any faster than the American battleship. *Achilles* was not asked to assist in the search.

As *Colorado* plowed southward, the battleship's commanding officer, Capt. Wilhelm Friedell, was monitoring the developing situation. In his official report of *Colorado*'s role in the search he described his perception of how things stood on that morning of July 4: "On the night of 3 and 4 July no signals were heard on the plane frequency by the *Itasca* or *Colorado*, but reports were received from Wyoming, Honolulu, Los Angeles, Australia and other points that signals, and in some cases voice reports, had been received from the plane. . . . There was no doubt that many stations were calling the Earhart plane on the plane's frequency, some by voice and others by signals. All of these added to the confusion and doubtfulness of the authenticity of the reports."[8]

Friedell's impressions were almost completely in error. During the night, *Itasca* heard numerous signals on the plane's frequency. The battleship's commanding officer did not know it because nobody knew it. Information was flowing in to *Itasca* about what other stations were reporting, but the cutter was silent about what its own operators were hearing. Captain Friedell's assumption that "many stations were calling the Earhart plane on the plane's frequency" was also wrong. The Coast Guard's San Francisco

Division had not told the navy about the precautions taken to avoid misunderstood signals.

The lack of communication was largely due to the absence of a centralized command structure for the search effort. Earhart and Noonan had been missing for forty-eight hours. The Coast Guard, the navy, Pan American Airways, and commercial radio stations in Hawaii were all doing their best to help find the lost fliers, but no one was in charge of the overall effort.

As *Itasca* began its third day of searching, Commander Thompson was grudgingly investigating the position reported by McMenamy and his friends. As he explained in his later report: "In view of possibilities of the plane being able to transmit on the water as indicated in prior information, [*Itasca*] stood west to this latest reported position for the purpose of proving or disproving the reports which could not be consistently ignored."[9]

As daylight returned, the cutter's radio room resumed its calls to Earhart on the plane's frequency. Throughout the day, every thirty minutes, on the hour and half hour, the operator on duty would transmit a long count in voice on 3105 kilocycles: "*Itasca* calling Earhart 1-2-3-4-5-6-7-8-9-9-8-7-6-5-4-3-2-1. If you get me, come in please."[10] But the airwaves were as silent as the sea was empty.

At one point during the day, *Itasca* received a position report from SS *Golden Bear*.[11] The Matson Line ship was about 350 miles northwest of Howland and almost exactly on the 157–337 degree line of position Earhart had said she was following. The ship had no voice radio capability and so was not a potential source of hoax messages.[12] *Golden Bear*'s only reason for contacting *Itasca* was to ask the cutter to relay its position to another of the company's passenger/cargo liners. *Itasca* complied with the request but made no attempt to enlist *Golden Bear*'s help in the search for the missing plane; nor did it advise Coast Guard headquarters or the navy that another ship was near the search area.

In an afternoon update to Treasury Secretary Morgenthau, Commander Thompson's tone was not optimistic:

Have searched area NW to NE of Howland [within] radius [of] 120 miles with negative results though visibility, weather, and sea conditions excellent. Extra and vigilant lookouts posted and continual use both high power searchlights during darkness.

Am reasonably certain party is not afloat in area indicated. Commenced rectangular search this morning at daybreak [from] 180 Meridian to Howland Island between Latitude 0.20° North and 1.30° North. Estimate origin this search well to westward and leeward of plane position if plane down west of island.

Will have covered indicated area to Howland by Tuesday evening 6
July. Estimate searching three thousand square miles daylight visibility
and one thousand five hundred square miles during night.[13]

The secretary of the treasury was not the only one asking Commander
Thompson for information. The newsmen aboard *Itasca* wanted to send
their wire services more details. Thompson contacted his superiors seeking permission to release the content of Earhart's communications: "Press
requesting release exact text Earhart messages. Aside from [necessity for]
long transmission and regulations, have no reason not to permit release.
Request permission to release."[14] Thompson appears to have been eager
to provide the press with specifics about what had happened on Friday. He
was increasingly doubtful that the search would end well, and the public
needed to know that he, his ship, and the Coast Guard were blameless. The
commandant's office approved the request, provided that the regulation
prohibiting the sharing of private communications (such as commercial
telegrams) was not violated and that the long transmission needed to send
the text did not interfere with search operations.[15]

Rather than give the two wire service reporters aboard *Itasca* access to
the radio room logs, Thompson composed his own version of events and
sent it to Washington. Coast Guard headquarters could then release the
story to the press.

Following text messages received by *Itasca* from Earhart morning 2
July . . . forwarded for headquarters release to Associated and other
presses.

All messages [were in] voice on 3105 kilocycles. Any press release
should clearly indicate that *Itasca* was at Howland as homing vessel
only and that this, with weather, was sole radio duty requested by
Earhart.

Ship met all Earhart requests with exception inability to secure
emergency radio bearings on 3105 kilocycles due [to] brief Earhart
transmissions and [her] use of voice.

With exception 0803 message, no *Itasca* message or request acknowledged by Earhart. Earhart apparently never received *Itasca* requests
[to] transmit on 500 kilocycles in order [for] *Itasca* to cut her in with
ship direction finder.[16]

Thompson then provided the requested "exact text" of the voice messages
received from Earhart. All of the transmissions he quoted were taken from
the log for position 2, the radio position dedicated to communicating with
the plane. In nearly every case there are significant discrepancies between

what the operators logged on the morning of July 2 and what Commander Thompson alleged two and a half days later. Thompson never claimed to have heard any of the transmissions himself.

0245 Recognized Earhart voice message. Not clear except "cloudy weather cloudy."[17]

Chief Radioman Leo Bellarts had the watch at that time. He was using headphones. Bellarts's radio log entry for 0245–48 was: "Heard Earhart plane but unreadable through static."[18]

0345 *Itasca* from Earhart. *Itasca* broadcast on 3105 kilocycles on hour and half hour. Repeat broadcast on 3105 kilocycles on hour and half hour. Overcast.[19]

Thompson's time and text agree with Bellarts's log entry except for the word "overcast."[20] Like "cloudy weather cloudy," Thompson was putting words in Amelia's mouth.

0453 Heard Earhart voice signals [but] unreadable with five [people] listening.[21]

Five people could not have been listening at 0453 because the signals were still only strength 1, not nearly strong enough to be put on the loudspeaker in the radio room. Only the two operators heard the transmission over their headphones. Bellarts logged: "Heard Earhart. Part cloudy." O'Hare, at the other position, was busy transmitting a message when "Earhart broke in on phone 3105." He logged the message as "unreadable."[22]

0512 Wants bearing on 3105 kilocycles on hour. Will whistle in microphone.[23]

No signal was heard at 0512. Bellarts logged the message Thompson quoted at 0614.[24]

0515 "About 200 miles out." Whistled briefly in microphone.[25]

Again, Thompson was an hour off. Bellarts logged the message at 0615.[26]

0545 "Please take bearing on us and report in half hour. I will make noise in microphone. About 100 miles out."[27]

The time should be 0646.[28]

0730 "We must be on you but cannot see you, but gas is running low. Have been unable reach you by radio. We are flying at 1000 feet."[29]

Galten logged the transmission at 0742, not 0730. The difference is only twelve minutes in this case, but it is an important discrepancy. Earhart was transmitting at quarter past the hour Greenwich Civil Time, just as she had said she would. A message at 0730 would be off schedule. Despite having earlier reported to headquarters that Earhart said she had only half an hour of gas left, Thompson was now quoting the "gas is running low" version of the transmission.[30]

0757 "We are circling but cannot see island. Cannot hear you. Go ahead on 7500 kilocycles with long count either now or on schedule time on half hour."[31]

Once again, when faced with ambiguity, Commander Thompson clarified the situation by changing the facts. Galten's original 0758 log entry was: "We are drifting but cannot hear you."[32] That did not seem right, so he erased "drifting" and typed in "circling." "We are circling but cannot hear you" still did not make much sense, so the captain changed it to something that did. "We are circling but cannot see island."

0803 "Earhart calling *Itasca*. We received your signals but unable to get minimum. Please take bearings on us and answer on 3105 kilo-cycles." Earhart made long dashes for brief period but emergency high frequency direction finder could not cut her in on 3105 kilocycles.[33]

This is the only message that Thompson reported just as it appears in the radio log.[34]

0844 Earhart called *Itasca*. "We are on the line of position 157 dash 337. Will repeat this message on 6210 kilocycles. We are now running north and south."[35]

It is obvious from the actual log entry for 0843 that Earhart's message took the operators by surprise. The message was received in two parts, and there was clearly some uncertainty about what she said.[36] None of that is reflected in Thompson's version. His account of events ends: "Nothing further heard from Earhart on 6210 or other frequencies. High frequency direction finder on Howland was set up as an additional emergency caution without Earhart's request or knowledge."[37] This was a not-so-subtle slam at Richard Black, who had brought the navy high-frequency direction finder along over Thompson's objections but had failed to mention it in his preflight messages to Earhart.

> *Itasca* had it [the high-frequency direction finder] manned throughout night but [was] never able to secure bearings due to Earhart [making] very brief transmissions and her use of voice.
>
> Earhart advised 28 June [that] *Itasca* direction finder frequency range [is] 550 to 270 kilocycles. *Itasca* ship direction finder [was] manned at 0725 and Earhart [was] repeatedly requested to transmit on 500 kilocycles to enable ship to cut her in. She neither acknowledged nor complied, though our advice indicates her ability to transmit on 500 kilocycles.
>
> Communications monitored throughout by Lieutenant Commander Baker, Lieutenant Commander Kenner, Ensign Sutter, and Lieutenant Cooper U.S. Army Air Corps.[38]

Baker and Cooper did not monitor the communications. Both officers were ashore on Howland all that morning.[39]

The story Commander Thompson sent to Washington was a self-serving portrayal of a stubborn woman who would not allow herself to be helped. Earhart ran into bad weather and got lost. Low on fuel, she went around in circles while refusing to cooperate with the Coast Guard's best efforts to save her. When last heard from, she was flying along a north–south line. The Coast Guard released Thompson's account, the Associated Press picked it up, and major newspapers ran it verbatim on page one without comment.[40] The press and the public were less interested in who was to blame than in the possibility that the damsel in distress might yet be rescued.

At Coast Guard headquarters in Hawaii, Sunday the Fourth of July was spent making plans for the coming night. The officers and operators had high hopes that darkness would bring more radio signals leading to the discovery of the missing Electra. Early in the day, the Hawaiian Section told *Itasca*: "Beginning after darkness, contemplate repeating organized listening operations 3105 [and] 6210 kilocycles of nite 3–4 July. Pan American Airways will follow same procedure with all stations concentration [*sic*] and endeavor obtain bearings. Suggest Howland direction finder be on standby for bearing if practicable." And as an afterthought: "Suggest *Itasca* remain silent 3105 and 6210 during listening period again tonight."[41]

Commander Thompson was generally in agreement, but *Itasca* was now more than two hundred miles west of Howland Island. He responded: "Will contact Howland as soon as possible and proceed as indicated. We are about out of range and possibly no contact until evening."[42] Thompson also thought it would be a good idea if *Itasca*, but only *Itasca*, were permitted to transmit on Earhart's frequencies from 8:00 PM until 9:00 PM:

> Submit desirability *Itasca* operating 3105 kcs, 6210 kcs and 7500 kcs between 2000 and 2100 this evening. If Earhart afloat in this area we are most favorably situated for communication.
>
> Our contacts [with] Earhart indicate her best reception on 7500 kcs and best transmission on 3105 kcs. If you approve, submit desirability radio silence those frequencies during period indicated except for this unit.
>
> We are sweeping east from 180 [degrees longitude]. Visibility excellent, slight sea, moderate swell, wind east 15 knots.[43]

The Hawaiian Section sent permission for Thompson to "proceed as you deem necessary."[44] Warner Thompson, however, was taking no chances. He sent the same request to San Francisco Division, noting that the commander of the Hawaiian Section had already approved his plan. San Francisco approved but cautioned that if *Itasca* intended to transmit Morse code signals to Earhart, its operators should "send at speed not greater than ten words per minute [and] sign [*Itasca's*] call letters in order [to] avoid any possible chance mistaken identity of signals."[45]

As the sun settled into the Central Pacific for the third time since the Electra had gone missing, San Francisco Division also passed along to *Itasca*, and all the other Coast Guard and navy stations involved in the search, some recently obtained information: "Reference Earhart transmitter. Due to design of transmitter, following frequencies are highly practicable. Odd harmonics of the 3105 crystals which the antennae will be resonant on without change of the dial settings 9315, 15525 and 21935. Other possible harmonic points 12420 and 18630."[46] Commander Thompson for some reason understood that this message "again indicated that the Earhart plane can possibly transmit on water."[47] The news about the harmonics bolstered the credibility of amateurs like Dana Randolph in Wyoming and Mr. Donaldson in Hawaii, but there is no indication that any of the government stations subsequently monitored the harmonic frequencies listed. As they had done on the first two nights, the Coast Guard, the navy, and Pan American Airways listened on Earhart's primary wavelengths of 3105 and 6210 kilocycles.

Earlier in the day, San Francisco had forwarded to the Hawaiian Section a request by George Putnam that "KGMB broadcast to Miss Earhart that help is on the way and that signals have been heard."[48] The Hawaiian Section contacted the commercial station, made the arrangements, and, just before sundown, sent a message to *Itasca*, *Swan*, *Colorado*, and the two major U.S. Navy radio stations in the Central Pacific: Radio Wailupe near Honolulu and Radio Tutuila in American Samoa:

> At 06:30 GCT KGMB [will] broadcast [on] 1320 kcs "To Earhart plane. We using every possible means establish contact with you. If you hear this broadcast please come in on 3105 kcs. Use key if possible, otherwise [use] voice transmission. If you hear this broadcast, turn [your] carrier on for one minute so we can tune you in, then turn carrier on and off four times, then listen for our acknowledgement at 0645 GCT."
>
> Broadcast will be repeated at 0700 and 0730 GCT. Request *Colorado*, *Itasca*, *Swan*, Tutuila, and Radio Wailupe report results after each broadcast.[49]

The Pan American direction-finding facilities at Mokapu in Hawaii, Midway, and Wake Island were also alerted. As the hour of the first KGMB broadcast approached—8:00 PM in Hawaii, 7:00 PM aboard *Itasca*, and 7:30 PM in Samoa—everyone had been alerted except for the stations on Howland and Baker. All of *Itasca*'s communication with Baker was being relayed through Howland Island, but the cutter had been unable to contact the operators there.[50]

The searchers were as ready as they were ever going to be. Now it was up to Earhart, if she was out there.

CHAPTER SIXTEEN

Bearings
the third night

As dusk came to the Central Pacific, Hawaiians who were not at a Fourth of July picnic or on their way to a fireworks display heard the KGMB Radio announcer interrupt the station's regular programming to make a special announcement: "Calling Earhart plane. Every effort being made to locate you. This station will call at 0630 GCT at which time please reply on 3105 kilocycles. Listen on 1320 as all communications originate here."[1] The preparatory call was made twice, once just before sundown at 6:30 PM and again an hour later.

At 0630 GCT, 8:00 PM Honolulu time, the experiment began: "To Earhart plane. We are using every possible means to establish contact with you. If you hear this broadcast please come in on 3105 kcs. Use key if possible, otherwise use voice transmission. If you hear this broadcast, turn your carrier on for one minute so we can tune you in, then turn the carrier on and off four times, then listen for our acknowledgement at 0645 GCT."[2] In Coast Guard and navy radio rooms around the Pacific, operators pressed their headphones to their ears, closed their eyes, and listened for a response.

Mother Nature was providing her own fireworks display that evening, and electrical storms in some areas filled the airwaves with crashing static. *Itasca* heard nothing in reply to the KGMB broadcast; nor did *Swan* and *Colorado*. The navy facilities at Wailupe and Tutuila did not hear a reply. The Coast Guard's Hawaiian Section, however, heard "answering signals, carrier broken."[3]

The best hope for pinning down Earhart's location rested on the Pan American Airways direction-finding stations at Mokapu near Honolulu, at Midway Atoll, and on Wake Island. Ten minutes before the KGMB broadcast, the operator in charge at Wake received a message from Mokapu advising him to "have men at DF and Receiver station, and one at hotel radio listening for KGMB broadcast." He complied, but Wake heard nothing in response to the commercial station's instructions for Earhart to send four dashes.[4]

Pan Am Midway also received the instructions from Mokapu. The direction finder began monitoring 3105, but in Midway's case, no one actually listened to the KGMB broadcast. Consequently, when the operator heard "a strange wobbly fone" that "cut out, remaining on the air for only short durations of time," he did not understand that he was hearing the intermittent transmissions the broadcast had asked for. As he listened, "A man's voice was distinctly heard but not of sufficient modulation to be understood or identified. . . . [A] quick shot was taken which resulted in a [bearing] of approximately 201, although the signal was of such a short duration that it was impossible to narrow it down properly."[5]

The operator at Midway informed Mokapu immediately. The Hawaiian station too had heard dashes in reply to the commercial broadcast. The *Honolulu Star Bulletin* captured the excitement.

> KGMB's first broadcast at 8 last evening brought electrifying results when several listening stations heard the signals turned on and off in conformity with instructions given by the broadcaster.
> "To Earhart plane, your signals have been heard," the hopeful announcer said in the third of the broadcasts which were continued at intervals of about 15 minutes for many hours.
> "Send two longs dashes if on sea, three if on land."
> The response to this message was too vague and weak to be deciphered, however, and hopes of quickly learning the plane's position were dashed.[6]

In their official reports, the Mokapu operators told a slightly different story. That evening, K. C. Ambler, the section supervisor, operated the direction finder, aided by his visiting boss, G. W. Angus, communication superintendent for the airline's Pacific Division. Both men heard "four distinct dashes on 3105 immediately following [the KGMB] broadcast."[7] Angus later reported:

> [W]e immediately called KGMB by phone and asked them to repeat the test. This was done and immediately after the second test, we again heard the same signals except at this time, only two dashes were received and the second dash trailed off to a weak signal as though the power supply on the transmitter had failed.
> During the time these dashes were heard, it was possible to observe an approximate bearing of 213 degrees from Mokapu.[8]

Ambler's log provides more details but is also more circumspect: "Occsionally signal strength rises sufficiently to hear voice but still too weak to distinguish a single word. Once it seemed as though it was a woman's voice but may only have been our imagination. Carrier heard from direction finder close to 3105 but signals so weak that it was impossible to obtain even a fair check. Average seems to be around 215 degrees—very doubtful bearings."[9] Doubtful though the bearings might be, they were virtually identical with those taken on a similar transmission the night before. In both cases, a voice signal on 3105 seemed to be coming from the direction of the Phoenix Islands.

The men at Mokapu were sure their receiver was correctly calibrated. As Angus explained, "We are certain of the frequency because the Coast Guard cutter, *Itasca*, had previously set their transmitter on this frequency in an effort to contact the plane. Shortly before, we had taken bearings on the *Itasca* on this frequency, obtaining an approximate bearing of 210 degrees."[10]

Mr. Angus was mistaken. Whatever station Mokapu took a bearing on, it was not *Itasca*. The cutter made its last call on 3105 at 5:00 PM Honolulu time. The Mokapu station did not start listening on 3105 until 7:30 PM.[11] What did Angus and Ambler hear that made them think it was the cutter trying to contact the plane? Did Mokapu hear the plane responding to KGMB's 7:30 PM preparatory broadcast? The bearing they took passed nowhere near *Itasca*'s position. For the third time in two nights, Mokapu had taken a bearing on a signal coming from the direction of the Phoenix Group. The Coast Guard was concerned that partially heard calls to the plane might be misunderstood to be calls from the plane. It appears that the reverse may have happened.

As the KGMB broadcasts continued, reception conditions improved and more stations began to hear the replies. After the eight-thirty broadcast, the navy radio station in Tutuila, Samoa, "heard four series of dashes." Fifteen minutes later they heard the same thing, as did the Coast Guard's Hawaiian Section.[12]

Itasca was still hearing nothing, but in accordance with the agreed-upon plan, at 9:30 PM Honolulu time (8:00 PM aboard the cutter), *Itasca* began broadcasting to Earhart. Radioman George Thompson made the first call in code on 3105. Five minutes later he repeated the transmission. At 8:15 and again at 8:20, he tried code on 6210. Next, at 8:30 and 8:35, Thompson sent code on 7500 kilocycles. Each time the call was the same, "NRUI, NRUI calling Earhart. Please answer."[13] And each time the only response was the crackle of static.

Earhart was now being called every fifteen minutes or so by KGMB on 1320 kilocycles, and by *Itasca* every five or ten minutes variously on 3105, 6210, and 7500 kilocycles. If there was ever a time when amateurs were likely to overhear and misunderstand calls to the plane as being distress calls sent from the plane, this would be it—and yet no amateur receptions were reported.

The special Coast Guard monitoring station in San Francisco was also listening and heard *Itasca*'s initial Morse code call to the plane. "Shortly after that [a] carrier was heard on 3105. Carriers were heard [on] 3105 at approximately 15 to 20 minutes past each hour to 05:05 PST seemingly [on] a prearranged schedule."[14] San Francisco Division's impression was correct. There was a prearranged schedule. Their own Hawaiian Section had arranged for KGMB to make broadcasts to the plane "at intervals of about 15 minutes for many hours," asking for a reply on 3105.[15] The Hawaiian Section, however, had not included San Francisco Division in its message alerting various ships and stations to the plan. The San Francisco operators, therefore, did not know about the KGMB broadcasts and so did not know that the signals they were hearing on 3105 exactly coincided with the commercial station's requests for Earhart to reply on that frequency.

If any of the responses to the KGMB broadcasts were hoaxes (and there is no evidence that any were), they did not originate in the mainland United States. Interference from two twenty-four-hour commercial stations—KID in Idaho Falls, Idaho, and KGHF in Pueblo, Colorado—operating on the same frequency as KGMB prevented listeners in the United States from hearing the Hawaiian station's calls to Earhart.[16]

At 8:45 PM aboard *Itasca*, George Thompson, for the first time that night, tried calling Earhart using voice on 3105 kilocycles.[17] He heard nothing in reply; nor did anyone else. Ten minutes later he tried again, but the result was the same. *Itasca*'s agreed-upon hour of transmitting to Earhart was over, but KGMB continued its periodic calls. Earhart could monitor only one frequency at a time. If she were listening to KGMB's broadcasts on 1320, she could not hear *Itasca*'s calls on 3105. At thirteen minutes past the hour, Thompson heard a weak carrier on 3105 that might be voice, but it was too faint for him to be sure.[18] Two minutes later he received a message from Hawaiian headquarters. They had heard the earlier responses to KGMB's broadcasts and, for the past hour, had heard the cutter calling the plane, but the replies seemed to have died out. "Unable to get response [to] last broadcast. Have you heard signals? Are you in communication with plane?"[19]

Before Thompson had a chance to reply, there was another weak signal in his headphones near 3105, and a few minutes later there was a "noise as of [a] generator starting up." Leo Bellarts had heard that same sound two nights before at the time of the *Achilles* incident. This time the noise was followed by a "weak carrier varying in frequency" and a "man's voice," but Thompson could not make out what the man was saying.[20]

A few minutes later, Hawaiian headquarters advised *Itasca*: "Baker Island reports heard following, "NRUI from KHAQQ" [in] voice short while ago. Howland heard weak voice."[21] Just as on the previous night, the operator on Baker Island had heard an understandable voice transmission from the plane on 3105 at the same moment that stations farther north were hearing a weak, unintelligible signal.

Freak receptions do occur. It is possible for a hoaxer in Hawaii, or even California, sending voice on 3105, to be heard clearly by a station in the middle of the Pacific but hardly at all by stations close to home. The probability of such an event is on the order of one in several tens of millions. The chance of the phenomenon occurring twice on successive nights approaches infinity. It appears that, whether genuine or bogus, the signals heard at Baker were sent from a location in the Central Pacific that was closer to that island than to Howland or *Itasca*. In other words, somewhere south of Baker Island there was a man sending voice signals on Earhart's frequency who was either Fred Noonan or an impostor.

Aboard the cutter, Radioman Thompson continued to hear the man's voice. Over the next few minutes the signal seemed to improve, but Thompson still could not make out what the man was saying.[22] At 10:00 PM, Thompson called the operator on Howland. All that afternoon and evening *Itasca* had been trying to reestablish radio communication with the island. When the ship began its search for Earhart, Radioman Frank Cipriani had been left behind on Howland to operate the high-frequency direction finder. He also had a portable Coast Guard radio with him, but it proved to be too weak to be of much use. Communication between the cutter and the island, such as it was, had been via Department of Interior operator Yau Fai Lum's amateur set. With *Itasca* searching hundreds of miles to the west, contact had been lost. Now the ship was working its way back eastward, and this time there was a reply. The following exchanges were all in Morse code and, according to the ship's radio log, were conducted between Radioman George Thompson aboard *Itasca* and Yau Fai Lum on Howland.

> *Itasca*: calling Howland Island, over.
> **Howland:** Go ahead.
> *Itasca*: Take bearings on any signals you hear on 3105 kilocycles and how about schedules, . . . wait a minute. . . . Take bearing now.
> **Howland:** Roger.[23]

Eight minutes went by with no word from the island. Thompson called again, but there was no answer. Four minutes later he tried yet again.

> *Itasca*: calling Howland Island.
> **Howland:** Go ahead.
> *Itasca*: Did you get a bearing?
> **Howland:** No, the antenna is being used to transmit.
> *Itasca*: Roger, do you hear anyone on 3105 now? Waiting.[24]

Two minutes later: "Howland Island, calling *Itasca*: Yes, at 2246 heard Earhart call *Itasca* and Baker heard Earhart plane strength 4, readability 7 last night at 8:20 PM."[25] Lum's casual statement was remarkable. He specifically claimed that he heard Earhart, not the Earhart plane or a man's voice, calling *Itasca*. A time check between the cutter and the island a few minutes later revealed the clock on Howland to be eight minutes slow, so the actual time of the call was fifty-four minutes past the hour. The cutter heard a man's voice for sixteen minutes, from thirty-seven until fifty-three minutes past the hour. It would appear, therefore, that between fifty-three and fifty-four minutes past the hour, the voice on 3105 switched from male to female.[26]

Earlier in the evening, the Pan American operator at Midway distinctly heard a man's voice. Shortly afterward, the Mokapu operators thought they heard a woman. Later, Baker heard a voice claiming to be KHAQQ calling *Itasca*. No gender was mentioned, but at the same time the cutter was hearing an unintelligible man's voice. Still later, the Howland operator seems to have heard a woman's voice.[27] Were Earhart and Noonan taking turns calling for help, or was there a hoaxer out there in the middle of the Pacific who either had a female accomplice or could convincingly mimic a woman's voice?

Coast Guard and navy authorities could not ponder such nuances because *Itasca* did not pass along the information. Even Commander Thompson's later report, "Radio Transcripts—Earhart Flight," mentions neither *Itasca* hearing a man's voice nor the strong, understandable call heard by Baker Island the night before; and Yau Fai Lum's, "Yes, at 2246 heard Earhart call *Itasca*" was changed to "Howland reports hearing KHAQQ at 2246."[28]

Asked about the report more than half a century later, Lum denied it completely: "I do not know anything about hearing signals from Earhart after she went down." He also had no recollection of Coast Guard radio-man Frank Cipriani being with him on the island and believed Cipriani's radio log to be a fabrication.[29] A second Chinese-American radio operator, Ah Kin Leong, supported Lum's recollection: "No idea who wrote the false log. I stand no radio watch on Howland Island. Cipriani, Henry Lau and me was on the Coast Guard Cutter *Itasca* when it left Howland Island looking for Earhart."[30]

Multiple primary source documents, including *Itasca*'s radio log, the ship's deck log, and diary entries by Richard Black and James Kamakaiwi, leave no doubt that Lum's and Leong's memories are incorrect. When *Itasca* departed Howland Island on July 2, ten men were left behind on the island. James "Jimmy" Kamakaiwi was in charge of five Hawaiian-American colonists (Albert Akana Jr., William Tavares, Joseph Anakalea, Carl Kahalewai, and Jacob Kaili) plus three Chinese-American licensed amateur radio operators: Yau Fai Lum (K6GNW), Ah Kin Leong (K6ODC), and Henry Lau (K6GAS). Coast Guard radioman Frank Cipriani also remained on the island to operate the navy's direction-finding equipment.[31]

Recollections often change over time to fit accepted versions of events. When asked in a 1973 interview whether "the guys on Howland and Baker ever heard" Earhart, *Itasca*'s former chief radioman, Leo Bellarts, replied, "No, they never heard her. They never heard her. We checked with them."[32]

As the night of July 4 wore on, *Itasca* received reports from Hawaii, Howland, and Baker. Commander Thompson and his executive officer, Lieutenant Commander Baker, were losing their skepticism about the radio calls and feeling the pressure from headquarters to find out where the signals were coming from. At 10:30, Howland Island received a stern message from the cutter: "This very important. From Mr. Baker here. Honolulu apparently getting Earhart signals. Want Howland keep loop in use especially at night. Use Chinese operators under your control. Keep Baker [Island] also on alert [for] plane data and to report to *Itasca* through Howland. Keep log. Captain expects results." Just to be sure, Radioman Thompson.

Itasca: Have you been calling us 3105?
Howland: No, we have been calling you on 24 [meters, or 12,500 kilocycles].
Itasca: Well we have been hearing [a] carrier on 3105 [with] a man's voice from 2137 to 2153.[33]

To make sure Lum understood the schedule and the urgency of the situation, and to make it clear that the Department of Interior radio operators were to follow Coast Guard orders, Thompson closed his message with:

Next schedule at 1 AM your time here. Use Interior's batteries if necessary. Mr. Black says Cipriani is in control and to keep continuous watch on 3105 and take bearings. Use Chinese operators. If you have trouble having the boys stand watches Mr. Black says to tell Jimmy [Kamakaiwi]. Baker heard plane calling NRUI tonight. Get direction finder in operation. *Itasca* [will be] going south of island tomorrow. If [not] possible to contact *Itasca* give all important information to Honolulu immediately. See you at 1 AM your time. How do you copy?

Lum replied: "Roger."[34]

At about this time, Commander Thompson had the radio room reply to the query Hawaiian headquarters had sent nearly an hour and a half earlier asking, "Have you heard signals? Are you in communication with plane?" He answered with a single word: "Negative."[35]

Once again the Pacific went quiet. No one heard anything for the next quarter hour. Then, at 10:43 PM, *Itasca* began hearing a "very weak rough carrier on 3105." The faint signal continued for the next fifteen minutes but was "impossible to make out." Just before the top of the hour, there was "another carrier now, smoother note on 3105. Slightly higher in frequency than [the] last one. Too weak to make out." Eighteen minutes later, "Still hear weak carrier on 3105 and now hear weak CW [Morse code] signals [a] little higher in frequency and about 20 words per minute but unread."[36] Twenty words per minute is a respectable speed. Whoever was tapping out code on a frequency slightly higher than 3105, it was not Earhart or Noonan.

Another fifteen minutes passed. The Pan Am direction-finding station at Midway resumed listening, and immediately "a strong carrier was heard on 3105 KC and a shot taken on it . . . resulting in a bearing of 175 which proved to be some unidentified station probably in South America or Russia and was later definitely disregarded as a possibility."[37] *Itasca* was still hearing unreadable twenty-word-per-minute code. On Howland, Cipriani too heard a signal and logged: "Weak carrier on 3105. No call [letters] given. Unilateral bearing impossible due to night effect.[38] Using small packed [presumably "pocket"] compass to determine relative direction. Bearing only approximate SSE or NNW."[39]

This was the first and only time during the entire search when two direction-finding stations were able to take simultaneous bearings. If Midway and Howland were hearing the same signal, if their respective bearings were reasonably accurate, and if the bearings cross, there is a high probability that the signals were coming from that point—quite literally, a case of X marking the spot. The bearings do, in fact, cross near Gardner Island, but the other questions are more difficult to answer.

The operator at Midway heard a strong carrier on 3105. Cipriani on Howland heard a weak carrier on the same frequency. Neither reported hearing code or voice. Were they hearing the same signal? Without some distinguishing characteristic reported by both stations, it is not possible to know for certain. *Itasca*, at that moment, was hearing a weak carrier on 3105 and twenty-word-per-minute code on a slightly higher frequency. None of the other stations around the Pacific reported hearing anything at that time.[40]

Midway's statement that the signal "proved to be some unidentified station probably in South America or Russia" is a non sequitur. If the station remained unidentified, nothing was proved. A 175 degree bearing from Midway passes nowhere near South America. If the source of the signals was in the opposite direction, the station was in eastern Siberia.

The bearing taken by Cipriani on Howland is even more difficult to pin down. He rotated the direction finder's loop antenna until he got a minimum signal and then determined the loop's orientation using a pocket compass. That gave him a line, not a direction, and a fairly imprecise line at that. The best he could say was that the signal seemed to be coming generally from either the north-northwest or the south-southeast. Whether by coincidence or not, Cipriani's line agreed with the 157–337 degree line Earhart had described in her last in-flight transmission.

In the end, what can be said about the simultaneous bearings taken by Midway and Howland on the night of July 4 is that both signals were of unidentified origin, either or both could have been sent from the missing plane, and neither station considered its bearing to be precise. A total of seven bearings had now been taken: four by Pan Am Mokapu, one by Pan Am Wake, one by Pan Am Midway, and one by Howland Island. None could be considered definitive, but five of the seven passed through the southwestern portion of the Phoenix Group in the vicinity of Gardner Island.

As midnight approached, *Itasca* continued to hear a faint carrier on 3105. Two, and sometimes three, other stations were sending code on nearby frequencies, but none of it was clear enough to be understandable.[41] The reported receptions by other stations were nonetheless encouraging. Perhaps *Itasca* should try to call the plane again. At twenty-five minutes into the new day, the cutter advised Hawaiian headquarters: "In view [of] Howland and Baker reports, we will open up at 0030 for one hour as earlier in evening. Suggest PAA listen for response. Estimate 7500 [is the] frequency she is receiving, from past experience."[42] It was a reasonable guess. On Friday, as the flight seemed to be drawing closer and closer to its destination, the only time Earhart had acknowledged hearing *Itasca* was when the ship transmitted on 7500 kilocycles. If they tried again, and if she received the signal, maybe she could at least indicate whether she was north or south of Howland. In any case, if she replied at all, Pan American might be able to take a bearing on the signal.

At half past the hour Leo Bellarts tapped out a Morse code message on 7500 kilocycles: "NRUI calling KHAQQ. Indicate reception by four long dashes and then give bearing Howland, north or south. This is NRUI."[43] The steady carrier on 3105 did not break in reply, but, on another receiver, a message came in from the U.S. Navy station in Tutuila, Samoa: "Following received from SS *Moorsby*, [call letters] GYSR, at 11:57 GCT, 'Hear continuous carrier wave 3105 kilocycles. Been going last couple of hours but no indication as to what it is. No way of getting in touch unless he can read Morse.'"[44]

Navy Radio Tutuila had the ship's name slightly wrong—it was actually SS *Moorby*—but the call letters were correct. Tutuila also relayed the British freighter's position as "4.5 on 185.28W."[45] The first number was clearly intended to be latitude, but was it 4.5 degrees south or north? The second number was nonsense. There is no longitude greater than 180 degrees. Despite the confusion, the message was more confirmation that some unknown station out there was transmitting continuously on 3105 kilocycles. *Itasca* was hearing it, Midway was hearing it, and now *Moorby* was hearing it.

Two minutes later Wake resumed its listening watch on 3105, and the operator in charge, R. M. Hansen, soon heard "a very unsteady voice modulated carrier." The signal was strong, strength 5, an unreadable male voice just like the one he had heard the night before. The signals continued for thirteen minutes, gradually fading to strength 2 before stopping. In his official summary, written a few days later, Hansen reported that, during that time:

> I was able to get an approximate bearing of 144 degrees. In spite of the extreme eccentricity of this signal during the entire length of the transmission, the splits were definite and pretty fair. . . . At the time I believed this bearing to be reasonable [sic] accurate and I am still of that opinion. After I obtained the observed bearing, I advised Midway to listen for the signal (couldn't raise Hawaii). He apparently did not hear it. . . . The characteristics of this signal were identical with those of the signal mentioned as being heard the previous night . . . with the exception that . . . the complete periods of no signal occurred during shorter intervals. . . . While no identification call letters were distinguished in either case, I was positive at the time that this was KHAQQ. At this date, I am still of this opinion.[46]

Hansen's statement was by far the most confident assertion that a reasonably accurate bearing had been taken on a signal sent from the missing plane. Like the majority of the other bearings, a 144 degree line from Wake passes near McKean and Gardner, the southwestern islands of the Phoenix Group.

His boss, Division Communication Superintendent G. W. Angus, did not share Hansen's opinion: "I do not believe the signals that Wake heard were from the Earhart plane inasmuch as they were unheard at Mokapu at this time. The signals heard at Wake were a continuous carrier for several minutes at a time and we [Angus and K. C. Ambler, the section supervisor for communications at Mokapu] were of the opinion that possibly these signals emanated from somewhere in Japan."[47]

Records show that no station in Japan was licensed to transmit voice on 3015, and Angus misinterpreted Hansen's report. Hansen did not say the carrier was continuous for several minutes at a time. He said he heard a signal "identical" with the intermittent voice signal with "rather wobbly characteristics" he had heard the night before, except this time "the complete periods of no signal occurred during shorter intervals."[48]

According to Mokapu's report, the operator at Midway heard it too but was able only to get a "very poor bearing" of 201 degrees.[49] The Midway operator considered the bearing to be so poor that the he did not mention it in his own report.

Angus and Ambler at Mokapu did not hear the transmissions, but just a few miles away at Radio Wailupe, three U.S. Navy operators had been

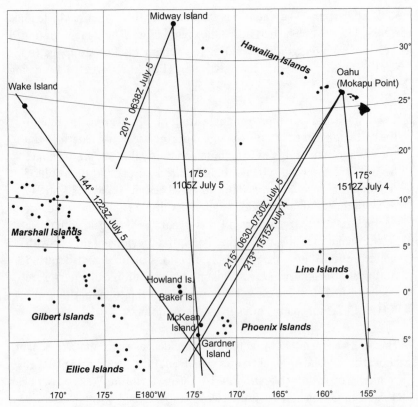

Directional bearings taken by Pan American Airways on possible distress signals sent from the Earhart plane.

puzzling over strange code messages on 3105 for the past hour. When the signals stopped, they contacted Coast Guard headquarters in Honolulu, which passed the news to *Itasca*: "Following copied Navy Radio Wailupe 11:30 to 12:30 GCT, '281 north Howland call KHAQQ beyond north don't hold with us much longer above water shut off.' Keyed transmission [but] extremely poor keying behind carrier. Fragmentary phrases but copied by three operators."[50]

After three days of fruitless searching, Commander Thompson felt that he finally had a solid lead. Here was a message, verified by three navy operators, that included Earhart's call letters and was clearly a cry for help. Most important, it contained information about the plane's position. Unfortunately, just how that information should be interpreted was not at all clear. *Itasca* received it via Coast Guard headquarters in Honolulu, not directly from the navy. Apparently someone at Wailupe telephoned the Coast Guard with a description of what they had heard. Whoever took the call at Hawaiian Section wrote it down, and the radio operator passed the report along to the cutter. Such a transfer of information offered plenty of opportunity for error, and many questions remained unanswered. How did the fragments of the message break down? For example, was it "281 north" . . . "Howland call KHAQQ," or was it "281 north Howland" . . . "call KHAQQ"? The reception was reported to have spanned a one-hour period. Was each phrase heard only once, or were they parts of a message sent over and over again?

If Commander Thompson was troubled by these questions, he did not say so. The reported phrases could be interpreted to support his long-held belief that the plane was afloat somewhere north of Howland. As he had done before, Thompson resolved ambiguities by adjusting the facts. He was sure the phrase "281 north Howland" meant 281 miles north of Howland, and he immediately ordered the ship's course altered to head for that spot.[51] Just before 3:00 AM he had the radio room send a message to the navy seaplane tender *Swan* still plodding southward toward the search area: "Official information indicates Earhart down 281 miles north of Howland. Suggest you search as indicated. *Itasca* proceeding."[52]

The phrases copied by the navy operators made it clear that the situation aboard the plane was now desperate, but Earhart's indicated position was nearly two hundred miles from *Itasca*'s present location. Even steaming at full speed, the cutter could not reach it before late in the day. Neither *Swan* nor *Colorado* could do better. At 3:14 AM, Commander Thompson had the radio room make a general broadcast for "nearest vessel [to] search 281 miles north [of] Howland."[53]

There was no response.

A few minutes later, Howland Island called with the first news of the bearing taken by Cipriani: "At 0035 Hawaiian Standard Time obtained bearing on a continuous wave of unknown origin indicating south southeast or north northwest on magnetic compass. Unable to obtain unilateral bearing due to night effect. No call [letters] given. Frequency is slightly above 3105 kilocycles."[54] Thompson took the report as further confirmation that he had been right all along. Now it was a life-or-death race against time.

The radio room had succeeded in establishing direct contact with SS *Moorby* long enough to get the freighter's correct position.[55]* It was about 250 miles northeast of the target area. After several unsuccessful attempts to reestablish radio contact, Thompson asked the navy stations at Wailupe and Tutuila to relay a message: "Following for GYSR, master SS *Moorby*: Earhart plane apparently down 281 miles north of Howland Island and

---

Moorby's position as recorded in *Itasca*'s radio log—latitude 5°59'N, longitude 163°41'W—is some eight hundred miles from the target area and cannot be correct based on where the ship was known to be a few hours later. The correct position was almost certainly latitude 5°59'N, longitude 173°41'W.

you are closest vessel. If you can divert, suggest search that vicinity. *Itasca* proceeding and will arrive this afternoon. Commander *Itasca*."[56]

While waiting to learn whether *Moorby* was willing to help, *Itasca* continued to send Morse code requests for the plane to reply with dashes, but heard no response. At times during the remainder of the night there was weak code on 3105 but no voice. Howland, too, heard a few weak signals and once picked up "distinct Japanese music on 3105."[57]

On one occasion, the Coast Guard's San Francisco monitoring station heard the cutter call the plane: "Almost immediately 4 dashes of approximately 4 or 5 seconds duration, spaces same length, [were heard] on 3105 and shortly afterward a carrier and a man's voice, the only distinguishable English being letter 'I.' This [was heard] at end of transmission. Duration voice transmission approximately 2 minutes. Dashes were heard by three radiomen and voice by two." San Francisco also mentioned that "local transport planes on 3105 were heard at various times." They were confident the signals in question were coming from the Central Pacific because the "monitors [were] using 6 receivers on 2 Honolulu diamond beam antennas."[58]

Dawn of the fourth day since Earhart and Noonan failed to arrive at Howland Island found *Itasca* steaming northward with renewed hope. The response to the KGMB broadcasts heard by multiple stations and the reports that Baker and Howland had heard the plane calling *Itasca* seemed to leave little doubt that the fliers were still alive. The fragmented message heard by the navy and the bearing taken by Howland could be interpreted to support Commander Thompson's established opinion that the plane had come down north of the island. The indicated course of action seemed clear.

It was time to brief headquarters. As soon as the sun was up, Commander Thompson sent a cautiously hopeful update to Washington: "For Secretary Morgenthau, Intercepts of ragged transmission indicate possibility Earhart plane still afloat two eighty one miles north [of] Howland. Bearings [by] radio direction finder on Howland confirmed approximate position. We will arrive indicated position this afternoon about 1700 [5:00 PM]."[59] His report to San Francisco Division was equally positive: "Reported position Earhart plane 281 north Howland apparently confirmed by radio compass bearing from Howland during night. We should arrive by dark. Will open up late afternoon on short wave and endeavor [to] get radio bearing from ship."[60]

The wire service reporters aboard *Itasca* were also eager to relate the results of the long, eventful night. Correspondent James Carey's story for the Associated Press was a mixture of fact, scuttlebutt, and misconception:

Aboard USCG *Itasca* en route north Howland. Most definite news [in] search [for] missing Earhart [and] Noonan heard Monday [at] two AM

Navy Radio Wailupe intercepted message "281 north Howland call KHAQQ beyond north won't hold with us much longer above water shut off."

Carey changed the reported phrase "don't hold with us much longer" to the more logical "won't hold with us much longer."

10:46 PM Sunday night Department [of] Interior stations Baker [and] Howland Islands report[ed] hear[ing] call "*Itasca* from KHAQQ," Earhart station call [letters]. Radio operator [aboard] *Itasca* thought [he] caught voice 12:30 AM [*sic*] today. *Itasca* radio called plane [on] both key [and] phone asking [Earhart to send] four dashes. After signal on 3105 kilocycles, *Itasca* receive[d] three dashes.[61]

Howland and Baker did report hearing the plane trying to contact *Itasca*, and the cutter's operator did hear voice several times during the night, but not at the time Carey claimed. His description of the cutter hearing three dashes is also inaccurate. At 1:00 AM, Bellarts logged: "Heard three dashes. Very ragged. Off frequency."[62] He heard the signals seven minutes after he called the plane in code on 7500 kilocycles.

At two A.M. *Itasca* west Howland approximately 300 miles from area [indicated in] Earhart message. [*Itasca*] immediately changed course [to] proceed there. Expect arrive five PM tonight.[63]

Carey had the anticipated time of arrival correct but not the distance. *Itasca* expected to cover 180 nautical miles in fifteen hours at an average speed of 12 knots, not 300 miles at 20 knots.

At four AM [during] regular schedule [between] *Itasca* and Howland, latter reported bearing approximately north to north northwest.[64]

Carey was echoing commander Thompson's half-truth. In reporting the bearing from Howland, Cipriani had specifically cautioned, "Unilateral bearing impossible due to night effect. . . . Bearing only approximate SSE or NNW."[65]

San Francisco monitor station report[ed] hearing four dashes this AM *Moorby*, British steamer, slightly south of Earhart position [at] time call received, unable [to] be contacted though calling continuously. Probably [due to] limited [radio] watches.[66]

In fact, *Itasca's* radio operators had been in direct contact with *Moorby* on at least two occasions during the night, but there was still no word as to whether the ship was willing to alter course and help search for Earhart.[67] Carey concluded on a note of cautious optimism.

Swan, 300 miles northeast [at] time call received, reported en route. All commercial stations, Pan American, [and] Navy radio constantly aid [in] listening [and] verify latest information [regarding the] search. Information considered best [so] far but not absolute.[68]

The account Howard Hanzlick filed with the United Press was similarly short on accuracy.

Most authentic signals of search received last night. *Itasca* turned [at] three A.M. Honolulu Standard Time [this] morning, speeding [to] point 281 miles northwest of Howland. Expect arrive six tonight.

The deck log shows that the ship made the turn at 1:20 AM *Itasca* time (2:20 Honolulu time).[69]*

11:47 PM July 4th, Howland reported hearing plane signals. Baker Island verified signals in code "NRUI de KHAQQ" meaning Earhart calling *Itasca. Itasca* operator reported hearing voice.[70]

Hanzlick again had the time wrong, and Baker Island heard voice, not code. At 9:40 *Itasca* time (10:40 Honolulu time), the Coast Guard operator in Hawaii called the cutter with the news that "Baker Island reports [that he] heard [the] following, 'NRUI from KHAQQ' [in] voice [a] short while ago. Howland heard weak voice."[71]

Itasca at 1:30 AM called plane [on] phone and key on 3105. Asked [plane to] send four dashes. Received three dashes [on] same frequency.[72]

This is the same distorted version of events that Carey reported. The three dashes were not in response to a call from *Itasca* on 3105. They were more likely a reply to a KGMB broadcast.

San Francisco Division heard *Itasca* call and four dashes reply.[73]

---

*Curiously, the deck log shows the cutter making the turn northward twenty-two minutes *before* receiving the Hawaiian Section's message about what Navy Wailupe heard.

San Francisco did not hear dashes until 2:47 AM *Itasca* time.[74]

[At] three AM Wailupe intercepted message "281 north Howland call KHAQQ beyond north won't hold with us much longer above water shut off."[75]

Navy Wailupe heard the fragmentary phrases between midnight and 1:00 AM *Itasca* time.[76]

Five AM Howland "obtained bearing on a continuous wave of unknown origin indicating south south east or north north west on magnetic compass. Unable to obtain unilateral bearing due to night effect. No call given. Frequency is slightly above 3105 kilocycles."[77]

Unlike Carey, Hanzlick accurately conveyed the ambiguous nature of the Howland bearing, but once more he had the time wrong. Cipriani took the bearing at 3:25 AM *Itasca* time (4:25 AM Honolulu time).[78]

British steamship *Mooreby* [*sic*] should be in approximately plane area. Have been unable contact since calls first received. *Swan* will be in area about same time [as] *Itasca* tonight. Weather; scattered clouds, sea calmer. Coast Guard headquarters Washington has text Earhart messages. Query for release [by] Washington. Not releasable here.[79]

No one aboard the cutter knew yet that Pan Am Wake had taken a bearing during the time Navy Wailupe was hearing the fragments of poorly sent code. The operator at Wake was "positive . . . that this was KHAQQ," and the bearing passed nowhere near the open sea 281 miles north of Howland.[80]
And *Itasca* still did not have the crucial piece of information that made the ship's rush to the rescue a fool's errand. The officers and men aboard the cutter were still interpreting clues and making search decisions based on their mistaken belief that the signals could be coming from a floating plane.

CHAPTER SEVENTEEN

Betty's Notebook
the fourth day

There was good news for America on Monday morning. It was official. Amelia Earhart was alive. The U.S. Coast Guard in Hawaii had confirmed that she was out there calling for help. Ships and planes of the U.S. Navy were hurrying to her rescue. Headlines across the country shouted:

HEAR AMELIA'S FAINT CALLS[1]

EARHART HEARD BY HONOLULU; DEFINITE SIGNALS
REPORTED BY COAST GUARD; WORD IS OFFICIAL[2]

NAVY RUSHES 60 PLANES TO EARHART SEARCH; HOPE
FOR SAFETY OF TWO FLYERS REVIVED AS SIGNALS BY
RADIO RECUR ALMOST HOURLY[3]

Many newspapers carried an Associated Press story in which Paul Mantz reiterated his earlier admonition that the plane could not transmit if afloat. Mantz now added his opinion that Earhart and Noonan "probably are sitting on an island."[4] The *Honolulu Star Bulletin* noted that Pan American bearings during the night "placed the transmitter roughly in the direction of Gardner and McKean Islands in the Phoenix Group, the same locality as the 'squeal' when it was first heard on Saturday night."[5]

San Francisco Division looked at the available evidence and sent a telegram to Coast Guard headquarters in Washington: "Suggest consideration be given proposal that State Department obtain cooperation British government in examination of the uninhabited portion of the islands of the Phoenix Group southeast of Howland Island. British cruiser *Achilles* recently in South Pacific nearby."[6] The suggestion came too late. The navy had already considered and rejected the idea of asking *Achilles* to help.

On July 5, the Japanese embassy in Washington notified the U.S. State Department Division of Far Eastern Affairs that it had received an urgent telegram from Tokyo offering the Japanese government's assistance in the search "in view of the fact that Japan had radio stations and warships in the Marshall Islands."[7] Now George Putnam asked Admiral Leahy, the chief of naval operations, what the Japanese were doing or might be willing to do. Leahy could not help him: "Replying to your dispatch: There is no information available here regarding any search being made by the Japanese. W. D. Leahy."[8]

Reports of receptions by amateurs continued to come in. Mrs. Thelma Dunham in Indianapolis said she had been listening on her shortwave set early Monday morning and heard a woman's voice say, "This is Amelia Earhart calling all stations. Sending equipment getting weak. Have landed on water. Don't know position. Navigator is trying to check longitude and latitude. Getting hungry but can survive for twenty-four hours." Mrs. Dunham said she heard the voice on a wavelength of "13 meters," or 23,077 kilocycles.[9] That frequency is nowhere near a harmonic of 3105, and, of course, the plane could not have sent signals if it had landed in the water. If Mrs. Dunham heard anyone, it was not Amelia Earhart.

In Los Angeles, Karl Pierson told the United Press that he heard *Itasca* call the plane "shortly before 5 AM and instruct the fliers to reply with 'four long dashes' if the call was received. Three long dashes were heard immediately on the slightly lower frequency."[10] His claim seemed credible at the time because it matched an event described in press releases filed by the wire service reporters aboard *Itasca*. Hanzlick and Carey, however, got the facts confused, and Pierson's account agrees with their flawed version of the incident rather than with the cutter's radio log. It appears that Pierson was once again bolstering his claim to have heard Earhart with information he gleaned by listening in on Coast Guard communications.

A man named Ray Mahoney in Cincinnati told a more plausible tale. The Associated Press reported that Mahoney "heard Amelia Earhart broadcasting distress signals at ten-minute intervals yesterday from a position which he interpreted to be within fifty-seven miles of Howland Island. 'The signals were weak,' he said. 'About all I could make out were the call letters of plane and apparently it had hit a reef or was near a reef.'"[11] The *New York Times* noted that Mahoney's report seemed to agree with the message Dana Randolph in Wyoming had heard the previous night in which Earhart gave the plane's call letters and said that she was on a reef.[12] If Mahoney gave specific times or a frequency for the transmissions, the press did not mention them. There is no reef within fifty-seven miles of Howland, but the islands of the Phoenix Group lie near the 157 degree arm of the line Earhart said she was "running on."[13]

While Coast Guard and navy headquarters were becoming more and more convinced that the plane was down on an island or reef in the Phoenix Group, *Itasca* was steaming at full speed in the opposite direction. At 9:30 AM aboard the cutter, Chief Radioman Bellarts was finally able to get through to the British freighter. The master of SS *Moorby* confirmed that he was "diverting and proceeding to 281 miles north of Howland."[14]

Although the sun was well up, Bellarts continued to monitor Earhart's frequency. Just before 10:00 AM he began hearing something on 3105. The signal was a "little low in frequency" and he could not make out any content.[15]

A girl in Florida seems to have had better luck. In the little house at 2027 Auburn Street South in St. Petersburg, it was late afternoon and fifteen-year-old Betty Klenck had just settled down in front of the family radio. The Klencks were not wealthy, but Betty's father, through his job at the local power company, had been able to get a good deal on a top-of-the-line set. Kenneth Klenck was an amateur radio buff, and he had rigged a special antenna from the house to the garage and across the backyard to a utility pole at the rear of the property. The resulting reception was phenomenal, and Betty spent many hours in front of the large console listening to music on local stations and cruising the shortwave dial for foreign programs. While she listened, she doodled pencil sketches of handsome men and glamorous ladies and jotted down the lyrics of her favorite songs in a notebook she kept by the set.

In tuning the dial this particular afternoon she stumbled upon a woman's voice, speaking in English and obviously quite upset. Betty listened for a while and was startled to hear the woman say, "This is Amelia Earhart. This is Amelia Earhart." For the next hour and three-quarters, Betty Klenck copied down, as best she could, the numbers and phrases that came through the radio speaker. The words came too fast for her to get everything, and often she got only a word or two of what was said. Sometimes the sound was distorted and the voice hard to understand. At other times the words seemed to make no sense at all. The signal faded in and out, often dying away completely for several minutes at a time before returning.

As Betty listened and wrote, the woman's pleas for help and attempts to give out information were often interrupted by verbal exchanges with a man who seemed to be in the same confined space. The man was irrational, and Betty had the impression that he was delirious from a head injury. The woman was trying to deal with the man's erratic behavior while struggling to maintain her own composure enough to use the radio. It was clear to Betty that both individuals were under tremendous physical and emotional stress.

Betty later explained, "I was home alone, until Dad got home from work and heard the last part of her cries for help." Kenneth Klenck immediately ran next door to see if his neighbor Russell Rhodes could also pick up the signal. "Russ couldn't get it . . . although he had the same kind of set but hardly any aerial."[16] Convinced that the distress calls were genuine, Klenck drove to the St. Petersburg Coast Guard station to report what he and his daughter had heard. The duty officer assured him that the Coast Guard was on top of the situation. "Mom was in town with my sister," Betty later recalled, "and got home before Dad got back from the Coast Guard. She came in and I was still at the radio to see if any more would come on from Amelia. I told her what had happened and she was so excited, she called Jean in (my sister) who had stayed out to play. Then Russ and Virgie Rhodes came over, then Dad got home, upset at the Coast Guard because of the way they wouldn't listen to him and do something for A.E."[17]

The Klenck family did not go to the press with their story. A few years later, while working as a long-distance telephone operator during World War II, Betty did try to get the attention of various officials in Washington. No one was interested. In 1942, Betty married U.S. Air Force gunner Oliver Brown. After the war, they moved to "Brownie's" hometown in Illinois, where they raised two children. In 1970, with Betty's permission, family friend John Hathaway wrote to Fred Goerner, author of *The Search for Amelia Earhart* (Doubleday, 1966). Goerner replied:

> I would be pleased to hear more information with respect to the message your friend received in 1937.
>
> Apparently, amateur radio operators in many parts of the country reported hearing signals from the Earhart plane, but unfortunately, they were largely discounted at the time by the U.S. Navy and U.S. Coast Guard.
>
> I do believe that many of the reports were founded on fact. Why the Navy and Coast Guard chose not to believe any of the amateur operators is a question yet to be answered.[18]

Hathaway replied with a full account of Betty's story. Goerner responded: "I can't make anything out of the messages Mrs. Brown received. The figures do not seem at all relevant, especially the supposed position reports. . . . Is there no way to determine what specific dates on which [*sic*] the broadcasts were received?" While recording what she heard, Betty had carefully noted the time of day but not the date. "I do appreciate your having taken the time to communicate with me about the matter," Goerner wrote. "I'm just afraid that without a great deal more clarification of the messages it would be impossible to make any determination from them."[19] Another thirty years would pass before sufficient information was compiled to make it possible to put the messages into context and assess their significance.

Today in her eighties, Betty Klenck Brown is the only person still living, as far as is known, who claims to have heard a distress call from Amelia Earhart. Aside from *Itasca*'s radio log, her carefully preserved notebook is the only known surviving real-time transcription of what might have been radio distress calls from the lost flier. If the voices Betty heard were those of Earhart and Noonan, her notebook provides a shatteringly intimate glimpse into their struggle to survive.

As a document dating from the summer of 1937, Betty's notebook appears to be authentic. The physical object and the notes on current films and popular song lyrics it contains are entirely consistent with the period.[20] Whether the five pages of notations relating to Amelia Earhart are transcriptions of genuine distress calls from the lost plane is a more difficult question to answer.

Were Betty and her family hearing and misunderstanding a radio play? The following year, thousands of Americans would be panicked by the broadcast of a radio drama based on the H. G. Wells story *War of the Worlds*. If Betty and her family were similarly fooled, they were alone in their gullibility. No one else reported hearing what Betty heard. During the search for Earhart, an episode of the popular CBS show *The March of Time* featured imagined messages from the lost plane. The show aired at 8:00 PM Eastern Standard Time on Friday, July 9, 1937, and presented a supposed radio conversation between Earhart and *Itasca*. *March of Time* dramatizations were half-hour programs broadcast via the local CBS affiliate and included narration, music, and, of course, commercials. The fragmented receptions Betty picked up on shortwave between 4:30 and 6:15 PM bore no resemblance to the CBS program. No other dramatization is known to have been broadcast during the search.

Were the Klencks victims of a hoax? If so, the hoaxer was apparently located a great distance from St. Petersburg, because their neighbor Russell Rhodes, lacking a sophisticated antenna, was unable to hear the signal. The only reported receptions of suspected transmissions from the plane that might coincide with Betty's transcriptions were logged by Leo Bellarts aboard *Itasca*.

The remaining possibility is that Betty did hear Earhart and Noonan. But could someone in Florida really pick up signals sent from the Electra's transmitter? Like Dana Randolph in Wyoming, Betty Klenck's receiver was connected to a specially built antenna. Betty did not make note of the frequency, but if, like Dana, she was tuned to a harmonic of 3105, it is theoretically possible that she received erratic but occasionally intelligible voice transmissions from the aircraft.[21]

Although Betty did not write down the date, the events described in her notebook dovetail with the *Itasca* radio log on the morning of Monday, July 5. Betty started hearing the woman's voice at around 4:30 PM, which was 10:00 AM in the Central Pacific.[22] The signal Bellarts logged on the morning of July 5 was the only one heard on 3105 at that hour of the daytime during the entire search.[23] As the operator aboard *Itasca* strained to hear what he thought might be a call from the plane, Betty was hearing the rapidly spoken words of a woman who was barely maintaining her composure.

Others had heard a similar voice the previous Friday morning. Commander Thompson described Earhart's last in-flight transmission as "hurried, frantic, and apparently not complete." Lt. Cdr. Frank Kenner was struck by the "desperate note" in the flier's voice. The sound still haunted Leo Bellarts years later. "She was just about ready to break into tears and go into hysterics," he remembered. ". . . I'll never forget it."[24] The voice Betty heard was also unforgettable. More than half a century later, recalling the woman's anguish brought tears to her eyes.

Betty made what notes she could; if she did not understand something, she wrote down the words she knew that were closest to the sound she heard. Any evaluation of the words and phrases the teenager transcribed must rely on the entries just as they appear on the pages of the notebook. Betty's later explanations and elaborations help make sense of her original notes, but like all oral histories, her recollections may or may not be accurate. Ultimately, the only way to judge whether Betty heard genuine transmissions from the Earhart plane is to ask whether other sources support the information and events portrayed in the notebook. Of special interest are any entries that appear to convey information that could have come only from Earhart herself.

The notebook originally had a total of eighty pages, but seven sheets toward the front of the book were torn out at some time. Betty's notes appear on five right-hand pages: 43, 45, 47, 49, and 51.

Page 43 contains the following notations:

158 mi.   44 N.E.
Help me
W40K Howland port
or W O J Howland port
waters high
here put your ear to it
This is Amelia Putnam
   "   "   "   "
SOS
stop—Amelia
speak
Uncle
Oh oh
(crying now)
help
help us quick
I can feel it
your right
Bob
come here just a moment

Betty later explained, "I was so floored at hearing 'This is Amelia Earhart' several times I didn't start writing right away until the numbers started being said. Several times she said something about '158 miles' and something else about '44 north east.' "[25] *

The woman said, "Help me," and then a garbled phrase Betty could not make out. It sounded something like "W40K Howlandport" or maybe "W O J Howlandport."[26] The phrase may have been "WPA Howland airport." During preparations for Earhart's world flight, the construction of the landing field on Howland Island was known as the "WPA airport project."

The woman then said "water's high."[27]

Aboard *Itasca*, Bellarts responded to the faint signal by calling Earhart on 3105 using Morse code.[28] Betty heard the woman say to the man who was with her, "Here, put your ear to it." Was Earhart holding up an earphone so that Noonan too could hear the dots and dashes? If so, she was receiving the signal over the loop antenna, because the belly antenna had been lost on takeoff in Lae, New Guinea.

The woman made another broadcast. Betty's notation reads: "This is Amelia Putman [*sic*]. SOS." The teenage girl thought Earhart's husband's name was "Putman," so that is the way she spelled it. Amelia almost never used her married name, but during her time in Australia and New Guinea she was invariably known as Mrs. Putnam. According to Betty's later recollection, the woman said, "This is Amelia Earhart Putnam," and repeated it several times.[29]

The woman's calls for help were interrupted by events in the background. "Stop!" the woman said to the man in an annoyed tone, and there followed quite a bit that Betty could not get. Then, "Amelia."

"Speak."

"Uncle." Or might the word have been "ankle"?

"Oh, oh." And the woman began to cry, apparently in pain.

She was broadcasting again, "Help. Help us quick."

Then to the other person, "I can feel it."

The man said, "Your right." Could it have been "you're right"? Or was it a reference to "Your right [ankle]"?

One of them said, "Bob," which seems to make no sense at all.

The woman to the man, "Come here just a moment."

Having reached the bottom of the sheet, Betty turned the page and kept writing. Page 45 of the notebook reads:

---

*Many years later, as an explanation for her children, Betty added a note to the upper left corner of page 43: "Time I heard Amelia Earhart call for help. Dad had put up a tall aireal [*sic*] from house to pole in lot in back of our house for short wave on our radio. I always came home from school and listened to short wave and all summer. We lived on Auburn St. So. #2027 in St. Petersburg, Florida."

58   338
send us help
Amelia take it
hear it
help help
I need air
Amelia things are
here I come—oh
let me out of here
different suffer
Amelia
take it away Howland
N.Y. N.Y. N.Y.
Marie   Marie
N.Y. N.Y.
Oh, if they could hear me
N.Y. N.Y.
Marie
It's going

The "58 and "338" at the top of the page resemble the notations "158 mi." and "44 N.E." at the top of the previous page. They are numbers that Betty heard spoken, but their significance is a mystery. Following the numbers came another broadcast plea from the woman, "Send us help."

The man said, "Amelia, take it. Hear it." Is he now passing the headset back to the woman? If so, the notebook again appears to match the *Itasca* radio log. Seventeen minutes after Bellarts's earlier transmission, he again tried to contact the plane.[30]

According to Betty it was the man who said, "Help, help, I need air. Amelia, things are." To which the woman replied, "Here I come—oh," crying out in pain again.

The statements and implications in Betty's notebook echo Mabel Larremore's claim that, on the night of July 2, she heard Earhart say that "her navigator Fred Noonan was seriously injured. Needed help immediately. She also had some injuries but not as serious as Mr. Noonan."[31]

To Betty, it sounded like the man would alternately struggle with the woman and try to get the microphone away from her, or panic and try to get out of the airplane. If she was really hearing Earhart and Noonan, the airplane had been on the ground for three days and three nights. Radio transmissions could be made only from the Electra's cramped cockpit, and the temperature inside a metal airplane parked in the tropical sun can easily exceed 120°F. If the airplane's rear cabin door was unusable for some reason, such as a collapsed left landing gear, the only way out would have been via the hatch directly over the pilot's seat. Using the hatch was cumbersome and meant standing on the seat and clambering over the edge and onto the wing. Someone trying to exit the plane while the pilot's seat was occupied might create just the sort of chaotic scene implied in the notebook.

The man said, "Let me out of here." The woman, apparently trying to reason with him, said something about ". . . different suffer." The man, speaking directly into the microphone, said something about "Amelia," and then, "Take it away Howland." The phrase appears to mimic a convention commonly used by commercial radio announcers at that time, as in, "We go now to our reporter in Chicago. Take it away, Chicago."

From what she heard, Betty gathered that the plane had crashed on land but that somehow water was coming in and getting deeper and deeper, as if the tide was rising. Two other amateurs—Randolph in Wyoming and Mahoney in Ohio—had described the aircraft as being on a reef. Mabel Larremore in Texas said Earhart was "down on an uncharted island. Small, uninhabited. The plane was partially on land, part in water."[32]

Most of the reefs in the Central Pacific are associated with atolls, and all are tidal. The few reefs that do not encircle islands are too sharp and ragged to permit a survivable landing by an airplane. However, some portions of the reefs surrounding the uninhabited atolls of the Phoenix Group are smooth enough to permit a normal, wheels-down landing and are dry at low tide. During the late morning hours of July 2, 1937, the time when the Electra could have arrived overhead, the tide was out in the Phoenix Islands.[33] Klenck, Randolph, Mahoney, and Larremore, therefore, were independently describing what could be the same set of circumstances: an aircraft that had made a relatively safe landing on a reef adjacent to one of the uninhabited atolls of the Phoenix Group.

The woman next said something that Betty wrote down as "New York, New York, New York."

The man, again speaking into the mike, said what sounded to Betty like "Marie, Marie." Noonan's wife's first name was Mary Bea.

The woman again, "New York, New York." "Oh, if they could hear me." "New York, New York." The woman's repetition of the phrase Betty recorded as "New York, New York" suggests that it was vital information, perhaps something that would lead to their rescue. What was the woman really saying?

Anyone stranded on an island and calling for help might reasonably be expected to transmit three essential pieces of information: their name, their desire for assistance, and their location. The most obvious way to describe an island is by its name, but conspicuously absent from all of the alleged distress calls is any mention of an island name. Several amateurs claimed to have heard Earhart give out latitude and longitude, but all of the coordinates were unintelligible, impossible, or subsequently lost. The fragmented code phrases copied by Navy Radio Wailupe seem to contain attempts to describe a location, but they include neither an island name (other than Howland) nor anything that might be a latitude/longitude position.

If Earhart and Noonan were alive and sending distress calls, they were on an island or a reef adjacent to an island. If the calls were genuine, it would appear that they did not know the name of the island and were unsure of its position. That supposition is reinforced by Mabel Larremore's claim that she heard Earhart describe the island as "uncharted."[34] In 1937 there were no uncharted islands in the Central Pacific. Some of the published coordinates were slightly off, and charts depicting the shape and features of some of the atolls were wildly inaccurate, but the existence and location of all of the islands in the region had been known and charted for many years.

For the radio to be usable, the plane had to be relatively undamaged. If the airplane was essentially intact, so were Noonan's navigational charts, almanacs, and instruments needed for celestial observations. Certainly, by the first night, he should have been able to accurately determine their position, and yet that apparently did not happen. Larremore's and Klenck's allegations that Noonan was injured are therefore consistent with the absence of an island name or sensible coordinates in the reported distress calls.

The man again said, "Marie," and exclaimed, "It's going." Betty later recalled that she had the impression that the plane had moved or shifted in a way that frightened the man.

Betty turned the page and continued to take notes. The entries on page 47 are:

since 4:30   5:10
airport
Marie
oh
where are you
waters knee deep—let me out
where are you going
we can't bail out
see
yes
Amelia—yes
oh oh ouch
are you so scared
what
Hello Bud

Amelia
South 391065 Z or E
fig 8—3. 30 500 Z
3E   MJ3B
Z 38 Z 13   8983638

The first notations on the page refer to time. After taking two pages of notes, Betty decided she should record when the receptions started and note the current time. "Since 4:30" represents her estimate of when she first heard the voices, and "5:10" is the time when she began writing on the third page. The first two pages of notes thus represent a period of roughly forty minutes.

The word "airport," spoken by the woman, might be another reference to the WPA airport at Howland.

Once again, the man called out, "Marie" and an exclamation, "Oh!" The woman asked, "Where are you?"

If the woman was who she claimed to be, she had to be sitting in the cockpit of the Electra to use the radio. If she could not see Noonan, he could only have been back in the cabin. Betty heard the man shout, "Water's knee deep—let me out." Under what circumstances could there be knee-deep water in the plane's cabin? "Knee deep" might be anywhere from one to two feet. The cabin floor of an Electra is normally three and a half feet off the ground. The airplane would therefore have had to be sitting in about five feet of water.

On the reefs of the southwestern Phoenix Group, late in the morning on Monday, July 5, 1937, it was roughly the midpoint of an incoming tide. Water levels on the reefs ranged from a few inches to a couple of feet, depending on the exact location, but even at full high tide the levels did not reach five feet.

There could be knee-deep water in the cabin if the plane was on its belly, but in that situation the radio would be submerged and inoperable. For the messages to be legitimate, it had to be possible to run the plane's right-hand, generator-equipped engine to recharge the battery. For the right-hand propeller to have clearance, the right-hand landing gear had to be supporting the engine.

Betty's notes suggest that the man could not use the cabin door. If the left-side landing gear failed during the landing, the cabin door, which was on the left side of the airplane, would be unusable. Down on its left side, the airplane could very well have knee-deep water in the rear part of the cabin. A rough landing that resulted in a collapsed landing gear leg could also explain the apparent injuries to the crew.

After the man said, "Let me out," there followed a series of confused and argumentative exchanges which Betty recorded in fragmented words and phrases.

The woman, "Where are you going? We can't bail out. See."

The man, "Yes."

The woman, "Yes."

The man, "Oh, oh, ouch."

The woman, "Are you so scared. . . .What."

The man, "Hello Bud. Amelia. . . ."

Betty did not hear everything, and sometimes the signal died away entirely for several minutes at a time. On at least one occasion, while waiting to see if the voices would return, Betty turned to an earlier page in her notebook to work on her sketches. When the signal suddenly returned, she made hasty notations. Among the crowded drawings on page 39 appear "KGMB" and, on another part of the page "31.05." The notations have obvious relevance in the context of the search, but they cannot be considered to be information that could have come only from Earhart. The call letters of the Hawaiian commercial station that sent broadcasts to the plane and the frequency on which signals were being heard by stations in the Pacific had been well publicized, and Earhart's 3105 kilocycle frequency can also be expressed as 31.05 megacycles.

A third notation on page 39, "11:H," is more unusual. If it means "eleven hours," it might represent local time in the Phoenix Group, which was Greenwich Civil Time minus eleven hours. There is a final stray notation on page 56 that may or may not be part of the transcriptions. It reads, "Life depends upon it."

Toward the bottom of Betty's third page of notes there is a flurry of numbers and letters. Betty wrote "South 391065Z or E" and later made a note of her own guess as to what it might mean, "S 309' 165° E." Any interpretation of the letters and numbers as a latitude and longitude indicates a position far from where the plane could possibly be. However, on March 14, 1937, during preparations for Earhart's originally planned flight from Howland Island to New Guinea, USS *Ontario* reported that it was "en route to plane guard station latitude 03 05 South, longitude 165 00 East for Earhart flight." The ship was assigned the same position, halfway between Lae and Howland, for the July flight.[35]

The spoken numbers "nine" and "five" sound so much alike that standard radio procedure today is to say "niner" to avoid confusion. Betty's "S 309° 165° E" seems too close to "S 3 05° 165° E" to be coincidence. *Ontario*'s assigned coordinates were not public information, but it is reasonable to assume that Noonan might have them written down on a chart or in his navigational notes aboard the airplane. With her position unknown and her navigator incapacitated, Earhart could have been desperately broadcasting any information she found in the hope it would make sense to someone.

The possible significance of other letters and numbers Betty heard is more puzzling: "Fig. 8 – 3.30 500 Z   3E MJ3B   Z 38 Z 13 8983638." How accurately the figures were copied and what they might mean remain a mystery.

The next page of Betty's notebook reads:

5:30   1 hr.
hurry
3.15
are you there—fuzzy
hear from me   hear from me
George
get the suitcase in my closet
Calf.
are you
Marie Hey!
Marie
Amelia Earhart
Hey
watch that battery
what did you tell me to do
SOS
Will you help me
Will you please
all night!

As on the previous page, the first notations refer to time. Betty has noted that it is now 5:30 and she has been hearing the transmissions for one hour. This page begins with another broadcast by the woman. "Hurry" echoes the urgency of "help us quick" on the first page, and "3.15" is very much like the "31.05" that appears on page 39.

Betty heard the woman say, "Are you there." Then the signal got "fuzzy." There was something about "Hear from me. Hear from me." And then, "George, get the suitcase in my closet . . . California."

On the surface, the directive seems trivial and inappropriate given the dire circumstances the rest of the transcript portrays. In fact, it strongly resembles very private instructions Earhart issued on another occasion when her future was in doubt.

The day after Christmas 1934, Amelia and George were aboard the Matson liner SS *Lurline* en route to Hawaii with Earhart's red Lockheed Vega lashed to the ship's deck. The plan was for Amelia to fly the twenty-four hundred miles back to California, thus making the first flight from Hawaii to the U.S. mainland. As they were about to dock in Honolulu, Earhart wrote a letter to her mother, Amy, who was house-sitting at the Putnams' new home in North Hollywood, California. The letter was newsy and very matter-of-fact, but toward the end Amelia wrote: "I have taken possession of the stuff in the zipper compartment of my briefcase. Put it away until I turn up and if I don't—burn it. It consists of fragments that mean nothing to anybody but me."[36]

Earhart had memorabilia that she wanted destroyed in the event of her death. In 1934, the material was in a briefcase in the house in California (the Putnams had another house in New York). About to undertake a dangerous flight, she instructed the family member living in the house to secure the items and burn them if she did not "turn up." In 1937, at a time when Earhart might again be contemplating her possibly imminent demise, Betty heard a woman claiming to be Amelia Earhart say, "George, get the suitcase in my closet," and specify that she means "California."

Earhart's 1934 letter to her mother did not become public until many years later. It seems safe to assume that, in 1937, no one outside Amelia's immediate circle knew there was "stuff" she wanted burned if she died. Even more than the coordinates of *Ontario*'s assigned position, the inclusion in the notebook of a request for "George" to "get the suitcase in my closet" appears to be information that could only have come from Earhart herself.

Betty's notes continued as the woman tried to broadcast information while trying to deal with the man's antics.

"Are you . . ."

"Marie, Hey! Marie."

"Amelia Earhart"

"Hey. Watch that battery."

The aircraft's main battery was mounted under the floor in the passageway leading from the cockpit to the cabin. If the floorboard was removed for access, a careless step could easily damage the battery.

The man, "What did you tell me to do?"

The woman, broadcasting again, "SOS," but then to the man, "Will you help me? Will you please . . . all night!"

The final page of Betty's notes includes the following numbers, words, and phrases.

6:00 end at 6:15
what are you doing
3Z rd36
J 3
Amelia here
quick

let me out
3630
knee deep over
stop
I won't make it
38-3
huh
are you here
3
darn
30
N.Y.
N.Y. or something that sounded like New York

The notations are similar to those on the other pages: numbers and letters with no known meaning and argumentative exchanges between the two people.

Betty had the impression that the airplane was slipping or being moved by the water. The woman banged herself on something. In her notebook Betty wrote "darn," but she later explained that the woman actually let out a string of swear words. Although it was certainly not part of her public image, Earhart was well known in aviation circles for her strong language when angered.

The final notebook entry is another repetition of the cryptic, "New York New York," to which Betty added "or something that sounded like New York."

Is Betty's notebook merely a transcription of yet another hoax? Compared with the known hoaxes, it seems unlikely. Alleged distress calls from the missing plane that were later confirmed to be bogus were specific and unambiguous in their content.

Thelma Dunham, for example, reported that she heard: "This is Amelia Earhart calling all stations. Sending equipment getting weak. Have landed on water. Don't know position. Navigator is trying to check longitude and latitude. Getting hungry but can survive for twenty-four hours."[37]

Mrs. Young of Wilmette, Illinois, said she heard a voice on her shortwave say: "From Amelia Earhart. We cannot last more than three hours longer. Position 42 miles north Howland Island."[38]

Charles McGill of Oakland offered a transparent elaboration on press reports of the message heard by Navy Wailupe. He claimed to hear: "NRUI NRUI KHAQQ. Two eight one north Howland. Cannot hold much longer. Drifting northwest. We above water. Motors sinking in water."[39]

By contrast, the near panic, incomplete information, and background chaos portrayed in Betty's notes read like the transcript of a modern 911 call. The situations described and implied in the notebook appear to match events documented in the *Itasca* radio log, the circumstances required for the plane to be able to make radio transmissions, and even the interior layout of Earhart's Electra. Finally, the notebook contains what seems to be private information that could only have come from Amelia Earhart.

Such compelling evidence for the transcription's authenticity merits an attempt to decipher what the woman was saying when Betty wrote "N.Y. N.Y. or something that sounded like New York." The only island in the region whose name might conceivably be mistaken for "New York" is "Duke of York Island" in the Tokelau group. The island is near the 157 degree line from Howland, but it is more than six hundred miles away and almost certainly beyond the plane's maximum fuel range. The atoll was settled sometime before 1841 and renamed by its Polynesian inhabitants. By 1937, most maps and charts showed its name as Atafu. The island's distance from Howland and the fact that it was an inhabited British possession would seem to disqualify it as the plane's landing place. Earhart, looking at an old chart, may have mistakenly thought she was on Duke of York, but the possibility seems remote.

Another, and perhaps more plausible, interpretation of Betty's notations is that she wrote "N.Y. N.Y." as shorthand for "New York City." Her note, "or something that sounds like New York," makes it clear that "N.Y." was an abbreviation for the words she heard. If Betty was hearing Amelia Earhart repeatedly say something that sounded like "New York City," the words may have been "Norwich City."

On the night of November 30, 1929, the British freighter SS *Norwich City* went aground in a storm on the reef surrounding Gardner Island in the Phoenix Group. The oil tanks ruptured and the ship caught fire. Eleven of the thirty-five-man crew were lost, and the survivors were rescued from the island a few days later. The burned-out hulk remained on the reef. Eight years later, its name was still legible on the hull. Marooned on an island whose name and position she did not know, Earhart may have broadcast the name on the wrecked ship as the only piece of information she had that might enable a listener to identify the island. By July 5, based on the Pan American radio bearings, Gardner Island was already considered a prime suspect for the plane's location, but neither San Francisco Division, nor the navy, nor, perhaps more significant, George Putnam ever had an opportunity to evaluate the transcriptions in Betty's notebook.[40]

Shortly after the voices on Betty's shortwave faded away for the last time, the Coast Guard's San Francisco Division informed *Itasca*: "Opinion of technical aids here that Earhart plane will be found on original line of position which indicated position through Howland Island and Phoenix Group. Radio technicians familiar with radio equipment on plane all state that plane radio could not function now if in water and only if plane was on land and able to operate right motor for power. No fears felt for safety of plane on water provided tanks hold as Lockheed engineers calculate 5000 pound positive buoyancy with plane weight 8000 pounds."[41]

In other words, if the plane was down at sea it could still be afloat, but if it was sending radio messages it had to be on land and was probably on one of the islands of the Phoenix Group. San Francisco was trying to get through to Commander Thompson that his interpretation of the message fragment "281 north Howland" could not be correct.

CHAPTER EIGHTEEN

281 North

the fourth night

Warner Thompson pressed on. Throughout the morning and afternoon of Monday, July 5, *Itasca* maintained a steady northward course at maximum speed. The radio room maintained its watch on Earhart's frequency, but the airwaves once again yielded only static. Nonetheless, anticipation aboard the cutter was running high. As evening approached, *Itasca* sent a message to the men on Howland Island: "Get everything in readiness for tonight as it will be a vital one in the search. We are nearly [at] Howland bearing and Navy position."[1]

Commander Thompson's interpretation of the ambiguous north-north-west or south-southeast bearing Frank Cipriani had taken and the fragments of code copied by Navy Wailupe had become, in his mind, "the Howland bearing" and the "Navy position." Once again, speculation had solidified into accepted fact.

The press knew that *Itasca* was drawing close to "281 north," and the National Broadcasting Company did not want to miss the story. An NBC executive sent an urgent message to Admiral Murfin in Hawaii:

Have talked to Chief of [Naval] Operations re Earhart and have been told [to] make request to you for permission to send Putnam, NBC man, and Paramount newsreel man from Honolulu to scene of Earhart rescue via navy patrol plane provided you can provide ship. Personnel involved would leave San Francisco [via] Pan American clipper Wednesday. Chief of Operations says if you relay our request they will approve. Please wire rush if you can supply such transportation. Chief of Operations requests [to] have copy [of] your answer to this wire.[2]

Murfin turned him down:

Sorry, do not consider it advisable to send patrol plane to Howland again. Plane to Howland must land in open sea and be serviced by such ship as may be available there. All available ships engaged in search and not available to tend plane. No anchorage for plane or servicing ship. Much danger involved except with fairly smooth sea.

In spite these conditions, plane was dispatched last Saturday because life was at stake. Will not take another chance except under similar extreme urgency.[3]

At about the same time, *Itasca* was also fending off a media request. The Coast Guard Hawaiian Section had advised Commander Thompson: "National Broadcasting Company and KGU respectfully request Earhart telephone statement for national release through RCA Kokohead if and when aboard *Itasca*." Thompson was tactful but noncommittal: "*Itasca* will be pleased cooperate as conditions permit. Entire matter problematical and no advance plans can be made. Radio now required exclusively to conduct search."[4]

As the sun set for the fourth time on *Itasca's* hunt for the missing plane, San Francisco Division tried again to provide a better picture of the situation to Commander Thompson.

Pan American Airways . . . report radio bearing on plane signal morning [of] fifth as 144 degrees from Wake Island and are reasonably certain of bearing. Possibility intersection [of] position line given just before last plane transmission, and latitude line 281 miles north of Howland using Howland as reference point, may be plane's position. Bearing from Wake Island places plane near line of position and intersection of radio bearings from Wake and Honolulu give indications of position in Phoenix Group. Which further substantiated by technicians who feel plane[']s radio could function only if on shore.[5]

The message summarized two competing theories. The plane might be afloat in the ocean near a point where Earhart's 337 degree line of position, the line of latitude at "281 north Howland," the north-northwest bearing from Howland, and the 144 degree bearing from Wake all crossed. For that to be true, the technicians who said the plane must be on land had to be wrong. The other possibility was that the technicians were right and the plane was on an island or reef in the Phoenix Group near where Earhart's 157 degree line of position, the south-southeast bearing from Howland, the 144 degree bearing from Wake, and the 213 degree bearing from Honolulu crossed. For that to be true, Thompson's interpretation of the "281 north" message fragments had to be wrong.

As soon as the sun was down, *Itasca* started trying to contact the plane by voice on 3105. Chief Radioman Bellarts made the calls, asking Earhart to reply with four long dashes and her bearing north or south of Howland. There was no response. Howland heard *Itasca's* calls, and from time to time both stations heard weak carriers on or near 3105. On one occasion, Bellarts could hear what he recognized as voice radio traffic from commercial aircraft on the U.S. West Coast, but there was nothing that sounded like it might be from the Earhart plane.[6]

Having reached the target area, Commander Thompson ordered the ship's speed reduced. Lookouts scanned the darkening ocean while searchlights flashed on and off in the hope of attracting a response from the floating fliers.[7] SS *Moorby* and USS *Swan* also arrived in the general area and started searching, but none of the ships was within sight of the others.

At 8:00 PM, *Itasca* received yet another clarification from San Francisco Division: "Information just received from Lockheed Aircraft Company states positively Earhart plane's radio transmitter could not, repeat not, operate if plane was in water." Commander Thompson clung to his theory. "Dashes as received here obviously from different set. Reports indicate messages received a little above 3105 kcs. Earhart set [on] night of flight was right on 3105." The cutter's commanding officer was arguing that the signals *Itasca* had been hearing must be coming from Earhart's "emergency set."[8]

He soon had reason to believe that vindication was imminent. Just before 9:00 PM, two lookouts and the officer of the deck saw a "distinct flare" arc up into the night sky on a bearing of 75 degrees. Bellarts sent a voice message on 3105: "Earhart from *Itasca*. Did you send up a flare? Send up another for identification." As Commander Thompson wrote in his later report, "A few seconds later another green light appeared bearing 75 degrees (25 witnesses)."[9]

Bellarts made another voice transmission on 3105: "Earhart from *Itasca*. We see your flares and are proceeding toward you." Navy Radio Wailupe overheard Bellarts's transmission and forwarded the word to other commands. Soon the Coast Guard Hawaiian Section was informing San Francisco Division: "*Itasca* sighted flares and proceeding toward them."[10]

At "281 north Howland" the drama continued. Minutes after assuring Earhart that help was on the way, Bellarts "heard Strength 3 phone right on 3105 but call so short that no check could be made." He immediately asked, "What station calling *Itasca* on 3105? What phone on 3105? Go ahead again." But there was no reply.[11]

The sky and the airwaves had again gone quiet. *Itasca* steamed at reduced speed across the dark water, sweeping and flashing its searchlights, every available hand lining the rail and the rigging, hoping for some sign of a floating plane or raft. The ship's deck log recorded a temperature of 84°F, a cloudless sky, unrestricted visibility, and a calm sea—a perfect night in the equatorial Pacific, except that what had to be there was not there.

At 9:45 PM there was more bad news. Another message from San Francisco Division shot down Thompson's theory about signals being sent from an emergency transmitter. "Plane carried no emergency radio equipment except

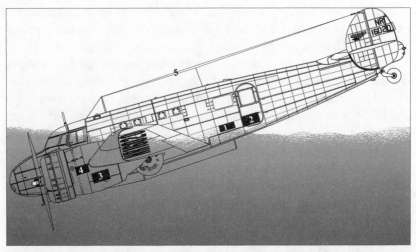

Location of radio elements in Earhart's Electra. The transmitter (1) was located on the floor in the back of the cabin and might have remained dry if the airplane was floating nose-down, as it almost certainly would. The auxiliary battery (2) nearby might provide current even if the main battery (3), located under the floor farther forward, was submerged. Before electrical power from either battery could be used by the transmitter, however, the voltage had to be boosted by a dynamotor (4) situated under the pilot's seat. That essential component would be submerged and useless unless the airplane was floating upside down, in which case the transmitting antenna (5) would be under water.

one spare battery in cabin. Dynamotors all mounted under fuselage and would positively be submerged if plane was in water. In absence of positive identity of signals suggest every effort be made to obtain direction finder bearings having in mind reciprocals from Howland. Roughness in note of plane radio could be caused by vibration and although set [is] crystal controlled [it is] possible [for] some slight deviation due to poor adjustment or fractured crystal."[12]

Moorby had not seen the flares, and Commander Thompson now thought that "it was a mistake and the signals seen were probably heat lightning."[13]

At the top of the hour, Bellarts checked in with the operator on Howland. Frank Cipriani had heard *Itasca*'s calls to the plane and also a man's weak voice in apparent reply, but he did not mention it to Bellarts. He did, however, have a comment about the flares: "Say, old man, we saw green flares on the east southeast horizon about 10 PM Honolulu Standard Time. . . . Did you see the flares?" Bellarts replied: "We think it was heat lightning."[14]

That pretty well clinched it. If the lights in the sky were visible on Howland, 281 miles away, they certainly were not flares fired from a floating plane or raft. Forty-five minutes later Thompson sent a message to the Hawaiian Section:

"Objects sighted were apparently meteors as Howland reported same effect." He later wrote in his report, "The flares were undoubtedly a meteoric shower. The position, appearance and timing gave credence to flares."[15]

Unfortunate timing created another problem. Just one hour passed between the time San Francisco found out that the cutter had sighted flares and the time *Itasca* sent notification that they were only shooting stars, but that was the hour that East Coast newspapers were being put to bed. The news that flares had been sighted arrived in time to make the morning papers. The word that the flares were only meteors did not.

The early edition of the *New York Herald Tribune* for Tuesday, July 6, 1937, carried the banner headline:

EARHART FLARES BELIEVED SIGHTED BY CUTTER RACING TO "281 NORTH HOWLAND" in PACIFIC[16]

The *New York Times* also headlined the good news:

EARHART SEARCHERS ARRIVE AT POINT REPORTED GIVEN BY PLANE ON RADIO

The paper reported, "The *Itasca* sent out a radio message to Miss Earhart: 'We see your flares and are coming toward you.' "[17]

Other news outlets quickly picked up the story and jumped to conclusions. At 9:00 AM in Washington, the Coast Guard commandant's office learned that radio news stations were reporting "Amelia Earhart's plane sighted by *Itasca*."[18] In the Central Pacific, it was still the wee hours of the morning after an exhausting and crushingly disappointing night. As the ship continued to search the dark and barren sea, the radio room was suddenly deluged with requests.

From the *New York Times*:
Commander Brown [*sic*] *Itasca*. . . . Greatly appreciate your wirelessing story Earhart rescue [to] *New York Times*.[19]

From the *London Daily Mirror*:
Captain US Coast Guard cutter *Itasca*. . . . Grateful you send us two hundred words on finding Earhart at our expense . . . reply prepaid $109.20.[20]

From Paramount Pictures:
Commander Coast Guard boat *Itasca*. . . . Advise if movie camera aboard. Anxious secure pictures search [and] rescue [of] Earhart.[21]

From NBC:
National Broadcasting Company and KGU respectfully request Earhart telephone statement for national release through RCA Kokohead if and when aboard *Itasca*.[22]

From Pathé News:
Desirous getting any movies made Earhart rescue. Please collect any made [of] their docking.[23]

The United Press urged Howard Hanzlick, its correspondent aboard *Itasca*, to be sure to "obtain pictures [in the] event [of] rescue."[24] The Associated Press wired its man, James Carey, "Please hold messages [to] twenty-five word maximum [pending] concrete developments. Also get all possible pictures. . . . Will pay crew well pictures Earhart rescue. Advise any obtain."[25]

In Washington, the commandant wanted to know what was going on: "Tropical Radio reports [they are] in communication with *Itasca* and steamer *Moorby*. Press services have been advised by Tropical Radio that Earhart plane located. Advise." Commander Thompson's one-word reply has the feeling of being sent through clenched teeth. "Negative." An hour later he sent a more informative message to Washington: "For Secretary Morgenthau: Searching area reported position Earhart plane since dusk yesterday. Results negative."[26]

Media requests continued to come in, sometimes through official channels. A message from Navy Radio Wailupe read: "Desire statement regarding Earhart search for Columbia Broadcasting System transcontinental broadcast at 0845 HST KGMB Honolulu." Thompson was tactful but firm: "Regret radio traffic relative search precludes."[27]

As the fifth day of the Earhart search began, Carey tried to clear up the night's confusion in a message to the Associated Press's San Francisco office: "Reports seen flares last PM in error. Merely meteors. Howland and *Swan* corroborate seeing same. Must refuel [from] *Colorado* prior further movements. Have taken measures secure photos event rescue. Will advise developments soon [as] possible. Coast Guard, Navy, myself, forward reliable information. Believe none other. Appears information plane afloat 281 north Howland inaccurate. *Moorby* proceeding next port: Carey."[28]

The night was also disappointing in terms of signals that might be from the plane. In marked contrast to the three previous nights, almost no signals were heard on 3105 by stations in the search area, in Hawaii, or by Pan American. The one exception occurred nineteen minutes after Bellarts sent his voice message, "Earhart from Itasca. We see your flares and are proceeding toward you." At 9:32 PM aboard Itasca, he heard a transmission "Strength 3 right on 3105"

that was too short to identify.[29] At that moment, two hams in California—
one in Los Angeles and one in Whittier—heard an "intermittent carrier"
on 3105.[30] Six minutes later on Howland, Cipriani logged "a man's voice,
very weak."[31] At virtually the same moment, two licensed ham operators on
Oahu and one in Maui heard "a rippling carrier right on 3105 kilocycles."
According to Navy Radio Wailupe, "One of them goes so far as to say that
it sounds like motor generator driven rather than DC."[32] Multiple stations
hearing the transmission, with the quality of reception being related to
distance from the Phoenix Group, fit the pattern of the signals heard on
the previous three nights.

In the United States, there was another flurry of amateur reports,
but most were questionable at best. San Francisco Division advised the
Hawaiian Section: "[We are] checking reports received at 05:55 PST on
3105 kilocycles, 3 July. Considerable belief in one report which stated
woman's voice made four distress calls followed by 'KHAQQ' followed
on key by '225 garbled off Howland, battery very weak, can't last long'
other garbled indicated 'sand' or 'bank.' Only banks charted are south and
east of Howland, however report may have been 225 NNW of Howland.
Investigating further."[33]

With the battleship *Colorado* due to arrive in the search area the next day,
San Francisco Division decided it would be best if *Itasca* were put under the
navy's control. A message to the commandant's office on Tuesday afternoon
read: "Propose to have Hawaiian Section direct *Itasca* to report for duty to
Commandant Fourteenth Naval District to assure coordination of effort
with increasing force of naval units. Approval requested." San Francisco
had a reply within the hour: "Authorized."[34]

It was just past midday aboard Itasca when orders arrived for
Commander Thompson from the Coast Guard's Hawaiian Section: "Report
to Commandant Fourteenth Naval District for assignment."[35] It was an
ignominious end to the Coast Guard's leadership of the Earhart search.
Clinging doggedly to his initial decision that the plane had come down at
sea, Warner Thompson had spent four crucial days and nights scouring the
ocean north of Howland despite mounting evidence that the Electra was
elsewhere. Believing that the plane had an emergency transmitter, he dealt
with the flood of reported distress calls by selecting and interpreting the
ones that seemed to fit his theory and rejecting the others.

Thompson orchestrated the three-ship dash to 281 north at a time when
San Francisco Division was becoming increasingly convinced that the plane
was on land somewhere in the Phoenix Group. Word finally arrived that
Earhart could not transmit if afloat just as his northern search was proving
futile. The flare incident, although not Thompson's fault, turned the whole
affair into a national embarrassment for the Coast Guard.

In his chagrin, Warner Thompson's reaction was to dismiss the possible authenticity of all of the distress calls rather than question his own interpretation of some of them. Although he spent days chasing first Walter McMenamy's "1.6 179" and then Navy Wailupe's "281 north Howland," in his later report he went so far as to deny that he took any of the messages seriously: "The *Itasca* was never convinced that signals were received from Earhart or that the plane was transmitting."[36]

As the 281 north fiasco came to an end, San Francisco Division sent a concisely worded summary of the situation to all of the ships and commands involved in the search.

Following from Putnam, "Please note, all radio bearings thus far obtained on Earhart plane approximately intersect in Phoenix Island region southeast of Howland Island. Further, line of position given by Noonan, if based on Howland which apparently [is a] reasonable assumption, also passes through [Phoenix] islands. Believe navigator, after obtaining such line, naturally would follow it to nearest indicated land. Additionally, if message stating position 281 miles north of Howland actually was 'south' instead of north, [the message] also indicates same region. Weather analysis indicates likelihood headwinds aloft much stronger than Noonan reckoned, with probability [that the plane] never got 100 miles from Howland as they thought. Lockheed engineers state positively [that the] plane could not operate its radio unless on shore and no islands apparently exist north of Howland. Therefore, [it is] suggested that planes from *Colorado* investigate Phoenix area as promptly as practicable."[37]

CHAPTER NINETEEN

The Most Likely Place

colorado arrives

The late-day edition of *New York Herald Tribune* for Tuesday, July 6, 1937, brought the disappointing news: "Earhart Plane Not at '281 North Howland,' Cutter's Dash on Radio Clew [*sic*] Is Fruitless." The press was openly critical of *Itasca*'s handling of the search: "Although Navy experts doubted that the message, which included the phrase '281 north Howland,' was intended to say that the Earhart plane was 281 miles north of the tiny island, the *Itasca* apparently accepted that interpretation."[1]

Expectations of an early rescue by the Coast Guard had flared and died with the falling meteors, and hopes that Earhart and Noonan would be found alive now rested on the U.S. Navy. For the first time, all of the U.S. government ships participating in the Earhart search were under the direction of a single commander, Rear Adm. Orin G. Murfin, commandant of the Fourteenth Naval District headquartered at Pearl Harbor. *Itasca*, now critically low on fuel, continued to steam at reduced speed far north of Howland, awaiting the arrival of USS *Colorado*. The seaplane tender USS *Swan* cruised nearby.

In the northern Pacific, the aircraft carrier USS *Lexington* and its escort of three destroyers pounded westward from California. They were scheduled to refuel in Hawaii on Thursday before heading south. It would be the following Monday, July 12, ten days after the plane vanished, before they joined the search. Until then, all eyes were on *Colorado*, and Murfin delegated the prosecution of the search to the battleship's commanding officer, Capt. Wilhelm L. Friedell. In a priority message, he ordered Friedell to "take charge of Naval and Coast Guard units in search area and direct and coordinate Earhart search until arrival [of the commander of the] *Lexington* Group who will then be directed to take charge. Keep Commandant Fourteenth Naval District advised of progress. Will keep you advised any pertinent information received [here]."[2]

Friedell replied: "Report[ing] for duty. Plan to fuel *Itasca* 7 July then, by plane, inspect Winslow Reef then each island Phoenix Islands including Carondelet reef."[3] Winslow reef was reported to be roughly halfway between Baker Island and McKean, the first island of the Phoenix Group; Carondelet was an ocean reef south of Gardner. Friedell's plan was based in part on a message he had received the night before from the Coast Guard's San Francisco Division. "Held consultation this date with persons familiar with navigation methods of Noonan . . . if short of gas, it was stated, he probably would follow line of position to nearest land."[4]

In a later report, Captain Friedell outlined his reasoning:

The line of position 337°–157° was given in one of the last reports received from the plane. It was also stated in a report that the plane was short of gas.

Considering the question as to what Mr. Noonan did do, it must be considered which way he would turn on the line. To the northwest of Howland was [sic] wide stretches of ocean, to the southeast were spots of land. To a seaman in low visibility, the thing to do when in doubt of own position would be to head for the open sea. To the Air navigator with position in doubt and flying a land plane it is apparent that the thing to do would be to steer down the line toward the most probable land. To the Air Navigator, land would be a rescue, just as the sea would be to the seaman. Would and did Mr. Noonan do this or had he other reasons to do otherwise? The answer was, of course, unknown, but logical deduction pointed to the southeast quadrant.[5]

Soon after sunup on Tuesday, Captain Friedell reported the ship's position to Admiral Murfin and informed him, "Expect begin searching with planes tomorrow, Wednesday, southeast of Howland Island."[6]

During the voyage southward, the men of *Colorado* tried to stay abreast of what was happening in the search. Every day, the ship's press yeoman put together a typed sheet of newsreports received by the radio room. Copies were distributed around the ship as the *Radio Press News*. The edition for July 6 included a report about *Itasca*'s disappointing search of "281 north," but it also carried more encouraging news:

WASHINGTON: The first authenticated reports from the Earhart Noonan plane were picked up at 5:15 EST at Howland Island. The radio distress signals were definitely identified as having come from Amelia Earhart and her navigator Capt. Fred Noonan. Coast Guard officials in Washington maintained constant communication with the Cutter *Itasca* which is sweeping the waters in the vicinity of Howland Island. The *Itasca* also picked up the distress calls at the same time that the radio receiving station at Howland heard the flashes from Miss Earhart.

Another story referenced the same event.

HONOLULU: The Coast Guard reported at 5:50 AM PST, that it had just received a radio message from Amelia Earhart. The Coast Guard said the message was picked up on a portable set at Howland Island. The message was also heard at Baker Island. The message was "KHAQQ calling *Itasca*." The Coast Guard said the *Itasca* now has a definite clew to the whereabouts of the missing plane.[7]

The news items were somewhat misleading. Although they appeared in the July 6 issue, the events described occurred on the night of July 4–5.

Another article suggested that *Colorado*'s mission to help search for Earhart might be of little consequence.

HONOLULU T.H.: . . . The famous navy airplane carrier *Lexington* was heading at full speed toward the scene of action with 72 aircraft on her decks. She left her base at San Diego for the four thousand mile run to Howland. Her planes can be sent on ahead, however, since they have a flying radius of three thousand miles [*sic*]. The battleship *Colorado* which left Honolulu Saturday night for Howland Island also reported that she expects to catapult three planes into the air to help search the area in which the *Itasca* is searching. It has been reported that the *Colorado* is not expected to be of much assistance.[8]

The story did not mention the aircraft carrier's need to refuel in Hawaii before speeding toward the scene of action, and the claim that the biplanes on its deck had a flying radius of three thousand miles was patently ridiculous.

These articles, interesting though they may have been to the crew members and NROTC students aboard *Colorado*, did not merit front-page coverage in the ship's *Radio Press News*. Page 1 on July 6 was dedicated to news of more immediate interest. The battleship's course would soon take it across the equator. With so many passengers aboard (including a number of college presidents and VIPs) who had never before crossed the Line, the portents of that event were ominous.

Considerable excitement and enthusiasm was experienced today by the arrival on board of the following dispatch:

"From: Neptune Rex, Ruler of Raging Main, On the Equator
"To: U.S.S. *Colorado*
"Captain Friedell; I have learned from good authority that your ship is heading for my domain with a cargo of eminent passengers. I am gratified to learn of their presence on board the *Colorado* and request

that you advise if they are all loyal Shellbacks or if you have aboard some Pollywogs, in order that a proper and fitting reception may be given them upon their arrival in my domain upon the Equator. . . ."

The enthusiasm was noted on the part of the Shellbacks only, but the excitement was prevalent among the Pollywogs also, although there was an unmistakable element of fear present.

The commanding Officer, Captain W. L. Friedell, U.S. Navy, replied as follows:

"From: U.S.S. *Colorado*

"To: Neptune Rex, Ruler of Raging Main, On the Equator

"I have your message and permission is requested to enter the eminent domain of Neptunus Rex of the Raging Main. It is regretted that there are on board the *Colorado* a large number of Pollywogs consisting of President Sieg, President Brittain, Dean Derleth, Dr. Bell, Commander Beary, members of ROTC units of the University of California and Washington, and members of the crew; but with the able assistance of the trusty Shellbacks as directed by your loyal subjects, I feel sure that they will be properly initiated into the mysteries of the deep; allowed to enter the realms of Neptunus Rex, Ruler of the Raging Main; and will in the future be welcome.

"Anticipating another visit with Your Royal Highness, I remain,

"Captain Friedell."[9]

The hazing of first-timers was an honored tradition, but on the day *Colorado* actually crossed the equator more urgent business took precedence. King Neptune would have to wait. At 7:00 AM Wednesday, on a calm sea, *Itasca* eased alongside the battleship to take on fuel oil and provisions. The transfer was completed in just under four hours, and by eleven o'clock *Colorado* was steaming southward again.

Back home, the *New York Times* headlines reported: "Earhart Search Shifting to Southeast of Howland after Fifth Fruitless Day . . . *Colorado* Is Heading for Winslow Bank, 175 Miles South of Isle . . . to Release Planes Today . . . Belief Grows That Flier and Her Navigator Are on an Island or Coral Reef."[10] At 2:30 PM, the battleship's three Vought O3U-3 "Corsairs" were launched to inspect the charted position of a "Reef and Sand Bank north of Winslow Reef."[11]

The aircraft were seaplanes, capable of landing only on water. They were carried on the deck and placed on steam-powered catapults—one on the fantail and one on top of a gun turret—by means of a large crane. The ship maneuvered so that the catapults could be swung into the wind for the planes to be launched. Recovering the planes was more involved. When the pilots returned from their mission, the ship steered a sharp turning course that created a stretch of relatively calm water on the inside of the turn. Each pilot landed and gunned his engine, bounding across the sea to catch up with a net, known as a "sled," being towed by the ship. Once on the sled, the pilot reduced power so that a hook on the underside of the plane's central float caught the net. With the plane now being towed via the sled, the ship's crane was swung out. The plane's observer in the rear cockpit climbed up, caught the cable, and attached it to a harness on the top wing. The aircraft was then hoisted aboard. *Colorado's* deck log records that the recovery procedure could be accomplished in as little as two minutes.[12]

The mission flown on July 7 went smoothly but failed to achieve its objective. Not only did the pilots and observers not find the lost fliers; they did not even find the place they were supposed to search. The ship's senior aviator, Lt. John O. Lambrecht, wrote up the experience for the weekly newsletter of the navy's Bureau of Aeronautics: "The exact locations of these reefs are not known and, indeed, there seems to be some doubt as to their existence. Several ships have, at various times, passed over the Latitude and Longitude of Winslow Reef without encountering any 'Rocks and Shoals' and without even seeing signs of anything but plain ocean. And that is exactly what the planes found."[13]

Lt. (j.g.) William Short was more descriptive in the diary of the voyage he was writing as a letter to his father:

> We . . . launched the planes about 2:30 and went out to look at the northernmost reef. (We crossed the equator on this hop.) It was a good idea only we couldn't find the damn thing. We had a moderate run out, of about 85 miles, and I'm reasonably certain that our navigation was fair enough because we hit the ship "on the nose" on our return. In addition, the visibility was excellent with moderate sea and swells. It there was a reef with breakers I don't see how we could have missed it.

Colorado's search for Earhart and Noonan was having an inauspicious beginning. Lieutenant Short privately expressed his misgivings about the overall mission.

> This whole business is certainly a royal pain in the neck—not but what I welcome this opportunity for a cruise down in this part of the world, mind you, but it's the principle of the thing. First place, I can't see it as anything but a publicity stunt. "Flying Laboratory" indeed! Even if she had been successful, what would have been proven thereby except that she was the first woman to fly around the world? As it stands now, she has only demonstrated once more that long flights over water in

a land plane are foolishly dangerous. It is my own personal opinion that she should never have been permitted to attempt this flight, or having once started it, more elaborate measures for safeguarding it should have been established.[14]

In Washington, the chief of naval operations was also uncomfortable with the battleship's participation in the search, but for different reasons. *Colorado* had been commandeered in the middle of its annual NROTC training cruise. Not only would the ship's civilian guests be late getting home, but there were also many Naval Reserve officers aboard who, by law, could not be held on active sea duty more than six weeks from the date of embarkation.[15] The battleship had sailed from Seattle on June 15 and so was already halfway through its allotted maximum time. On Wednesday, the CNO informed Admiral Murfin: "In view *Colorado* schedule, desire release that vessel as soon as practicable. Recommendation requested." Murfin replied: "Expect to release *Colorado* and direct her proceed on previously assigned duties upon arrival *Lexington* Group in search area."[16]

That day, Wednesday, July 7, the admiral assured the gentlemen of the press that the answer to the question on everyone's mind would soon be answered: "Admiral Orin G. Murfin, directing the search, said today it should be known by mid-afternoon Monday whether the round-the-world flier and her navigator are still alive. . . . [T]he aircraft carrier *Lexington* should reach the search area Monday morning. If it used all its planes, it would be able to scout thoroughly 36,000 square miles about the Phoenix Islands in six hours."[17]

Others felt the evidence warranted a more exhaustive examination of the islands. "Friends of George Palmer Putnam, Miss Earhart's husband, expressed belief there would be grounds for continuing the search another two weeks, even if no further word came from the lost plane. . . . The five feverish nights of radio manifestations so convinced observers of Miss Earhart's safety that they said there would be justification for searching the southern island area over and over. . . . Mr. Putnam reiterated his theory that Miss Earhart was on solid footing somewhere in the Phoenix Islands area."[18]

Whether *Lexington*'s sixty-three airplanes and three-destroyer escort were to spend six hours or two weeks searching for the lost Electra, there was general agreement that the Phoenix Group was the place to look. A surviving map from Fourteenth District Headquarters documents the rationale for Murfin's remarks and suggests a special focus on McKean and Gardner islands. The map is physically quite large, measuring three feet by four and a half feet, and is festooned with hand-drawn lines and notations. It covers the North-Central Pacific east to west from Hawaii to the Marianas, but it extends southward only as far as latitude 2°S—not far enough to show the Phoenix Group. Drawn on the map are Earhart's route from Lae to Howland and various notations about ship positions. Lines of latitude and longitude have been added by hand at the bottom of the map, but only two of the eight islands of the Phoenix Group are plotted: McKean and Gardner. Drawn and labeled are Earhart's 157–337 degree line of position through Howland, Pan American's 144 degree bearing from Wake and 213 degree bearing from Mokapu, and Cipriani's south-southeast bearing from Howland. All four lines cross near Gardner Island.

Back in the United States, reports of radio distress calls from the plane had dwindled to a trickle. The next morning, Thursday, July 8, 1937, under the headline "Warship's Planes Start Search for Miss Earhart; No Definite Signals Heard," the *New York Times* stated that "weak carrier wave signals, possibly from the radio of Amelia Earhart's missing monoplane, were reported heard again by the Coast Guard just as hope for the safety of the foremost woman flier sank to its lowest point since she disappeared with her navigator in mid-Pacific last Friday."[19] Throughout the day as *Colorado* steamed southward, the ship's aviators made three separate attempts to locate Winslow Reef or any other associated reefs or sandbanks, and each time they returned frustrated. Lieutenant Lambrecht wrote in his newsletter article: "Anyhow, the Senior Aviator wants to go on record as saying that the mariners (?) who saw and reported these reefs are probably the same ones who are constantly reporting having seen sea serpents!!"[20]

While *Colorado*'s planes scouted in vain for the elusive reefs, two thousand miles to the north the four ships of the *Lexington* Group arrived in Hawaii for refueling before heading south to join the search. The three destroyers proceeded directly to the fueling dock at the navy base, but the aircraft carrier did not come into the harbor. In earlier radio exchanges with the ship and with the Navy Department in Washington, Admiral Murfin had noted that no *Lexington* class carrier had ever entered Pearl Harbor and that the narrow entrance channel might be hazardous, especially in high winds. On the other hand, he cautioned, fueling the carrier at an anchorage outside the harbor would be "a long process." The chief of naval operations in Washington decided to play it safe. He ordered the ship to refuel in Lahaina Roads off Maui from the oiler USS *Ramapo*.[21]

On the day the Earhart flight disappeared, before sending *Colorado* south, Admiral Murfin had called a meeting of senior officers to review the available information and solicit opinions. On *Lexington*'s anchoring at Lahaina six days later, he again convened a conference. At noon, a patrol plane from Fleet Air Base landed alongside *Lexington* to take the ship's commanding officer, Capt. Leigh Noyes; two officer assistants; and the officer in charge of the *Lexington* Group, Capt. J. S. Dowell, to Fourteenth Naval District

Headquarters.[22] Captain Dowell returned to Lahaina late that night aboard one of the destroyers, but Captain Noyes stayed ashore and continued consultations with Admiral Murfin the next morning, returning to his ship by plane at 10:30 AM.

During the meetings at Pearl Harbor, the admiral's subsequent report stated, "all available information and studies of the weather and probable location of the Earhart plane were made available to the *Lexington* Group."[23] The available information is described in a six-page paper entitled "Discussion as to the Best Area in Which to Conduct Search." The unsigned, undated paper was included as part of the "Report of Earhart Search—U.S.S. *Lexington*, July 1937" later submitted by Captain Noyes. It appears to have been written after the July 8 conference but before the *Lexington* Group reached the search area on the eleventh.

The document represents a major shift in the search for the missing fliers. Before the conference, the navy had identified the islands of the Phoenix Group, especially McKean and Gardner, as the most likely place for the plane to be found. That decision was based on evidence that emerged during the first few days after the disappearance as *Colorado* hurried south to join the search. *Itasca* had reported that Earhart said she was running on a 157–337 degree line. As Captain Friedell put it, navigational logic dictated that "to the Air navigator with position in doubt and flying a land plane it is apparent that the thing to do would be to steer down the line toward the most probable land."[24] The Coast Guard and the navy had received what they believed were genuine radio calls from the missing plane. Numerous amateurs also claimed to have heard Earhart, and at least some had been checked out and judged to be credible. Lockheed technicians who were familiar with Earhart's Electra were adamant that the plane had to be on land and able to operate the right-hand, generator-equipped engine to be able to transmit. The most confident bearings taken by Pan American indicated that the signals were coming from the vicinity of Gardner Island.

Whether the lost fliers were really there or not, the facts on which the navy based the decision to search the islands were at least accurately presented. Unfortunately, much of the data used to formulate the *Lexington* Group's search plan were not. The analysis of Earhart's flight in the "Discussion as to the Best Area in Which to Conduct Search" is based on information selected from Commander Thompson's contradictory and often distorted descriptions of Earhart's in-flight radio transmissions. The report, for example, states as fact that at "0742 Howland time (1912 GCT) Earhart reported '30 minutes gas remaining, no landfall, position doubtful.'"[25] The cutter's radio log shows that at 0742 *Itasca* time (not Howland time), the radio operator assigned to monitor Earhart heard her say, "We must be on you but cannot see you, but gas is running low. Have been unable reach you by radio.

We are flying at 1000 feet." The operator tasked with handling other radio traffic overheard the transmission and logged it as "Earhart on now. Says running out of gas. Only ½ hour left. Can't hear us at all."[26]

Noyes's report indicates that the last in-flight transmission *Itasca* heard occurred at "0855 Howland time (2025 GCT)." The cutter's radio log has it being heard at 0843.[27]

After summarizing the available information, which was presumed to be accurate, the report went on to list "Assumptions." These include the following:

- That [Noonan] was closest to Howland Island at 0758 (based on strength of radio signals received by *Itasca*) and that he may have been on any course at that time.
- That 57 minutes later the fuel gave out and the plane was forced to land.
- That the plane landed shortly after 0855 [on July 2] on the water within 120 miles of Howland Island, actual position unknown, but approximately on a line running through Howland Island in a direction 157–337 [degrees].[28]

Noyes explained the reasoning behind these assumptions as follows:

Having arrived at the navigator's position of the island, the plane maneuvered to make a landfall, circling first and then running north and south indicating that they were fairly certain of their longitude. With the gasoline supply practically exhausted (½ hours gas supply remaining was reported at 0745) it is not likely that the plane ventured more than 40 miles from the navigator's best position. Assuming that the gasoline gave out when the plane was at the end of one of these runs farthest from the island, the distance from Howland would be only 100 miles.[29]

The report discusses other scenarios but concludes that only two are possible:

1. That the plane may have landed well to the north of its intended course. This is substantiated by several radio messages supposed to have been sent out by the plane. One message stated "281 north"; another "225 NNW." Broadcast experiment of KGMB indicated that the plane was north of Howland and on the water.*

---

*The KGMB broadcasts established only that someone was responding on Earhart's frequency with the requested dashes.

2. That the plane may be well to the south of Howland. This is substantiated by dubious radio bearings supposed to have been taken on the plane
two or three days after it landed. . . . The *Colorado*, *Itasca*, and *Swan*
are investigating the area to the south and it need not be considered by
the Lexington group.[30]

The report estimates how fast, how far, and in what direction a floating
plane or rubber boat might drift in eleven days and concludes that the missing fliers "may be anywhere from the position at which the forced landing
occurred to a position 528 miles to the leeward."[31] It relies entirely on the
supposed "30 minutes gas remaining, no landfall, position doubtful" message to justify its conclusion that the plane ran out of gas hours before it
should have. It even revives the by that time thoroughly debunked notion
that the "281 north" message "substantiated" an ocean landing well north of
Howland. *Colorado* had not yet begun its inspection of the Phoenix Group,
but bad information and unwarranted assumptions had already sidetracked
the next phase of the navy's search.

That night of July 8, *Itasca*, now under orders from *Colorado*'s commanding officer, was crisscrossing the ocean immediately to the south of
Howland and Baker islands. Richard Black, who had virtually disappeared
from official message traffic from the time Earhart went missing, reported
in to his superiors at the Department of the Interior: "Searching as unit in
Navy organization. . . . Hope remains that plane search in Phoenix might
be successful; Black."[32]

Aboard *Colorado*, Lieutenant Short resumed his letter to his father:

You can imagine what a nightmare it must be for the Captain in
command of one of U.S. Navy's best battleboats charging around
in waters where the latest charts and Sailing Directions provide such
reliable information.

Tomorrow we expect to look over the westernmost islands of the
Phoenix Group, Mckean I., Gardner I. and Carondelet Reef and possibly Hull I. We at least ought to be able to find the islands—I hope.

The ship crossed the "Line" yesterday (Wednesday) afternoon but
due to the search operations, his Majesty, King Neptune Ruler of the
Raging Main postponed His arrival on board to greet His loyal subjects
and to mete out just punishment to the lowly polywogs, until tomorrow
morning. As the schedule calls for an early morning launching for us
I will probably miss most of the fun. However, if I can only keep my
date with Amelia it will be worth it![33]

CHAPTER TWENTY

Signs of Recent Habitation
the search of the phoenix group

At 6:56 AM on Friday, July 9, 1937, *Colorado*'s quarterdeck catapult hurled Plane 4-0-4 into a clear tropical Pacific sky of light winds and a few scattered clouds. Senior Aviator Lt. John Lambrecht was at the controls in the front cockpit; Seaman 1st Class J. L. Marks was riding as observer in the rear seat. Thirty seconds later, the high catapault launched Plane 4-0-6, flown by Lt. (j.g.) Leonard O. Fox. In the rear cockpit was Radioman 3rd Class Williamson. He could communicate with the ship using Morse code, but the planes could not talk to each other. The pilots signaled to each other using hand gestures. Lieutenant Short's mount, Plane 4-0-5, left the quarterdeck catapult at exactly seven o'clock. Along for the ride as Short's observer was the ship's assistant first lieutenant, Lt. Charles F. Chillingworth.[1]

The three planes joined up in loose formation and set off on a heading calculated to bring them to the charted position of McKean Island, forty-five miles and about a half hour away. In the article Lambrecht later wrote, he noted that

> M'Kean Island was visited first and when first sighted was about a half point to port, bearing out the statement in Sailing Directions that the island's actual position is somewhat WNW of that shown on the chart.
>
> M'Kean did not require more than a perfunctory examination to ascertain that the missing plane had not landed here, and one circle of the island proved that it was uninhabited except for myriads of birds.[2]*

The pilots also saw evidence that people had once lived on the island. "Signs of previous habitation remained and the walls of several old buildings apparently of some sort of adobe construction, were still standing."[3]

---

*A 1968 survey by ornithologists from the Smithsonian Institution found McKean Island to be home to the world's largest known colony of lesser frigate birds (*Fregata ariel*), an estimated 85,000 individuals, plus more than 150,000 seabirds of other types. See Eric Clapp, "SIC #19 Preliminary Report, McKean Island, 13–15 July 1968."

Beginning in 1859, the Phoenix Guano Company began mining the accumulated bird dung in McKean's shallow lagoon as fertilizer. Thirty to forty Hawaiian laborers lived in crude huts made from piled slabs of coral. Working under horrific conditions of heat and filth, the "Kanakas" shoveled guano into bags that were stored until the next ship arrived to transport the valuable phosphate to markets in the United States and Europe. By the turn of the twentieth century, the Pacific guano trade had been abandoned and McKean once again belonged exclusively to the birds.[4] Lambrecht described a desolate scene:

> M'Kean is perfectly flat and no bigger than about one square mile. Its lagoon, like those of several of the smaller islands of the Phoenix Group, is very shallow and almost dry. This island had no vegetation whatsoever. As in all of these atoll formations coral extends out from the shoreline a distance of 100 to 150 yards and then drops precipitously into water many fathoms deep. There is no anchorage off any of these islands.
>
> As in the case of the subsequent search of the rest of the Phoenix Islands one circle at fifty feet around M'Kean aroused the birds to such an extent that further inspection had to be made from an altitude of at least 400 feet.[5]

The senior aviator's caution was justified. The wingspan of an adult lesser frigate bird often exceeds seven feet. A midair collision could bring down an O3U-3.

"From M'Kean," Lambrecht continued, "the planes proceeded to Gardner Island (sighting the ship to starboard en route) and made an aerial search of this island which proved to be one of the biggest of the group."[6] The run from McKean down to Gardner was sixty miles, or about forty minutes for the Colorado's Corsairs. Allowing five minutes for the "perfunctory examination" of McKean, the planes arrived over Gardner at about 8:15 AM local time. Lambrecht noted that "Gardner is a typical example of your south sea atoll . . . a narrow circular strip of land (about as wide as Coronado's silver strand) surrounding a large lagoon."[7] Coronado is the town adjacent to the North Island Naval Air Station in San Diego, California. The Silver Strand is a long, narrow isthmus of beach connecting North Island to the mainland, well known and popular with navy pilots. Lambrecht was not writing an official report, but rather a newsletter article intended for his fellow naval aviators.

"Most of this island is covered with tropical vegetation with, here and there, a grove of coconut palms," he noted.[8] There were 111 coconut palms, to be exact, in five groves; they were counted during a British visit later that year. The palms were the last survivors of a failed planting. In 1892, twenty laborers employed by British entrepreneur John T. Arundel cleared brush and planted trees on the west end of the atoll. Drought defeated the effort, and by 1894 the island was once again uninhabited.[9]

Lieutenant Short described his impression of the atoll to his father: "Gardner was very different [from McKean]—a ring of land surrounding a lagoon about 2½ miles long by about a mile wide. Almost completely covered with short bushy trees including two small groves of coconut palms."[10] Gardner's lagoon was actually three and a half miles long, and the "short bushy trees" were as much as sixty feet tall.

Flying at an altitude of at least four hundred feet to avoid the birds, and with nothing on the ground of known dimensions to provide a sense of scale, it was difficult for the pilots to accurately assess size and distance. Objects of known size, such as people or an airplane, would appear much smaller than the searchers expected. Nonetheless, Lambrecht saw something that made him think someone might be down there: "Here signs of recent habitation were clearly visible but repeated circling and zooming failed to elicit any answering wave from possible inhabitants and it was finally taken for granted that none were there."[11]

Unfortunately, Lambrecht did not elaborate on what he meant by "signs of recent habitation." Gardner had been uninhabited for nearly a half century. There should have been no signs of recent habitation on the island. "At the western end of the island a tramp steamer (of about 4000 tons) bore mute evidence of unlighted and poorly charted 'Rocks and Shoals.' She lay high and almost dry head onto the coral beach with her back broken in two places."[12]

Lieutenant Short's estimate of the ship's size was a little different from Lambrecht's. "There was the wreck of a fairly large steamer—of about 5000 tons hard up on the beach—her back broken in two places and covered with red rust, but otherwise fairly intact. Apparently it had been there less than ten years."[13] Short's guess was quite good. *Norwich City* was a ship of 5,587 tons, and it had gone aground eight years earlier.

Vegetation covered the land areas on Gardner, and the sand beaches were narrow and steeply sloped. Lambrecht saw the lagoon as the best place for an emergency landing: "The lagoon at Gardner looked sufficiently deep and certainly large enough so that a seaplane or even an airboat could have landed or taken off in any direction with little if any difficulty. Given a chance, it is believed that Miss Earhart could have landed her plane in this lagoon and swam or waded ashore. In fact, on any of these islands it is not hard to believe that a forced landing could have been accomplished with no more damage than a good barrier crash or a good wetting."[14]

Lambrecht did not know that there was a better place to land an Electra at Gardner Island. As he had noted, "in all of these atoll formations coral extends out from the shoreline a distance of 100 to 150 yards and then drops precipitously into water many fathoms deep." In Gardner's case, the protecting reef is a broad, flat expanse of hard coral. At high tide, upward of four feet of water cover the surface, but at low tide, the reef flat at Gardner is dry or covered by only a thin film of water. At such times, from the air, the island looks like it is surrounded by a giant parking lot. In many places, especially near the ocean's edge, the reef surface is smooth enough to ride a bicycle—or land an airplane. On the morning of July 9, 1937, the tide was high at Gardner Island, and a photograph of the shoreline taken from one of the search planes shows lines of surf running across the flat to the beach. Heavy breakers all along the reef's seaward edge hide anything that might have been there.

Satisfied that Earhart had not come down on Gardner Island, the pilots moved on. "From Gardner," Lambrecht reported, "the planes headed southeast for Carondelet Reef, sighting its occasional breakers a good ten miles away. No part of the reef is above water and, although it could be plainly seen from the air, the water over it must have been at least ten to twenty feet in depth. Finding nothing here the planes returned to the ship."[15]

The pilots were at least gratified that their navigational abilities had been vindicated. Lieutenant Short wrote that "we felt right good about finding [Carondelet Reef] at all under all these conditions after a run of 80 miles from Gardner Is. And this confirmed our conviction that Winslow and that other reef either don't exist or are a hell of a long way from their charted positions."[16]

Colorado's log shows that the ship changed course to begin receiving the returning flight at 10:20 AM.[17] The planes had been gone three hours and twenty minutes and had covered 272 nautical miles at their cruising speed of ninety knots.[18] They thus spent a total of no more than twenty minutes over their three objectives. A reasonable estimate might be five minutes at McKean, ten minutes at Gardner, and five at Carondelet Reef.

Upon being hoisted aboard, Lt. Short found that "all the pollywogs were converted to shellbacks this morning and now they are all going around sitting down as little as possible and that very gingerly. I can well sympathize with them as this constant exposure to a parachute for three hours at a clip has much the same effect."[19] Short's bottom would have little time recover; the pilots were scheduled to fly another search mission after lunch.

At noon, the United Press correspondent aboard *Colorado* sent the disappointing word about the morning flight to his company's Honolulu office: "Planes unsuccessfully search Mclean [*sic*] Gardner [and] Carondelet and water between this morning, dropping low over islands [to] insure thoroughness. Unceasing search [of] radio waves continues. [Planes will] scout Hull [and] Sidney this afternoon, then upswing [for] rendezvous [with] *Swan*

[at] Canton Island [on] Saturday [to] obtain plane gas. KGU [and] KGMB broadcast excellent signal."[20]

Admiral Murfin's reaction to the news was to affirm his exit strategy in a message to Captain Dowell, the commander of the *Lexington* Group: "I intend to abandon the search when the area discussed in our conference has been searched if Earhart and Noonan have not been located by that time or in case something unexpected happens."[21]

The admiral was also concerned that Dowell not bite off more than he could chew. The officers at the conference had calculated that "*Lexington* and 3 destroyers will have sufficient fuel upon arrival at Howland to conduct the search for a period of 7 days, in which time an area of about 200,000 square miles can be efficiently and thoroughly searched. This is an area about 400 × 500 miles."[22] Murfin urged restraint: "Referring to our conference about [the] area for systematic scouting, please bear in mind the likelihood of possible unfavorable weather. Because of this, area should be confined to what can be searched in seven days." Dowell responded: "Extremely advantageous *Colorado* make such coverage Phoenix Islands that same may be eliminated from *Lexington* plans."[23]

Aboard *Colorado*, Lieutenant Short settled his sore bottom into the cockpit of his airplane and went back to work.

We catapulted again at 2:00 this afternoon and went out some 90 miles to Hull I. This is very similar to Gardner only it is slightly larger and is inhabited. The population consists of one white man and some 30 or 40 natives who tend the coconut groves—the principal export being copra [dried coconut meat]. Johnny Lambrecht (our Senior Aviator) landed in the lagoon and talked with the white overseer in hopes that he might have heard or seen the plane passing. He had not even heard about the flight in the first place—lucky fellow![24]

The "lucky fellow" was John William Jones, supervisor of the Burns Philp Company's copra-harvesting operations on Hull and Sydney Islands. As Lambrecht described him:

He was a man of about medium height, deeply tanned, and dressed as may have been expected, in white duck trousers, white shirt and a straw hat, which he removed to wave at us. His appearance led one to believe that his nationality was German, due, no doubt, to his closely cropped hair and rotund face, but his accent proclaimed him British.

We told him we were searching for a plane which we believed may have been forced down somewhere in the Phoenix Islands, that the plane had left Lae, New Guinea for Howland Island a week past and had not [been] heard of since, and we wondered whether he'd seen or heard of it. He replied that he hadn't and added that he possessed a radio receiver but heard nothing on it. He was ignorant of the flight but evinced quizzical surprise when told it was being made by Amelia Earhart. He then asked where we had come from and was considerably startled when we told him "Honolulu." We hastily explained, however, that our ship was some fifty or sixty miles to the westward, awaiting our return.

After informing him that we expected to search the rest of the islands, we took off, rendezvoused with the other planes, and returned to the ship.[25]

Jones had the only known radio in, or anywhere near, the islands of the Phoenix Group. Was he able to transmit on 3105 kilocycles? Was he the source of the signals heard by *Itasca*, Howland, Baker, Tutuila, and Hawaii? Were the bearings taken by Pan American Airways at Mokapu, Midway, and Wake Island, and by Cipriani on Howland, taken on transmissions sent by Jones? Were Mabel Larremore, Dana Randolph, Betty Klenck, and other amateurs victims of an elaborate hoax perpetrated by the overseer on Hull Island? Apparently not. When Jones told Lambrecht that he had heard nothing on his radio receiver, he was telling the truth. The overseer had been without a functioning radio since early June, and a new set was not delivered and installed until the end of August.[26] British colonial officer Eric Bevington later related the circumstances surrounding the loss of Jones's radio:

The trouble started just before the total solar eclipse of 1937 [June 8]. One day the labour refused to turn out for work. So he told them that unless they turned out to cut copra . . . he would black out the sun at midday. This threat was met with the derision it apparently deserved. The natives did not turn out . . . so Captain Jones repeated his threat. Next day, Tuesday, he would black out the sun at midday.

Tuesday morning came with a bright sun. . . . and how stupid the "Kaben" (Captain) looked. But as the morning wore on, to their horror and amazement, the Tokelaus noticed that the sun was losing its shape, it was darkening at one side, the whole world was darkening. Terror struck. They watched in utter disbelief; then suddenly one panicked, then all panicked. They rushed to the shack where the Kaben was reporting the eclipse on his radio, all tried to get in at once to beg him to restore the sun, and in the melee, vital radio equipment was smashed and the station put out of action.[27]

Aboard *Colorado*, the senior aviator's adventuresome landing quickly became the talk of the ship, and his fellow officers proclaimed that, henceforth, the lagoon at Hull Island should be known as Lambrecht Lagoon.[28]

On Saturday morning, July 10, the battleship's planes continued their inspection of the Phoenix Group with a morning flight to Sydney Island. Lambrecht wrote: "Upon dropping down for an inspection of that island [we] could discover nothing which indicated that the missing flyers had landed there. The lagoon was sufficiently large to warrant a safe landing but several circles of the island disclosed no signs of life and a landing would have been useless."[29]

In relating what he saw on the ground at Sydney, Lambrecht used some of the same language he had used in his description of Gardner: "There were signs of recent habitation and small shacks could be seen among the groves of coconut palms, but repeated zooms failed to arouse any answering wave." At least in this context Lambrecht's "signs of recent of recent habitation" were something other than dwellings, which he mentioned separately. The small shacks on Sydney belonged to eleven of Hull Island's Tokelau laborers, who until recently had been on the island harvesting copra.[30]

According to a press release filed by a correspondent aboard *Colorado*, the pilots also saw "letters scooped in Sidney [*sic*] beach spelling dozens [of] Polynesian words including 'kele, fassau, molei' seen from air, but pilots said life unsighted, discounting possibility [that the words] were messages relating [to the] lost plane."[31] Kele is a common male name in Tokelauan. Fassau, if actually "faasau," is a Samoan female name. Molei is the Polynesianized form of "Murray."[32] Apparently the workers had written their names and the names of wives or girlfriends in the sand. Man-made marks in the beach sand, soon obliterated by wind or waves, might well be taken as signs of recent habitation, and many years later, Lambrecht described what he saw on Gardner as "markers of some kind."[33] If Lambrecht saw marks in the sand on Gardner, he did not interpret them as any kind of distress signal, but only as evidence that someone had been there recently.

From Sydney Island the planes continued on to inspect Phoenix, Enderbury, and Birnie—small, barren islands that offered no clue to the lost fliers' fate. After lunch, the three Corsairs were launched for a search of Canton Island, the largest and northernmost atoll of the Phoenix Group. Lambrecht wrote, "It held the *Colorado*'s only remaining hopes of finding Miss Earhart and her missing navigator. Search here, however, proved as fruitless as that of the other islands and hopes of locating the unfortunate fliers were virtually abandoned."[34]

The eight islands of the Phoenix group had been covered in four flights, two on Friday the ninth and two on Saturday the tenth. Lieutenant Short finished

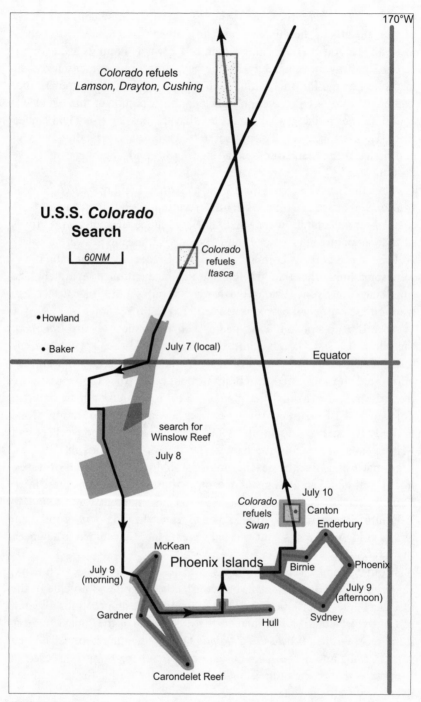

USS *Colorado*'s search pattern.

his letter to his father, "Well, our part in the search has been completed and we are headed for the barn."[35]

That evening, Captain Friedell sent a message to Admiral Murfin: "With completion [of] flight this afternoon, all islands Phoenix Group have been located and carefully searched for any sign of Earhart plane or inhabitants with exception Winslow reef and reef and sandbank to the northward. The charted position of these places and for several miles in vicinity was covered twice without locating them."[36] *Colorado*'s search was over. The United Press correspondent aboard the battleship described the mood as "disappointed and search weary."[37]

A few hundred miles to the north, the pilots who were about to take up the torch were not optimistic about their own prospects for success. A representative for International News aboard the aircraft carrier *Lexington* reported that the some of the officers were offering even money on bets that they would find Amelia. There were "no takers" as plans for the search were completed.[38]

CHAPTER TWENTY-ONE

"We Will Find Amelia Tomorrow"
lexington's search

I t was July 10, 1937, and Amelia Earhart's Electra had been missing for eight days. The navy had been in charge of the entire search for four days, and the *Lexington* Group's strategy had been in place for two days, when Admiral Murfin decided it would be a good idea to get some basic information about the missing airplane. That morning, he sent a message to his counterpart at the Eleventh Naval District in California asking him to contact the Lockheed Aircraft Company in Burbank for the answers to four questions about the aircraft's capabilities. What was the plane's total fuel capacity? How far could it fly on 1100 gallons of gas? What was its economical cruising speed? And what was the maximum distance the plane could fly at an average fuel consumption of 53 gallons per hour? He explained that his inquiries were "based on established facts that Earhart plane took off with eleven hundred gallons fuel and remained in air about twenty and three quarter hours."[1]

Murfin based his certainty about the plane's fuel load on a July 5 message sent out by the Coast Guard's San Francisco Division: "Lae verified that Earhart took off with 1100 gallons gas. Estimated flight time 24 to 30 hours."[2] His "established fact" that the Electra remained in the air for only twenty and three-quarters hours, however, was not a fact at all. It was speculation based on the assumption that the plane ran out of gas about half an hour after the last in-flight radio transmission heard by *Itasca*. The 53 gallons-per-hour figure assumed that the plane burned through 1100 hundred gallons of fuel in 20.75 hours.

Lockheed answered Murfin's questions promptly. Earhart's Electra could hold a total of 1151 gallons of gas. With 1100 gallons aboard, discounting headwinds or tailwinds, it could cover 3600 miles at its economical cruising speed of 150 miles per hour. But the engineers and technicians at Lockheed said that 53 gallons per hour was the wrong number. They also disagreed with the statement that the plane ran out of gas after only 20.75 hours: "Earhart, to our best belief, in air twenty-four and half hours. Took off with 1100 gallons. Her average cruising speed should have been 150 miles per hour. Her maximum flight should have been about 3600 miles in still air. We figure her average economical fuel consumption at 45 gallons an hour.

... Base all estimates on fact that plane would average forty-five gallons per hour fuel consumption and approximately 150 miles per hour ground speed still air."[3]

Lockheed's response was inconvenient. Forty-five gallons per hour and twenty-four and a half hours aloft fit well with the idea that the plane might have reached one of the islands in the Phoenix Group, but the navy's new search plan was based on the assumption "that the plane landed shortly after 0855 [on July 2] on the water within 120 miles of Howland Island."[4] On Sunday morning, July 11, 1937, three hours after he received Lockheed's comments, Murfin ordered Captain Dowell to "take charge all units in search area. Search of Phoenix Group area considered completed."[5]

While Admiral Murfin was clinging to his established facts, San Francisco Division was coming up with some of its own. That night, in a message to the Hawaiian Section, with copies to Murfin and Dowell, San Francisco reported: "Further investigation this date of radio reports made by amateurs at Los Angeles on night of 3 July confirmed by four separate stations and indicate credibility of receipt of distress call from Earhart plane."[6] This was the report by McMenamy and his friends alleging that they had heard Earhart say "179 and what sounded like 1 point 6."[7] Commander Thompson had interpreted the numbers to mean longitude 179°W, latitude 1.6°N, but his search of that area found nothing.[8] San Francisco Division now believed the message was supposed to mean longitude 176°E, latitude 1.6°S.[9] That would put the plane near the islands of the southern Gilberts. The message continued:

Conferred with wife of Noonan this date and she states characteristic of Noonan was to turn back when in doubt. This appears reasonable assumption in view of prevailing winds and apparent sufficient fuel for about three hours, computed from actual time in air of slightly over 20 hours to last radio contact, and established fact that fuel consumption was 42 gallons per hour at cruising speed of about 130 knots [150 miles per hour].

Technical advisor for Earhart states plane could operate at slow speed on 30 gallons per hour and positively states that radio could not be used in water. Above indicates possibility plane may be in Gilbert Group.[10]

Aboard *Lexington*, Captain Dowell considered this new information. The plane's performance described in the Coast Guard message—twenty-three hours aloft at 42 gallons per hour, and possibly longer at reduced speed—was similar to the manufacturer's belief that the Electra had remained in the air for twenty-four and a half hours at 45 gallons per hour. Nonetheless,

Dowell's plan to confine the aerial search to areas of open ocean remained unchanged.

The navy, however, was not opposed to searching the Gilberts. The previous day, Secretary of State Cordell Hull had sent a "rush" telegram to Joseph Grew, the American ambassador in Tokyo:

> The authorities of the Navy Department and the relatives of Miss Earhart express the opinion that if Miss Earhart's plane was forced down on the ocean it may have drifted, because of the prevailing currents, in the general direction of the Gilbert islands. In view of the urgency of the time element involved, please endeavor to advise the appropriate authorities of the Japanese Government immediately of these facts and state to them that, because of the generous offer of assistance tendered by the Japanese government, and because of the continuing interest which the Japanese government has taken in the search for Miss Earhart's plane, your government suggests that if any suitable vessels or airplanes of the Japanese Government are located in or near the Gilbert Islands they may be asked to be on the lookout for Miss Earhart's plane. Please telegraph such reply as may be made to you by the Japanese Government; Hull.[11]

The Gilbert Islands, as the State Department well knew, were not part of the Japanese Mandate. The archipelago was part of the British Empire, administered by the Colonial Office as part of the Gilbert and Ellice Islands Colony of the Western Pacific High Commission. The United States was growing increasingly suspicious of Japan's intentions in the Pacific. Hull's query may have been at least in some respects a ploy to find out whether the Japanese had warships or airfields in the Marshall Islands a few hundred miles north of the Gilberts.

A few hours later, Grew replied: "Contents of Department's telegram under reference communicated immediately to senior aide to the Navy Minister who stated that no Japanese aircraft in that area but survey ship *Koshu* has proceeded toward Marshall Islands and should now be there. Japanese radio stations have been ordered to be on continuous watch for Earhart signals and many Japanese fishing craft in and to east of Marshall Islands have been instructed to be on lookout. The senior aide expressed greatest willingness to cooperate. Grew."[12]*

---

*Later investigations of the prewar Japanese military buildup in the Pacific indicate the navy minister was telling the truth. Construction of the first airfields and seaplane ramps in the Marshalls did not begin until 1940. See Thomas Wilds, "How Japan Fortified the Mandated Islands," *U.S. Naval Institute Proceedings* 81, no. 4 (April 1955): 2.

Shortly after receiving San Francisco's suggestion that the plane might have landed on one of the Gilbert Islands, Captain Dowell ordered *Itasca* to "proceed immediately at most economical speed laying course for Arorai [*sic*] Island, Gilbert Group."[13]

The Earhart search had reached another turning point. For the first five days after the Earhart flight disappeared, the burden of trying to locate and rescue the missing fliers had fallen entirely on *Itasca*. The cutter's commanding officer, convinced that the plane had come down at sea, had scoured the ocean to the north and west of Howland without success. On July 6, the search entered a second phase with the arrival of the battleship *Colorado* and the transfer of all operational authority to the navy. Based on general agreement among Coast Guard, navy, and civilian authorities that legitimate distress calls had been received, the focus of the search shifted to the land areas near where the radio bearings crossed—the reefs and atolls of the Phoenix Group. When *Colorado* declared the islands carefully, but fruitlessly, searched, Admiral Murfin passed operational command to the arriving *Lexington* Group and put a seven-day limit on the third and final phase of the search.

With the Phoenix Group eliminated, the consensus about where to search broke into two opposing camps. Admiral Murfin in Hawaii and Captain Dowell aboard *Lexington* returned to Commander Thompson's original belief that the plane had run short of fuel far earlier than expected and had come down at sea not very far from Howland. In California, the people at Lockheed, who had built the airplane and flown with Earhart to develop her long-range fuel management techniques, and Paul Mantz, the technical adviser who sat beside her on the flight to Hawaii, were sure the navy was wrong. For their part, the Coast Guard's San Francisco Division remained convinced that at least some of the radio distress calls were genuine and that the plane must be on land. If it was not in the Phoenix Group, maybe it was in the Gilberts.

The odds that the plane was down and unreported somewhere in the Gilberts were slim. The islands were densely inhabited. Overpopulation was such a problem, in fact, that British authorities were considering expanding the colony into the uninhabited Phoenix Group.

The curtain went up on act three of the Earhart search at dawn on Tuesday, July 13, 1937. On reaching a point roughly fifty miles northwest of Howland Island on Earhart's reported line of position, USS *Lexington* turned into the wind. At 6:36 AM, the first of sixty planes roared down the flight deck and lifted into the Pacific sky. As the squadrons launched and assembled to begin their sweep, 450 miles to the southwest, *Itasca* was just arriving off Arorae to begin its search of the Gilberts.

Lexington's planes made two flights that day, two more on the fourteenth, and another two on the fifteenth, working constantly westward into the area where the plane or life raft could conceivably have drifted. The pilots saw nothing of interest except "huge whales."[14]

Itasca and *Swan* made inquiries at several atolls in the southern Gilberts, but no one had any information. On the afternoon of July 15, as Itasca stood off Tarawa Atoll, Commander Thompson reported to Captain Dowell: "Senior District Officer in close contact with this group and Taritari reports negative for plane passage or wreckage. Island[s] all thickly inhabited and communication frequent. Do not believe further investigation this portion of Gilberts necessary and in view fuel situation request permission proceed Howland." Dowell agreed: "Permission granted to proceed Howland. Conserve fuel. Continue reports."[15]

Itasca's long search for Earhart and Noonan was over. That same day, the State Department sent a wire to the American embassy in London: "Developments of the search have led to the dispatch of the Coast Guard cutter *Itasca* and the Navy minesweeper [*sic*] *Swan* to the Gilbert Islands to make a careful search of the uninhabited islands and to establish contact with residents of inhabited islands. Inquire whether this action has the approval of the British government. Hull."[16] The British government granted its permission two days later.

Swan still had two more islands to visit in the southern Gilberts, but what hope remained for finding the lost fliers rested primarily on *Lexington*'s ocean search. Based on their calculations of the effect of wind and currents on a floating plane or raft, Dowell's team made a prediction to the International News Service correspondent aboard the carrier: " 'We will find Amelia tomorrow' [is the] belief [of] strategists on *Lexington* as planes returned [from] third unsuccessful day."[17]

That night, Admiral Murfin and Captain Dowell were asked to shift the navy's search to an entirely new area. A message from the Coast Guard's San Francisco Division read: "For reasons which apparently possess plausibility, Putnam requests, if possible, you arrange immediate plane reconnaissance vicinity 170 degrees East longitude and about 9 minutes North latitude for drifting plane. Request advise results if flight made."[18] San Francisco did not explain where Putnam got the coordinates and why he considered them plausible. The numbers do not appear in any of the reported radio distress calls, and the position they describe is in open ocean about two hundred miles west of the Gilberts—far beyond the designated search area. Murfin and Dowell ignored Putnam's request.

At dawn the next morning, Friday, July 16, Lexington's flight deck was a forest of wings and struts as dozens of biplanes were positioned for launch. Clouds of blue smoke whipped aft as forty-two engines coughed to life and the carrier came up to speed. According to the ship's Associated Press reporter, the pilots rolled up their sleeves and smeared their faces with grease against the tropical sun while laughing at news broadcasts that described their search as futile. "Confidence well based," the reporter agreed. "Success today or tomorrow if Amelia afloat since all data point [to] planes entering 'most probable area.' "[19] A local rain squall drenched the deck as the planes took off, formed up, and began their sweep.

In California, it was early afternoon and no one had replied to Putnam's plea. San Francisco tried again: "Putnam requests *Itasca* search area if impracticable to use planes."[20]

Itasca was already on its way home via Howland. That evening, with still no response from Murfin or Dowell, George Putnam took his plea to Washington. In a telegram to Chief of Naval Operations Adm. William Leahy he wrote:

Deeply grateful if steps be taken to search area slightly north of intersection of longitude 170 east and equator contemporaneously with search of Gilbert Island[s]. Because [of] peculiar intimate nature [of the] alleged information, this is a confidential personal request to you. Most compelling unusual circumstances dictate, although sole obvious reasonableness lies in westward prevailing drift which might well [have] carried floating plane through Gilberts to designated area. Anyway cannot pass up this bet, forlorn as it may be. George Palmer Putnam.[21]

Since the day the plane went missing, Putnam had been bombarded with advice from clairvoyants and psychics. Not all of the visions were unsolicited. According to the Associated Press, he appealed to Amelia's "girlhood neighbor," the "internationally known psychic" Gene Dennis, for help. She worked with Putnam "in a series of long distance telephone conversations," and he sent her "a pair of Miss Earhart's stockings and a handkerchief of Miss Earhart's navigator, Fred Noonan, to aid her psychic efforts." The same day San Francisco transmitted Putnam's request to Murfin and Dowell, Gene Dennis offered her reading that Amelia was "alive and safe on a South Seas island. The name 'Gelbert' has come to me." She predicted that "fishing boats or a fishing boat will discover the flyers . . . possibly this weekend."[22] Whether the location Putnam gave the navy came from Gene Dennis or someone else, it seems apparent that the coordinates were given to him by someone who claimed to have received them from the beyond.

By late morning, July 17, Putnam had received no reply from Washington. The search for Earhart and Noonan was scheduled to end the next day. He sent another telegram to Admiral Leahy: "Appreciate, if possible, confirmation that request contained my dayletter yesterday evening will be acted upon. To you alone I venture to say [that my] conviction they still live is vivid beyond my power to express, for intimate reasons one cannot rationalize or wisely make public. Please believe this is written by one [who is] essentially practical minded. G P Putnam."[23]

An hour and a half later there was still no answer. Putnam asked San Francisco to try Murfin and Dowell again: "Following from Putnam 'Request you secure definite confirmation that region requested will be searched, also southern Gilberts, especially Beru and islands adjacent.'" An hour later Murfin responded with bad news: "Regret impracticable search area requested. All Gilbert Islands have been searched."[24]

Nearly five hours later, unaware of Admiral Murfin's reply to San Francisco, Admiral Leahy interceded on Putnam's behalf in a wire to Murfin: "Request that, if practicable before termination of search on eighteen or nineteen July, that search be extended to cover point 170 degrees East longitude and 0 degrees latitude and area slightly to northward of that point. Reply desired." Murfin's response to his superior was tactful but firm: "Search suggested [in] your despatch this date possible but impracticable. Would require abandoning remainder scheduled search plan and use most economical speed with possibility *Lexington* requiring some fuel at Pearl Harbor before proceeding San Diego. To search the area requested would require four days steaming to accomplish one days search. Will not search this area unless directed to do so by [Navy] Department."[25]

George Putnam had not become a successful businessman by taking no for an answer. He sent another telegram to Admiral Leahy: "Thanks for message and for all your great helpfulness. If humanly possible please have at least one plane examine area, the western edge of which is nine minutes north of equator at intersection of 170 longitude East. My last request, terribly urgent. George Palmer Putnam." Leahy tried to explain: "Commandant at Honolulu reports it is impracticable to send *Lexington* to 170 East longitude without abandoning remainder of scheduled search. All possible drift from vicinity anywhere near Howland Island will be covered by plan of present search. Admiral William D. Leahy."[26]

Putnam persisted: "Thanks for message. Realize authorities on ground are doing everything possible. My suggestions was not for *Lexington* to proceed to area indicated but that, if possible, a couple of planes give it one quick reconnaissance which forever would put my mind at rest. George Palmer Putnam." There was finality in Leahy's response: "Replying to your telegram. Firmly believe that, allowing for rate of drift, the area between Howland and the point mentioned has been thoroughly searched. Be assured that no possibility has been neglected. William D. Leahy, Chief of Naval Operations."[27]

While Putnam pleaded, *Lexington's* operations proceeded as planned. As the optimistic pilots began their search on the sixteenth, Captain Dowell sent a message to Commander Thompson aboard *Itasca*: "Assuming that Earhart plane or rubber boat still afloat, please submit your estimate as of noon today most probable position first of plane, secondly of rubber boat." Thompson replied as ordered. His estimates of the plane's and rubber boat's present positions agreed with Dowell's calculations.[28] In justifying his estimates, Commander Thompson offered a new version of the events of July 2: "End of flight clear blue sky south and east of Howland. Heavy cloud banks approximately 50 miles north and west of Howland."[29] This was the first time Thompson had mentioned the presence of heavy cloud-banks north and west of Howland. According to the weather observations recorded in *Itasca's* deck log on July 2, there was "blue sky with detached clouds" throughout most of the day, including when the ship was searching north and west of Howland. The only time the sky was "mainly cloudy" was around 1:00 PM. At that time the ship was about twenty miles directly north of the island.[30] An observation taken at noon on Howland found cumulus cloud covering five-tenths of the sky with bases at 2650 feet.[31]

Thompson also told Dowell that "*Itasca* had laid heavy smoke screen for two hours which had not disintegrated and clearly visible from south and east for 40 miles or more at altitude 1000."[32] At 1000 feet, in perfect visibility, the horizon is 41.6 statute miles away, but Thompson could not possibly know what could actually be seen from the air that day from 40 miles away. According to the cutter's log, *Itasca* began making smoke at 6:14 AM. The log does not note when the ship ceased making smoke, but it is difficult to explain how the procedure could have continued for more than about half an hour without risking severe damage to the ship's power plant.

"Doubtful if visible over 20 miles from north and west," Thompson added.[33] Thompson offered no explanation for his opinion. Throughout the day on July 2, the cutter's deck log recorded the surface visibility at the maximum value, 9 (defined as "prominent objects visible above 20 miles").[34] "Signal strength and line of position would indicate Earhart reckoning correct as for distance, though she probably carried line of position east before circling and afterward probably flew north and south on this line."[35] *Itasca's* radio logs support Thompson's reasoning that Earhart reached a fairly accurate line of position drawn through Howland and then flew north–south along that line. There is no support in the logs for his supposition that she continued eastward, and the notation about circling is clearly a later overtype of the partially erased word "drifting."

Thompson's statement that Earhart's "reports indicate high flight with overcast and cloudy weather and evidently flying in clouds until the last few minutes of flight" is not supported by the cutter's radio logs either.[36] "Signal

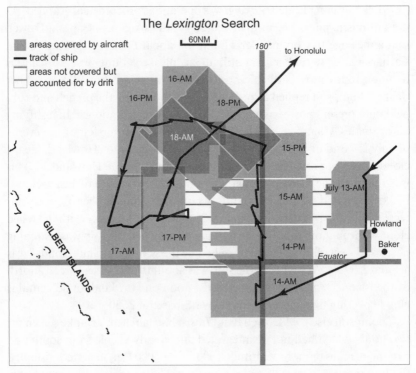

USS *Lexington's* search track.

strength indicates the maximum distance 250. Estimated plane down within 250 miles of Howland between 337 and 45 true and not nearer than 30 miles. At latter distance could not have failed to see smoke screen if she passed south."[37] Thompson had expanded his estimate considerably since July 2, when he told San Francisco Division, "Judge she came down between 337° and 90° from Howland and within 100 miles."[38]

Later that evening, Captain Dowell reported the day's results to Admiral Murfin: "*Swan* searched Taputeuea and Onutt [Onatoa] thus completing search of Gilbert[s] by surface craft. Results [of] aircraft search today negative."[39] The previous day's brave predictions of success now sounded like whistling in the graveyard. Looking for some good news to report, Dowell told Murfin about Commander Thompson's agreement with the *Lexington* Group's calculations: "*Itasca* was asked by despatch at 0910 today to submit estimate most probable position as of noon today, Friday—firstly [for] Earhart plane and secondly [for] Earhart rubber boat. Reply received gave area bounded by lines between following four points, 2° North, 179°30' East; 5° North, 178°15' East; 5° North, 175°45' East; 2° North, 177° East. Consider this a very interesting coincidence since no previous communication with *Itasca* in this regard."[40] The coincidence was hardly remarkable.

Starting from the same assumption about where the plane came down, both Dowell and Thompson had observed the same winds and currents and come up with similar projections.

The next morning, Saturday, July 17, Admiral Murfin advised the chief of naval operations: "*Lexington* Group ordered discontinue search evening 18th if flying conditions practicable [on] 17th and 18th. Otherwise discontinue evening 19th."[41]

Aboard the aircraft carrier, flight operations got under way at dawn. Forty-one aircraft were launched, but two aborted. The remaining thirty-nine saw nothing but the blue Pacific and returned shortly after 10:00 AM. During landing operations, one of the planes missed the arresting gear, hit the barrier, and ended up against one of the gun turrets. No one was injured, but the aircraft suffered major damage. The search planes were again sent out after lunch. By five o'clock, all were back aboard without incident, and without finding any sign of the lost fliers. This flight completed the coverage of the designated search area.

Flight operations on the next day were dedicated to "cleaning up rain holes" (areas previously skipped due to local squalls).[42] As the afternoon flight came up over the carrier to begin landing operations, Captain Dowell sent a message to Admiral Murfin: "Search today, Sunday, completed as scheduled."[43] At two minutes before 5:00 PM on July 18, 1937, the last plane of the last squadron caught the wire and lurched to a stop. The navy's search for Amelia Earhart and Fred Noonan was over. In Hawaii, Murfin passed the news to Admiral Leahy in Washington: "All search for Earhart terminated."[44]

CHAPTER TWENTY-TWO

Banquo's Ghost
explaining failure

The greatest rescue expedition in flying history" had failed.[1] The enticing clues, the carefully reasoned theories, and the confident assurances of imminent success had come to naught. No trace of the missing fliers had been found: no silver Lockheed parked on a reef or adrift at sea, no joyful survivors waving from a beach or rubber boat, no debris washed up on an island shore or afloat on the ocean—nothing.

In contrast to the utter dearth of physical evidence was the abundance of electronic clues. For three frantic nights after Earhart and Noonan went missing, professional operators and private citizens reported dozens of radio transmissions reputedly sent from the lost plane. Investigators discovered some reports from amateurs to be hoaxes but judged others to be genuine. Directional bearings taken by Pan American Airways radio installations and the Coast Guard pointed to the southeastern arm of the navigational line Earhart had said she was following. Confirmation from Paul Mantz and Lockheed that the plane carried no emergency radio set and had to be on land to transmit led to the navy's decision to search the islands and reefs of the Phoenix Group. When *Colorado*'s captain reported the area thoroughly inspected, *Lexington*'s planes searched the open ocean west of Howland while *Itasca* and *Swan* made inquiries in the Gilberts. Again the results were negative. Sixteen days after Earhart and Noonan disappeared, the U.S. government abandoned all official efforts to find them.

As the ships steamed homeward, the specter of the radio distress calls hung over the failed search like Banquo's ghost. If even one of the nearly two hundred alleged transmissions from the plane was authentic, then Earhart and Noonan had been alive and on land, and might even now be standing on some island shore watching the horizon for a rescue that would never come.

As the commanders wrote their reports, each dealt with the body of radio evidence in his own way. Because his ship was released while the search was still under way, *Colorado*'s captain, Wilhelm Friedell, did not have to explain the distress calls. He needed only to show that they had not come from the area he searched.

"Resumé Earhart Search by the U.S.S. *Colorado* (in Charge Search Group)" was completed July 13, 1937, as the battleship left the search area for Hawaii, San Francisco, and ultimately its home port, Tacoma, Washington. In the report, Friedell reviewed the rationale for the Phoenix Islands search and offered brief summaries of what the search planes saw at the various islands. "McKean Island showed unmistakable signs of having at one time been inhabited." "Carondelet Reef was under water but plainly could be seen from the plane at a distance of 10 miles." At Hull, "A European Resident Manager came out in a canoe to meet the plane."[2]

In describing the overflight of Gardner Island, Friedell mentioned the "four thousand ton tramp steamer," but he also stated that "no dwelling appeared at Gardner or any other signs of inhabitation." As if to reinforce the notion that there was nothing of interest on Gardner, he also wrote, "Sydney was the only island which showed any signs of recent habitation and, in appearance, was much the same as Gardner Island."[3]

Friedell concluded his report with a categorical affirmation that he had accomplished his assigned mission: "As this is written the Lexington Group is approaching the Search Area and will be able to conduct an extensive search over a large water area. The Colorado has, however, searched the land area within a radius of 450 miles of Howland Island and definitely ascertained that the Earhart Plane is not on land within the region unless on an unknown, uncharted and unsighted reef."[4]

Captain Friedell's confidence was misplaced. In 1937, the techniques and standards of aerial searching were in their infancy. According to present-day Civil Air Patrol Probability of Detection (POD) tables, the chance of *Colorado*'s planes locating the aircraft in the course of a single inspection of each island was on the order of 10 to 20 percent.[5] In other words, if the Earhart plane was on one of the islands of the Phoenix Group, there is an 80 to 90 percent chance that *Colorado*'s search missed it.

On July 16, as *Colorado* anchored off the entrance to Pearl Harbor, Lieutenant Lambrecht finished writing "Aircraft Search of Earhart Plane" for the weekly newsletter of the navy's Bureau of Aeronautics. He subsequently submitted it to his commanding officer, Captain Friedell, who passed it up the chain of command when the ship reached its home port later that month. Lambrecht's description of the search largely agrees with Captain Friedell's version, except for one glaring discrepancy. Friedell had said, "No dwelling appeared at Gardner or any other signs of inhabitation." But the man who had been there reported that "signs of recent habitation were clearly visible."[6]

How did Friedell get it wrong? If Lambrecht gave his commanding officer written after-action reports following each search flight, they have not survived; nor is there any reference to such reports in the ship's records.

It appears likely that the debriefings were verbal. The flight that inspected McKean, Gardner, and Carondelet Reef arrived back aboard the ship just as the pollywog initiation festivities were winding down. Lambrecht might not have mentioned the signs of recent habitation on Gardner, or Friedell might not have taken good notes.

In any event, both accounts of the search appear to have remained aboard *Colorado* until the ship reached the U.S. mainland. If in reviewing Lambrecht's article Friedell noticed that his own report was in error about what the senior aviator had seen on Gardner Island, he apparently did not think it was worth correcting. For Lambrecht's part, junior officers are seldom asked to proofread their commanders' reports, so he probably never had a chance to point out the mistake.

Captain Dowell's "Report on Earhart Search" for the *Lexington* Group left the door open to the possibility that distress calls had been sent. His account, dated July 20, 1937, was written aboard "U.S.S. *Lexington*, Flagship, Enroute Hawaiian Area." In his transmittal memo to Admiral Murfin, Dowell made a point of saying, "An effort has been made to confine the substance of this report to matters of fact rather than opinion."[7]

Dowell began with a ten-page section entitled "Estimate and Decisions" in which he reviewed the reasoning behind his conclusions concerning where the *Lexington* Group should search. He took it as fact that at 7:42 AM Earhart had said, "One-half hour fuel and no landfall." He was also sure that the plane carried "a two man rubber life boat, life belts, flares, and emergency water and rations." The rubber boat "had a pair of oars and could be kept afloat by patching material and hand pump."[8] No one knew, and to this day no one knows, what emergency equipment was aboard the plane when it left Lae. An army inventory taken of the Electra in Hawaii after the crash that ended the first attempt to fly to Howland included life preserver vests but not a boat.[9] Dowell acknowledged that the plane's "normal radio power supply was so located that it would not have been used with plane on the water." But he also stated as "known fact" that "the plane was equipped with an orange box kite to be flown as distress signal, and by means of which an emergency antenna might be carried to a moderate height."[10]

Despite his promise to confine the substance of his report to matters of fact rather than opinion, Dowell included a sixteen-item list of "Probabilities Arising from Rumor or Reasonable Assumptions." Among these was: "That the plane was equipped with an emergency radio set that could be operated from battery power supply." Dowell concluded that at about 9:00 AM local time on July 2, the plane most probably "landed on the sea to the northwest of Howland Island, within 120 miles of the island." Implied, but unstated, was the possibility that distress calls had been sent from the floating plane or rubber boat, which sank before *Lexington* arrived on the scene.[11] Dowell followed the list of probabilities with a sixteen-page "Narrative of Earhart Search" recounting the daily operations of the ships and planes under his command and ending with the statement, "No sign nor any evidence of the Earhart plane was discovered."[12]

The report continued with four pages of "Aerological Data" describing weather conditions experienced during the search, followed by a nine-page "Report of Earhart Search Operations 3–18 July 1937" by *Lexington*'s commanding officer, Capt. Leigh Noyes. Noyes's facts and assumptions largely echo those of his superior officer, but, unlike Dowell, he took an aggressive stand on the alleged radio distress calls: "Numerous radio messages were reported to have been received by various agencies, particularly amateur radio operators, which purported to give information received direct from the plane after it landed. Many of these messages were in conflict and many of them were unquestionably false. None could be positively verified. These messages were a serious handicap to the progress of the search, especially before the arrival of the *Lexington* Group."[13]

Captain Noyes ended his narrative with a pat on his own back: "Although unfortunately the fate of the missing flyers remains a mystery, it is considered that the search made was efficient and that the areas covered were the most probable ones, based on the facts and information available."[14]

On July 18, *Itasca* stopped briefly at Howland to pick up Frank Cipriani and the others who had been left on the island when the search began. That day, Warner Thompson received a request from headquarters that he submit "a written report of communications throughout the entire expedition with the Commanding Officer's recommendations for the information of the [San Francisco] Division office."[15]

He began assembling the report the next day and finished the 106-page document on the twenty-third, the day before the ship reached Hawaii. He was undoubtedly aware that the secretary of the treasury, Henry Morgenthau, and his family were due to arrive in Honolulu aboard the Matson Line's SS *Lurline* the same day the cutter was scheduled to make port. Although Morgenthau was technically on vacation, the intense interest he had shown in the Earhart search made it likely that he would want a personal briefing from *Itasca*'s commanding officer.[16]

Although Warner Thompson titled the report "Radio Transcripts—Earhart Flight," it was much more than that. He described his intention in the opening paragraph.

For purposes of clarity, this report will trace the Earhart flight from the communications angle from the time the *Itasca* was first ordered in connection with the flight on 9 June until the *Itasca* was released by Navy on 16 July, 1937. The report is divided into three sections,

(a) Before Flight; (b) The Flight; (c) The Search. Comments are made directly as events occur. Summary of opinion is made at the end of each section and at the end of the report. This report has been made "confidential" due to the fact that it contains a large number of personal messages and that further it discusses, frankly, certain matters which might be considered as controversial. This has been done to present an accurate picture of *Itasca*['s] opinion.[17]

Thompson's report is a chronological reproduction of 526 official communications sent and received by *Itasca* in the course of its involvement with the flight preparations, the flight from Lae, and the subsequent search. Interspersed among the messages are Thompson's comments, complaints, and explanations. Many of his representations are inaccurate. Twice in the report he asserted that Richard Black was designated by Putnam to be Earhart's representative aboard *Itasca*.[18] Black was not working for Putnam. He was a field representative employed by the Interior Department's Division of Territories and Island Possessions with orders to be the "leader of the expedition and coordinator of government assistance to Earhart flight as regards Howland Island."[19] Prior to the first world flight attempt, Putnam asked Black to be Earhart's press representative at Howland, and Black declined.[20] There is no record of the request being repeated for the second attempt.

Thompson complained about micromanagement during preflight preparations. Referring to an exchange of messages on June 21, 1937, he wrote: "We now have the following persons endeavoring to control the Earhart flight communications, Mr. Putnam; Mrs. Hampton in Washington; San Francisco division and Mr. Black on *Itasca*." He complained about Black's use of the ship's radio facilities: "Black's government messages were burdening a Navy–Coast Guard network with undue traffic which could readily be relieved by Coast Guard–Navy procedure. The commanding officer *Itasca* willingly stood ready to transmit any information Mr. Black deemed necessary to disseminate provided it be done in a Navy–Coast Guard manner."[21]

In one of his comments he correctly identified the problem with Earhart's choice of frequencies in her message to Black on June 26.

It will be noted that the frequencies requested were high frequencies with the exception of *Ontario*. This is contradictory to the last message received from Commander San Francisco Division suggesting 333 and 545 kilocycles. It will also be noted that the requested 7.5 megacycles is beyond the frequency range, that at least to our knowledge, of the plane direction finder. . . . In view of the contradictory matter obtained in Earhart dispatch it was deemed necessary that the *Itasca* handle the situation.[22]

But *Itasca* did not handle the situation. The cutter never sent Earhart a message questioning her choice of frequencies. Referring to himself in the third person, Thompson explained why.

> The *Itasca*'s technical opinion as to Earhart's radio desires was never consulted. The Commanding Officer only contacted Earhart once directly by radio as to the arrangements. This was done because the Commanding Officer fore-saw the chance of disaster and desired personal and special precautions on the Earhart departure and final radio plans."[23]*

Thompson felt that Black had put him in an unintended and untenable situation: "The Coast Guard had no intention of navigating Earhart to Howland. The high frequency direction finder obtained from the Navy by Mr. Black was set up on Howland and manned by an *Itasca* radioman. This was in accordance with Mr. Black's request. Records show that Earhart was not advised by this vessel of the high frequency direction finder's existence. Mr. Black states that he did not inform Earhart. This fact is very important as shown in Section (b)."[24] In "Section (b) The Flight," Thompson continued to claim that Earhart had reported "overcast" weather conditions. The "excerpts from *Itasca* radio log" he included in the report were embellished with his own additions and interpretations.[25]

Thompson was highly critical of Earhart's conduct. In various parts of the report he noted that:

> Earhart never answered *Itasca* questions and never gave a position. Earhart messages lacked any useful information and consisted of generalities.
> Earhart asked *Itasca* to take bearings on her. This was never planned. Earhart knew that *Itasca* could give her accurate bearings on 500 and yet never transmitted on 500 in order for *Itasca* to assist her.
> Earhart was on air very briefly and apparently over modulated. The attempts of the radioman on Howland to secure cut failed.[26]

In the picture Warner Thompson painted, his ship's valiant efforts to meet Earhart's unreasonable requests had been defeated by the flier's own incompetence.

---

*Thompson was referring to the telegram he sent to Darwin and Lae on June 23 while Earhart was still in Bandoeng: "Request you advise this vessel 12 hours prior to your departure from New Guinea full information regarding your desires in matter of radio frequencies and communication schedule. We will conform to any frequencies desired. Important anticipate your departure as communication via Port Darwin very slow."

Thompson's discussion of the search mounted a full frontal assault on the notion that radio calls had been sent from the plane after it was down: "Since 10:00 in the morning *Itasca* had been endeavoring to contact the Earhart plane by repeatedly calling the plane as the *Itasca* searched the immediate sector where it thought the plane was down. From this time on the *Itasca*'s signal as picked up by other units are steadily reported as possible signals from other sources. A careful check of the *Itasca* radio logs shows that in most cases the signals were originated by *Itasca*."[27] The statement is patently untrue. A careful check of *Itasca*'s radio logs shows that not one of the purported receptions from the plane corresponds with a transmission by the cutter. In fact, *Itasca*'s own radio operators logged more unexplained signals on Earhart's frequency—forty-four in all—than any other station.

Over the first several days of the search, information flowed in to *Itasca* about the suspected distress calls received by the Coast Guard Hawaiian Section, Navy Radio Wailupe, Pan American, and various amateurs. The cutter, however, shared virtually no information about what its own radio operators were hearing. After the search, Thompson did not include the ship's complete radio logs as part of his report. The few excerpts in "Radio Transcripts—Earhart Flight" appear to be the only representations of the logs seen by anyone other than the ship's own officers and radiomen.*

Thompson's report does not reveal that on the night of July 4, the radio operator on Howland unequivocally reported that he had recently "heard Earhart call *Itasca*." In the same message, the Howland operator passed along the information that "Baker [Island] heard Earhart plane QSA 4 [strength 4 of 5], R7 [readability 7 of 9] last nite at 8:20 PM."[28]

Thompson, in fact, specifically denied that such receptions had been reported: "The *Itasca* was never convinced that signals were received from Earhart or that the plane was transmitting. The *Itasca* with two (2) operators, the *Swan*, Howland and Baker were closest to the signals. None of these units heard the apparently faked messages. Samoa, listening on 3105, did not hear them. Throughout, *Itasca* opinion was that if the plane was down some of these units would get the traffic." Thompson went on to explain why he did not believe the plane was transmitting: "*Itasca* was of the opinion that the traffic would consist of some useful information and not just call signs and dashes. Both Earhart and Noonan could use code. Why should a plane in distress waste time on repeated calls or on making special signals. If the plane was using battery the carrier signals were out of all proportion to the length of time the battery could stand up."[29]

----

*Leo Bellarts and Thomas O'Hare kept the original radio logs as souvenirs; they surfaced only in the 1970s. The logs are now in the National Archives.

At the end of the report, Thompson offered a "Summary of Search" that included the following:

Earhart plane went down after 0846, July 2nd, and apparently sent no distress message.

Amateurs reported several messages, all probably criminally false.

Pan American, Howland and others took bearings on a carrier [wave signal] some place in the Pacific.

Itasca signals calling Earhart, the *March of Time* program and other signals were interpreted as from Earhart.

If Earhart was down and sending messages, the guards maintained by *Itasca*, *Swan*, Samoa, Howland, *Colorado*, Baker, Plane 62c [the PBY], Wailupe, Pan American, San Francisco Radio, Honolulu Coast Guard Radio, and British stations in the Gilbert Islands should have intercepted legitimate Earhart traffic, whereas the only interceptions were by amateurs, with the exception of one Wailupe interception.

All available land areas were searched therefore Earhart plane was not on land. Was not in Gilberts.

Extremely doubtful that Earhart ever sent signals after 0846, 2 July.

Reports causing diversion of searching vessels should be, and were, carefully investigated. Once the searching vessel receives such a report it is required by public clamor to investigate.

Itasca's original estimate after three (3) weeks of search problem still appears correct, that plane went down to northwest of Howland.[30]

A more complete catalog of distortion, unwarranted assumption, and outright falsehood is difficult to imagine. To his credit, Thompson also presented a disclaimer.

The *Itasca* has been so close to the matter of the flight and search that it may be that this report lacks proper perspective and proportion.

The failure of Earhart to reach Howland and the failure of the search efforts to find her was felt by every officer and man on the *Itasca*. The ship's company fully appreciates the responsibility of the ship to the Service and the public.

In the course of time, opinions on the Earhart flight and its communications will definitely be formulated. Many of our opinions would probably be changed if Miss Earhart were able to give her side of the picture. It is with this in mind that the foregoing report has been frankly written and it is considered that on this date (July 23) it represents *Itasca*'s thought.[31]

Commander Thompson closed "Radio Transcripts—Earhart Flight" with a series of recommendations. Most of his suggestions concerned the need for better planning and preparation for Coast Guard support of future flights. Thompson expressed his opinion "that viewed from the fact that Miss Earhart's flight was largely dependent upon radio communication, her attitude towards arrangements was most casual to say the least." He also recommended "that immediate action be taken looking toward the suppression of amateur radio stations who repeatedly, upon occasions of this kind, spread rumors and originate false messages."[32]

At 11:10 AM on Saturday, July 24, 1937, *Itasca* moored at Pier 27 in Honolulu.[33] Commander Thompson met with Morgenthau and, given the tone of his recently completed report, undoubtedly gave the secretary an earful.

While navy and Coast Guard officers made their case that all had been done that could be done, George Putnam was still trying to find his wife. On July 20, President Roosevelt's head secretary, Marvin McIntyre, wrote FDR a memo saying: "Gene Vidal has been in very close touch with the Earhart story, talking several times a day with her husband, Mr. Putnam. He has some very interesting sidelights and some speculations, which are probably true, as to what happened. You might find it interesting to spend 15 minutes with him." Roosevelt jotted a response on the bottom of the note, "Mac—I would like to see him for 5 or 10 minutes."[34]

Putnam was still convinced that the plane had reached an island. On July 23 he sent a telegram to the secretary of the navy.

Please accept my gratitude for Navies [*sic*] generous and efficient conduct of Amelia Earhart search. Respectfully request your good offices in obtaining cooperation of British and Japanese in continuing search, especially regarding Ellice, Gilbert and Marshall Island, Ocean Island and area north east of same. Also, if possible, request some examination of island northerly and north westerly of Pago Pago. Seek leave nothing undone. Looking toward securing information. What ever it may be possible to do will be sincerely appreciated; George Palmer Putnam.[35]

The area northeast of Ocean Island was the mysteriously inspired location he had so desperately urged the navy to search in the earlier series of telegrams to Admiral Leahy. The islands north of Pago Pago were the Tokelaus, far beyond the plane's expected range. Putnam was truly seeking to leave nothing undone.

The next day, the secretary of the navy replied: "Navy Department has been informed that British and Japanese have given assurance their shipping operating in area concerned will maintain particular lookout for lost plane and fliers."[36] Merely keeping an eye out was not what Putnam had in mind.

The meeting between FDR and Gene Vidal took place on Friday, July 30. Vidal conveyed Putnam's strong belief that the plane might have landed there, despite the negative results of the inquiries by *Itasca* and *Swan* in the Gilberts. Putnam wanted the State Department to ask the British to conduct a real search of the islands, and he was willing to back up his request with a reward. Roosevelt apparently agreed to the plan, because that same evening the secretary of state sent a message to Joseph Kennedy, the American ambassador in London.

> Evidence, which to many sources seems positive, indicates that Amelia Earhart (Mrs. Putnam) was on land the two nights following her disappearance. In the circumstances, we should appreciate your getting in touch with the Colonial Office or other appropriate authority and telling them: (1) That if the authorities could send a boat from the Gilbert Islands to continue a thorough surface search in those islands, Mr. Putnam would be glad to defray the expenses involved, and (2) That word might be circulated that there is a reward of $2,000 offered for any evidence leading to a solution of her disappearance whether in the nature of wreckage or more positive indication of what happened. Hull.[37]

The next day, Saturday, July 31, Putnam wrote to thank McIntyre for the "friendly personal cooperation which you have extended all along in our present troubles." He also asked, "Is there any way of ascertaining what the Japanese are actually doing—especially as regards a real search of the eastern fringe of the Marshall Islands? That is one of the most fruitful possible locations for wreckage."[38]

On Sunday, Putnam had another favor to ask of the State Department. In a telegram to Sumner Wells, his principal contact at State, Earhart's husband wrote:

> Supplementing action taken Friday following Gene Vidal conference requesting local British authorities Gilbert Island cooperation, now urgently request specific immediate search at my expense, if appropriate, [of] following position; 174°10' East longitude, 2°36' North latitude. This is only 85 miles from Tarawa. On making island, bearing thence 106° True. Have apparently authentic information from former commander copra vessel substantiated by reliable American that [an] uncharted reef exists [at] that point which [is] frequently visited for turtle eggs, etc., by older Gilbertese natives. Believe Captain I. Handley

of Tarawa know[s] about it. Confidentially, this information astonish-
ingly corroborates the position actually repeatedly given [to] me during [the] last ten days from other sources probably disclosed by Vidal
which, [in] themselves, [are] interesting in their independent unanimity,
if not necessarily convincing because of their nature. Grateful for word
on outcome. George Palmer Putnam.[39]

In his desperation, Putnam was listening to psychics again. According
to an article published in *Popular Aviation* two years later, Putnam had
that morning received a telegram from Hamilton, Ontario, saying: "Amelia
Earhart alive on coral shoal on one of Gilbert Islands, latitude 2 above
equator 174 longitude. This messaged [*sic*] received by Mr. L—— New
York Medium."[40]

After much back-and-forthing among Putnam, the State Department,
and the British, Captain Handley eventually checked out the position of the
supposed uncharted reef. On August 31, 1937, Putnam received a telegram
with news of the result. "I regret to inform you that Foreign Office, London
advises us that High Commissioner at Suva has telegraphed that Captain
Handley has returned from the position you specified without finding any
trace of reef or plane. Cordell Hull, Secretary of State."[41]

While Putnam grasped at straws, at the Coast Guard's San Francisco
Division, Commander Thompson's scathing "Radio Transcripts—Earhart
Flight" was causing second thoughts about the authenticity of the radio
distress calls. On July 26, an Associated Press article in the *New York Times*
quoted the division communications officer as saying that "aviators in
the Eastern States probably were the senders of radio signals which were
reported as possible distress calls from Amelia Earhart."[42]

If San Francisco Division now agreed with *Itasca*'s captain that none of
the distress calls was legitimate, Pan American Airways apparently felt otherwise. That same day, the airline drafted a "Proposed Joint Rescue Procedure
for Use in Aircraft Distress Cases in Vicinity of Honolulu." The paper was
submitted to the Coast Guard commandant's office in Washington. No copy
of the document seems to have survived, but its general content is readily
discernible from various Coast Guard responses to it.[43] The first six pages
were introductory statements that the Coast Guard's chief communications
officer felt "might be subject to controversy." Pan Am seems to have suggested that at least some of the distress calls from Earhart were authentic
and that better coordination among the various government and private
organizations involved in the search might have made it possible to figure
out where she was and get to her in time to effect a rescue.

The rest of the paper was a communications plan that the chief communications officer found "to be based on sound practice and to be entirely

practicable." On December 14, 1937, he recommended to the commandant that "a final plan should be drawn up by a joint conference in Honolulu of representatives of the Pan American Airways, Navy, Coast Guard, and other interested parties such as the Matson Steamship Company."[44]

As 1937 drew to a close, a new search for the missing fliers was taking shape, this time as a private venture. On December 23, the state of California recognized the "Amelia Earhart Foundation, a non-profit corporation." One of the organization's primary purposes was "to conduct an expedition to clear up the mystery surrounding the disappearance of Amelia Earhart the lost aviatrix, and Frederick J. Noonan, her navigator, and to establish beyond a doubt whether or not they are still alive." The foundation had George Putnam's support and encouragement, but the board of directors was made up of Amelia's friends and business associates: Nellie G. Donohoe, G. Earle Whitten, Kenneth C. Gillis, James A. Maharry, and E. H. Dimity.[45]

In the foundation's charter, the organizers clearly articulated their reasons for continuing the search.

At the time Miss Earhart's plane disappeared, the Navy Department came forward and offered its services and ships to conduct a search. It is well known that the Navy and Coast Guard made as thorough a search as was humanly possible under the hurried and unfavorable conditions prevailing at the time.

In view of the well known aeronautical skill of Amelia Earhart and the navigating ability of Captain Frederick J. Noonan, it would seem more than reasonable that, after they had passed over numerous islands, fighting a head wind, with their gasoline supply low, they attempted to retrace their path. In this case, they may well have landed on one of the many islands they had previously sighted.

From time to time, various amateur radio operators picked up messages, some of which were thought to be authentic. Although messages indicated that the fliers were down on land, they were so garbled that no definite information could be gleaned as to their whereabouts. A careful and lengthy analysis of messages and data obtained during and since the search, together with checking of American and British charts of the Pacific waters, has led the investigators to believe that some of the messages were authentic and that it is more than possible that the fliers came down on land. This belief has been further strengthened through checking information collected with a number of the oldest and best known Pacific Ship masters. A number of these, who have spent many years of their lives in sail and power in these Pacific island waters, believe a strong possibility exists that Miss Earhart and her navigator landed safely on some small island

and may be still alive and awaiting rescue. One of them states: "I am firmly convinced that there is far more than an even chance of Miss Earhart and her navigator having landed on one of the hundreds of islands in that area, where any kind of a ship might not touch for a year or many years."

In addition, there are instances where persons have been marooned on islands in this vicinity and have been able to sustain life for various lengthy periods.[46]

To raise the money needed for the proposed expedition, the foundation formed a National Sponsor's Committee. Amelia's friend Eleanor Roosevelt agreed to act as honorary chairman, and the list of committee members soon boasted names such as Mrs. Juan T. Trippe, wife of the founder of Pan American Airways; Mrs. Louise Thaden, often described as America's second most famous female flyer; Judge Florence E. Allen, the first woman ever appointed to a federal circuit court; and a virtual who's who of New York society.[47]

On January 6, 1938, the Coast Guard commandant approved Pan American's "Proposed Joint Rescue Procedure" and sent the plan to Capt. Stanley Parker, commander of the San Francisco Division. The commandant authorized Parker, at his discretion, to have the Hawaiian Section confer with Pan Am, the navy, and the other organizations involved with a view toward adopting the plan.

Parker waited until March 22 before sending the proposed plan to the commander of the Hawaiian Section. In his four-page transmittal memo he strenuously objected to Pan American's characterization of the events and circumstances surrounding the Earhart flight:

The matters stated in paragraph 6 [of the Pan Am paper] are entirely in error. The statement that "The U.S. Coast Guard was officially charged with the safeguarding of the flight" had no basis in fact. The Coast Guard was not ordered or designated to safeguard the flight. Messrs. Miller and Black of the Department of the Interior had more information on the flight and were representing Mr. Putnam aboard the *Itasca*. The *Itasca* was ordered to Howland Island for the purpose of acting as a radio homing beacon and plane guard at Howland.[48]

Parker's objection was essentially correct. Commander Thompson's orders had been "to act as Earhart plane guard at Howland and furnish weather."[49] Black, however, was not representing Putnam, and Miller was not even there.

It was very evident after the flight started that the entire flight was
badly managed, and that Mr. Putnam, at San Francisco, was not aware
of all facts, and that the information which he furnished was often at
variance with that received from Miss Earhart.[50]

Again, the record supports Parker's complaint.

Miss Earhart was specifically warned by the San Francisco Division
against attempting to use the high frequencies for direction finding
purposes.[51]

Parker was mistaken. No such warning appears in any of the messages
sent to Earhart.

The statement in paragraph 8, last sentence, is at absolute variance with
the facts and no basis exists for such a statement. Neither the Navy nor
the Coast Guard was expected to arrange a search for the plane. There
was no lack of coordination between any of the military forces.[52]

Parker's assertion that the Coast Guard was not expected to arrange a
search is difficult to reconcile with his statement that *Itasca* was there as
"plane guard."
The commanding officer of San Francisco Division also vehemently
rejected Pan American's premise that some of the distress calls had come
from the missing plane.

Not one of the amateur reports received during the Earhart search was
accurate, and all reports of receipt of such of signals from the Earhart
plane were definitely known to be false, as the San Francisco Division
had a continuous intercept watch at three separate locations guarding
3105 and 6210 kc. using beam receiving antennas, with better equipment than is available to amateurs, and no signals were heard other
than those of the *Itasca* on 3105 kc [emphasis in the original].[53]

Parker seems to have forgotten the message his own experts sent to *Itasca*
on July 4.

Unconfirmed reports from Rock Springs, Wyoming state Earhart
plane heard 16,000 kilocycles. Position on a reef southeast of Howland
Island. This information may be authentic as signals from mid-Pacific
and Orient often heard inland when not audible on coast. Verification
follows.[54]

Parker went on to say,

> However, no reports were discarded until after due investigation by
> either the Coast Guard or a representative of Mr. Putnam, on the
> chance that radio signals had actually been heard by the amateurs
> due to the vagaries of radio.[55]

Captain Parker's memory seems to have failed him again. Some of the
amateur reports were investigated; most were not. In some cases, hoaxes
were exposed, but on other occasions government investigations judged
amateur reports to be credible.

Pan American's "Proposed Joint Rescue Procedure" appears to have died
on the vine, as did the Amelia Earhart Foundation's plan to send an expedition to the Pacific. No dedicated private search was mounted, but in 1940,
the foundation commissioned Capt. Irving Johnson, whose yacht *Yankee* was
making an around-the-world tour, to make inquiries in the British Central
Pacific. In May of that year, Johnson called at several islands in the Ellice
and Gilbert groups. A missionary on Beru told him of local reports that "the
Earhart plane had flown eastward high up over the island of Taputeouea
[Tabiteuea]."[56] If the stories were true, it meant that the flight was slightly
south of course when it was five hundred miles from Howland.

Otherwise, the news was discouraging. "[N]ot a particle of a wrecked
plane or any wreckage that could possibly be from airplane had been found
on any of the islands although the natives often walk along the reefs to see
what they can pick up in the way of drift, especially as their islands are so
heavily populated that anything they can get is useful." *Yankee* also visited
several islands in the Phoenix Group, but because he had no permission
from British authorities, Johnson avoided the three atolls that had recently
been colonized—Sydney, Hull, and Gardner.

In a June 4, 1940, letter to one of the foundation members, Johnson wrote,
"It is my opinion and that of all those with whom I have talked in this area
that the search be considered finished and that everything that is humanly
possible had been done to find any trace of Miss Earhart."[57]

The U.S. government never conducted an independent review of the disappearance of Amelia Earhart and Fred Noonan or the subsequent search by
the U.S. Navy and Coast Guard. The Bureau of Air Commerce investigated
other accidents in far-flung U.S. territories—the Wiley Post–Will Rogers
crash in Alaska in 1935 and the Pan American Clipper loss off Samoa in
January 1938—but the closest thing to an official verdict in the Earhart case
was a memo from the chief of the bureau's Accident Analysis Section to
the Registration Section on May 5, 1938.

Subject: NR-16020–Lockheed 10-E

The subject aircraft was presumably washed out in an accident in the Pacific Ocean near Howland Island, on July 2, 1937, while being piloted by Amelia Earhart, owner.

Inasmuch as it is presumed that Miss Earhart was fatally injured in the above accident, no further action is being taken by this section.[58]

EPILOGUE

Telegram from Gerald B. Gallagher, Officer-in-Charge, Phoenix Islands Settlement Scheme, to Resident Commissioner Barley, Gilbert & Ellice Islands Colony, September 23, 1940:

Some months ago working party on Gardner discovered human skull—this was buried and I only recently heard about it. Thorough search has now produced more bones (including lower jaw) part of a shoe a bottle and a sextant box. It would appear that

(a) Skeleton is possibly that of a woman,
(b) Shoe was a woman's and probably size 10,
(c) Sextant box has two numbers on it 3500 (stencilled) and 1542—sextant being old fashioned and probably painted over with black enamel.

Bones look more than four years old to me but there seems to be very slight chance that this may be remains of Amelia Earhardt [*sic*]. If United States authorities find that above evidence fits into general description, perhaps they could supply some dental information as many teeth are intact. Am holding latest finds for present but have not exhumed skull. There is no local indication that this discovery is related to wreck of the "Norwich City."

NOTES

The sources cited in the notes and elsewhere in this book are drawn from a wide variety of archival collections. These include: Archives of New Zealand, Auckland, New Zealand; Army Center of Military History, Fort McNair, Washington, D.C.; Bishop Museum, Honolulu, Haw.; George Palmer Putnam Collection of Amelia Earhart Papers, Purdue University Library Special Collections, West Lafayette, Ind.; Hawaii State Archives, Honolulu, Haw.; Kiribati National Archives, Tarawa, Republic of Kiribati; Library of Congress, Washington, D.C.; National Archives, College Park, Md.; National Archives Pacific Region, San Bruno, Calif.; Naval Historical Center, Washington, D.C.; Pan American World Airways [PAA] Collection, University of Miami Library, Miami, Fla.; Public Records Office, Kew, England; Schlesinger Library, Radcliffe College, Cambridge, Mass.; Smithsonian National Air and Space Museum Library, Washington, D.C.; The International Group for Historic Aircraft Recovery [TIGHAR] Earhart Collection, Wilmington, Del.; University of Delaware Library, Wilmington, Del.; and University of Hawaii Library, Honolulu, Haw. Many of the documents are also available at TIGHAR's Web site: www.tighar.org.

The DVD that accompanies this book contains Adobe Acrobat™ PDF images of most of the sources cited in the text and notes plus a wealth of other documents, reports, and studies relevant to Earhart's disappearance. To view a particular document referenced in the text, insert the DVD into any computer's DVD drive and click on "Notes." Select the chapter and individual note you would like to view and click on the italicized link to go directly to an image of the document. You can also browse folders containing letters, reports, analytical studies, and so on. See the "Read Me" file on the DVD for complete instructions.

Chapter 1. An Airport in the Ocean: The American Equatorial Islands

1. J. S. Wynne, Chief, Airports Section, letter to R. L. Campbell, December 14, 1936, National Archives, Record Group [RG] 237, file 835, William T. Miller Files.
2. Amelia Earhart, letter to Eleanor Roosevelt, June 15, 1932, Schlesinger Library, Radcliffe College, Cambridge, Mass., ref: 83–M69.
3. *Poughkeepsie Eagle-News*, November 20, 1932.
4. E. H. Bryan Jr., *Panala'au Memoirs* (Honolulu: Pacific Scientific Information Center, Bernice P. Bishop Museum, 1974), pp. 1–12.
5. Ibid.
6. Cordell Hull, Secretary of State, memorandum to President Franklin D. Roosevelt, February 18, 1936, Franklin D. Roosevelt Library, Hyde Park, N.Y.
7. Ruth Hampton, Acting Director, Department of the Interior [DOI] Division of Territories and Island Possessions, to Black, November 16, 1936.
8. Ibid., November 17, 1936.
9. George P. Putnam, letter to Eleanor Roosevelt, June 1936, Earhart Collection, Purdue University Library.

10. Malvina Schneider, secretary to Eleanor Roosevelt, note to Richard Southgate, June 29, 1936, Franklin D. Roosevelt Library.
11. Earhart, letter to President Franklin D. Roosevelt, November 10, 1936, Earhart Collection, Purdue University Library.
12. Paul Bastedo, Navy Department, memorandum to Chief of Naval Operations [CNO], November 16, 1936, U.S. Navy Archives.
13. Commander, Aircraft Base Force, U.S. Fleet, memorandum to Commander in Chief, U.S. Fleet [CINCUS], November 29, 1936, U.S. Navy Archives.
14. Eugene Vidal to William Miller, November 17, 1936.
15. CNO to CINCUS, December 4, 1936.
16. Poindexter to Ernest H. Gruening, Director, DOI Division of Territories and Island Possessions, December 12, 1936.
17. Hampton to Black, December 7, 1936.
18. Vidal to Robert L. Campbell, Bureau of Air Commerce engineer, December 8, 1936.
19. Wynne to Campbell, December 14, 1936.
20. Campbell to Wynne, December 21, 1936.
21. Ibid.
22. Wynne to Campbell, December 28, 1936.

Chapter 2. Kamakaiwi Field: Preparations for the First World Flight Attempt

1. Campbell to Wynne, December 23, 1936.
2. Campbell to Wynne, January 5, 1937.
3. Poindexter (Black) to Gruening, January 7, 1937.
4. Earhart, telegram to FDR, January 7, 1937.
5. USCG *Duane* to Commandant, Coast Guard [COM CG], January 22, 1937.
6. Black to COM CG, January 24, 1937.
7. Commander, Hawaii Section [COMHAWSEC] (Campbell) to Wynne, February 5, 1937.
8. Poindexter (Black) to Gruening, February 12, 1937.
9. Gruening to Black, February 15, 1937.
10. Wynne to William Miller, quoting Campbell to Black, March 5, 1937.
11. Miller to Black, March 5, 1937.
12. Miller to Black, March 6, 1937.
13. Miller to Putnam, March 6, 1937.
14. Miller to Black, March 8, 1937.
15. Miller to Commandant, Fourteenth Naval District [COM14], etc., March 8, 1937.
16. Poindexter (Black) to Miller, March 8, 1937.
17. Ibid.
18. Putnam to Miller, March 8, 1937.
19. Wynne to Black, March 9, 1937.
20. Poindexter (Black) to Miller, March 9, 1937.
21. Earhart, telegram to Eleanor Roosevelt, September 15, 1936, Franklin D. Roosevelt Library.
22. J. Carroll Cone, Assistant Director of Air Commerce, letter to George P. Putnam, October 20, 1936, National Archives, RG 237, file 835.

23. Miller to Robert R. Reining, Chief, Bureau of Air Commerce [BAC] Registration Section, March 10, 1937.
24. Reining to Miller, March 11, 1937.
25. Reining to Miller, March 9, 1937.
26. R. D. Bedinger, BAC Inspector, to Reining, March 11, 1937.
27. USCG *Shoshone* to Wynne via COM CG, March 13, 1937.
28. Keane, Associated Press reporter aboard *Shoshone*, to the Associated Press, March 15, 1937.
29. Bedinger to Reining, March 13, 1937.
30. Fred D. Fagg, BAC Director, to Bedinger, March 14, 1937.
31. Miller to Commandant, San Francisco Division [COMFRANDIV] et al., March 15, 1937.
32. "Earhart Flight Delayed a Day By Head Winds," *New York Herald Tribune*, March 15, 1937, p. 1.
33. "One in a Million," *Time*, July 19, 1937, p. 45.
34. Naval Station San Diego to Secretary of the Navy, March 15, 1937.
35. Miller via COMFRANDIV to CINCUS et al., March 16, 1937.
36. Miller to CINCUS et al., March 17, 1937.

Chapter 3. Hawaiian Debacle: The Luke Field Accident

1. U.S. Army Proceedings, "Investigation of Earhart Crash, Luke Field, March 20, 1937, Exhibit A—Work Performed," p. 1, National Archives, RG 395.
2. Ibid.
3. Miller to CINCUS et al., March 18, 1937.
4. Memorandum from Lt. Arnold E. True to CNO, April 6, 1937, Naval Historical Center.
5. U.S. Army Proceedings, "Exhibit A—Work Performed," p. 2.
6. COMHAWSEC to USCG *Taney* and *Shoshone*, March 18, 1937.
7. U.S. Army Proceedings, "Exhibit E—Depot Report," p. 2.
8. U.S. Army Proceedings, "Exhibit A—Work Performed," p. 2.
9. U.S. Army Proceedings, "Exhibit D—Luke Field Operations," p. 1.
10. Fleet Air Base, Pearl Harbor, to USCG *Shoshone*, March 19, 1937.
11. U.S. Army Proceedings, "Exhibit E—Depot Report," p. 4.
12. U.S. Army Proceedings, "Exhibit O—Newspaper Clippings."
13. U.S. Army Proceedings, "Exhibit D—Luke Field Operations," p. 2.
14. Ibid.
15. U.S. Army Proceedings, "Exhibit O—Newspaper Clippings."
16. U.S. Army Proceedings, "Findings," p. 5.
17. U.S. Army Proceedings, "Exhibit O—Newspaper Clippings."

Chapter 4. Reversals: Preparations for the Second World Flight Attempt

1. Richard B. Black, Field Representative, DOI, report: "Tenth Cruise to the American Equatorial Islands," p. 2, TIGHAR Collection, photocopy of original document.
2. Putnam to Black, March 20, 1937.
3. Miller to Black and Campbell, March 22, 1937.

4. Putnam to Roper, March 20, 1937.
5. Roper to Putnam, March 22, 1937.
6. Adjutant General Conley to General Drum, April 22, 1937.
7. Secretary of the Navy to Miller, March 25, 1937.
8. "Earhart Wrecks Ship after Setting an Ocean Record," *Newsweek*, March 27, 1937, p. 27; "Mourning Becomes Electra," *Time*, March 29, 1937, p. 36.
9. "Maj. Al Williams Rips Earhart Flight as Stunt," *Cleveland Press*, March 31, 1937.
10. "Proceedings of a Board of Officers Appointed to Investigate the Crash of Miss Amelia Earhart at Luke Field, March 20, 1937."
11. Ibid., p. 5
12. R. S. Boutelle, letter to Earhart, April 19, 1937, Earhart Collection, Purdue University Library.
13. Manning interview with author Fred Goerner, as related by Goerner at an Amelia Earhart Symposium held at the National Air and Space Museum in 1983; notes in TIGHAR Collection.
14. Earhart to Rear Adm. Russell R. Waesche, April 27, 1937; Waesche to Earhart, April 27, 1937.
15. CNO to Naval Station Tutuila, April 28, 1937.
16. Hampton, letter to Black, April 29, 1937, National Archives, RG 126, file 9-12-21.
17. Black to Gruening, April 21, 1937.
18. Hampton to Black, April 22, 1937.
19. Black to Hampton, April 22, 1937.
20. Hampton to Black, encrypted, April 23, 1937.
21. Black to Hampton, April 24, 1937.
22. Capt. Edwin Musick, "Route of Clipper Is Found the Best," *New York Times*, March 31, 1937, p. 6.
23. Black to Hampton, June 1, 1937.
24. Hampton to Black, June 2, 1937.
25. Putnam, letter to Southgate, May 5, 1937, National Archives, RG 59, file 800.79611.
26. Putnam, letter to Admiral Leahy, May 8, 1937, Naval Historical Center, RG 26: Proposed Flight Correspondence.
27. Southgate, letter to Putnam, May 8, 1937, National Archives, RG 59, file 800.79611.
28. Earhart, letter to President Franklin D. Roosevelt, November 10, 1936, Naval Historical Center, RG 26.
29. Amelia Earhart, *Last Flight* (New York: Harcourt Brace, 1937), p. 43.
30. Ibid., p. 44.
31. J. M. Johnson, letter to Secretary of State, May 14, 1937, National Archives, RG 59, file 800.79611.
32. R. E. Dake, Bureau of Air Commerce Inspection Report, May 19, 1937, Federal Aviation Administration [FAA] Archives.
33. "Miss Earhart Set to Fly Eastward around the World," *New York Herald Tribune*, May 30, 1937, p. 1.

Chapter 5. Not for Publication: Crossing the South Atlantic

1. Earhart, in-flight notes, Earhart Collection, Purdue University Library.
2. Pan American Airways memorandum, "Hawaiian Flight of NR823M—Navigation," April 29, 1935, Pan Am Archives, University of Miami Library.
3. U.S. Shipping Board, Service Record for Frederick Joseph Noonan, November 20, 1928, National Archives, files pertaining to U.S. Shipping Board.
4. Jon E. Krupnick, original press reports and photographs reproduced in *Pan American's Pacific Pioneers: A Pictorial History of Pan Am's Pacific First Flights, 1935–1946* (Missoula, Mt.: Pictorial Histories Publishing Company, 1997), p. 149.
5. William Stephen Grooch, *From Crate to Clipper with Captain Musick, Pioneer Pilot* (New York: Longmans Green, 1939), p. 212.
6. Associated Press story datelined El Paso, Texas, March 3, 1937.
7. Earhart, *Last Flight*, p. 47.
8. *Oakland Tribune*, March 13, 1937.
9. Noonan, telegram to Martinelli, March 19, 1937, in private collection of Elgen Long.
10. "Noonan Takes Oakland Bride," *Oakland Tribune*, March 29, 1937.
11. "Bride of Plane Navigator Hurt in Fresno Crash," *Fresno Republican*, April 5, 1937 p. 1.
12. Fred Noonan, letter to Helen Day, June 5, 1937, TIGHAR Collection.
13. "Miss Earhart Flies Ocean to Africa in 13-Hour Hop," *New York Herald Tribune*, June 8, 1937, p. 1.
14. Sailing chart of South Atlantic, Earhart Collection, Purdue University Library.
15. Fred Noonan, letter to Eugene Pallette, June 9, 1937, TIGHAR Collection.
16. Earhart, notes made during South Atlantic crossing, June 7, 1937, Earhart Collection, Purdue University Library.
17. Ibid.
18. Noonan, note given to Earhart during South Atlantic crossing, June 7, 1937, Earhart Collection, Purdue University Library.
19. Ibid.
20. Noonan, letter to Pallette, June 9, 1937.
21. Ibid.

Chapter 6. Stand to Sea: Preparations for the Flight to Howland Island

1. COM CG to COMFRANDIV, June 7, 1937; COMFRANDIV to COM CG, June 7, 1937.
2. COMFRANDIV to COM CG, June 7, 1937.
3. COM CG to COMFRANDIV, June 8, 1937.
4. COMFRANDIV to Commandant, Southern Section [COMSOSEC], June 9, 1937.
5. Putnam, letter to Hampton, June 4, 1937; Hampton, letter to Putnam, June 8, 1937, National Archives, RG 126, file 9-12-21.
6. Hampton to Black, June 8, 1937.

7. COMFRANDIV to COMHAWSEC, June 10, 1937.

8. Black to Hampton, June 9, 1937.

9. Putnam, letter to Hampton, June 9, 1937, National Archives, RG 126, file 9-12-21.

10. Admiral Waesche, letter to Putnam, June 7, 1937, Naval Historical Center, RG 80.

11. Putnam to Black, March 20, 1937.

12. Hampton to Black, June 10, 1937.

13. Black to Hampton, June 10, 1937.

14. COMFRANDIV to COM CG, June 10, 1937; COM CG to COMFRANDIV, June 11, 1937.

15. *Itasca* to COMFRANDIV, June 11, 1937; COMFRANDIV to *Itasca*, June 11, 1937.

16. COMFRANDIV to *Itasca*, June 12, 1937.

17. COMFRANDIV to COM CG, June 12, 1937.

18. COM CG to COMFRANDIV, June 15, 1937; West to Black, June 15, 1937.

19. Hampton, letter to Putnam, June 16, 1937, National Archives, RG 126, file 9-12-21.

20. Poindexter (Black) to Hampton, June 15, 1937.

21. COMHAWSEC to COMFRANDIV, June 18, 1937; Black, "Tenth Cruise to the American Equatorial Islands," p. 1.

22. Warner Thompson, U.S. Treasury Department report: "Radio Transcripts—Earhart Flight," July 19, 1937, p. 5, National Archives, RG 26.

23. COMFRANDIV to *Shoshone*, March 13, 1937.

24. Thompson, "Radio Transcripts—Earhart Flight," p. 5.

25. Black to Hampton, June 16, 1937.

26. Putnam to CNO, COMFRANDIV, and Hampton, June 16, 1937.

27. Hampton to Black, June 18, 1937.

28. Poindexter (Black) to Hampton, June 15, 1937; Hampton to Black, June 18, 1937; Putnam, letter to Hampton, June 17, 1937, National Archives, RG 126, file 9-12-21.

29. Black to Hampton, June 19, 1937.

30. Putnam, letter to Johnson, June 17, 1937; Johnson, letter to Putnam, June 18, 1937, National Archives, RG 237, file 835.

31. COMFRANDIV to COMHAWSEC, June 18, 1937; COMHAWSEC to COMFRANDIV, June 18, 1937.

32. Warner Thompson, U.S. Treasury Department report: "Cruise Report 4 June to 24 July 1937—embracing Earhart flight and Equatorial Island cruise," p. 3, Naval Historical Center, RG 26.

33. COMFRANDIV to *Itasca*, June 18, 1937; *Itasca* to COMFRANDIV, June 18, 1937.

34. Black to Putnam via Hampton, June 19, 1937.

35. Ibid.

36. Putnam to Black via Hampton, June 20, 1937.

37. *New York Herald Tribune*, June 1–9, 1937; June 10–12, 1937; June 13–21, 1937.

38. "Amelia Earhart Has Java to N.Y. Chat on Phone," *New York Herald Tribune*, June 22, 1937, p. 1.

39. Noonan, letter to Helen Day, June 22, 1937, TIGHAR Collection.

40. "Amelia Earhart Has Java to N.Y. Chat on Phone," p. 11.
41. Noonan, letter to Day, June 22, 1937.
42. "Miss Earhart Waits in Java as Dutch Work on Her Plane," *New York Herald Tribune*, June 24, 1937, p. 1
43. Putnam, letter to Hampton, June 23, 1937, National Archives, RG 126, file 9-12-21.

Chapter 7. The Long Road to Lae: Delays on the Way to New Guinea

1. Black to Earhart via Samoa, June 23, 1937.
2. *Itasca* to Earhart via Samoa, June 23, 1937.
3. COMFRANDIV to *Itasca*, June 23, 1937; *Itasca* to COMFRANDIV, June 23, 1937.
4. "Putnam and Amelia Chat by Phone from Cheyenne to Java at Cost of $24," *Wyoming Tribune Eagle*, June 25, 1937, p. 1.
5. Thompson, "Cruise Report 4 June to 24 July 1937," July 24, 1937, p. 3.
6. Daniel Cooper, U.S. Army report: "Expedition to the American Equatorial Island in Connection with Amelia Earhart Flight," July 27, 1937, p. 3, National Archives, RG 94/407, file 581.81.
7. Carey to Associated Press, June 24, 1937; Hanzlick to United Press, June 24, 1937.
8. *Itasca* to *Swan*, June 24, 1937; Black to Hampton, June 24, 1937.
9. "Miss Earhart Back in Bandoeng to Have Instruments Repaired," *New York Herald Tribune*, June 25, 1937, p. 1.
10. COMFRANDIV to *Itasca*, June 25, 1937.
11. Ibid.
12. Ibid.
13. Black to Earhart via Samoa, June 23, 1937.
14. COMFRANDIV to *Itasca*, June 26, 1937.
15. Ibid.
16. Black to Earhart via Samoa, June 23, 1937; *Itasca* to Earhart via Samoa, June 23, 1937.
17. Earhart to Black, June 26, 1937.
18. *Itasca* to COMFRANDIV, June 26, 1937.
19. COMFRANDIV to *Itasca*, June 25, 1937; COMFRANDIV to *Itasca*, June 26, 1937.
20. Thompson, "Radio Transcripts—Earhart Flight," p. 22.
21. "Bendix D-Fs," *Aero Digest* (August 1937): 42.
22. COMFRANDIV to *Shoshone*, March 13, 1937.
23. COMFRANDIV to *Itasca*, June 25, 1937.
24. COMFRANDIV to *Itasca*, June 26, 1937.
25. Noonan, letter to Day, June 27, 1937, TIGHAR Collection.
26. "Amelia Earhart Flies Timor Sea to Port Darwin," *New York Herald Tribune*, June 28, 1937, late ed., p. 1.
27. Black, "Tenth Cruise to the American Equatorial Islands," p. 6.
28. C. L. A. Abbott, letter to Albert M. Doyle, American Consul, August 3, 1937, National Archives, RG 59, file 800.79611.
29. Earhart, *Last Flight*, p. 128.

30. "Mrs. Putnam at Darwin," Sydney, Australia, newspaper [name unknown], June 28, 1937, Earhart Collection, box 5, Purdue University Library.
31. Amalgamated Wireless to Lae, June 28, 1937.
32. Vacuum to Lae, June 28, 1937.

Chapter 8. "Denmark's a Prison": Confusion and Frustration in Lae

1. Eric Chater, letter to Frank Griffin, July 25, 1937, TIGHAR Collection.
2. Earhart to Black, June 26, 1937.
3. Governor of Samoa to Earhart, June 28, 1937.
4. Ibid.
5. Ibid.
6. Earhart to *Itasca*, June 30, 1937.
7. Chater letter, July 25, 1937.
8. Earhart to Putnam, June 30, 1937.
9. Hampton to Black, June 18, 1937.
10. Earhart to *Itasca*, June 30, 1937; Earhart to Putnam, June 30, 1937.
11. Black to Earhart, June 23, 1937.
12. Chater letter, July 25, 1937.
13. Ibid.
14. Earhart, "Amelia Earhart Ready to Fly to Howland Island," *New York Herald Tribune*, June 30, 1937, p. 1.
15. "Amelia Earhart Quits Australia for New Guinea," *New York Herald Tribune*, June 29, 1937, p. 1.
16. Earhart to Putnam, June 30, 1937.
17. Putnam to Earhart, June 29, 1937.
18. Earhart to *Itasca*, June 30, 1937.
19. *Itasca* to Fleet Air Base, Pearl Harbor, June 29, 1937.
20. *Itasca* to Earhart, June 29, 1937.
21. Fleet Air Base to Earhart, June 29, 1937.
22. *Itasca* to Earhart, June 29, 1937.
23. *Itasca* to COMFRANDIV, June 30, 1937.
24. Earhart to Black, June 30, 1937.
25. Chater letter, July 25, 1937.
26. Earhart to Black, July 1, 1937.
27. COMFRANDIV/Putnam to Earhart, June 30, 1937.
28. Chater letter, July 25, 1937.
29. Fleet Air Base to Earhart, June 30, 1937.
30. Earhart to *New York Herald Tribune*, July 1, 1937.
31. Chater letter, July 25, 1937.
32. Bureau of Air Commerce, Aircraft Inspection Report, May 19, 1937, FAA Archives.
33. Chater letter, July 25, 1937; James Collopy, letter to the Secretary, Civil Aviation Board, August 28, 1937, Earhart Collection, box 5, Purdue University Library.
34. C. L. Johnson and W. C. Nelson, "Lockheed Report No. 487—Range Study of Lockheed Electra Bimotor Airplane," June 4, 1936, p. 6, TIGHAR Collection.
35. Earhart, *Last Flight*, p. 35.

36. Earhart to *New York Herald Tribune*, July 1, 1937.
37. William Shakespeare, *Macbeth*, act 3, scene 5.

Chapter 9. Lost: Communications Failure on the Flight to Howland Island

1. Leo G. Bellarts, transcript of interview, April 11, 1973, p. 36, TIGHAR Collection.
2. Ibid.
3. Ibid.
4. Ibid., p. 2.
5. Earhart to Black, July 1, 1937.
6. *Itasca* to Fleet Air Base, July 1, 1937.
7. Fleet Air Base to Earhart, July 1, 1937.
8. Chater letter, July 25, 1937.
9. *Itasca* Radio Log, position 1 [RLP1], 1645, July 1, 1937.
10. *Itasca*, RLP1, 1750, July 1, 1937.
11. COMFRANDIV to *Itasca*, July 1, 1937.
12. *Itasca* Deck Log, July 1, 1937, National Archives, RG 26.
13. Carey to Associated Press, July 1, 1937.
14. Earhart to Commanding Officer USS *Itasca*, June 30, 1937.
15. Chater letter, July 25, 1937.
16. *Itasca* Radio Log, position 2 [RLP2], July 1, 1937.
17. Chater letter, July 25, 1937.
18. Thompson, "Radio Transcripts—Earhart Flight," p. 36.
19. Howland Radio Log, 2200, July 2, 1937.
20. *Itasca*, RLP1, 2151, July 1, 1937.
21. Telegram from U.S. Consul in Australia to State Department, July 3, 1937.
22. *Itasca*, RLP2, raw version, 0236, July 2, 1937.
23. Ibid., 0245–48.
24. Thompson, "Radio Transcripts—Earhart Flight," p. 39.
25. Bellarts interview, April 11, 1973, p. 48.
26. *Itasca*, RLP2, 0345, July 2, 1937.
27. Earhart to Black, June 26, 1937.
28. COMFRANDIV to *Itasca*, June 26, 1937.
29. Earhart to Black, June 30, 1937.
30. COMFRANDIV to *Itasca*, June 26, 1937.
31. *Itasca*, RLP2, 0345, July 2, 1937.
32. Thompson, "Radio Transcripts—Earhart Flight," p. 40.
33. Ibid.
34. Cooper, "Expedition to the American Equatorial Island."
35. *International Radiotelegraph Conference, Madrid, 1932: Report to the Secretary of State by the Chairman of the American Delegation, with Appended Documents* (Washington, D.C.: Government Printing Office, 1934).
36. *Itasca*, RLP1, 0358, July 2, 1937.
37. *Itasca*, RLP1, 0440, July 2, 1937.
38. *Itasca*, RLP1, 0445–50, July 2, 1937.
39. *Itasca*, RLP2, raw version, 0453, July 2, 1937.
40. *Itasca*, RLP1, 0455, July 2, 1937.
41. *Itasca* Deck Log, July 2, 1937.

42. *Itasca*, RLP2, raw version, 0614, July 2, 1937.
43. *Itasca* to Earhart via Samoa, June 28, 1937.
44. Bellarts interview, April 11, 1973, pp. 72, 73.
45. Ibid., p. 74.
46. *Itasca*, RLP1, 0620, July 2, 1937.
47. Howland Radio Log, 0717, July 3, 1937, p. 1.
48. *Itasca* Deck Log, July 2, 1937.
49. Thompson, "Radio Transcripts—Earhart Flight," p. 43.
50. See description of *Itasca* at http://www.uscg.mil/hq/g-cp/history/
    WEBCUTTERS/Itasca_1930.html, which references Donald Canneym,
    U.S. Coast Guard and Revenue Cutters, 1790–1935 (Annapolis: Naval
    Institute Press, 1995), among other sources.
51. *Itasca* Deck Log, July 2, 1937.
52. *Itasca*, RLP2, raw log, 0645 and 0646, July 2, 1937.
53. *Itasca*, RLP1, 0642–45 and 0647, July 2, 1937.
54. Bellarts interview, April 11, 1973, p. 76.
55. Howland Radio Log, 0747, July 3, 1937, p. 1.
56. *Itasca*, RLP2, raw version, 0715, July 2, 1937.
57. *Itasca*, RLP2, raw version, 0718 and 0725, July 2, 1937.
58. James C. Kamakaiwi, Daily Log for Howland Island, March 21–July 18,
    1937; July 2, 1937, National Archives, RG 237, William T. Miller Files.
59. *Itasca*, RLP2, raw version, 0730, July 2, 1937.
60. *Itasca*, RLP2, raw version, 0735–40 and 0741, July 2, 1937; *Itasca*, RLP1,
    0740, July 2, 1937; Bellarts interview, April 11, 1973, p. 81.
61. Bellarts interview, April 11, 1973, p. 24.
62. *Itasca*, RLP2, raw version, 0742, July 2, 1937.
63. *Itasca*, RLP1, 0740, July 2, 1937.

Chapter 10. Probably Down: The Last In-Flight Radio Messages

1. Bellarts interview, April 11, 1973, pp. 22, 81.
2. Ibid., pp. 63, 23.
3. Cooper, "Expedition to the American Equatorial Island," pp. 7, 8.
4. Bellarts interview, April 11, 1973, pp. 22, 35.
5. Thompson, "Radio Transcripts—Earhart Flight," p. 42.
6. *Itasca*, RLP2, raw version, 0749–50–57, July 2, 1937; Howland Radio Log,
   0845, July 3, 1937.
7. *Itasca*, RLP2, raw version, 0758, July 2, 1937.
8. *Itasca*, RLP2R, 0800–03, July 2, 1937.
9. Bellarts interview, April 11, 1973, pp. 84, 85.
10. Ibid.; Howland Radio Log, 0859, July 3, 1937.
11. *Itasca*, RLP2, raw version, 0805, July 3, 1937.
12. Ibid., 0811.
13. Ibid., 0815.
14. Bellarts interview, April 11, 1973, p. 84.
15. Black, "Tenth Cruise to the American Equatorial Islands," p. 1.
16. Ibid.
17. Howland Radio Log, 0926, July 3, 1937.
18. *Itasca* press release to Unipress [United Press], 1330Z, July 3, 193

19. *Itasca*, RLP2, raw version, 0827, July 2, 1937.
20. *Itasca*, RLP2, raw version, 0845, later changed to 0843.
21. Bellarts interview, April 11, 1973, p. 56.
22. *Itasca*, RLP2, raw version, 0843, July 2, 1937.
23. Thompson, "Radio Transcripts—Earhart Flight," p. 47; Frank Kenner, letter to Eve Kenner, August 10, 1937.
24. Bellarts interview, April 11, 1973, p. 45.
25. *Itasca*, RLP2, raw version, 0844–46, 0847, and 0854–0907, July 2, 1937.
26. *Itasca* Deck Log, July 2, 1937.
27. *Itasca*, RLP1, 0935, July 2, 1937; Howland Radio Log, 1000, July 3, 1937.
28. *Itasca*, RLP1, 1005, July 2, 1937.
29. *Itasca* to COMFRANDIV, 2145Z, July 2, 1937.
30. *Itasca* to COMHAWSEC, 2148Z, July 2, 1937.
31. Ibid.
32. Thompson, "Radio Transcripts—Earhart Flight," p. 47.
33. Kenner letter, August 10, 1937.
34. Thompson, "Radio Transcripts—Earhart Flight," p. 47.
35. Ibid.
36. Ibid.
37. See "The Lae Takeoff" on the DVD.
38. Thompson, "Radio Transcripts—Earhart Flight," p. 43.
39. *Itasca* press release.

Chapter 11. The Search Begins: The First Day

1. COM CG to COMFRANDIV, 2315Z, July 2, 1937.
2. COMHAWSEC to *Itasca*, 0031Z, July 3, 1937.
3. Putnam, telegram to CNO, 0042Z, July 3, 1937.
4. CNO to COM14, 0040Z, July 3, 1937.
5. *Itasca* to COMFRANDIV, 0045Z, July 3, 1937.
6. *Itasca* to all ships, 0103Z, July 3, 1937.
7. COMHAWSEC to *Itasca*, 0031Z, July 3, 1937.
8. *Itasca* to COMFRANDIV et al., 0132Z July 3, 1937.
9. Ibid.; *Itasca* Deck Log, July 2, 1937.
10. K. C. Ambler, PAA Section Supervisor, Communications, Honolulu, memorandum to Division Superintendent, Communications, Alameda, July 10, 1937, PAA Collection, University of Miami Library.
11. U.S. Navy Hydrographic Office, San Francisco, to all ships, 0245Z, July 3, 1937.
12. COMFRANDIV to *Itasca*, 0310Z, July 3, 1937.
13. *Itasca* to COMFRANDIV, 0403Z, July 3, 1937; COMFRANDIV to *Itasca*, 0410Z, July 3, 1937.
14. *Itasca* Deck Log, July 2, 1937.
15. Warren Harvey, letter to Mrs. S. D. Harvey, July 24, 1937, TIGHAR Collection.
16. Ibid.
17. COM14 to CNO, 03:30Z, July 3, 1937.
18. Wilhelm Friedell, "Resumé Earhart Search by the USS *Colorado*," July 13, 1937, p. 1, National Archives, San Bruno, Calif., RG 181, file A4-3 Earhart.

19. Ira Dye, "Liberty Lost Pursuing a Legend," *Naval History* 11, no. 3 (May–June 1997): 42.
20. Ibid.
21. Lt. (j.g.) William Short, letter to his father, July 22, 1937, TIGHAR Collection.
22. Ibid.
23. COM14 to *Colorado*, 0745Z, July 3, 1937; Friedell, "Resumé Earhart Search," p. 3.
24. *Itasca* to COMFRANDIV et al., 0132Z July 3, 1937.
25. Friedell, "Resumé Earhart Search," p. 3.
26. Short letter, July 22, 1937.
27. Dye, "Liberty Lost Pursuing a Legend."

Chapter 12. "Think It Is Plane?": The First Night

1. *Itasca*, RLP2, 1800, July 2, 1937.
2. *Itasca*, RLP2, 1801, July 2, 1937; *Itasca*, RLP1, 1800 and 1801, July 2, 1937.
3. *Itasca*, RLP2, 1807, July 2, 1937.
4. *Itasca*, RLP2, 1812, July 2, 1937.
5. *Itasca*, RLP2, 1824, July 2, 1937; *Itasca*, RLP1, 1825, July 2, 1937.
6. Ambler memorandum, July 10, 1937.
7. *Itasca*, RLP1, 1830, July 2, 1937.
8. *Radio* Tutuila to *Itasca*, 0730Z, July 3, 1937.
9. *Itasca*, RLP2, 1834 and 1836, July 2, 1937; *Itasca*, RLP1, 1830, July 2, 1937.
10. Radio Tutuila to *Itasca*, 0730Z, July 3, 1937.
11. *Achilles* to Radio Tutuila, 22xxZ, July 3, 1937.
12. *Itasca*, RLP1, 1837, July 2, 1937.
13. *Itasca*, RLP2, 1840 and 1841, July 2, 1937.
14. *Itasca*, RLP1, 1856, July 2, 1937.
15. *Itasca* to COMFRANDIV, 0710Z, July 3, 1937.
16. Ibid.
17. Ibid.
18. COM14 to *Itasca*, 0720Z, July 3, 1937.
19. *Itasca*, RLP2, 1950, July 2, 1937.
20. COMHAWSEC to *Itasca*, 0802Z, July 3 (Greenwich), 1937.
21. Radio Tutuila to *Itasca*, 0730Z, July 3, 1937.
22. *Itasca* to COMFRANDIV, 0710Z, July 3, 1937.
23. COMHAWSEC to *Itasca*, 0810Z, July 3, 1937.
24. Author's telephone interview with Mabel Larremore Duncklee, October 2, 1990.
25. Mabel Duncklee, letter to TIGHAR, received October 2, 1990; Duncklee interview, October 2, 1990.
26. Duncklee letter, October 2, 1990.
27. Ibid.
28. Ibid.
29. For a technical discussion of harmonics and how they apply to reports of signals heard from the Earhart plane, see "Harmony and Power: Could Betty Have Heard Earhart on a Harmonic?" on the DVD.

30. COMHAWSEC to *Itasca*, 0810Z, July 3, 1937; *Itasca*, RLP2, 2103 and 2105, July 2, 1937.
31. PBY to Fleet Air Base, 0835Z, July 3, 1937.
32. *Itasca*, RLP2, 2107, July 2, 1937.
33. *Itasca*, RLP2, 2110, July 2, 1937.
34. *Itasca*, RLP2, 2113, July 2, 1937.
35. Page W. Smith, interview, August 6, 1993.
36. Radio Coast Guard, San Francisco, to *Itasca*, 1210Z, July 3, 1937.
37. U.S. Consul, Sydney, Australia, telegram to U.S. State Department, 1200Z, July 3, 1937.
38. *Itasca*, RLP2, 2130 and 2132, July 2, 1937.

Chapter 13. Hoaxes and Hopes: The Second Day

1. KPH to Radio Coast Guard, San Francisco, 101xZ, July 3, 1937.
2. COMFRANDIV to *Itasca*, 1020Z, July 3, 1937; *Itasca* to COMFRANDIV, 1140Z, July 3, 1937.
3. COMFRANDIV to *Itasca*, 1145Z, July 3, 1937.
4. "Miss Earhart Forced Down at Sea," *New York Times*, July 3, 1937, p. 1.
5. Ibid.
6. Ibid.
7. Ibid.
8. *Oakland Tribune*, July 3, 1937.
9. Ibid.
10. COMFRANDIV to *Itasca*, 0750Z, July 4, 1937.
11. "Radio Aid Sure Earhart Plane Is Safe on Reef," *New York Herald Tribune*, July 9, 1937, p. 5.
12. COMFRANDIV to COMHAWSEC, 0640Z, July 12, 1937.
13. COMFRANDIV to *Itasca*, 1840Z, July 3, 1937.
14. COMFRANDIV to *Itasca*, 2240Z, July 6, 1937.
15. *Ashland* (Ky.) *Daily Independent*, July 9, 1937.
16. Ibid.
17. Nina Paxton, letter to Fred Goerner, July 22, 1968, TIGHAR Collection.
18. Ibid.; Paxton, letter to Goerner, August 23, 1968, TIGHAR Collection.
19. COM14 to CNO, 2028Z, July 3, 1937.
20. CNO to COM14, 0040Z, July 3, 1937.
21. CNO to CINCUS, 2145Z, July 3, 1937.
22. COMFRANDIV to COMHAWSEC, 1830Z, July 3, 1937.
23. Commandant, Twelfth Naval District [COM12] to COM14, 2015Z, July 3, 1937.
24. "2 Aids Believe Earhart Plane Safe on Pacific Atoll," *New York Herald Tribune*, July 4, 1937, p. 1.
25. COMFRANDIV to *Itasca*, 0750Z, July 4, 1937.
26. *Itasca* to COMHAWSEC, 1930Z, July 3, 1937; COMHAWSEC to *Itasca*, 2026Z, July 3, 1937.
27. COMHAWSEC to COMFRANDIV, 2135Z, July 3, 1937.
28. COM CG to *Itasca*, 2256Z, July 3, 1937.
29. *Itasca* to COM CG, 0020Z, July 4, 1937.
30. COM CG to *Itasca*, 0140, July 4, 1937.

31. *Itasca* to United Press, 0215Z, July 4, 1937.
32. Carey to Associated Press, 0216Z, July 4, 1937.
33. *Itasca* to COM CG, 0450Z, July 4, 1937.
34. Telegram from U.S. Consul, Sydney, Australia, to U.S. State Department, 1200Z, July 3, 1937.
35. *Itasca* to COM CG, 0450Z, July 4, 1937.
36. COMFRANDIV to *Itasca*, 1145Z, July 3, 1937.
37. *Itasca* to COMFRANDIV.
38. COMFRANDIV to *Itasca*, 0120Z, July 4, 1937.
39. COMFRANDIV to COMHAWSEC, 0420Z, July 3, 1937.

Chapter 14. Voices: The Second Night

1. *Itasca*, RLP2, 1806, July 3, 1937.
2. Ibid.
3. *Itasca*, RLP2, 1915 and 1923, July 3, 1937.
4. *Itasca*, RLP2, 2216, July 4, 1937.
5. A. Frederick Collins, *The Radio Amateur's Handbook*, 14th ed. (West Hartford, Conn.: American Radio Relay League, 1937), p. 364.
6. COMHAWSEC to *Itasca*, 0846Z, July 4, 1937.
7. *Itasca* to United Press, 0815Z, July 4, 1937.
8. *Itasca* to COMFRANDIV et al., 0132Z, July 3, 1937; *Itasca* to COMFRANDIV, 0710Z, July 3, 1937.
9. *Itasca* to United Press, 0815Z, July 4, 1937.
10. Ambler memorandum, July 10, 1937.
11. *Itasca*, RLP2, 2120, July 3, 1937.
12. *Itasca*, RLP2, 2205, July 3, 1937.
13. Ambler memorandum, July 10, 1937.
14. *Itasca*, RLP2, 2233, July 3, 1937.
15. Ambler memorandum, July 10, 1937; COMHAWSEC to *Itasca*, 1035Z, July 4, 1937.
16. COMHAWSEC to *Itasca*, 1035Z, July 4, 1937.
17. *Itasca*, RLP2, 2306, July 3, 1937.
18. COMFRANDIV to *Itasca*, 1200Z, July 4, 1937.
19. COMHAWSEC to *Itasca*, 1340Z, July 4, 1937; R. M. Hansen, PAA Operator in Charge, Communications, Wake Island, memorandum to Communications Superintendent, Alameda, July 10, 1937.
20. Radio Wailupe to *Colorado*, *Itasca*, et al., 1415Z, July 4, 1937.
21. *Itasca*, RLP2, 0120 and 0150, July 4, 1937.
22. "Plane's Letters Heard on Radio at Los Angeles," *New York Herald Tribune*, July 5, 1937, p. 2.
23. Ibid.
24. Ibid.
25. *Itasca* to United Press, 0815Z, July 4, 1937.
26. *Itasca*, RLP2, 0200, July 4, 1937; G. H. Miller, PAA Operator in Charge, Communications, Midway Island, memorandum to Division Communications Superintendent, Alameda, July 11, 1937.
27. Miller memorandum, July 11, 1937.
28. COMHAWSEC to *Itasca*, 1610Z, July 4, 1937.

29. "First Radio Contact with Miss Earhart Made by Springs Boy," *Rock Springs Rocket*, July 6–7, 1937, p. 1.
30. Ibid.
31. COMFRANDIV to *Itasca*, 2310Z, July 4, 1937.
32. COMFRANDIV to *Itasca*, 0057Z, July 5, 1937.
33. See "Post-loss Radio Probability Analysis," on the DVD.
34. *Rock Springs Rocket*, July 6–7, 1937.
35. Ibid.
36. Ibid.
37. Ibid.; COMFRANDIV to *Itasca*, 2310Z, July 4, 1937.

Chapter 15. Negative Results: The Third Day

1. "Storm Turns Back Plane Sent to Find Miss Earhart; Several Radio Calls Heard," *New York Times*, July 4, 1937, p. 1.
2. "Storms Balk Navy Plane on Earhart Hunt," *New York Herald Tribune,* July 4, 1937, p. 1
3. Ibid.
4. CNO to CINCUS, 1700Z, July 4, 1937.
5. Friedell, "Resumé Earhart Search," p. 3.
6. *New York Herald Tribune*, July 4, 1937, p. 1.
7. Radio Tutuila to *Achilles*, 1800Z, July 4, 1937.
8. Friedell, "Resumé Earhart Search," p. 4.
9. Thompson, "Cruise Report 4 June to 24 July, 1937," p. 6, National Archives, RG 26 file 601.
10. *Itasca*, RLP2, 0930–1600, July 4, 1937.
11. *Golden Bear* to *Itasca*, time unknown, July 4, 1937.
12. Bureau of International Telecommunication Union, *List of Coast Stations and Ship Stations* (Berne, Switzerland, 1937), p. 332.
13. *Itasca* to COM CG, 0245Z, July 5, 1937.
14. *Itasca* to COM CG, 2205Z, July 4, 1937.
15. COM CG to *Itasca*, 2355Z, July 4, 1937.
16. *Itasca* to COM CG, 0630Z, July 5, 1937.
17. Ibid.
18. *Itasca*, RLP2, 0245–48, July 2, 1937.
19. *Itasca* to COM CG, 0630Z, July 5, 1937.
20. *Itasca*, RLP2, 0345, July 2, 1937.
21. *Itasca* to COM CG, 0630Z, July 5, 1937.
22. Cooper, "Expedition to the American Equatorial Island," p. 6; *Itasca*, RLP2, 0453, July 2, 1937; *Itasca*, RLP1, 0455, July 2, 1937.
23. *Itasca* to COM CG, 0630Z, July 5, 1937.
24. *Itasca*, RLP2, 0614, July 2, 1937.
25. *Itasca* to COM CG, 0630Z, July 5, 1937.
26. *Itasca*, RLP2, 0615, July 2, 1937.
27. *Itasca* to COM CG, 0630Z, July 5, 1937.
28. *Itasca*, RLP2, 0646, July 2, 1937.
29. *Itasca* to COM CG, 0630Z, July 5, 1937.
30. *Itasca*, RLP2, 0742, July 2, 1937; *Itasca* to COMFRANDIV, 2145Z, July 2, 1937.

31. *Itasca* to COM CG, 0630Z, July 5, 1937.
32. *Itasca*, RLP2R, 0758, July 2, 1937.
33. *Itasca* to COM CG, 0630Z, July 5, 1937.
34. *Itasca*, RLP2R, 0803, July 2, 1937.
35. *Itasca* to COM CG, 0630Z, July 5, 1937.
36. *Itasca*, RLP2R, 0843, July 2, 1937.
37. *Itasca* to COM CG, 0630Z, July 5, 1937.
38. Ibid.
39. Black, "Tenth Cruise to American Equatorial Islands," p. 13.
40. "Earhart Flares Believed Sighted by Cutter Racing to '281 North Howland' in Pacific," *New York Herald Tribune,* July 6, 1937, p. 1.
41. COMHAWSEC to *Itasca*, 2025Z, July 4, 1937.
42. *Itasca* to COMHAWSEC, 2140Z, July 4, 1937.
43. Ibid.
44. COMHAWSEC to *Itasca*, 0225Z, July 5, 1937.
45. *Itasca* to COMFRANDIV, 0535Z, July 5, 1937; COMFRANDIV to *Itasca*, 0605Z, July 5, 1937.
46. COMFRANDIV to *Itasca*, 0555Z, July 5, 1937.
47. Thompson, "Radio Transcripts—Earhart Flight," p. 68.
48. COMFRANDIV to COMHAWSEC, 0326Z, July 5, 1937.
49. COMHAWSEC to *Itasca* et al., 0445Z, July 5, 1937.
50. *Itasca*, RLP2, 1810, July 4, 1937.

Chapter 16. Bearings: The Third Night

1. *Honolulu Star Bulletin*, July 5, 1937, p. 1.
2. COMHAWSEC to *Itasca* et al., 0445Z, July 5, 1937.
3. COMHAWSEC to *Colorado, Swan*, Tutuila, *Itasca*, 0730Z, July 5, 1937.
4. Hansen memorandum, July 10, 1937.
5. Miller memorandum, July 11, 1937.
6. *Honolulu Star Bulletin,* July 5, 1937.
7. Ambler memorandum, July 10, 1937.
8. G. W. Angus, PAA Division Communication Superintendent, Pacific Division, Alameda, memorandum to Chief Communication Engineer, Communications, New York, July 10, 1937, PAA Collection, University of Miami Library.
9. Ambler memorandum, July 10, 1937.
10. Angus memorandum, July 10, 1937.
11. *Itasca*, RLP2, 1600, July 4, 1937; Ambler memorandum, July 10, 1937.
12. Radio Tutuila to COMHAWSEC, 0745Z, July 5, 1937; COMHAWSEC to *Itasca*, 0845Z, July 5, 1937.
13. *Itasca*, RLP2, 2000, 2005, 2015, and 2020, July 4, 1937.
14. COMFRANDIV to *Itasca*, 1930Z, July 5, 1937.
15. *Honolulu Star Bulletin*, July 5, 1937.
16. Robert Brandenburg, "Analysis of Radio Direction Finder Bearings in the Search for Amelia Earhart," p. 21, TIGHAR research document, TIGHAR Collection.
17. *Itasca*, RLP2, 2045, July 5, 1937.
18. Ibid., 2113, July 5, 1937.

19. COMHAWSEC to *Itasca*, 0845Z, July 5, 1937.
20. *Itasca*, RLP2, 2128 and 2137, July 4, 1937; *Itasca*, RLP2, 1834, July 2 1937; *Itasca*, RLP2, 2141, July 5, 1937.
21. COMHAWSEC to *Itasca*, 0910Z, July 5, 1937.
22. *Itasca*, RLP2, 2141–49, July 5, 1937.
23. *Itasca*, RLP2, 2202, July 5, 1937.
24. *Itasca*, RLP2, 2210 and 2214, July 5, 1937.
25. *Itasca*, RLP2, 2216, July 5, 1937.
26. *Itasca*, RLP2, 2233, July 5, 1937.
27. Miller memorandum, July 11, 1937; Ambler memorandum, July 10, 1037; COMHAWSEC to *Itasca*, 0910Z, July 5, 1937; *Itasca*, RLP2, 2233.
28. *Itasca*, RLP2, 2216; Thompson, "Radio Transcripts—Earhart Flight," p. 69.
29. Letter from Yau Fai Lum to Thomas F. Gannon, January 10, 1989, TIGHAR Collection; John P. Riley, "The Earhart Tragedy: Old Mystery, New Hypothesis," *Naval History* 14, no. 2 (August 2000): 22–28.
30. Riley, "The Earhart Tragedy," p. 26.
31. Black, "Tenth Cruise to the American Equatorial Islands," p. 13.
32. Bellarts interview, April 11, 1973, p. 49.
33. *Itasca*, RLP2, 2232, July 5, 1937.
34. *Itasca*, RLP2, 2240, July 5, 1937.
35. COMHAWSEC to *Itasca*, 0845Z, July 5, 1937; *Itasca* to COMHAWSEC, 1008Z, July 5, 1937.
36. *Itasca*, RLP2, 2243, 2258, 2259, and 2317, July 5, 1937.
37. Miller memorandum, July 11, 1937.
38. For an explanation of "night effect," see Robert Brandenburg, "Analysis of Radio Direction Finder Bearings in the Search for Amelia Earhart," on the DVD.
39. *Itasca*, RLP2, 2335, July 5, 1937; Howland Radio Log, 0035, July 5, 1937.
40. Miller memorandum, July 11, 1937; Howland Radio Log, 0035, July 5, 1937; *Itasca*, RLP2, 2335, July 5, 1937.
41. *Itasca*, RLP2, 2335, July 5, 1937.
42. *Itasca*, to COMHAWSEC, 1155Z, July 5, 1937.
43. *Itasca*, RLP2, 0030–35, July 5, 1937.
44. Radio Tutuila to *Itasca*, 1210Z, July 5, 1937.
45. Ibid.
46. Hansen memorandum, July 10, 1937.
47. Angus memorandum, July 10, 1937.
48. Hansen memorandum, July 10, 1937.
49. Angus memorandum, July 10, 1937.
50. COMHAWSEC to *Itasca*, 1312Z, July 5, 1937.
51. *Itasca* Deck Log, July 5, 1937.
52. *Itasca* to *Swan*, 1425Z, July 5, 1937.
53. *Itasca*, RLP2 0314, July 5, 1937.
54. *Itasca*, RLP2 0035, July 5, 1937.
55. *Itasca*, RLP2 0307, July 5, 1937.
56. *Itasca* to Wailupe and Tutuila, 1449Z, July 5, 1937.
57. Howland Radio Log, 0518, July 5, 1937.
58. COMFRANDIV to *Itasca*, 1930Z, July 5, 1937.

59. *Itasca* to COM CG, 1810Z, July 5, 1937.
60. *Itasca* to COMFRANDIV, 1955Z, July 5, 1937.
61. *Itasca* to Associated Press, 2030Z, July 5, 1937.
62. *Itasca*, RLP2, 0100, July 5, 1937.
63. Carey to Associated Press, 20:30Z, July 5, 1937.
64. *Itasca* to Associated Press, 2030Z, July 5, 1937.
65. Howland Radio Log, 0035, July 5, 1937.
66. *Itasca* to Associated Press, 2030Z, July 5, 1937.
67. *Itasca*, RLP2, 0307 and 0500, July 5, 1937.
68. *Itasca* to Associated Press, 2030Z, July 5, 1937.
69. *Itasca* Deck Log, July 5, 1937.
70. *Itasca* to United Press, 2030Z, July 5, 1937.
71. COMHAWSEC to *Itasca,* 0910Z July 5, 1937.
72. *Itasca* to United Press, 2030Z, July 5, 1937.
73. Ibid.
74. COMFRANDIV to *Itasca*, 1930Z, July 5, 1937.
75. *Itasca* to United Press, 2030Z, July 5, 1937.
76. COMHAWSEC to *Itasca*, 1312Z, July 5, 1937.
77. *Itasca* to United Press, 2030Z, July 5, 1937.
78. Howland Island to *Itasca*, 1455Z, July 5, 1937.
79. *Itasca* to United Press, 2030Z, July 5, 1937.
80. Hansen memorandum, July 10, 1937.

Chapter 17. Betty's Notebook: The Fourth Day

1. *Oakland Tribune*, July 5, 1937, p. 1.
2. "Wyoming and Ohio Listeners Believed She Was Trying to Give Position Near Howland," *New York Times*, July 5, 1937, p. 1.
3. "Mantz Believes Fliers Are 'Sitting on an Island,'" *New York Herald Tribune*, July 5, 1937, p. 1.
4. Ibid., p. 2.
5. *Honolulu Star Bulletin*, July 5, 1937, p. 1.
6. COMFRANDIV to COM CG, 1845Z, July 5, 1937.
7. U.S. State Department memorandum: "Search for Plane of Amelia Earhart," July 5, 1937.
8. Putnam to CNO, 1659Z, July 8, 1937; CNO to Putnam, 18xx, July 8, 1937.
9. "Woman Asserts She Got Communication by Voice," *New York Herald Tribune*, July 6, 1937, p. 2.
10. "Amateur Gets Message," *New York Herald Tribune*, July 6, 1937, p. 2.
11. "Wyoming and Ohio Listeners Believed She Was Trying to Give Position Near Howland," *New York Times*, July 5, 1937, p. 1.
12. Ibid.; *Rock Springs Rocket*, July 6-7, 1937.
13. *Itasca*, RLP2, raw version, 0843, July 2, 1937.
14. *Moorby* to *Itasca*, 2100Z, July 5, 1937.
15. *Itasca*, RLP2, raw version, 0957, July 5, 1937.
16. Betty Klenck Brown, email to Ric Gillespie, September 28, 2000.
17. Ibid.
18. Fred Goerner, letter to John Hathaway, August 21, 1970.
19. Goerner to Hathaway, September 4, 1970.

20. Scanned images of each page of the notebook are included on the DVD.
21. See Robert Brandenburg's study, "Harmony and Power: Could Betty Have Heard Amelia on a Harmonic?" on the DVD.
22. Betty Klenck's notebook [BN], p. 53.
23. *Itasca*, RLP2, raw version, 0957, July 5, 1937.
24. Thompson, "Radio Transcripts—Earhart Flight," July 19, 1937, p. 47; Frank Kenner, letter to Eve Kenner, August 10, 1937; Bellarts interview, April 11, 1973, p. 45.
25. Brown, email to Gillespie.
26. BN, p. 49.
27. Ibid.
28. *Itasca*, RLP2, raw version, 1000, July 5, 1937.
29. Brown, email to Gillespie.
30. *Itasca*, RLP2, raw version, 1022, July 5, 1937.
31. Mabel Duncklee, letter to TIGHAR, received October 2, 1990, TIGHAR Collection.
32. Ibid.
33. See "Tidal Study," on the DVD.
34. Duncklee letter to TIGHAR.
35. *Ontario* to CINCAF, 0310Z, March 14, 1937; CNO to Naval Station Tutuila, 1700Z, April 28, 1937.
36. Amelia Earhart, letter to her mother, December 26, 1934, Schlesinger Library, Radcliffe College.
37. "Woman Hears Call," *New York Herald Tribune*, July 6, 1937, p. 2.
38. Commandant, Ninth Naval Division [COM9] to CNO, 0530Z, July 6, 1937.
39. COMFRANDIV to *Itasca*, 1625Z, July 6, 1937.
40. *Honolulu Star Bulletin*, July 5, 1937, p.1.
41. COMFRANDIV to *Itasca*, 2325Z, July 5, 1937.

Chapter 18. 281 North: The Fourth Night

1. *Itasca* to Howland, 0407Z, July 6, 1937.
2. Carey NBC to COM14, 0316Z, July 6, 1937.
3. Messages from COM14 to Carey NBC, 0521Z, July 6, 1937.
4. COMHAWSEC to *Itasca*, 0036Z, July 6, 1937; *Itasca* to COMHAWSEC, 0455Z, July 6, 1937.
5. COMFRANDIV to *Itasca*, 0535Z, July 6, 1937.
6. *Itasca*, RLP2, 1840 and 2010, July 5, 1937.
7. *Itasca* Deck Log, July 5, 1937.
8. COMFRANDIV to *Itasca*, 0730Z, July 6, 1937; *Itasca* to COMFRANDIV, 0740Z, July 6, 1937.
9. *Itasca* Deck Log, July 5, 1937; Thompson, "Radio Transcripts—Earhart Flight," pp. 75, 76; *Itasca*, RLP2, 2105, July 5, 1937.
10. *Itasca*, RLP2, 2113, July 5, 1937; Radio Wailupe to COMM OFFICE NYD PH et al., 0845Z, July 6, 1937; COMHAWSEC to COMFRANDIV, 0913Z, July 6, 1937.
11. *Itasca*, RLP2, 2132 and 2133, July 5, 1937.
12. COMFRANDIV to *Itasca*, 0915Z, July 6, 1937.
13. Thompson, "Radio Transcripts—Earhart Flight," p. 76.

14. *Itasca*, RLP2, 2200, July 5, 1937.
15. *Itasca* to COMHAWSEC, 1015Z, July 6, 1937; Thompson, "Radio Transcripts—Earhart Flight," p. 76.
16. *New York Herald Tribune*, July 6, 1937, p. 1.
17. "Earhart Searchers Arrive at Point Reported Given by Plane on Radio," *New York Times*, July 6, 1937, p. 1.
18. Jacksonville Beach to COM CG, 14xxZ, July 6, 1937.
19. *New York Times* to *Itasca*, 15xxZ, July 6, 1937.
20. *London Daily Mirror* to *Itasca*, 15xxZ, July 6, 1937.
21. Paramount Pictures to *Itasca*, 15xxZ, July 6, 1937.
22. Honolulu (Thurston) to *Itasca*, 15xxZ, July 6, 1937.
23. New York Pathé News to *Itasca*, 15xxZ, July 6, 1937.
24. United Press to Hanzlick, 15xx, July 6, 1937.
25. Honolulu Press/Associated to Carey, 15xx, July 6, 1937.
26. COM CG to *Itasca*, 1658Z, July 6, 1937; *Itasca* to COM CG, 1754Z and 1850Z, July 6, 1937.
27. Radio Wailupe to *Itasca*, 1900Z, July 6, 1937; *Itasca* to Radio Wailupe, 1914Z, July 6, 1937.
28. Carey to Associated Press, 2030Z, July 6, 1937.
29. *Itasca*, RLP2, 2113 and 2132, July 5, 1937.
30. Radio Wailupe to COM14, 1005Z, July 7, 1937.
31. Howland Radio Log, 2238.
32. Radio Wailupe to COM14, 1005Z, July 7, 1937.
33. COMFRANDIV to COMHAWSEC et al., 1040Z, July 6, 1937.
34. COMFRANDIV to COM CG, 2038Z, July 6, 1937; COM CG to COMFRANDIV, 2133Z, July 6, 1937.
35. COMHAWSEC to *Itasca*, 0001Z, July 7, 1937.
36. Thompson, "Radio Transcripts—Earhart Flight," p. 75.
37. COMFRANDIV to COMHAWSEC et al., 1010Z, July 6, 1937.

Chapter 19. The Most Likely Place: *Colorado* Arrives

1. *New York Herald Tribune*, July 6, 1937, p. 1.
2. COM14 to *Colorado*, 0135Z, July 7, 1937.
3. *Colorado* to COM14, 0225Z, July 7, 1937.
4. COMFRANDIV to *Itasca* and *Colorado*, 0752Z, July 7, 1937.
5. Friedell, "Resumé Earhart Search," p. 8.
6. *Colorado* to CNO, 1615Z, July 6, 1937.
7. USS *Colorado*, *Radio Press News*, July 6, 1937, p. 5, TIGHAR Collection.
8. Ibid.
9. Ibid., p. 1.
10. "Earhart Search Shifting to Southeast of Howland after Fifth Fruitless Day," *New York Times*, July 7, 1937, p. 1.
11. Friedell, "Resumé Earhart Search."
12. *Colorado* Deck Log, July 8, 1937.
13. Lt. John O. Lambrecht, "Aircraft Search for Earhart Plane," *Bureau of Aeronautics Weekly Newsletter*, July 16, 1937, p. 2, National Archives, RG 72, file BB45/A9.
14. Short letter, July 22, 1937.

15. CNO to COM14, 2021Z, July 9, 1937.
16. CNO to COM14, 2112Z, July 7, 1937; COM14 to CNO, 0130Z, July 8, 1937.
17. "Warship's Planes Start Search for Miss Earhart; No Definite Signals Heard," *New York Times*, July 8, 1937, p. 1.
18. "Warship's Planes Join Earhart Hunt" and "Putnam Keeps up Hope," *New York Times*, July 8, 1937, p. 12.
19. "Warship's Planes Start Search."
20. Lambrecht, "Aircraft Search for Earhart Plane," p. 3.
21. COM14 to COMDESRON2, 0319Z, July 6, 1937; CNO to *Ramapo*, 1445Z, July 6, 1937.
22. Capt. Leigh Noyes, "Report of Earhart Search—U.S.S. *Lexington*," July 1937, p. 2, National Archives, San Bruno, Calif., RG 181, file A4-3 Earhart.
23. Rear Adm. Orin G. Murfin, "Report of Earhart Search, 2–18 July, 1937," p. 5, National Archives, San Bruno, Calif., RG 181, file A4-3 Earhart.
24. Friedell, "Resumé Earhart Search," p. 8.
25. Noyes, "Report of Earhart Search," p. ii.
26. *Itasca*, RLP2, raw version, 0742, July 2, 1937; *Itasca*, RLP1, 0740, July 2, 1937.
27. Noyes, "Report of Earhart Search"; *Itasca*, RLP2, raw version, 0843, July 2, 1937.
28. Noyes, "Report of Earhart Search," p. iii.
29. Ibid., p. v.
30. Ibid., p. iii.
31. Ibid., p. v.
32. Black to Gruening, 1145Z, July 9, 1937.
33. Short letter, July 22, 1937.

Chapter 20. Signs of Recent Habitation: The Search of the Phoenix Group

1. *Colorado* Deck Log, July 9, 1937, National Archives, RG 24.
2. Lambrecht, "Aircraft Search for Earhart Plane."
3. Ibid.
4. Jimmy M. Skaggs, *The Great Guano Rush: Entrepreneurs and American Overseas Expansion* (New York: St. Martin's Press, 1995), pp. 80–81.
5. Lambrecht, "Aircraft Search for Earhart Plane."
6. Ibid.
7. Ibid.
8. Ibid.
9. H. E. Maude, "Colonization of the Phoenix Islands by the Surplus Population of the Gilbert and Ellice Islands," p. 7, Public Records Office, Kew, London, Great Britain, CO225/309/860593.
10. Short letter, July 22, 1937.
11. Lambrecht, "Aircraft Search for Earhart Plane."
12. Ibid.
13. Short letter, July 22, 1937.
14. Lambrecht, "Aircraft Search for Earhart Plane."
15. Ibid.
16. Short letter, July 22, 1937.

17. *Colorado* Deck Log, July 9, 1937.
18. Lambrecht answers to Goerner, undated.
19. Short letter, July 22, 1937.
20. *Colorado* to United Press 2304Z, July 9, 1937.
21. COM14 to COMDESRON2, 2331Z, July 9, 1937.
22. Noyes, "Report of Earhart Search," p. v.
23. COM14 to COMDESRON2, 2331Z, July 9, 1937; COMDESRON to COM14, 2040Z, July 10, 1937.
24. Short letter, July 22, 1937.
25. Lambrecht, "Aircraft Search for Earhart Plane."
26. Captain, HMS *Leith*, "Report of Proceedings: Island Cruise—Second Part," September 18, 1937, Public Records Office, Kew, London, Great Britain.
27. Eric R. Bevington, *The Things We Do for England—If Only England Knew!* (Acorn Bookwork: Hampshire, U.K. 1990), p. 25.
28. Lambrecht, "Aircraft Search for Earhart Plane."
29. Ibid.
30. Ibid.; H. E. Maude, "Colonization of the Phoenix Islands," *Journal of the Polynesian Society* 61 (1952): 71–75.
31. *Colorado* to Associated Press, 0825Z, July 11, 1937.
32. Foua Tofinga, letter to Dr. Thomas F. King, October 5, 1999, TIGHAR Collection.
33. Fred Goerner, letter to Dr. Thomas King, February 29, 1992, TIGHAR Collection.
34. Lambrecht, "Aircraft Search for Earhart Plane."
35. Short letter, July 22, 1937.
36. *Colorado* to COM14, 0600Z, July 11, 1937.
37. *Colorado* to United Press, 0425Z, July 11, 1937.
38. Brooks to International, 0100Z, July 11, 1937.

Chapter 21. "We Will Find Amelia Tomorrow": *Lexington*'s Search

1. COM14 to COM11, 2215Z, July 10, 1937.
2. COMFRANDIV to *Itasca* et al., 2219Z, July 5, 1937.
3. COM11 to COM14, 1705Z, July 11, 1937.
4. Noyes, "Report of Earhart Search," p. iii.
5. COM14 to *Colorado* and COMDESRON2, 2015Z, July 11, 1937.
6. COMFRANDIV to COMHAWSEC et al., 0640Z, July 12, 1937.
7. "Noonan Sends SOS from Earhart Plane," *Oakland Tribune*, July 3, 1937, p.1.
8. *Itasca* to COMFRANDIV 1145Z, July 3, 1937.
9. COMFRANDIV to COMDESRON2, 1200Z, July 12, 1937.
10. COMFRANDIV to COMHAWSEC et al., 0640Z, July 12, 1937.
11. State Department to American Embassy, Tokyo, 1900Z, July 10, 1937.
12. Tokyo to State, 0200Z, July 11, 1937.
13. COMDESRON2 to *Itasca*, 0920Z, July 12, 1937.
14. Welty to Associated Press, 2323Z, July 15, 1937.
15. *Itasca* to COM14 and COMDESRON2, 0230Z, July 16, 1937; COMDESRON2 to *Itasca*, 0444Z, July 16, 1937.
16. U.S. State Department to American Embassy, London, 2200, July 15, 1937.
17. Brooks to International 0845Z, July 16, 1937.

18. COMFRANDIV to COM14 and COMDESRON2, 0735Z, July 16, 1937.
19. Welty to Associated Press, 2009Z, July 16, 1937.
20. COMFRANDIV to COM14 and COMDESRON2, 2120Z, July 16, 1937.
21. George Putnam to CNO, 0220Z, July 17, 1937.
22. "Woman Psychic Asserts Amelia Earhart Is Safe," *New York Herald Tribune*, July 16, 1937, p. 11.
23. Putnam to CNO, 1908Z, July 17, 1937.
24. COMFRANDIV to COM14 and COMDESRON2, 2035Z, July 17, 1937; COM14 to COMFRANDIV, 2130Z, July 17, 1937.
25. CNO to COM14, 0212Z, July 18, 1937; COM14 to CNO, 0845Z, July 18, 1937.
26. Putnam to CNO, 1910Z, July 18, 1937; CNO to Putnam, 1920Z, July 18, 1937.
27. Putnam to CNO, 2053Z, July 18, 1937; CNO to Putnam, 23xxZ, July 18, 1937.
28. COMDESRON2 to *Itasca*, 2040Z, July 16, 1937; *Itasca* to COMDESRON2, 2330Z, July 16, 1937.
29. *Itasca* to COMDESRON2, 2330Z, July 16, 1937.
30. *Itasca* Deck Log, July 2, 1937.
31. Black to Miller, 0840Z, July 22, 1937.
32. *Itasca* to COMDESRON2, 2330Z, July 16, 1937.
33. Ibid.
34. *Itasca* Deck Log, July 2, 1937.
35. *Itasca* to COMDESRON2, 2330Z, July 16, 1937.
36. Ibid.
37. Ibid.
38. *Itasca* to COMFRANDIV et al., 0132Z, July 3, 1937.
39. COMDESRON2 to COM14, 0730Z, July 17, 1937.
40. Ibid.
41. COM14 to CNO, 2025Z, July 17, 1937.
42. COM14 to CNO, 1950Z, July 18, 1937.
43. COMDESRON2 to COM14, 0321Z, July 19, 1937.
44. COM14 to CNO, 0520Z, July 19, 1937.

Chapter 22. Banquo's Ghost: Explaining Failure

1. "Greatest Rescue Force in History of Aviation," *New York Herald Tribune*, July 5, 1937, p. 1.
2. Friedell, "Resumé Earhart Search," p. 11.
3. Ibid., pp. 10, 11.
4. Ibid., p. 13.
5. Civil Air Patrol, *Mission Aircraft Reference Text*, Chapter 9: "Search Planning and Coverage," section 9.2.1: "Probability of Detection Table," Civil Air Patrol.
6. Friedell, "Resumé Earhart Search," p. 10; Lambrecht, "Aircraft Search for Earhart Plane."
7. J. S. Dowell, Commander *Lexington* Group, memorandum to Commandant Fourteenth Naval District, July 20, 1937, National Archives, San Bruno, Calif., RG 181, file A4-3 Earhart.

8. J. S. Dowell, "Report of Earhart Search," July 20, 1937, Annex A: "Estimate and Decisions," pp. 1, 2, National Archives, San Bruno, Calif., RG 181, file A4-3 Earhart.

9. Lt. D. M. Tites, USAAC, "Inventory NR16020," March 26, 1937, sheet 3, item 53, in U.S. Army Proceedings, "Investigation of Earhart Crash, Luke Field, March 20, 1937."

10. Dowell, "Report of Earhart Search."

11. Ibid., pp. 3, 5, 8.

12. Dowell, Annex B, "Narrative of Earhart Search," p. 16.

13. Dowell, Annex D, "Report of Earhart Search Operations 3–18 July 1937," p. 4.

14. Ibid., p. 9.

15. Thompson, "Radio Transcripts—Earhart Flight," p. 105.

16. Ibid.; CNO to COM14, 2020Z, July 16, 1937.

17. Thompson, "Radio Transcripts—Earhart Flight," p. 1.

18. Ibid., pp. 7, 34.

19. Black, "Tenth Cruise to the American Equatorial Islands," p. 1.

20. Black to Miller, 0333Z, March 5, 1937.

21. Thompson, "Radio Transcripts—Earhart Flight," pp. 12, 15–16.

22. Ibid., p. 22.

23. Ibid., p. 34; *Itasca* to Earhart via Samoa, June 23, 1937.

24. Thompson, "Radio Transcripts—Earhart Flight," p. 34.

25. Ibid., pp. 1, 40.

26. Ibid., p. 46, 47.

27. Ibid., p. 52.

28. *Itasca*, RLP2, 2216, July 4, 1937.

29. Thompson, "Radio Transcripts—Earhart Flight," p. 75.

30. Ibid., p. 105.

31. Ibid.

32. Ibid., p. 106.

33. Ibid., p. 9.

34. Marvin McIntyre, memorandum for the President, July 20, 1937, Earhart Collection, Purdue University Library.

35. Putnam to Secretary of the Navy, 1645Z, July 23, 1937.

36. Secretary of the Navy to Putnam, 1810Z, July 24, 1937.

37. U.S. State Department to American Embassy, London, 0000Z, July 31, 1937.

38. G. P. Putnam, letter to Marvin McIntyre, July 31, 1937, Earhart Collection, Purdue University Library.

39. Putnam to U.S. State Department, unknown time, August 1, 1937.

40. Dean S. Jennings, "Is Amelia Earhart Still Alive?" *Popular Aviation* (December 1939): 76.

41. U.S. State Department to Putnam, 2133Z, August 31, 1937.

42. "Says Calls Were Not Earhart's," *New York Times*, July 26, 1937, p. 17.

43. J. F. Farley, memorandum to the Commandant, December 14, 1937, National Archives, RG 26, file 651, box 751.

44. Ibid.

45. Articles of Incorporation, Amelia Earhart Foundation, article IIb, Earhart Collection, Purdue University Library.

46. Charter of the Amelia Earhart Foundation, "An Unsolved Mystery," December 23, 1937, Earhart Collection, Purdue University Library.
47. Amelia Earhart Society, "National Sponsors Committee as of April 16, 1938," as shown on letterhead, letter to E. W. Libbey from Ernest B. Chamberlain, June 15, 1938, Earhart Collection, Purdue University Library.
48. COMFRANDIV, memorandum to COMHAWSEC, March 22, 1937, p. 2.
49. COMHAWSEC to COMFRANDIV, June 18, 1937.
50. COMFRANDIV memorandum, p. 1.
51. Ibid., p. 2.
52. Ibid., p. 3.
53. Ibid., p. 4.
54. COMFRANDIV to *Itasca*, 2310Z, July 4, 1937.
55. COMFRANDIV memorandum, p. 4.
56. Letter from Capt. Irving Johnson to Bessie Young, June 4, 1940, Earhart Collection, Purdue University Library.
57. Ibid.
58. Jesse W. Langford, memorandum to Registration Section, Bureau of Air Commerce, May 5, 1937, FAA Archives.

INDEX

ABOUT THE AUTHOR

The son of a decorated World War II pilot, Richard E. Gillespie grew up around airplanes and learned to fly while he was still in high school. After graduating from the State University of New York at Oswego with a BA in history he flew professionally until going on active duty with the U.S. Army in 1970. Gillespie completed Infantry Officer Candidate School and attended the army's Advanced Radio Systems School before being assigned to the First Cavalry Division, where he served as communications officer for an aviation battalion. Following his military service, he embarked on a career as an aviation risk manager and accident investigator for the aviation insurance industry. Servicing his clients throughout the northeastern United States, he logged many thousands of hours in single and twin-engined light, and often poorly equipped, aircraft in all kinds of weather. As Ric says, "It was a pretty good simulation of 1930s' flying."

In 1985 he left the insurance business and, with his wife, Patricia Thrasher, founded The International Group for Historic Aircraft Recovery. Known by its acronym TIGHAR (pronounced tiger), the nonprofit foundation has an international membership of several hundred scholars, scientists, and enthusiasts whose volunteer expertise and financial contributions support the organization's mission to promote responsible aviation archaeology and historic preservation. As TIGHAR's executive director, Gillespie has conducted dozens of educational seminars at air museums around the United States and has organized and moderated conferences of air museum professionals in Britain and Europe. Gillespie has also led more than three dozen aviation archaeological expeditions to remote areas of the United States, Canada, Europe, Micronesia, and New Guinea.

Since launching TIGHAR's investigation of the Earhart disappearance in 1988, he has led eight expeditions to the Phoenix Islands. Gilllespie's writings on the Earhart disappearance have appeared in the organization's journal TIGHAR Tracks and in the Naval Institute's *Proceedings* and *Naval History* and in *LIFE* magazine.

For more information about TIGHAR, including membership and educational opportunities, visit the TIGHAR website at www.tighar.org.

The Naval Institute Press is the book-publishing arm of the U.S. Naval Institute, a private, nonprofit, membership society for sea service professionals and others who share an interest in naval and maritime affairs. Established in 1873 at the U.S. Naval Academy in Annapolis, Maryland, where its offices remain today, the Naval Institute has members worldwide.

Members of the Naval Institute support the education programs of the society and receive the influential monthly magazine *Proceedings* and discounts on fine nautical prints and on ship and aircraft photos. They also have access to the transcripts of the Institute's Oral History Program and get discounted admission to any of the Institute-sponsored seminars offered around the country. Discounts are also available to the colorful bimonthly magazine *Naval History*.

The Naval Institute's book-publishing program, begun in 1898 with basic guides to naval practices, has broadened its scope to include books of more general interest. Now the Naval Institute Press publishes about seventy titles each year, ranging from how-to books on boating and navigation to battle histories, biographies, ship and aircraft guides, and novels. Institute members receive significant discounts on the Press's more than eight hundred books in print.

Full-time students are eligible for special half-price membership rates. Life memberships are also available.

For a free catalog describing Naval Institute Press books currently available, and for further information about subscribing to *Naval History* magazine or about joining the U.S. Naval Institute, please write to:

Member Services
U.S. Naval Institute
291 Wood Road
Annapolis, MD 21402-5034
Telephone: (800) 233-8764
Fax: (410) 571-1703
Web address: www.navalinstitute.org